Cuming
2/1788

P9-CSS-230

The Path to Vietnam

The Path to Vietnam

ORIGINS OF THE AMERICAN COMMITMENT TO SOUTHEAST ASIA

Andrew J. Rotter

Cornell University Press

ITHACA AND LONDON

Copyright © 1987 by Cornell University

All rights reserved. Except for brief quotations in a review, this book, or parts thereof, must not be reproduced in any form without permission in writing from the publisher. For information, address Cornell University Press, 124 Roberts Place, Ithaca, New York 14850.

First published 1987 by Cornell University Press.

International Standard Book Number 0-8014-1958-1
Library of Congress Catalog Card Number 87-47603
Printed in the United States of America
*Librarians: Library of Congress cataloging information
appears on the last page of the book.*

*The paper in this book is acid-free and meets the guidelines for
permanence and durability of the Committee on Production Guidelines
for Book Longevity of the Council on Library Resources.*

For my parents,
Muriel and Roy Rotter

Contents

Preface

It has become a cliché to say that Americans of my generation—I turned eighteen in 1971—must "come to terms" with the Vietnam War. In a general sense, my desire to understand the war led me to write my doctoral dissertation, and now this book, on the origins of the United States' commitment to Vietnam. I did not fight in Vietnam, nor did I go to jail, flee to Canada, fail a draft physical, or become a conscientious objector. Richard Nixon was Vietnamizing the war when the draft lottery for my cohort was held, and my number came up 318. As it turned out, no one who had entered college in the fall of 1971 would be called to Vietnam, but we didn't know that in early 1972, so one friend (lottery number 8) got braces on his teeth, and another (number 13) swallowed hard and joined the Reserve Officers Training Corps. Although I was relieved not to have to make these choices, in a perverse way I felt left out: I had been deprived of a chance to come to terms with Vietnam. So I confronted the war in my own ways, continuing to march in antiwar demonstrations and writing an undergraduate seminar paper on the United States and Great Britain in Southeast Asia following World War II. The demonstrations reflected and sharpened my distaste for the war. The paper ultimately provided the foundation for this book.

I started this project with a simple question: why had the United States gotten involved in Vietnam in the first place? I was surprised by the complexity of the answer that emerged from the evidence. Vietnam, I discovered, came up in diplomats' discussions of communism in China, the dollar balance of the sterling area nations, and the possible rearmament of West Germany. By the time I finished following all the unexpected leads, I found the manuscript was not really about Vietnam anymore. Instead, it was a study of U.S. postwar efforts to reconstruct the global political economy, in which efforts Southeast Asia, and especially Vietnam, would play a critical role.

The result is a book that examines American ideology and the pattern of United States Cold War policy a good deal more thoroughly than I once imagined it would. It is not strictly an economic interpretation of the origins of U.S. involvement in Vietnam, though I think how much I owe to historians who emphasize the importance of economics in American foreign policy will be evident. Also, although the book describes the application of the containment doctrine in East Asia, other works say a good deal more about that subject. I am interested here in examining the imagined world American policymakers hoped to create on their side of the containment barrier and in reporting on their efforts to bring it about.

Looking both backward and forward from the American decision of May 1950 to provide the nations of Southeast Asia with economic and military aid, the book locates the reasons for that decision in the foreign policy dilemmas that the United States in 1949 faced throughout the world. The victory of communism in China, the persistent economic woes of Japan and Great Britain, and the fragmentation of Western Europe, caused partly by French unwillingness to countenance the reconstruction of West Germany, were problems linked by their connections with Southeast Asia. American policymakers attempted to reach solutions by reviving Southeast Asia economically and inoculating the region against the Communist expansionism they feared. By the time the Korean War broke out in June 1950, the United States had in place a sophisticated policy to support and defend colonialism in Southeast Asia, designed to ensure the recovery of the developed, non-Communist world.

Because it has wandered so far off course, this book may not help anyone else "come to terms" with Vietnam. It will not chase the demons of a veteran, give comfort to a bereaved parent, or exculpate foreign policymakers. I do hope it will challenge some currently fashionable thinking about the war and be a source of ideas for Americans who face their future in the light of lessons of the past.

Writing this book has left me with an astonishing number of debts. I despair of repaying many of them; let me simply acknowledge them.

I received financial support for my early research and writing from several sources: the Stanford University Graduate School, the David

M. Potter and James Birdsall Weter funds (both within Stanford's Department of History), and the Institute for Humane Studies in Menlo Park, California, which provided a hefty summer fellowship and stimulating company as I started my research in 1978. I am also grateful to the Center for Research on International Studies and its director, Ronald Herring, for awarding me a "write-up" grant during the spring and summer of 1980. The Faculty Development Fund of Saint Mary's College paid my travel expenses to and from London in 1982 and Washington in 1983, and an Albert J. Beveridge Research Grant from the American Historical Association helped me prepare the manuscript for publication in the summer of 1984.

Men and women in libraries and archives across the country and in England endured my questions with remarkable patience and capably guided my research. Grace Hawes of the Hoover Institution on War, Revolution and Peace at Stanford University introduced me to R. Allen Griffin, head of the U.S. economic mission to Southeast Asia in early 1950, and assisted me with his papers. Mr. Griffin himself graciously submitted to an interview. The staff at the Stanford Government Documents Library was enormously helpful, especially W. David Rozkuszka. The intelligence and energy of the staff at the Harry S Truman Library in Independence, Missouri, are legendary among scholars of the Truman period; I must single out Dennis Bilger for his ability to find answers to even the vaguest requests. Those in charge of the Burton Historical Collection at the Detroit Public Library facilitated my use of the Joseph M. Dodge papers, and I am grateful to Joseph M. Dodge, Jr., of Austin, Texas, for permission to quote from the papers. Milton Gustafson, along with his staff in charge of State Department records at the National Archives, guided me through those important materials. The cooperativeness and courtesy of the staff at the Public Record Office in Kew made my research in England a pleasure.

Most of my debts are intellectual. Walter LaFeber of Cornell University kindled my interest in American foreign relations and presided over a very early version of Chapter 7. Professor LaFeber's association with Cornell University Press makes it particularly satisfying for me to publish this book there. Profound thanks go to three professors at Stanford, all of whom read my dissertation. Alexander George made me sensitive to the imprecision of foreign policymaking and the perils of absolutes and advised me with humor, wisdom, and compassion. More than anyone else, David Kennedy forced me to grapple with my fuzzy or foolish ideas and held me to account on matters of style and evidence, all the while reassuring me that things were far better than he made them sound. My adviser, Barton Bernstein, set for me an example of meticulous scholarship, ~~demanded that~~ I be fair, and provided me with dozens of insights about the United States and the Cold War, many of which I cheerfully appropriated without proper attribution. He, at least, will recognize them and know how grateful I am.

Many friends and colleagues read all or part of the manuscript while it was in various states of disrepair. Bertram Gross of Saint Mary's College and Walter Salant of the Brookings Institution read a version of Chapter 1; Mr. Salant saved me from several errors. Gary Hess of Bowling Green State University and Waldo Heinrichs of Temple University offered useful comments on an earlier version of Chapters 3 and 7. My colleagues in the Department of History at Saint Mary's—Benjamin Frankel, Carl Guarneri, Ronald Isetti, and Katherine Roper—helped me clarify my thinking about American ideology. Professor Guarneri in particular offered shrewd advice and considerable moral support. Gerald Eisman of the Saint Mary's Department of Mathematics taught me how to use a personal computer and otherwise contributed to my delinquency. My friends Anthony Fels at Stanford and David Alvarez at Saint Mary's bravely read the entire dissertation and helped me with revisions, and Thomas McCormick of the University of Wisconsin, Jonathan Utley of the University of Tennessee, and two anonymous readers read and commented on the penultimate draft of the manuscript. I am especially grateful to Professor Richard Immerman of the University of Hawaii, who seemed to agonize as much as I did over the last stage of rewriting and offered many valuable suggestions. I thank them all.

Material from Chapters 3 and 7 was originally published in *The International History Review*, 6, no. 3 (1984), and is reprinted here by permission of the editors.

Nancy Riley typed my dissertation with terrific speed and skill. My editor at Cornell, Peter Agree, has been so cooperative that it is almost impossible to avoid making a pun on his name, and Allison Dodge has been a splendid copy editor. My greatest debt is to my wife, Padma. With her coaxing, explaining, supporting, with her intelligence and good humor and her love, she has made this book possible. She has made everything possible.

ANDREW J. ROTTER

Hamilton, New York

The Path to Vietnam

Are you really asking me this goddamn silly question?

Walt W. Rostow, when asked why the United States got involved in Vietnam

What trouble is beyond the range of man?
What heavy burden will he not endure?
Jealousy, faction, quarreling, and battle—
The bloodiness of war, the grief of war.
And in the end he comes to strengthless age,
Abhorred by all men, without company,
Unfriended in that uttermost twilight
Where he must live with every bitter thing.

Sophocles, *Oedipus at Colonus*

Introduction

On May 1, 1950, President Harry S Truman allocated $10 million in military aid for the French-sponsored governments of Indochina and approved "in principle" a program of economic assistance for the same states. The amount of money involved was paltry, especially in light of the billions the United States had provided Western Europe under the Marshall Plan, and no one at the time believed the president's decision was darkly portentous. In retrospect, however, this decision might well be considered what the authors of the *Pentagon Papers* later called "a tangible first step" toward deeper American involvement in Vietnam.

Why was the decision made? Years ago, when I set out to explore the origins of U.S. military intervention in Vietnam, this seemed a question of at least modest significance. As it turned out, my straightforward question led me into regions I had scarcely anticipated. The fate of Southeast Asia, it seemed, was connected to the destinies of nations throughout the world. The region was mentioned in conversations between American policymakers and their Japanese, British, Dutch, and French counterparts. Instability in Southeast Asia indirectly jeopardized the future of West Germany. By 1949, American policymakers had concluded that Southeast Asia was a likely potential victim of Communist expansionism. If Southeast Asia was so important after early 1949, however, the relatively trivial sum offered the region by the United States seemed an insufficient reflection of weighty American concerns.

This paradox compelled me to shift the focus of the study. The Truman administration's decision to provide economic and military

1

assistance to Southeast Asia was not, I concluded, the ultimate expression of American policy toward the Far East, but was one of several hallmarks denoting the reorientation of American policy toward East Asia and the world following the summer of 1949. The decision implanted the United States firmly in Southeast Asia and particularly in Vietnam, and as such it was an important step toward American military intervention in the region. An exploration of U.S. policy toward Southeast Asia after mid-1949, however, taken as a whole, offers insights that are, I think, even more significant. Following the summer of 1949, American policymakers found that Southeast Asia was the critical theater in their efforts to contain communism and to effect the recovery of the developed, non-Communist nations. By the spring of 1950, the administration concluded that Southeast Asia was the fulcrum on which the recovery of the developed nations rested, and it was prepared to take several steps, including the extension of economic and military aid to Southeast Asia, to secure the success of these nations.

The distinction between containment and the pursuit of free world recovery is worth emphasizing. The objectives, of course, were complementary: containment, properly implemented, would prevent Communist encroachments on the non-Communist world, and the economic revival of Western countries would make their inhabitants less susceptible to Communist subversion or persuasion. Yet though the point seems simple, scholars have been reluctant to recognize that during the late 1940s American policymakers sought both objectives. Containment was a negative strategy; it defined what policymakers did not want, and it was not by itself adequate to restore prosperity and stability to those nations the United States counted as its closest allies and best trading partners. The West also needed a program for recovery on its side of the containment barrier. Until mid-1949, American policymakers believed this program should be based on a distinctly American ideology.

By ideology I mean a coherent system of assumptions, through which people view the world and to which they would have the world conform; it is, then, both prismatic and prescriptive. Those who hold the same ideology do not necessarily believe precisely the same things, for an ideology is flexible enough to allow its adherents to emphasize its different components. At the same time, an ideology is not so elastic that it can expand to include every assumption a group might hold. If it were, it would be useless as a way of explaining human perception or behavior.

Many scholars have attempted to characterize the ideology of U.S. foreign policymakers. The eminent revisionist historian William Appleman Williams (who calls ideology "weltanschaung") argues that since the late nineteenth century policymakers have demanded an economic and a political "open door" throughout the world. Political scientist Robert A. Packenham stresses the importance of the "liberal tradition" in the "unarticulated premises" of American ideology; Gabriel Kolko believes capitalism itself sufficiently explains American policy. Alexander George and John Lewis Gaddis do not use the concept of ideology in their work on the Cold War, but they write of a policymaker's "operational code," in Gaddis's words "a set of assumptions about the world, formed early in one's career, that tend to govern without much subsequent variation the way one responds to crises afterwards." The distinction between this and my definition of ideology appears to me small.[1]

It is difficult to label the ideology of American diplomacy, probably because of its comprehensiveness. Among its features are: (1) the belief that people have the right of self-determination; (2) the belief that no people truly exercising self-determination will choose communism or authoritarianism because all people desire representative political institutions; (3) the belief that economic progress and political freedom can exist only where the means of production are, for the most part, privately owned; (4) the idea that full, unfettered trade among all nations—multilateralism—will keep the world prosperous; (5) the belief that economies should specialize in what they do best—developed nations should export manufactured goods and underdeveloped countries should sell food and raw materials; and (6) the idea that political and economic reforms, carefully guided by elected governments, are necessary for human progress and to blunt the sharp edges of the free market and are essential to prevent discontent that might lead to revolution. Behind these ideas is a faith that America's moral rectitude is absolute and a confidence that American power is sufficient to persuade the unconvinced.

These ideas are the basis of what N. Gordon Levin, in his work on Woodrow Wilson, calls "liberal capitalism."[2] I prefer this term for several reasons. First, it is more precise than the term "open door." Unlike "liberalism" alone (or the "liberal tradition"), "liberal capitalism" acknowledges economic elements in the ideology; unlike "capitalism" alone it accommodates factors that are not exclusively economic. Moreover, I think the term emphasizes the similarities between the foreign policy ideologies of the Wilson and Truman administrations, the continuity of thought that characterized American efforts to reconstruct the postwar world in 1920 and 1945. I do not claim that Wilson's and Truman's ideologies were identical. Wilson was more sophisticated and doctrinaire than Truman, more often given to ruminations on the international system than the accidental president from Missouri. But Truman deeply admired Wilson—he believed Wilson was the third greatest president, behind Washington and Jefferson[3]—and his leading foreign policy advisers held Wilsonian principles. As it had been since the Progressive era, liberal capitalism was the ideal of American foreign policy following the Second World War.

The thesis of this book is that by 1949 the liberal capitalist ideal had been hopelessly compromised. This process began in 1947 with the Truman administration's acceptance of the containment doctrine. Containment itself was an acknowledgment that those nations within the Soviet sphere of influence would be, at least temporarily, beyond the reach of political and economic freedom. The Americans had also discovered that the mere imposition of liberal capitalism on the developed, non-Communist world was insufficient to ensure its recovery. The revival of the West demanded the infusion of American capital on an enormous scale. The European Recovery Program, approved by Congress in early 1948, did not represent the abandonment of liberal capitalism, but it signified the American recognition that the ideal world was still a few years off.

As it turned out, even the massive increase of American assistance was not enough. By the summer of 1949, the success of U.S. foreign policy seemed in jeopardy. The economic recovery of Great Britain, considered by American policymakers a crucial postwar goal, had not occurred, and in response to a mild American recession, British dollar reserves dipped dangerously low. The French government was opposed by France's powerful Communist labor movement and, largely because of French unwillingness to consider West German participation in the North Atlantic alliance, Western Europe remained vulnerable to invasion, political subversion, and economic collapse. In the Far East, China had fallen to the Communists with stunning speed, there were rebellions in Indochina, Burma, British Malaya, and Indonesia, and Japan limped toward the 1950s still helplessly dependent on American economic aid. All these events, policymakers believed, took place in the shadow of increased Soviet hostility and enhanced Soviet capacity for militarism.

How could the United States respond? Liberal capitalism, even buttressed by the European Recovery Program, was at best a temporary failure. The developed, non-Communist nations did not seem to possess the resources or imagination to solve their own problems. In a way that was impressionistic and halting rather than clear and confident, President Truman made the first contribution to the new policy of 1949. Truman's announcement of the Point Four program in his inaugural address of January 1949 marked the administration's initial step toward a comprehensive policy for what was known as the underdeveloped world. Point Four combined a proposal for a small amount of American technical assistance for underdeveloped nations with an attempt to encourage business to invest in these countries.

At the time of the inaugural speech, the president had only a dim notion of why such a policy was necessary, but he justified it in lavish terms that masked his uncertainty. As 1949 wore on and as the intensification of the problems of the non-Communist world made Point Four itself increasingly obsolete, the conceptual basis for the new policy grew directly from the grandiose rationale offered for Point Four. Truman and proponents of Point Four had vaguely recognized that the underdeveloped world demanded American attention, yet they were unsure precisely what form their concern should take. By the fall of 1949 officials had lowered their expectations for Truman's modest proposal, but had appropriated its rationale for their conceptually bolder plans. During those months, policymakers realized that the problems of the most important developed nations in the non-Communist world—Japan, Great Britain, France, and West Germany—were linked to dislocations in the underdeveloped world. Permanent solutions to these problems could be found only by improving conditions in the underdeveloped nations, and this would require considerably more than Point Four promised.

Along with the recognition that the stability of the developed world was linked to that of the underdeveloped came the understanding that Southeast Asia was the most important region in the underdeveloped half of the linkage. The administration "discovered" Southeast Asia at the intersection of its policies toward China, Japan, Great Britain, and France. China was, by the fall of 1949, a Communist state, and the non-Communist world had thus been deprived of a vital listening post, a strategic bulwark against the Soviet Union, and, it seemed to many, a potentially vast market for European and Japanese exports. These responsibilities now fell to Southeast Asia. The recovery of Japan was made more urgent by the Communist victory in China and appeared to depend on the growth of trade between Japan and Southeast Asia. The reduction of Great Britain's dollar debt, essential to the recovery of the British economy, was possible only if the sterling area as a whole could increase its exports to the dollar-rich United States. The partial solution to this problem could be found in the revival of triangular trade between the United States, Great Britain, and British Malaya, which held the key position in the triangle because its rubber and tin were important dollar earners for the sterling area. Finally, the Truman administration understood that French political problems and the unification of Western Europe, including West Germany, could be addressed most effectively if the French committed their resources to strictly European concerns. Their struggle in Indochina prevented the French from attending to matters of higher priority in Europe. At the same time, American policymakers believed it was essential for France to fight communism in Southeast Asia, and they sought to relieve the French of part of their burden while nevertheless strengthening the resistance to Asian communism.

Southeast Asia itself was in turmoil, the result of ongoing poverty, Japanese depredations during World War II, the attempted reimposition of colonial control over nations with powerful nationalist movements, and the presence of a Communist China at the region's northern border. By late 1949, American policymakers were actively considering enlisting the United States in the battle to stabilize Southeast Asia. Economic recovery was one obvious priority: it was vital that Southeast Asia become productive, exporting, as it had before the war, rice and raw materials, and importing from Japan and Western Europe any finished goods it needed. To this end, American policymakers encouraged Southeast Asian governments to trade with Japan, and they agreed to import more Malayan rubber and tin to diminish the British dollar debt. Ultimately, they consented to a small program of economic aid to the anti-Communist governments of Southeast Asia. Policymakers hoped this program would assure the recovery of Southeast Asia and in the process assist the recovery of Japan, Great Britain, France, and West Germany as well.

But economic recovery was meaningless in a region threatened by strife. The rebellions that raged throughout Southeast Asia prevented the achievement of stability required to include the area in the world system. The fighting in Vietnam was the major worry of American policymakers because of its intensity and the strategic position of the country. Despite American ambivalence about French policy in Indochina, in the end policymakers were persuaded that military aid was a necessary supplement to economic assistance. So, for the sake of the developed non-Communist world, it too was provided.

These decisions undermined the ideology of liberal capitalism. As the underdeveloped world—and particularly Southeast Asia— became a greater concern of American foreign policymakers, U.S. interest in democracy and free trade receded into the background. If Southeast Asia was to provide the basis for the recovery of Japan and Western Europe, and if this recovery was an urgent matter, the Americans could not afford to insist on strict adherence to principle. If communism was to be contained, the United States could not wait for democracy to flower in those nations that occupied the front ranks in the struggle. Recovery and containment demanded that the ideology be compromised. It was difficult to find democratic nations in Southeast Asia, but it was not hard to find non-Communist ones. The eccentric socialist government of Burma qualified; so did the military dictatorship of Marshal Phibun Songkhram in Thailand. For Japan to recover economically, Japanese exports had to receive favored treatment by Southeast Asian states and Southeast Asian food and raw materials had to provide payment for these exports. This arrangement demanded a form of Far Eastern regionalism, a clear contravention of multilateralist doctrine. Great Britain's economic fortunes rested substantially on the pacification of Malaya, and France's potency and credibility in Europe depended on a victory over communism in Vietnam. The success of the European countries thus required American acceptance of colonialism in Southeast Asia. There could be no more dramatic rejection of liberal capitalism than this.

At this juncture, it is appropriate to expose one of the critical assumptions of this book. As introductions will, this one has described "American policy" as if it were at all times cohesive, purposeful, and directed by a single actor. It was not, of course. A recent book on American aid to Southeast Asia in 1950 demonstrates that U.S. Far Eastern policy during this period was neither uniformly devised nor adeptly implemented. Instead, it was the product of months of struggle by competing bureaucracies within the foreign policymaking establishment and more than occasionally the hostage of right-wing representatives and lobbyists, who insisted that something be done to save China and the Orient from communism. The Department of State, which had primary responsibility for advising the president on foreign affairs, was itself divided over what to do about the Far East.[4]

But the fractious process by which foreign policy is made should not obscure several important axioms. First, some competitors in the policymaking process are stronger than others. Harry Truman followed the advice of Secretary of State Dean Acheson more often than he heeded Defense Secretary Louis Johnson or Senator William Knowland. Acheson, in turn, placed great trust in Philip Jessup and W. Walton Butterworth and not much in George Kennan or John Snyder. Second, no matter how foreign policy decisions get made, they do get made. Decisions may reflect compromise, but they indicate resolve; to make a decision is to be decisive. Finally, the bureaucratic quarreling that occurs within the foreign policymaking elite exists within a framework of shared values. American policymakers often differ over tactics—how to do something—but they generally agree on strategy, the larger issue of what to do. I use the word "strategy" here in the broadest sense, and I would argue that it is shaped by ideology. It is, I suppose, a modest contribution to assert that American foreign policy during the late forties and early fifties was made by people who held similar assumptions, that these assumptions came under the rubric of liberal capitalism, and that this was an ideology. The point, however, is worth making, if only as a reminder that explorations of the policymaking labyrinth too often highlight confusion and conflict at the expense of reason and calculation. All were present.

Here I am left with what seems a contradiction. If American policymakers shared a belief in liberal capitalism, how could they have capitulated in late 1949 and accepted protectionism, despotism, and colonialism? Strange as it may sound, I do not think these changes meant the abandonment of the ideology. Compromises were made because policymakers believed it was necessary to suspend temporarily the rigid application of liberal capitalism in order to assure its ultimate success. The United States acquiesced uncomfortably in these changes because the urgency of Cold War problems gave it no choice. When the problems had been solved, the United States would guide the free world back toward peace, freedom, and prosperity, all of which could be attained permanently only through liberalism and capitalism.

There was irony in this idea. I disagree with scholars who regard American remonstrance against Asian despotism and European colonialism as insincere. Instead, I accept at face value the public and private declarations of policymakers who expressed dismay at the undemocratic cast of anti-Communist governments in Southeast Asia and the constraints of colonialism. Certainly Harry Truman wanted a liberal capitalist world, and it was with genuine reluctance that he gradually abandoned this ideal to temporary (as he saw it) support of despotic and colonial solutions. The endorsement of colonialism, Truman hoped, would be a means to a democratic end. By May 1950, however, this idealism had all but disappeared from U.S. policy toward Southeast Asia, subverted by several compromises too many. In retrospect, it is clear that colonialist and despotic means had not served liberal capitalist ends but had engulfed them; the disjunction between rhetoric and reality was complete.

PART I

THE STAGE IS SET:
THE REDISCOVERY OF ASIA

1

The Domestic and Foreign Contexts of the United States' Southeast Asian Policy, 1948–1949

On the morning of November 3, 1948, Americans awoke to find they had elected Harry S Truman president of the United States. Defying nearly every prediction, Truman had defeated his Republican rival, Thomas Dewey, and had survived challenges from the left and right wings of his own party as well. For Truman the victory was particularly satisfying: it offered him four full years to prove he was something other than Franklin Roosevelt's unlikely successor.

The hiatus between the election and the inauguration gave the administration the opportunity to reassess its foreign policy. Secretary of State George Marshall was in poor health and would retire in January; his successor, Dean Acheson, would doubtless have some ideas of his own. The results of the election seemed to dictate continuity, but the world was changing, rapidly and dangerously. Reflection, at least, seemed imperative.

The Truman administration's policymaking was undertaken in the context of Soviet-American hostility. The administration believed the postwar world was frozen into two irreconcilable blocs and that the Communist bloc, under the control of the Soviet Union, sought to extend its rule throughout the world. Following the advice of the Soviet expert George F. Kennan, the administration had since early 1947 pursued a policy of containment of the Soviet bloc. The United States offered a combination of political, economic, and (to Kennan's dismay) military support to its allies in the non-Communist world to inoculate these countries against Communist expansion or subversion and to help rebuild their economies in order to assure a high volume of open, multilateral trade. American policy, in short, was designed to ensure the success of liberal capitalism.

Foreign Aid for the Underdeveloped World

The key front in this effort was Western Europe, especially Great Britain, France, and West Germany and, to a lesser extent, Italy and the Benelux countries. The Truman Doctrine, announced by the president on March 12, 1947, was the political embodiment of containment. Specifically, Truman had in mind a program of economic and military aid for staunchly anti-Communist regimes in Greece and Turkey. At the same time, using harsh, anti-Communist rhetoric, he declared support for all "free peoples . . . resisting attempted subjugation." Three months later, on June 7, Secretary of State Marshall offered extensive U.S. economic aid to Europe. The Marshall Plan spoke simultaneously to many concerns. The direct dollar grant to Western European nations would, in theory, raise living standards and thus reduce the attractiveness of communism. The availability of dollars in Western Europe would assure a continued high level of American exports to the region, and the stimulus to production provided by the grant would bring trade between the United States and Western Europe into balance. American policymakers hoped the supranational agencies created to administer the Marshall Plan would promote the unification of Western Europe. On the last day of March, 1948, the House of Representatives approved $4 billion in Marshall Plan aid, and by early summer the aid began to arrive in Europe.

The Truman Doctrine and the Marshall Plan were the major political and economic solutions the administration offered for the problems of Western Europe. In early 1948, policymakers on both sides of the Atlantic recognized a third dimension to the Western European crisis. In February, a pro-Soviet faction took over the government of Czechoslovakia. American policymakers and the leaders of moderate governments in Great Britain, France, and Italy saw Czechoslovakia as a victim of the internal subversion the Soviets conducted through European Communist parties. France and Italy had large, powerful Communist organizations supported by leading labor unions, and both governments feared domestic uprisings fomented by the Soviet Union. In early 1948, the United States encouraged the formation of an Atlantic alliance aimed at countering Soviet aggression in Europe. A vague aggregation—British Foreign Minister Ernest Bevin christened it "a sort of spiritual federation of the West"[1]—the North Atlantic alliance was not yet the imposing military organization it was to become, but the manifestation of an American promise to stand by Western Europe in resisting Soviet encroachment. The alliance was an American effort to establish a psychological climate of increased confidence, within which Western European moderates could confront the lingering problems of the postwar period. By late 1948, although the North Atlantic Treaty had not yet been signed, this fundamental purpose had been made clear; only the details of the alliance remained to be worked out.

The effect on European problems of these American actions, though unquestionably mixed, warranted at least cautious optimism among policymakers during late 1948. Yugoslavia had defected from the Soviet camp in June, signaling dissension in the Communist world. United States aid had bolstered Turkey and Greece. Disagreements between the United States and the Netherlands over the decolonization of Indonesia were overshadowed by the surprising economic recovery of the Benelux nations. The Soviets had blockaded Berlin in June, but by December the Western airlift to the city seemed a success, an imaginative stroke that avoided the perils of a shooting war while demonstrating American resolve in Western Europe. For moderate Western European governments, 1947 had been a dismal year economically and politically, but the beginning of Marshall Plan aid in 1948 brought an apparent reversal of fortunes. In April, West Germans and Italians had elected Christian Democratic governments that promised increased industrial production and crackdowns on Communists. Industrial output increased in France, and, in November, the French government confidently broke a miners' strike. In Great Britain, too, economic indications were bright. After a nearly disastrous winter in 1947-1948, production rose significantly during the spring and summer and exports to the United States increased, making possible a reduction of Great Britain's troublesome dollar debt.

Problems remained of course. West Germany was not yet fully integrated into the Western sphere; the striking French miners had seen their wages decline in value and were thus unable to share in the prosperity of the middle class; and, despite improvement, the sterling-dollar gap persisted. But American policymakers were satisfied that trends were good. The United States and the West had seized the initiative in Europe and, as Dean Acheson observed, "We are not doing badly."[2]

Acheson could not have said the same for U.S. policy toward China in 1948. The Nationalist Chinese government of Generalissimo Chiang Kai-shek was disintegrating. What the administration wanted in China—a unified, non-Communist nation accessible to Western and Japanese trade and investment—was manifestly unattainable. Chiang Kai-shek's regime was ineffectual and shot through with corruption, and almost no one in Washington believed otherwise. By 1948 few policymakers doubted that the Communists would win the civil war, and most officials acknowledged that continuing aid to China was like throwing money "down the rat-hole." Yet the administration persisted. While they ruled out American military intervention, policymakers would neither totally abandon their profligate ally nor would they open themselves to Republican charges that they were sympathetic to communism.

If the administration was largely resigned to the Communist victory in China, it was determined not to lose its grasp on the Far East. Officials' halfhearted requests for more economic aid for Chiang were accompanied by the State Department's renewed interest in the recovery of Japan. An economically strong Japan had figured in American plans at least since 1946, and now the loss of China made the strengthening of Japan imperative and urgent. United States aid for Japan increased dramatically in 1948. Policymakers hoped Japan would become the workshop of the Far East and an anti-Communist bulwark against Sino-Soviet expansionism. But in late 1948 the recovery of Japan remained in doubt. Production had risen only slowly, and foreign trade, vital to the health of the Japanese economy, had not approached pre-war levels. Japanese workers, many of them Communists, grew increasingly restive as their purchasing power declined. A start had been made, but more would have to be done, for Japan was now to be the Far Eastern bastion of the non-Communist world.

Elsewhere in the world of late 1948, American policy was characterized by neglect and incoherence. The United States had offered no underdeveloped nation the extensive economic aid it provided for Western Europe, China, and Japan. In the Far East, the United States had reaffirmed its commitments to its anti-Communist allies in South Korea and the Philippines. The turmoil in China brought the problems of South and Southeast Asia into focus, and by late 1948 American policymakers were beginning to show more interest in these areas. But the region remained primarily the responsibility of the Western European colonial powers. If American objectives in the Middle East were clear—opposition to perceived Soviet expansionism in Turkey and Iran, insistence on full access to oil, and support for the new state of Israel—there was no consistent effort to carry out these objectives, no systematic program of economic aid. Africa, when American policymakers contemplated it at all, was generally left to the Europeans or to its own devices.[3] The United States had offered no economic aid package for Latin America. The Western hemisphere nations had agreed on a mutual defense pact at Rio de Janeiro in August 1947, and the Organization of American States, established at the Bogota Conference in May 1948, formed a basis for potential regional cooperation. Nevertheless, Latin American nations, like most nations in Africa and Asia, received no extensive, consistent American economic aid in late 1948.[4]

Perhaps this lack of aid was unsurprising. Economic aid was a new idea in 1948, and the administration had committed itself to unprecedented expenditures in Europe. Still, Harry Truman seems to have believed the absence of an aid program for the underdeveloped world weakened American foreign policy. The president concluded that an initiative had to be taken, some audacious gesture made in the direction of the underdeveloped world.

Following the election, and between vacations in Independence and Key West, the president stopped in Washington and asked his staff and members of the cabinet to prepare drafts of the inaugural and state of the union addresses. Truman told Robert Lovett, the acting secretary of state, that he hoped to make the inaugural "a kind of democratic manifesto addressed to the people of the world."[5] Lovett referred the matter to Francis H. Russell, director of the State Department's Office of Public Affairs. And the president's instructions jogged Russell's memory.

The previous month, Russell had been approached by his deputy, Benjamin Hardy, who had an idea about the poverty in the underdeveloped world and what the United States might do about it. Hardy urged the creation of "a program that will hold out to these people the hope of acquiring the things that science and the know-how of the twentieth century can provide for them" as a way of raising living standards among those who would otherwise be "ripe for revolution." Russell had listened sympathetically, and so when Lovett called, Russell summoned Hardy. The two of them wrote a memo incorporating Hardy's idea—its title was "Use of U.S. Technological Resources as a Weapon in the Struggle with International Communism"—and, on November 23, sent it to Lovett. It was soon returned. Lovett claimed he liked the idea, but thought it unsuitable for the inaugural address.[6]

17

Despite this rejection, Hardy persisted. Urged on by his wife, he decided to risk reprimand by circumventing the State Department. On December 15, he took the memo directly to White House aide George Elsey.[7] Elsey liked the memo, and immediately showed it to Clark Clifford, special counsel to the president and Truman's most influential adviser. Clifford shared Truman's belief that the inaugural provided an opportunity for a declaration on foreign policy. He was looking for "a significant and dramatic topic," "something fresh and provocative that would make people think." The Hardy memo fit this need admirably. Clifford and Elsey took the memo to Truman, who read it, "kicked it around" briefly, and then approved the idea with the breezy remark that "we can work out the operating details later."[8]

The inaugural address was written over the next month, and Truman delivered it on January 20. Hardy's proposal had become Point Four in the speech, what the president called a "bold new program." Truman described the poverty of the underdeveloped nations in Latin America, Africa, and Asia and argued that the United States' "technical knowledge" could provide the solution to this problem. No large flow of capital would accompany the technical aid, but the president added that "in cooperation with other nations" the United States "should foster capital investment in areas needing development."[9] There were, then, two components of Point Four: technical assistance and private investment, encouraged by the federal government, for the underdeveloped world.

Truman had in mind several objectives for Point Four, and several others evolved as the program was designed by the State Department. Certainly the president hoped that Point Four would combat the misery of people in the underdeveloped world.[10] He also promoted Point Four as a new weapon in the Cold War; the president recalled that Point Four was "a practical expression" of the American will to resist the "Communist domination" of the underdeveloped world.[11]

Fundamentally, however, Point Four was a program of economic means and ends. American policymakers recognized the need for the United States to obtain raw materials—particularly oil, rubber, and metal ores—and acknowledged that supplies of some of these products in the developed, non-Communist world were nearing exhaustion. Technical aid and investment in the underdeveloped nations, some policymakers hoped, would encourage these nations to extract more raw materials.[12] Point Four might also encourage a steady flow of American exports to the underdeveloped nations: the dollars generated through investment in these nations could be used to purchase American products.[13] Finally, Point Four would contribute to the expansion and specialization of world trade. American policy-makers believed that the free exchange of goods over the widest possible area was the first and most important step toward world economic recovery. Truman noted "that an improvement of only two percent of the living standards of Asia and Africa would keep the industrial plants of the United States, Great Britain, and France going at full tilt for a full century just to keep up with the increased demand," and the State Department emphasized Point Four's potential contribution to the economic recovery of Western Europe.[14] Officials also believed in the need for an international division of labor, in which the underdeveloped nations produced food and raw materials and the developed nations generated manufactured goods. The State Department hoped Point Four aid would enable underdeveloped countries to grow more food and extract more raw materials. Sale of these resources would provide the foreign exchange needed to buy "the types of goods produced more efficiently abroad."[15]

Despite the president's enthusiasm, the Point Four program was not easily implemented. Dean Acheson claimed he first heard of Point Four when Truman announced it in the inaugural speech.[16] Officially he was not secretary of state (he would be sworn the following day), but his sense of responsibility in assuming the office must have been pricked by Truman's declaration of "a bold new program" about which Acheson apparently knew nothing. Acheson had a history of government service, having served most recently as Truman's under secretary of state between August 1945 and June 1947. Highly intelligent, witty, a superb debater, Acheson was at heart a conservative whose tough anticommunism made him an ideal director of Truman's foreign policy. Acheson was intensely loyal to Truman, who in turn trusted and admired him. While the theatrical introduction of Point Four seems to have offended him, Acheson's dedication to the larger aims of the president's foreign policy allowed him to put aside his apparent displeasure, and he resolved to oversee the program.

The secretary and the Department of State immediately ran into problems. Acheson first had to deflate expectations excited by the sketchiness of Truman's proposal and the grandiose language with which he proclaimed it. "Unfortunately," Acheson recalled, "the hyperbole of the inaugural outran the provisions of the budget."[17] The secretary spent his first press conference cautioning underdeveloped nations against anticipating a program the magnitude of the Marshall Plan and emphasizing the president's statement that private, not government capital would be involved.[18] This point was difficult to put

19

across, though administration spokespersons made it at every opportunity.[19] At the same time, no one had bothered to consult potential investors about their interest in the new program. As it happened, the business and banking communities proved reluctant to commit their resources to underdeveloped nations.[20]

Nor was Congress enthusiastic about Point Four. On June 24, Truman brought two Point Four bills from the State Department to Capitol Hill. One authorized the Export-Import Bank to "guarantee United States capital" in order to stimulate private investment abroad. The other asked for a technical assistance program.[21] Both bills were greeted with skepticism and subjected to amendment and delay. The Senate withheld approval of the investment guarantee bill until 1951, when it was adopted in another guise.[22] The president's request for technical assistance money was trimmed by the House, but it did eventually pass as Title IV of the Foreign Economic Assistance Act of 1950, signed by Truman on June 5. The actual appropriation was delayed three months, and then it had to survive a final attempt by the Senate to cut the allocation drastically. On September 8, 1950, Truman signed an executive order giving Acheson the primary responsibility for administering the program. The administration had previously committed $12.5 million to United Nations technical aid programs, so Acheson had $22.5 million with which to finance the bold new program.[23]

This evidently was not quite what President Truman had in mind when he announced Point Four. But from the beginning, some officials recognized that the program's ambitious objectives were incompatible with its limited scope. One of these officials was Walter S. Salant, a member of the senior staff of the Council of Economic Advisers. Throughout the struggle to implement Point Four, Salant contended that the program's sponsors would be successful only if they abandoned their cautious commitment to technical aid and private investment abroad and embraced instead the principle that extensive aid from the U.S. government was necessary to strengthen the economies of the underdeveloped nations.

In two meetings during December 1948, Salant suggested to presidential adviser David Lloyd that Western European economies could recover if underdeveloped nations had more dollars to purchase European products. Salant pointed out that the Marshall Plan would end well before Western European countries could pay for necessary imports. United States assistance to underdeveloped nations would act as small Marshall Plans, however, enabling these countries to pay for more imports from Western Europe, among other places. Aid would inspire trade. "Obviously," Salant wrote later, "this approach emphasized the capital aspect of aid."

Lloyd was interested. He told Salant that the idea was similar to one presented in a memo recently received by the White House, but that the memo mentioned only technical assistance; this, of course, was Benjamin Hardy's paper. Lloyd asked Salant to prepare a memo on capital export by the end of that day and implied that it might be used "in a major speech by a top official." Lloyd later told Salant that he had approached Clark Clifford with the Salant memo and that both technical assistance and capital export were being "favorably considered," apparently for insertion in the inaugural speech.[24]

Salant's ideas did not explicitly find their way into the president's inaugural address. Truman's emphasis on private investment was certainly not what Salant envisioned, and the State Department's subsequent focus on technical aid indicated that policymakers had ignored Salant's capital export proposal.[25] In early April, Salant drafted a proposed letter from Truman to Acheson, urging the secretary to stress the "financial aspects" of Point Four as well as its technical aid component.[26] Later that month, Salant noted the inability of technical assistance alone to achieve the president's ambitious goals and pleaded that Point Four be developed "as a program of capital export for resource development."[27] But the Point Four bills presented to Congress in June bore no evidence of Salant's influence.

The reasons Salant gave for government investment in the underdeveloped world were as precise and sophisticated as the administration's defense of private investment was vague and half-baked. Salant argued that aid to these nations was essential for the restoration of international trade at a high level. Salant hoped immediate investment by the United States in the underdeveloped world would help Europe through triangular trade: the European dollar deficit to the United States would be offset if the Europeans could sell to the underdeveloped nations, which would pay with American aid dollars. In the summer of 1949, at the height of a British financial crisis, Salant endorsed devaluation of the pound in the belief that it would lower the prices of sterling area goods. Lower prices would make British products generally more attractive in world markets, and the underdeveloped nations could then use dollars from Point Four loans to make their purchases in the sterling area.[28] Foreign investment, Salant explained to Lloyd, "would contribute to European viability if conducted so as to make underdeveloped countries better market[s] for European capital and other goods. Europe would continue having [a trade] deficiency with [the] U.S. . . . , but could finance it through export surpluses with the rest of the world."[29]

Salant believed Asia should receive most Point Four capital. Not only would this distribution best serve Western Europe, but more dollars in underdeveloped Asia would expand the market for Japanese exports as well.[30] Finally, Salant warned that the United States risked a drastic reduction in its export surplus unless it sent more dollars abroad to pay for American products.[31] The expansion of world trade was the only possible replacement for the Marshall Plan, which would end in 1952.[32]

Salant's plan to turn Point Four into a program of government investment in the underdeveloped world was shrewd and imaginative. It was also ahead of its time and was therefore ignored by many of the proponents of Point Four, who during the fall of 1949 insisted to Congress that technical assistance and government guarantees of private loans were adequate to achieve American foreign policy objectives. One exception was presidential adviser David Lloyd, who had become an admirer of Salant and a critic of the State Department's handling of Point Four. Lloyd promoted Salant's ideas on foreign investment to Clark Clifford, George Elsey, and Truman.[33] In December, Lloyd complained that the State Department lacked the proper enthusiasm for Point Four.[34]

The extent to which Salant's ideas actually influenced leading policymakers is uncertain. It is clear, however, that by late 1949 the administration had begun to see that the underdeveloped world had an important role to play in the reconstruction of the developed nations. Even as officials defended the Point Four program, events affecting the underdeveloped world, especially the Far East, rendered the limited scope of the Point Four bills obsolete.

During 1949, a change occurred in the international economic thinking of the Truman administration. The president's Point Four proposal in January reflected an economic orthodoxy that rested on faith in private enterprise and balanced federal budgets. The administration viewed the Marshall Plan as an extraordinary act demanded by an unprecedented situation, not a permanent feature of U.S. foreign policy. Despite calls by public figures for an Asian Marshall Plan, there was never any possibility that the United States would create one. At the same time, the intensification of postwar crises during 1949 compelled the White House and the State Department to abandon the hope that a handful of technicians and investments by the private sector in the less developed countries would be sufficient to assure the success of liberal capitalism. Policymakers recognized that political and economic problems in the underdeveloped world prevented the return of stability and prosperity in the developed world. Because the recovery of developed, non-Communist nations in Western Europe and East Asia was the major, positive goal of the United States after 1945, and because this goal appeared increasingly unattainable unless the United States addressed the problems of the underdeveloped world, the administration moved slowly away from the cautious Point Four legislation and toward Salant's prescription for exports of government capital. Technical aid and private investment were innovative concepts, and they were adequate for nations on the periphery. By late 1949, the administration no longer regarded the difficulties of some underdeveloped nations as peripheral concerns.

On January 4, 1950, almost a year after Truman announced Point Four, the president delivered his state of the union address. He urged Congress to pass the Point Four legislation. But much of Truman's earlier imprecision was gone. First, the president now thought the program would "require the movement of large amounts of capital from the industrial nations, and particularly from the United States." This idea was in pointed contrast to the entreaty to the investment community embodied in the investment guarantee bill and suggested that the U.S. government might take a more active role in the export of capital. Second, Truman recognized the larger benefits of aid to the underdeveloped world in a way that must have gratified Walter Salant. "An expanding world economy," the president explained, "requires the improvement of living standards and the development of resources in areas where human poverty and misery now prevail. Without such improvement the recovery of Europe and the future of our own economy will not be secure." Finally, while Truman still referred generally to the problems of the "underdeveloped areas," the program had acquired a focus: Point Four, said the president, was needed "particularly in the Far East."[35]

What the president wanted was not really Point Four, at least as he had described it in January 1949 and as it was reflected in the two bills then languishing in Congress. The new demands placed on American foreign policy during 1949 required a more genuinely ambitious response, one that included capital assistance for the underdeveloped world and revitalization of commerce between the developed and underdeveloped nations. The recovery of Europe remained imperative, and 1949 was a difficult year on the Continent and in Great Britain. American policy toward the Far East sought redefinition. The administration's new concern for the region, expressed by Truman in the state of the union address, was stimulated by the tardiness of Japanese recovery and the increasingly ominous implications of conflict in Southeast Asia. It was the Communist victory in China, however, that principally engaged the interest of American policymakers throughout the summer and autumn of 1949.

The Communization of China and Its Implications

The president's concern for the Far East was nothing new. It reflected ongoing American unhappiness with instability and radicalism in China. Since the late 1920s, China had been tormented by civil war, frustrating American hopes that it would become a vast market for American goods and a strong, cooperative friend in the Far East. The Chinese government was tenuously controlled by the Nationalist, or Kuomintang, party (KMT), led by Generalissimo Chiang Kai-shek. The United States supported Chiang's regime, although policymakers acknowledged that Kuomintang rule was corrupt and increasingly unpopular. Opposing Chiang was the Chinese Communist Party (CCP), led by Mao Tse-tung. The Communists, in contrast to China's ruling party, were scrupulously sensitive to the needs of the Chinese peasantry and therefore enjoyed broad support in the countryside. They also espoused economic and political doctrines that were anathema to American officials.

By late 1948, any hope American officials still held for the salvation of a non-Communist China had evaporated. In early November the Communists cleared Manchuria and captured Tsinan, capital of the Shantung peninsula, thereby encircling the Nationalist army of General Fu Tso-yi. General Fu surrendered in January 1949. Meanwhile, the Communists drove another Nationalist army south to the area between the Hwai and Yangtze rivers. There, in the pivotal battle of the civil war, the Communists smashed the Nationalists, killing 600,000 men and taking 327,000 prisoners. By early January, the Communists stood, unopposed, on the north bank of the Yangtze, preparing for the decisive attack on south China.[36] On November 6, 1948, Ambassador John Leighton Stuart reported from Nanking that the fall of Chiang's government was "inevitable."[37] David Barrett, a military attaché in Peking, knew the end was near when he saw the Nationalist generals evacuating their gold bars and concubines from northern China.[38]

The imminent demise of the Kuomintang left the administration with two major options. Many China experts argued that the United States should accommodate the Chinese revolution and attempt to negotiate with the Communists. The traditional open door policy, contended these experts, would be served best by endeavoring to influence the Communists as friends, rather than by cutting off communications and leaving Mao to pursue alliances elsewhere. Other policymakers insisted, however, that it was already too late. Because communism was by definition malevolent and expansionist, there was nothing left to do but quarantine China and resolve to prevent the revolution from spreading out.

The first of these alternatives, that the United States might ease its unrelenting support for Chiang Kai-shek and open negotiations with the Communists, predated the actual collapse of Kuomintang rule on mainland China. Between 1944 and 1949, a distinguished group of American officials, both military and civilian, urged Roosevelt and Truman to consider this option. Among these "negotiators" were General Joseph W. Stilwell, American chief of staff in China during World War II; John Stewart Service, Stilwell's political adviser; diplomats John Carter Vincent, John Paton Davies, and Ambassador John Leighton Stuart—the "trinomial Johns" later vilified by Joseph McCarthy—John Cabot and O. Edmund Clubb, consuls general at Shanghai and Peking, respectively; and Economic Cooperation Administration officials Roger Lapham and R. Allen Griffin. These officials were supported by many American businesspeople, missionaries, journalists, and scholars.[39]

None of these officials wanted a Communist-dominated China, but all of them argued that negotiations with the CCP offered the best opportunity to achieve American goals there. Stilwell had argued that Nationalist cooperation with the Communists was essential to victory over Japan. Service, Vincent, and the others recognized the Communists' strength and knew that Chiang could not destroy them on the battlefield. They urged that the United States encourage Chiang to enter a political coalition with the CCP, on the hopeful assumption that the popularity of the Communists and the political moderation of the KMT would fuse and lead to the establishment of a benign government.

The Truman administration flirted with the negotiation option. George Marshall, who had preceded Dean Acheson as secretary of state, had been in China from December 1945 to January 1947 and came away convinced that Chiang Kai-shek was the leading obstacle to peace and democratic reform. Marshall believed discussions with the Communists might put pressure on Chiang, resulting in a compromise government led by liberals, whom he praised as "a splendid group of men."[40] Harry Truman was not totally unsympathetic to the negotiators' position. The president genuinely hoped liberals would gain influence in China—"there were a great many liberals in China," he told reporters, and "he had talked with one the day before yesterday"[41]—and administration officials were willing to speak bluntly to Chiang and even threaten him with an aid cutoff. Truman did not consider military intervention in China to save Chiang. Secretary Acheson, for his part, lingered for months over the possibility of conciliating the Communists.

These attitudes, however, marked the limits of the administration's flexibility. Though the United States continued to exhort Chiang to reform his repressive and corrupt regime, neither Truman nor leading foreign policymakers ever declared that the United States would withdraw its economic and military support of Chiang if the Generalissimo failed to comply. Chiang Kai-shek was the indispensable man. Support for Chiang seemed to violate the ideology of liberal capitalism but was judged the only policy that even hinted at its ultimate success. By late 1948, most policymakers had concluded that as unsound as Chiang's government appeared, the alternatives to it were indiscernible or inconceivable.

Truman and his chief advisers viewed communism as a malign, indivisible force. In early 1946, Truman had rejected the idea that the Soviet Union was a conservative power, seeking to expand, as it had even under the czars, only to assure itself of defensible borders. Instead, the president concluded that the Soviet Union was a revolutionary power, expanding in response to the demands of Communist ideology and bent, ultimately, on conquering the world.[42] According to this viewpoint, a nation's allegiance to its Communist ideology overrode its identification as a traditional nation-state. It was true for the Soviet Union; it was true for Communist China as well. This was the basic assumption underlying what would become the "containment" position that governed American policy toward China.

This assumption about Communist ideology was the reason the negotiation option was quashed each time it was raised. Despite George Marshall's evident willingness to be stern with Chiang, Truman had rigged the general's mission from the start. Following his final briefing with the president, Marshall noted "that in the event I was unable to secure the necessary [conciliatory] action by the Generalissimo . . . it would still be necessary for the United States government, through me, to continue to back the National Government of the Republic of China."[43] Lest anyone miss the point, Truman declared publicly that "we did not want any Communists in the Government of China or anywhere else if we could help it."[44] John Leighton Stuart's continued efforts to promote a Kuomintang-Communist coalition met with indifference or rejection. Marshall put it plainly to the ambassador in August 1948: "The US Govt must not, directly or indirectly, give any implication of support, encouragement or acceptability of coalition govt in China with Communist participation."[45] The administration believed that any serious overture to the Communists would be inconsistent with the fundamental principles of containment.

Moreover, despite Truman's evident interest in promoting the careers of Chinese liberals, this policy, too, proved ineffectual. Even while policymakers pleaded with Chiang to reform and rummaged futilely through the Kuomintang hierarchy in search of a mythical democratic alternative, the United States continued to sustain Chiang's government with extensive economic and military aid. The administration grew increasingly frustrated with Chiang's autocratic rule, but officials stopped well short of doing anything to undermine it. "There was constant pressure to replace Chiang Kai-shek," recalled Marshall, "but no one ever suggested anyone could take his place."[46]

The impending victory of the Communists in late 1948 seemed to change the terms of the debate. The administration was committed to Chiang, but what would its policy be when Chiang no longer led the Chinese government? The negotiation option emerged once more in policymaking circles. The negotiation advocates' primary goal was to prevent the extension of Soviet influence over Comunist China, and they firmly believed this could be accomplished. In 1948, John Paton Davies, then with the State Department's Policy Planning Staff, wrote that the ability of the Soviets to shape events in China was "severely qualified by . . . demographic, economic and political" conditions there.[47] In a memo to Harlan Cleveland, head of the Economic Cooperation Administration's China branch, R. Allen Griffin of the ECA declared, "I most emphatically believe that the United States . . . has a fighting chance to separate the communism of China from control by Moscow."[48] The tactics suggested by the negotiators to achieve this objective were both political and economic: the diplomatic recognition of the People's Republic of China by the United States and the continuation of Chinese-American and Chinese-Japanese trade.[49]

Again, the administration was not without sympathy for the possibility of negotiation. Secretary of State Acheson in particular remained throughout 1949 and into 1950 ambivalent on the issues of U.S. recognition of the People's Republic of China and Sino-Japanese trade. However, the thrust of the administration's China policy after late 1948 was skeptical. The administration decided to wait and see what direction Communist China took, while seeking to minimize the impact of the Communist victory by vigorously supporting China's non-Communist neighbors. This policy was, of course, an expression of the containment option.

In late 1948, American policymakers responded to the debacle by continuing publicly to support Chiang Kai-shek, but privately working to cut their losses and endeavoring to retain freedom of action in China.[50] The administration continued to send economic aid to China, largely to prevent Republican charges that the administration's refusal to aid Chiang had caused his defeat and partly to buy time to allow a rethinking of U.S. policy.[51] Marshall described an earlier, narrower version of this policy as "a stay of execution" for Chiang, and Acheson characterized the American attitude as letting "the dust settle."[52] As George Kennan, head of the Policy Planning Staff, wrote, "The disappearance of the Chinese National Government, as now constituted, is only a matter of time and nothing that we can realistically hope to do will save it."[53] The illusions were gone.

Military assistance was also continued, but by late 1948 the administration began to tighten the conduit. In mid-December the joint chiefs of staff recommended that military aid be temporarily sustained, but urged that "emphasis on its priority and tempo . . . be relaxed."[54] Truman accepted this recommendation on February 7, 1949; as Acheson recorded it: "wherever possible, it is desirable that shipments be delayed where this can be done without formal action."[55] The Joint United States Military Advisory Group, conceived as an adjunct to the Nationalist army and activated on October 28 after several months of discussion, was substantially dismantled before the year was out.[56] On February 24, the day Acheson told congressional representatives he was waiting for the dust to settle, he scribbled notes to himself prior to the meeting: "No amount of monetary aid with or without military advice can help so discredited and inefficient an outfit . . . . Thus again—and for a time—the middle of the road view is crowded out."[57] The following month, at Acheson's request, the president authorized the preparation of a "white paper" study of the American failure in China.[58]

As a result of these efforts to divorce itself from Chiang Kai-shek, the administration found itself at odds with its uneasy allies in the containment constituency: the conservative China lobby in Congress.[59] Already in a sour temper because of Truman's unexpected victory in November, members of the China lobby saw in the administration's attempt to restrict the flow of aid to Chiang a betrayal of a loyal ally who alone could withstand communism in the Far East. Though they never seriously challenged the administration's refusal to intervene militarily, China lobby members demanded that the president do anything else necessary to bolster Chiang's desperate regime.

Truman, of course, did not agree with the China lobbyists that Chiang should be given increased military aid. He did not share the delusion that Chiang was an unselfish patriot and knew that Nationalist incompetence, not American penuriousness, had caused the debacle in China. While China lobbyists argued that Soviet imperialism, and the unwillingness of the United States to stop it, had closed the door in China, the administration insisted that Chiang had made it impossible for the United States effectively to resist Communist expansionism. On the issue of what to do about the accomplished fact of Communist China, however, there was less to distinguish the analyses of the president and his right-wing critics. All believed that Communist China, like the Soviet Union, would prove an ideological state. It would be a closed society, impervious to reason and aggressive, and therefore naturally antagonistic to the United States.

This interpretation of the People's Republic struck directly at the negotiation advocates' central assumption. Advocates of containment argued that the ideological loyalties of the Chinese leadership submerged China's nationhood. In his letter of transmittal, issued with the *China White Paper* in August 1949, Dean Acheson asserted that "the communist leaders have forsworn their Chinese heritage and have publicly announced their subservience to a foreign power, Russia."[60] Exponents of containment argued that it was naive to expect a cleavage to develop spontaneously between the Chinese and Russian Communists.

If the Soviet Union and Communist China were cast in the same mold, it followed that the method for dealing with them should be the same. As it had in Europe, the administration applied the containment policy to the Far East. China had gone Communist, but it might not stay that way if forced to confront its domestic problems without the distractions provided by an expansionist foreign policy. The Chinese must be hemmed in. While the negotiation advocates pleaded for the preservation of the open door in China, their opponents concluded that the United States should instead slam doors shut along China's periphery.

The containment alternative had implications for two Asian regions in particular. First, like the negotiators, those who recommended containment believed the communization of China gave new urgency to the restoration of Japan. However, while the negotiators saw the revival of Sino-Japanese trade primarily as a means of retaining influence in China, the containment advocates dismissed the possibility that Communist China could be relied on as a trade partner and hoped instead to contain China by strengthening Japan. The plan to make China a responsible ally had failed. Japan would now take China's place as an anti-Communist bulwark in the Far East.

But within the framework of the containment position, this hope held a paradox. Containment advocates recognized that Japan's economic weakness stood in the way of its becoming a great power and that foreign trade, through which Japan could obtain food and raw materials in exchange for manufactured goods, was essential for full recovery. Before the war, China had been Japan's principal trading partner, but as a Communist state, China could not fill this role. If Japan was to replace China as policeman of the Far East, the United States would have to find alternative commercial partners for the Japanese. Although the administration would not offer military aid to Chiang on Taiwan, it was willing to consider the island a prospective market for the Japanese. South Korea, apparently more secure, was another attractive prospect. The most intriguing possibility, however, was Southeast Asia.

Southeast Asia was the second region for which the communization of China had serious implications. The economic implication, if indirect, was clear enough: the nations of the region were potential trade partners for Japan. There were political implications as well. To American policymakers, the existence of a Communist China on the northern border of Southeast Asia was itself ominous. China was a seductive and sinister example of revolution for people struggling against European colonialism. Communist China offered a sanctuary to Ho Chi Minh's guerrillas, who were fighting the French in Vietnam. Moreover, the nations of Southeast Asia harbored large Chinese minorities, people whose loyalties to their governments were estimated, at best, to be mixed. The administration believed that, like the Soviet Union in Western Europe, the Chinese would put pressure on Southeast Asian countries by encouraging subversion through their agents abroad. Some American policymakers feared Communist China might actually invade Southeast Asia.[61]

The imperatives of containment did not require that policymakers abandon all hope of accommodation with the People's Republic of

China. Even in the first months of 1950, Acheson continued to hope weakly that the Chinese Communists, perhaps enticed by the prospect of American diplomatic recognition, would follow the example of Yugoslavia and reject subordination to the Soviet Union.[62] Ultimately, however, Truman's commitment to the containment of the Communist threat allowed that position the last word in the American debate over China policy in 1949 and 1950. Recognition was not extended, Sino-American trade rapidly fizzled, and Sino-Japanese trade, sanctioned by the administration and undertaken principally for the restoration of Japan rather than out of hope for China, was soon considered secondary to trade contacts between Japan and Southeast Asia. Most important, the administration argued that Communist China threatened both polities.

By 1949, the Truman administration had started a fundamental reevaluation of its policies in the underdeveloped world and particularly the Orient. The president's vague sense that something ought to be done for the underdeveloped nations—Point Four—was crystallizing into the idea that a good deal of American capital was essential to the economic success of these countries. The recovery of the underdeveloped world would in turn stimulate international trade, strengthening the economies of developed nations. Coincidentally, the communization of China drew special American attention to the underdeveloped states of the Far East. More than anything else, the threat to Asia of Chinese communism exposed technical assistance and toothless guarantees to private investors as inadequate solutions to increasingly dangerous problems. In this way, the administration's heightened willingness to provide assistance to have-not nations meshed with its growing concern about China's neighbors, and shaped the context for a sophisticated new strategy designed to contain communism and ensure the prosperity of the developed, non-Communist world.

PART II

THE PROBLEMS UNFOLD, 1948–1949

2

Japan: The New Urgency
of Reconstruction

The stunning power of the atomic bomb, coupled with the threat of Soviet military entry, brought a sudden end to the war in the Pacific on August 14, 1945. The unconditional surrender of Japan found the allies quarreling over the exact form of the incipient occupation. On the basis of their contributions to the war, Great Britain, China, and the Soviet Union laid claim to a portion of the occupation authority. But no one questioned that the future of the conquered nation would be primarily the responsibility of the United States; here, unlike in Germany, "there would be no zones of occupation."[1] In Japan the United States had a relatively free hand in reconstructing a nation shattered by the war.

The early disagreements over occupation policy were temporarily resolved at the Moscow Conference in December 1945, when the allies created two councils charged with vague governing tasks. The Allied Council for Japan (ACJ) included representatives of the four nations judged most responsible for the defeat of Japan and was designed to "consult and advise" the Supreme Commander for the Allies in the Pacific (SCAP)—the imperious General Douglas MacArthur.[2] The Far Eastern Commission (FEC), based in Washington, represented eleven nations that had fought the Japanese. The FEC was to "formulate general policies for the Occupation," but the United States was left with the power to issue "urgent unilateral interim directives" should international squabbling or inertia prevent the FEC from making policy quickly enough to satisfy MacArthur.[3] The terms of the occupation were set by the State-War-Navy Coordinating Committee (SWNCC) in the "U.S. Initial Post-Surrender Policy for Japan," approved by Truman on September 6, 1945. The directive promised the United States would make "every effort" to consult its allies on occupation policy, but "in the event of any differences of opinion among them, the policies of the United States will govern."[4]

What followed for the duration of the occupation was entirely predictable: MacArthur used the ACJ and FEC when it suited him, and, when it did not, he simply made policy for the United States. After early 1948, MacArthur consulted the councils less and less frequently.[5] One SCAP official observed that MacArthur "ignored the FEC" and "sneered at the ACJ," which MacArthur's chief political adviser regarded as "a thorn in the side of SCAP."[6] Despite foreign protests that were by no means confined to the Soviet delegates, the United States retained nearly unilateral control in Japan.

The occupation was largely a military affair. The heads of all but one of the SCAP administrative "sections" were military men, and MacArthur himself rigorously enforced army protocol. However, aside from differences in timing or emphasis, often caused by an expectation of military-civilian mistrust and exacerbated by MacArthur's near paranoia about scheming officials in Washington, there was ultimately little to distinguish civilian policymakers' plans for Japan and the army's practices there. All American officials agreed on the general objectives of the occupation. They wanted, first, to punish the Japanese responsible for instigating and conducting the war. They hoped to liberalize Japanese political institutions, undermining the system of loyalty and deference that allowed the ultranationalists to lead the nation into war. Naturally, policymakers wished to build a strongly anti-Communist Japan. Finally, the United States intended to integrate an economically vigorous Japan into the system of non-Communist, multilateral trading nations. Policymakers anticipated that this would require altering the Japanese economy in a way that complemented a representative government.

In the abstract, these objectives were entirely harmonious. The desires to purge Japanese ultranationalism and prevent communism were consistent with American liberalism, and the effort to remake Japan as a republic with privately owned economic institutions sustained by multilateral trade was an assertion of capitalism. The attempt to achieve all these things at once, however, was quickly paralyzed by contradictions. By late 1947, the vehement effort by the occupation authorities to detoxify Japanese nationalism and liberalize Japanese political life threatened to impede the struggle against communism and inhibit the attainment of a viable Japanese economy. The purge from public life of those Japanese associated with the war left the nation without its most experienced political leaders. The attacks on Japan's great economic combines, the zaibatsu, menaced the traditional forms of Japanese economic organization. The insistence by the Allies that Japan pay reparations further threatened the nation's recovery, and SCAP's requirement that industry recognize labor unions seemed to offer a forum to Communists whose views might otherwise be suppressed. The occupation's emphasis on political reform jeopardized the possibility of Japanese economic recovery and allowed communism a foothold.

As a result of these difficulties, during 1947 American policymakers acknowledged the contradiction among their objectives, decided that political reform had gone far enough, and shifted from their political to their economic goals. It is customary to divide the occupation into reform (1945–1947) and recovery (1948–1952) phases.[7] As with most attempts to pronounce historical watersheds, this periodization is too sharp: for example, MacArthur urged a more lenient reparations policy beginning late in 1946.[8] In general, though, the reform-recovery dichotomy accurately conveys what policymakers concerned with the occupation thought they were doing. This shift in occupation policy was strenuously debated within the administration and SCAP throughout 1947.[9] On January 22, 1948, an SWNCC directive was revised by the organization's successor—the State-Army-Navy-Air Force Coordinating Committee (SANACC)—and became U.S. policy. The document noted that "exceptional progress" had been made in creating democratic institutions in Japan. "However," it continued, "the establishment of a self-supporting economy in Japan . . . has not yet been accomplished." SCAP was directed to "take all possible and necessary steps" to revive Japan's economy.[10] Four months later, the Central Intelligence Agency concluded, "In the final analysis the political stability and the cooperation of Japan with [the] U.S. depends largely on the attainment of a viable economy."[11] The policy of reform had capitulated to the requirements of recovery.

The reason for this shift in American policy was the persistent weakness of the Japanese economy in the context of the increasingly ominous situation in China. The war had destroyed 30 percent of Japan's industrial capacity and 80 percent of its shipping. Production had increased during 1947, but only slowly, and it remained roughly a third of what it had been in the mid-1930s.[12] Wholesale prices were ten times their 1946 level.[13] American support for Japan had reached $600 million by late 1947. Moreover, simultaneously with the American decision to encourage the restoration of West Germany in late 1946, policymakers made more frequent references to the need to restore Japan as "the workshop of Asia."[14] American officials believed it was undesirable to keep Japan in a state of total dependence on the United States. Persuaded that the political reforms already instituted would prevent Japanese aggression, policymakers began to relax the restrictions they had placed on Japan's economy.

The imminent collapse of the Chiang Kai-shek regime made Japanese economic recovery urgent. MacArthur was not greatly concerned that the Communist victory in China would strengthen Japanese communism, which he regarded as little more than a "nuisance factor."[15] But the administration hoped that Japan would replace China as the anti-Communist bulwark and economic hub of the Far East. Robert Barnett, a State Department representative in Japan, recalled that occupation officials spoke of a " 'crankup' program for Japan" because it was "futile to think of China as being of much value to us."[16] Joseph M. Dodge, the Detroit banker put in charge of stabilizing the Japanese economy, was directed by Truman to attend to "the economic situation in Japan and its relation to what has been happening in China."[17] This created the paradox noted earlier: if Japan were to recover sufficiently to replace China, it would have to trade finished goods for food and raw materials, and China had always been Japan's best trading partner. The effort to resolve this paradox formed the core of the American response to the new urgency of Japanese economic recovery in 1948 and 1949.

With the "crankup program" in mind, the administration sent a number of missions to Japan to study economic conditions. A mission of industrial engineers, led by Clifford Strike, reported in April 1947 that political reforms had prevented self-sufficiency.[18] In the spring of 1948, the State Department, concerned that the new plans for the Far East had not fully gotten through to MacArthur, sent George Kennan to Tokyo. At the same time, a mission headed by William Draper, the under secretary of the army who had successfully urged a reduction in German reparations and who now championed a modified Marshall Plan for Japan, and Percy H. Johnston, chairman of Chemical Bank, arrived in Japan. The Johnston report, released in May, stressed Japan's need for increased trade, especially with Asian nations. In June, a group led by Ralph Young of the Federal Reserve reported on economic stability and suggested a ten-point program for obtaining it.

The reports of these missions recommended a number of measures to enhance Japanese economic recovery. All urged increased industrial production and an energetic search for trade partners. The Young and Dodge programs advised fewer imports and lower wages to foster economic stability. And all agreed that the success of the recovery relied on the abandonment of reform policies that reduced the ability of the Japanese to marshal their resources and compete for foreign markets. As one analyst put it, it was time to "put the cartel before the hearse."[19]

There were several reforms to be undone. One involved the large corporations owned by the leading Japanese industrial families, the zaibatsu. The dissolution of these corporations had been mandated by the SWNCC paper "U.S. Initial Post-Surrender Policy for Japan" in September 1945.[20] To accomplish this goal, MacArthur appointed a Holding Company Liquidation Commission (HCLC) to designate Japanese combines for dissolution. By late 1947 the HCLC had selected ten zaibatsu combines holding a total of 1,197 subsidiaries. In December, the Japanese Diet, on SCAP's insistence, passed the deconcentration law, which empowered the HCLC to reorganize combines. In the meantime, in May 1947 SWNCC had submitted to the FEC a statement demanding an attack on the zaibatsu. The document, known as FEC-230, argued that "the dissolution of excessive private concentrations of economic power is essential to the democratization of Japanese economic and political life" and was therefore "one of the major objectives of the occupation." FEC-230 went on to outline a stringent set of guidelines for effecting and enforcing dissolution. It was a ringing declaration of war against the Japanese trusts.[21]

It also became a rallying point for conservative opponents of the occupation. Writing in *Newsweek* in December 1947, James Lee Kauffman, a lawyer who visited Japan in the summer of 1947, exposed FEC-230 and assailed the administration for prescribing a program "far to the left of anything tolerated in this country."[22] Two weeks later, William F. Knowland, the prominent China lobbyist, obtained a copy of FEC-230 and waved it before the Senate, charging that its policy represented a "very unusual and distinctly un-Anglo-Saxon philosophy" and demanding that Congress be consulted on future initiatives in Japan.[23] Secretary of the Army Kenneth Royall reportedly "hit the ceiling" when the document was exposed.[24] In early January, Royall told the San Francisco Commonwealth Club that the government realized "that deconcentration must stop short of the point where it unduly interferes with the efficiency of Japanese industry" and promised that the policy contained in FEC-230 was being reevaluated.[25] Following the reassessment, the administration quietly withdrew its support of FEC-230 and instructed the American representative to the FEC, Major General Frank McCoy, to vote against the measure should another representative bring it to the floor.[26] Washington had begun to reverse its policy on deconcentration.

Occupation authorities apparently were not fully enamored of the shift in policy, but MacArthur and the HCLC nevertheless slowly backed off from their ardent pursuit of the zaibatsu. MacArthur responded to Knowland with a spirited defense of the deconcentration program, but at the same time proposed the creation of a Deconcentration Review Board (DRB) to comment on (though not contravene) the HCLC's designations for dissolution and advise him accordingly.[27] Despite the apparent latitude permitted by the deconcentration law, the HCLC thereafter moved only cautiously to reorganize the combines, designating 325 for modification by February 22.[28]

George Kennan arrived in Tokyo March 1, 1948, the day before the administration withdrew its support for FEC-230. MacArthur, predictably, was unenthusiastic about Kennan's arrival—"I'll have him briefed to the ears," he reportedly muttered[29]—but agreed to meet with him to discuss the occupation. The meeting proved surprisingly congenial. MacArthur was at first defensive, asserting that most Japanese welcomed the destruction of the zaibatsu and that he had often been forced to moderate even more radical directives on deconcentration coming from Washington. Other than finishing the work of the HCLC, MacArthur felt the occupation's reform program was nearly consummated. Kennan suggested a legalism MacArthur might use to circumvent the FEC. The general was delighted with the suggestion and "slapped his thigh in approval." "We parted," Kennan thought, "having reached a general meeting of the minds."[30]

Kennan had reason to be satisfied, for his presence in Japan proved influential in several ways. Kennan persuaded the State Department to request withdrawal of a June 1947 department paper on decartelization; the paper was subsequently withdrawn.[31] Following his return to Washington, Kennan submitted a report recommending that SCAP not introduce any more reform legislation. As for legislation already in effect, "SCAP should be advised to relax pressure steadily but unobtrusively on the Japanese Government." This recommendation became part of National Security Council (NSC) document 13/2, "Recommendations with Respect to United States Policy toward Japan," approved by the president in October.[32] And MacArthur had come around on deconcentration. In late March he proclaimed that only those combines "interfering seriously with economic recovery" should be subject to reorganization, and a SCAP headquarters memo in mid-April specified that "no more than twenty companies" were to be affected by the deconcentration law. The HCLC promptly exempted 194 of the 325 firms it had designated for review and freed 31 more by July 1. The DRB took over from there. Made up of five American businessmen who were appointed by SCAP, the board went beyond its mandate and further reduced the HCLC's list. The DRB finished its work in August 1949. At a press conference, Roy S. Campbell, chairman of the DRB, declared that competition had been introduced to the Japanese economy. In fact, only nineteen concerns had been reorganized.[33]

A similar reversal occurred on the issue of the purge. The 1945 SWNCC "Post-Surrender Policy" called for the removal from any position of responsibility of those who had been "active exponents of militarism and militant nationalism" and provided for the punishment of war criminals.[34] Almost immediately, occupation officials began compiling lists of those to be purged, including anyone attached to the armed forces, many educators, and political and business leaders who could not prove they had resisted the war effort. In April 1946, indictments were brought against twenty-eight suspected war criminals.[35] The purge lists eventually contained 220,000 names.[36]

The quest for reform removed from political and economic institutions many capable and experienced Japanese, and as the emphasis of the occupation shifted to economic recovery, the purge became increasingly intolerable. In January 1948, W. Walton Butterworth, director of the State Department's Office of Far Eastern Affairs, complained about the effects of the purge on "Japanese economic revival and governmental efficiency" and urged that the administration reconsider its program. Charles Saltzman, assistant secretary of state for the occupied areas, agreed.[37] A month later, from Tokyo, Kennan recommended that the purge be stopped and found MacArthur blamed Washington for the purge; it had not been his choice, he told Kennan, "to eliminate all those brains from public life."[38] The dissent was overwhelming, and the purge was terminated on May 10.[39]

This termination, of course, did not meet the problem directly. Kennan now argued that those already on the purge lists should have their cases reviewed with an eye toward their possible rehabilitation and reentry into Japanese society. Reflecting Kennan's concern, NSC-13/2 contained procedures for reinstating the accused.[40] Individual appeals were encouraged, and some purge categories were simply dropped. By 1952, only 8,700 Japanese remained on the list.[41] In October of that year, 139 formerly purged politicians were elected to the lower house of the Diet.[42] The purge, once considered by policymakers central to the occupation's task, had been halted, then undone.

MacArthur had for several years complained that the Allied policy of extracting Japanese industrial equipment for reparations frustrated his efforts to rebuild Japan's economy. In early 1947, Clifford Strike's mission had recommended a sharp reduction in the amount of war damages Japan had been asked to pay, and a year later the Johnston mission report warned that the threat of confiscation for reparations made Japanese industrialists wary of becoming too productive and thus conspicuous targets.[43] Despite the evident need to curb or end reparations to promote Japan's economic recovery, this problem had to be approached with delicacy: the nations that had suffered because of Japanese imperialism continued to press for the payments. Kennan made no recommendation on reparations following his trip to Japan, and none appeared that October in NSC-13/2. But the persistent stagnation of the Japanese economy ultimately convinced the administration that MacArthur was right. By the spring of 1949, Acheson told British Foreign Minister Ernest Bevin that reparations were constricting the Japanese economy and that the United States planned to "let them fall into oblivion." In early May, over the vigorous objections of its allies, the administration unilaterally terminated Japanese reparations payments.[44]

The administration also moved to strengthen the Japanese economy directly through a program of "stabilization." In June, Congress approved $125 million in aid for Economic Recovery in the Occupied Areas (EROA), meaning Japan, South Korea, and the Ryukyus.[45] Using as a prototype the recommendations of the Young mission (May–June 1948), the government on December 10, 1948, prescribed a nine-point austerity program that ordered, among other things, a balanced budget, wage stability, and increased procurement of domestic raw materials.[46] The following day, Truman asked Joseph M. Dodge, the conservative banker, to take charge of Japanese economic recovery. The problems of the Japanese economy, the president told Dodge, "had moved to the highest level of consideration" by the administration.[47] A week later, as Dodge arrived in Japan, MacArthur submitted the austerity program to Japanese Premier Yoshida.[48]

This became the Dodge Plan. In part, it reflected the administration's belief that the Japanese had not made sufficient economic sacrifices following the war. The plan, however, as a State Department official recalled, had "a more fundamental purpose—the expansion of Japanese foreign trade to permit the attainment of a self-supporting economy."[49] Increased production for export was the logical focus of the stabilization program—a quarter of Japan's industrial production was exported—and the Johnston report and leading occupation officials emphasized this need.[50] But American policymakers recognized that production itself relied on Japan's ability to import raw materials and that increased production would in fact be dangerous for Japan if it had no foreign buyers to purchase the anticipated surplus.[51] Foreign trade was the vital ingredient for Japan's recovery.

As with the reparations question, MacArthur's thinking outran that of most Washington policymakers. Just two years after Japan's surrender, members of the news media meeting with MacArthur concluded that he sought a "co-prosperity sphere" for the Far East, with Japanese factories processing the raw materials of the less developed Asian nations.[52] The Johnston report acknowledged that trade was the cornerstone of Japanese recovery, and Kennan asserted that "Japan's industrial strength has got to operate in a realm much wider than the Japanese Islands themselves."[53] In early August 1948, Secretary of State Marshall informed American diplomats that U.S. policy was to ensure "the revival of Japan's foreign trade" in order to encourage "world economic recovery, particularly in Asia and Southeast Asia," and to relieve the United States of the financial burden of sustaining Japan.[54] Both civilian and military authorities justified continued American aid for Japan with the argument that the donated funds could be used to buy raw materials that would be refined, then sold to East Asia.[55] These objectives reflected American occupation policy by mid-1948: the dependence of Japan on the United States was unacceptable, and Japanese foreign trade would be revived only if Far Eastern markets could be found. The United States promoted a new economic regionalism in the Far East, anchored by a benignly industrializing Japan in peaceful commercial exchange with underdeveloped Asian nations.

Many policymakers continued to hope China would remain one of these nations. Despite the primacy of the containment option in U.S. policy toward China, the State Department explored Sino-Japanese trade contacts during the first nine months of 1949. NSC-41, approved in February, urged SCAP to seek trade with China "on a *quid-pro-quo* basis."[56] In the spring, O. Edmund Clubb, consul general at Peking, reported a number of overtures by Chinese Communist officials regarding the continuation and expansion of Sino-Japanese trade, and the administration offered no objections to initiating contacts. Similarly, the administration approved requests by MacArthur to open trade negotiations in mid-November.[57] A State Department document circulated in December stressed the importance of Sino-Japanese trade and argued that to prevent "such trade would inevitably result in a heavy and continuing drain on the United States to support the Japanese economy."[58] The Japanese themselves were determined to trade with the Communists, and even into 1950 the administration acknowledged the potential fruitfulness of Sino-Japanese trade.[59]

But like the test for distinguishing an optimist from a pessimist, the question for the administration was whether the door to China was half open or half closed. In 1949, as the Chinese Communists extended their control throughout the mainland, the defense establishment worried that Sino-Japanese trade would strengthen the CCP, and even civilian policymakers doubted the permanence of China's receptiveness to Japanese trade. The authors of NSC-41 sounded a note of caution when they recommended that Japan "avoid preponderant dependence" on the China trade.[60] Further, the administration had no intention of allowing the Japanese to sell to China any equipment that might be converted to military purposes or that might be transshipped to the Soviet Union. The administration forbade the sale to China of items having direct military utility and required that capital goods having potential military uses be approved by the Commerce Department before they were exported to Far Eastern nations.[61] Acheson hoped to use the Japan trade as a lever with which to pry concessions from the Chinese, but during the summer of 1949 Communist harassment of American personnel in China intensified, and the secretary grew more doubtful of rapprochement.[62] Finally, the well-entrenched assumption that communism meant economic autarchy led even relative optimists like John Leighton Stuart to doubt that the Chinese Communists would consistently welcome Japanese trade.[63] Japanese economic recovery was urgent. Japan needed foreign trade; China could not be relied upon to provide it. Therefore, as the influential Ambassador-at-Large Philip Jessup wrote in the fall of 1949, "the alternative outlets for Japanese goods and skills must be examined."[64] These outlets were located in the Far East.

During the 1930s, Japan had sent more than 60 percent of its exports to Far Eastern nations and had obtained more than 50 percent of its imports in the region. Since the collapse of the co-prosperity sphere, Japan had come to rely almost exclusively on exports from the United States, paid for with American aid dollars.[65] While American policymakers and businessmen hoped to maintain a lucrative trade with Japan, they argued that the Japanese could not foreseeably produce much that Americans needed, and Congress refused to continue subsidizing Japanese recovery. Instead, the United States, through SCAP, attempted to encourage Japanese trade with the Far East. There was "a natural complementarity" between the Japanese and other Far Eastern economies, and an increased volume of trade was judged by an observer to be "absolutely indispensable" to maintain subsistence living standards in Japan.[66] A February 1949 report prepared by the Department of the Army argued that only Japan could offer "the manufactured goods requisite for rehabilitating the Asian economy."[67] Dean Acheson pointed out that economic relations between Japan and the non-Communist Far East were the "only hope" for a peaceful Japan friendly to the United States.[68] Policymakers hoped their de-emphasis of political reform and Dodge's austerity program would equip the Japanese for economic competition throughout the world, but only trade with East Asia would allow Japan to assume its intended role as anti-Communist bulwark and economic nexus in the Far East.

Policymakers believed there were a number of Asian nations with which the Japanese might trade. Two possibilities were the sterling nations of southern Asia, India and Pakistan. An arrangement with these states would allow Japan to pay for imports with pounds, not the dollars that had to be supplied by the United States.[69] U.S. officials held some hope for Taiwan, a former Japanese possession that traded extensively with the home islands before the war. By early 1949, however, there appeared every prospect that Taiwan would soon be controlled by the Chinese Communists, placing the island in the same position as the mainland with regard to Japanese trade. An important possibility was northeast Asia, especially South Korea, and this area was carefully explored.[70]

But by the autumn of 1949, the Americans and Japanese were interested primarily in Southeast Asia: the states of Indochina, Burma, Thailand, British Malaya, and Indonesia. The Japanese, of course, understood the value of Southeast Asia to their economy: in 1940, following a partial U.S. embargo on oil, they had invaded the region to gain access to Tonkinese coal, Malayan tin and rubber, and Indonesian oil. Before the war, Indochina, Burma, and especially Thailand had produced surplus rice. If Japan could manufacture industrial goods and textiles, it might trade with Southeast Asia for the raw materials and food it needed so badly.[71] This trade would have obvious advantages for the beleaguered Southeast Asian nations as well. By late 1949, American policymakers began mapping strategy to achieve an intraregional trading system in the Far East anchored by Japan. At the end of the thread the administration had traced from Communist China to Japan, it now discovered Southeast Asia. The region had grown in importance for two related reasons: the containment of China and the restoration of Japan.

There were sizable obstacles to the realization of these hopes for

Southeast Asia. First, like much of the world outside the United States, the nations of Southeast Asia suffered a severe shortage of dollars, which occupation officials continued to insist be used to purchase Japanese products.[72] There remained in Southeast Asia and throughout the Far East an antagonism toward the Japanese. American plans to revive Japanese industrialism using the food and raw materials of less developed Far Eastern nations sounded very much like the reimposition of the East Asian co-prosperity sphere, and four years after the end of the war, memories of Japanese brutality remained fresh. As Ernest Bevin put it dourly, "The people who live near the Japanese are anxious about them."[73]

The most critical problem with the American design was the economic and political chaos in Southeast Asia itself, exacerbated in 1948 and 1949 by the advent of Communist China. During this period, the French were fighting in Indochina, the British in Malaya, and the Dutch in Indonesia. The Burmese were fighting each other. With the partial exception of Malaya, the instability in Southeast Asia prevented the recovery of food and raw materials production. Even if the colonial powers and indigenous collaborators could revive agriculture and the extractive industries, it was doubtful that they could then protect them. The United States could perhaps reshape Japan as it wished, but it had no control over Southeast Asia. It essentially had no policy there.

This lack of policy could be remedied. By the summer of 1949, the imminent "loss" of China, the continuing economic difficulties of Great Britain, and the persistent weakness of Western Europe, caused in good part by the drain on the French economy of the war in Indochina, had drawn the attention of U.S. policymakers to Southeast Asia. The region's importance for Japanese economic recovery provided an additional reason for American concern. The United States could thus attain several objectives at once if it could do something to pacify Southeast Asia and revive it economically as a producer of food and raw materials and a consumer of developed nations' manufactured goods. One way to do this was to offer aid to Southeast Asian countries. In November, U. Alexis Johnson, the deputy director of the State Department's Office of Northeast Asian Affairs, noted: "With regard to Japanese trade with south and southeast Asia the problem involves the maximizing of the food and raw materials production in those areas, thereby enabling the acquisition of foodstuffs and raw materials by Japan in exchange for industrial products." Japanese economic recovery depended on "increasing the food and raw materials production of south and southeast Asia, possibly by . . . loans and Point Four assistance."[74] This kind of assistance was not of the magnitude hoped for by Walter Salant, but a State Department official had nonetheless raised the possibility that the United States could enhance Japanese chances for success by providing aid to increase the productivity of Southeast Asia.

The compromise of American ideology began in Japan in 1947. Liberalism, manifest in the postwar efforts by occupation authorities to purge imperialists, dissolve the zaibatsu, and accede to European and Asian demands for Japanese reparations, was suspended when the Americans stopped or reversed these policies. Multilateral trade, at first, was less obviously jettisoned. American plans to establish a Japanese–East Asia trading sphere, however, demanded special arrangements that implicitly discriminated against nations outside the region. To guarantee Japan these East Asian markets, policymakers would find it necessary to create the sort of preferential agreements against which they had battled for years.

Ironically, this policy shift met stern opposition from a vocal advocate of economic protectionism, Great Britain. The British and their Commonwealth allies Australia and New Zealand supported Japanese economic recovery but opposed Japan's becoming the workshop of East Asia.[75] Great Britain had interests of its own there, and required an active Far Eastern trade to escape the enormous dollar debt it had incurred during the war. The Japanese, encouraged and underwritten by the United States, potentially could produce the same sorts of goods the British did, and with relatively low wages, geographic proximity, and American subsidized exports would ultimately undersell the British and push them out of their Far Eastern markets.[76] F. R. Hoyer Millar, minister at the British embassy in Washington, cautioned the Foreign Office in November that "we shall probably need to be vigilant over the extent to which the Americans will seek to expose South-East Asia to Japanese penetration."[77] The British ambassador in Thailand went further: "SCAP policy seems to me . . . to play into the hands of Moscow and Peking and thereby to be contrary to America's own desire to contain the communist menace in this part of the world."[78]

At the same time, the British recognized that their opposition to the nascent American interest in reviving Southeast Asian production subverted their own purposes in the region. British policymakers knew it was essential to the success of their nation's economy to reinstate the previously lucrative triangular trade between the United Kingdom, Asia, and the United States. This trade had failed in part because of conditions in Southeast Asia. If Southeast Asian—and particularly Malayan—productivity could be restored, if the United States would abandon its wartime habits and agree again to import Malayan raw materials, and if the United States could be induced to help protect Southeast Asia from Communist-inspired nationalism, then perhaps Great Britain could fully reenter the system of non-Communist world trade and assure the success of its economy. Despite their protests about American help for Japan in Southeast Asia, the British understood that their need in the Far East was the same as that of the Japanese: to foster U.S. interest in the economic recovery and political stability of Southeast Asia.

3

Great Britain and the Dollar Gap: The Malayan Link

Early in February 1949, the White House received a plaintive letter from May and Samuel Charles Wright, recently retired mistress and master of a London school. The Wrights wanted to travel from England to Pennsylvania to meet Father Divine, the noted evangelist whom the Wrights believed was "the long looked-for God" appearing in fulfillment of biblical prophecy. All their arrangements had been made, wrote the couple, save one: they had not been allowed to convert their sterling savings into dollars. Would the president help?

If the Wrights ever managed to meet Father Divine, it was not because of the administration's assistance. The letter was referred to an official in the State Department, who replied stiffly that the matter was in the hands of the British government.[1] In the winter of 1949, pounds were not directly convertible into dollars. Concerned that traders throughout the world would immediately exchange their sterling holdings for dollars, thereby undermining the pound and jeopardizing the United Kingdom's position as banker for the sterling area, the British government refused to permit convertibility. The Wrights' predicament symbolized the profound economic problems of Great Britain during the postwar period.

The United Kingdom operated both within and outside of the sterling area, a bloc of nations that had been or were still members of the British Empire and that conducted their economic relations in pounds sterling.[2] The Second World War had seriously eroded the influence of Great Britain within the empire and the sterling area as a whole, and by 1947 the British had relinquished political control in Palestine, India, and Burma and faced the prospect of a less domi-

49

nant relationship with colonies and former colonies in Africa and Asia. "The great thing was," recalled the British under secretary of state, ". . . to try to establish a new and, if possible, an intimate relationship with old dependencies which, in our weakened state, it was impossible to hold down by force, even if that was desirable."[3] The Labour government of Prime Minister Clement Attlee, elected in 1945, hoped to replace political control with strategic and particularly economic links that would transform the United Kingdom from policeman of the empire to banker of the sterling area.[4] But even this more modest position would prove difficult for the British to achieve. During the war, the British government had created within the bloc a sterling-dollar pool, through which all dollars received for sterling area exports were funneled to the desperate United Kingdom in exchange for promissory notes payable in sterling. In 1945, Great Britain owed sterling debts—known as "sterling balances"—of £2.723 billion.[5] In five years, Great Britain had gone from a creditor to a debtor nation within the sterling bloc.

Great Britain's debtor status within the sterling area was a post–World War II phenomenon, but the nation had had a negative trade balance with the dollar area nations since World War I. This problem became acute during the Second World War, when the United States provided a $390 million loan, along with Lend-Lease grants totaling $27 billion. It was apparent that these funds were not sufficient to ensure the restoration of British economic strength in the postwar period, and another sizable American loan seemed necessary for the British to be able to purchase from the dollar area the materials essential for survival and reconstruction. As difficult as the outstanding sterling balances made the British position within the Commonwealth, the "dollar gap" proved the most serious and intractable problem in British postwar economic relations. Its solution, as the Labour leadership came to recognize, depended ultimately on the Americans' willingness to suspend temporarily their cherished vision of a world free of colonialism and invigorated by expanding, multilateral trade and an understanding by the Truman administration of the crucial role played by the underdeveloped sterling nations, especially British Malaya, in the restoration of Great Britain's economic potency.

Throughout the war and into the postwar period, U.S. policymakers regarded their most important task as the reconstruction of Western Europe, including Great Britain. They pursued this goal for the sake of Western Europeans, who otherwise faced privation and instability; for Americans, who felt a kinship with Western Europeans and had an interest in the recovery of freely trading European economies; and for the entire non-Communist world, which could retain its freedom only as long as Soviet expansionism was halted and Communist subversion, which seemed to feed on social distress, was discouraged. Great Britain was the mainstay of Western European recovery, the United States' largest prewar market, and America's closest ally. America's postwar objectives would be realized only with the revitalization of the British economy.

While American and British authorities agreed on the necessity for British recovery, the allies differed sharply over the suitable means for achieving it. Since the depression of the 1930s, the United States had struggled to destroy the British system of imperial preference, which protected sterling markets by discriminating against exports from dollar nations. The Roosevelt administration, and particularly Secretary of State Cordell Hull, insisted that the solution to depression and war was free trade, unencumbered by high tariffs and state trading. Though few American policymakers believed as zealously as Hull in the multilateralist panacea, most in essence shared his view and labored during and following the war to break down the imperial system.

That the Truman administration inherited these assumptions was apparent from the conditions the United States attached to the \$3.75 billion British loan, approved in December 1945 following an autumn of acrimonious bargaining. At American insistence, the British agreed not to discriminate against American exports, to negotiate within the Commonwealth a scaling down of the sterling balances (thus generally loosening the colonial tie and opening Commonwealth markets to American exporters), and to allow sterling-dollar convertibility within one year of the effective date of the agreement. The British were unhappy with these stringent terms, but had no choice and could only accept. "We have done our level best to move [the] Americans," wrote the ambassador, Lord Halifax. "I am sorry we have failed."[6] In the United States, many congressional skeptics who regarded the loan as unsound were won over by negotiator Will Clayton's assurance: "If the agreement is ratified, we will have multilateral trade."[7]

It did not work. Unable to discriminate against exports from dollar nations, the British watched helplessly as dollars streamed out of the country, used to purchase badly needed food and raw materials from the United States and Canada. As the dollar gap widened, the sterling gap between Great Britain and other pound-holding nations narrowed only slightly; the underdeveloped countries that held the balances were not much inclined to reduce them simply because the United States hoped they would. British compliance with the American demand for sterling-dollar convertibility nearly proved disastrous. The convertibility clause went into effect on July 15, 1947. Immediately, holders of sterling throughout the world betrayed their suspicions of the pound by converting to dollars. British dollar reserves dwindled at the rate of $115 million a week in the latter half of July and $150 million a week in August. Eighteen months from its beginning, the British loan neared exhaustion. On August 20, Chancellor of the Exchequer Sir Stafford Cripps suspended convertibility, and the British prepared to face the consequences of this violation of the terms of the loan.[8]

The failure of multilateralist principle coincided with the intensification of the Cold War. In March 1946, Winston Churchill delivered his famous "Iron Curtain" speech at Fulton, Missouri. Joseph Stalin responded by spurning the World Bank and the International Monetary Fund, announcing a new five-year plan, and increasing diplomatic pressure on Iran and Turkey. Attempts to secure agreements on the control of atomic weapons and the future of divided Germany foundered on what the Americans regarded as Soviet ambition and what the Soviets believed was United States intransigence. By early 1947, the American containment doctrine began to take shape. In March, Truman announced plans to supply beleaguered Turkey and Greece with economic and military assistance, wrapping his request for funds in an excoriation of the Communists that he and his advisers hoped would frighten Congress into making the appropriation. The Truman Doctrine speech further chilled relations between the two great powers.

In the wake of this growing hostility and the absence of economic recovery in Europe, the Americans changed course slightly and combined their demands for pure free trading with a policy of giving substantial economic aid to their Western European allies. Under the Marshall Plan, or European Recovery Program (ERP), Great Britain became the largest beneficiary of U.S. economic aid, receiving $1.24 billion. The Marshall Plan did not signal the administration's abandonment of multilateralism, but reflected a new awareness that it was too soon after the war to demand sweeping reforms without the proper underpinnings. The United States now pursued multilateralism second hand, through the medium of large-scale economic assistance.

For a time the new strategy seemed to work. The British economy improved in 1948. Agricultural and industrial production each rose

12 percent, and investments increased with the rise in investor confidence. The adverse balance of payments with the United States was reduced by nearly one-third.[9] It appeared that the British had finally begun to bridge the dollar gap.

But Stafford Cripps, at least, recognized that recovery had come under highly favorable conditions and thus remained tenuous. Serious problems still existed. The British economy had not yet proved it could survive in a world of free convertibility. The sterling balances had not been scaled down. Most critically, despite modest progress, the dollar gap remained enormous. Cripps's "Economic Survey for 1949," released in February, declared that "the outstanding problem with which we are now faced is the large and continuing deficit with the Western hemisphere, and in particular with the dollar area." British exports to the United States were one-third of British imports from the U.S.[10] "It is becoming increasingly clear," concluded the cabinet's Economic Policy Committee, "that, unless in the next two or three years we can greatly increase our exports to Canada and the U.S.A., we cannot become independent of ERP Aid without a reduction in our present standard of living."[11] In the meantime, Great Britain remained vulnerable to any disruption of its delicate economic relationship with North America.

The jolt came in the late spring of 1949, when a months-old recession in the United States suddenly intensified and began to have an impact on foreign trade. Some American economists had predicted a serious postwar depression, so most were relieved when the recession stayed mild. In Great Britain, the subsequent decline in American imports of British and sterling area products and the continued rise of U.S. exports caused the dollar gap to widen again. At the beginning of 1949, the dollar gap was £82 million (about $330 million). Following the second quarter of the year, the gap was nearly twice that and rapidly increasing. The statistics, reported a Foreign Office man, had "awful implications," and officials at the American embassy in London thought "Cripps exhibited more concern than we have ever seen him show."[12] In the florid prose of the *New York Times*, Great Britain was "nervously taking her own economic pulse, feeling her head for signs of fever and ransacking the medicine cabinet for commercial cure-alls." More soberly, the paper added, "Now the time of jubilation has passed."[13]

The crisis intensified through June and July. Lewis Douglas, the American ambassador in London, sent a flurry of cables to the State Department, describing the steady erosion of the British dollar position. The London stock market plunged, and a state of emergency was declared to cope with a strike by dockworkers.[14] On June 22, Foreign Minister Ernest Bevin wrote to Dean Acheson that his nation's predicament was "more serious than I supposed" and requested "urgent consultation" with Treasury Secretary John Snyder, who was scheduled to visit the Continent in early July. Bevin concluded: "Unless firm action is taken I fear much of our work on Western Union and the Atlantic pact will be undermined and our progress in the Cold War will be halted. Indeed, the effects of a continued recession in the United States may drag us all down."[15] It would require more than increased American aid to assure recovery. As a Bank of England official put it, "even the great concept of Marshall Aid, which has buoyed up the hopes and maintained the fabric of the Western Europe democracies during the last two years, now seems unlikely to achieve the ends for which it was designed."[16]

John Snyder arrived on July 8 and held two days of meetings with British officials and Canadian Finance Minister Douglas Abbott. Snyder and Cripps did not get on well. The treasury secretary was a doctrinaire multilateralist who deplored the British loyalty to "international state trading" and had little patience for Cripps's bland requests for a lower U.S. tariff and price supports for Malayan rubber. Snyder was unhappy with the proposed British import reduction and thought it more sensible to curtail Labour socialism or devalue the pound. Following the first meeting, Snyder cabled Acheson that "we now seem to be facing squarely a fundamental difference" between the American and British strategies for coping with the dollar gap. When the meetings ended, the parties issued a vague communique, indicating little more agreement than a resolve to continue the talks on a more specific level in Washington during early September.[17]

Despite its differences with the Americans, the Labour government moved with dispatch and determination to solve the crisis. Some steps could be taken within Great Britain. First, convertibility had to be temporarily forsworn; any return to free dollar-sterling exchange must come, the Board of Trade decided, only "in our own time."[18] Next, the article of the British loan agreement that prohibited discrimination against American exports would have to be ignored. In his quarterly balance of payments report to the House of Commons on July 6, Cripps called the dollar gap the nation's "most difficult problem" and reluctantly urged a reduction of dollar imports as "an evil necessity."[19] "Non-discrimination is nonsense," declared a report by the Board of Trade, and in August Cripps announced dollar import cuts of $400 million for 1949–50, a reduction of 25 percent.[20] Finally, Cripps and other government officials exhorted British exporters to abandon readily accessible sterling markets in favor of more competitive but potentially more rewarding dollar markets. While the sterling balances practically guaranteed British exporters automatic payment in pounds for their products and thus provided a strong temptation to sell to balance-holding countries, sales for sterling yielded none of the dollars needed by the British to buy essential goods from the dollar area. Selling for sterling was also inflationary because it raised the amount of spendable currency in the United Kingdom without increasing the number of goods available for purchase. For these reasons, Cripps appealed "most earnestly and with all my strength to our manufacturers and exporters to redouble their efforts to sell their goods in dollar markets."[21]

But domestic measures alone would not make the problems go away. Sterling-dollar convertibility had not caused the latest downturn. Imports could be slashed only so far if the British standard of living was not to be reduced to a politically perilous level. Most significant, British exporters favored sterling over dollar markets not solely because of their desire for easy profit. In fact, British manufacturers did not produce much of what Americans wanted. There seemed little future for Great Britain's machinery, vehicles, and textiles in the American market. Elsewhere within the sterling area, however, there were resources that might attract American dollars to places where the British might get at them. As Cripps told John Snyder, only one-third of the recent dollar loss was due to a decline in British exports. Two-thirds of the loss was attributable to a fall in dollar receipts for sterling area raw materials. Two of the most important of these, rubber and tin, were primarily produced by the colony of British Malaya.[22]

Before the war, Great Britain had avoided a serious trade imbalance with the dollar area through a system of triangular trade. The British had been creditors to underdeveloped sterling nations, sending more in value of manufactured goods to these nations than it accepted in value of raw materials from them. Of course, Great Britain was in debt to the dollar area, particularly the United States. A balance, however, was maintained by the third link in the system: the underdeveloped sterling nations exported raw materials to the United States, and, because their modest needs for finished goods were largely met by the British, they obtained American dollars in payment for their raw materials. The British then accepted these dollars as payment for their surplus exports to the other sterling nations. The entire sterling area was thus involved in balancing the British dollar deficit.[23]

The most important and fragile link in the operation of the triangle was the Malayan trade surplus with the United States. In 1937, the United States bought more from Malaya than from any other nation except Canada. (Malaya ranked only thirty-ninth on the U.S. export list.) The largest dollar earner for the sterling area before the war was natural rubber, and 90 percent of it came from Malaya. The United States bought three-quarters of its prewar rubber from the sterling area. The sterling area's second largest dollar earner was tin, mostly in the form of smelted tin metal, almost all of it exported by Malaya. During the depression, rubber and tin made the most significant contributions to narrowing the dollar gap. In 1937, while Great Britain languished $591 million behind in its trade balance with the dollar area, Malaya had a trade surplus with the United States and Canada of $247 million.[24]

The war disrupted triangular trade. The Japanese invaded Malaya the day after Pearl Harbor and occupied it until the end of the war. Maintaining trade with Malaya was inconceivable. For the British this meant no dollars were available from what was ordinarily their most prolific source. For the Americans, the occupation of Malaya cut off the principal source of rubber and tin, which were essential to the war effort. In response, the U.S. government subsidized the development of synthetic rubber and built the nation's first tin smelter at Texas City, Texas. Synthetic rubber was not an exact substitute for the natural product, and it was still necessary to obtain tin ore for the smelter. But the twin developments made the sterling bloc's chief dollar earners far less necessary than they had been to the U.S. economy. By 1949, the decline of triangular trade appeared serious to many Britons. A high ranking official pointed out that while "public opinion in Canada and the United States tended to assume that our current difficulties were due to a drop in exports of United Kingdom manufactured goods to dollar markets . . . in fact, our difficulties were more largely due to a drop in the volume and value of exports to dollar markets of primary products from the rest of sterling area."[25] Even so, rubber and tin were in 1949 the second and fifth most valuable sterling exports to the United States, and Malaya was easily the most important dollar earner in the sterling area.[26] The promise of a successful triangular relationship remained.

And so, during the postwar period, while the Labour government imposed austerity at home, the British lavished effort and money on their Southeast Asian colony of Malaya in an attempt to reconstruct triangular trade. First, they endeavored to revive rubber and tin production. Second, the government encouraged producers to increase exports of rubber and tin to the United States, the largest source of dollars. Finally, when rebellion broke out in the colony in 1948, the British moved with alacrity to suppress it and protect their precious investment. At the same time, and more broadly, British officials tried to persuade their American counterparts to provide economic aid to the underdeveloped nations in the sterling area and Southeast Asia. The permanent reduction of the dollar gap depended on the success of all these efforts.

The British government believed it essential to give special attention to the rehabilitation of the rubber and tin industries. Between 1945 and 1949, the government spent £86 million on Malaya in grants and loans, and much of this was directed at rubber estates and tin mines.[27] In rubber, a record 600,000 tons produced in 1941 had fallen to 400,000 tons in 1946. Machinery had been broken, the jungle had reclaimed portions of the plantations, and the labor force had dissolved.[28] The tin mines had been severely damaged, and most of the dredges used to bring the ore from the mines had been destroyed; of the 126 dredges operating in 1941, only 18 remained five years later. Tin production, which had reached roughly 110,000 tons in 1940, was in 1946 a meager 8,500 tons.[29]

British efforts to revive the Malayan extractive industries met with some success. Rubber production increased rapidly, and by 1947 tonnage exceeded that of 1941. The production of tin rose more slowly, but in 1947 showed an improvement of more than 30 percent over the previous doleful year. Both industries expanded in 1948.[30] But the American recession slowed rubber and tin exports and exposed the frailty of British progress. In response to market conditions, rubber production slumped, and tin inched ahead too slowly to soften the impact of the crisis. Fact-finding missions scurried into the field. British officials exhorted Malayan producers to work harder, and the Colonial Office drew up a five-year development plan for the colony.[31] Along the first front, the British had won a partial victory: Malayan rubber production had recovered from the war and tin had nearly done so, but both extractive industries remained highly sensitive to economic conditions in the United States.

Though the British might battle alone to revive the Malayan rubber and tin industries, it was obvious that the second part of the effort to restore triangular trade required American cooperation. The dollars needed to reduce the dollar gap would come principally through American purchases of Malayan tin and rubber. The British government used a number of tactics to convince the Americans to buy more of these products. Since the end of the war, the United States had purchased large amounts of foreign raw materials for the strategic stockpile, and foreign economic requirements had always figured in American decisions to buy. The stockpile appropriation had expired in February 1949, and bureaucratic squabbling, congressional inertia, and the effects of the recession combined to prevent the approval of a new appropriation until October. In the meantime, purchases dropped off.[32] British policymakers stressed the injury to sterling area dollar earnings caused by infrequent stockpile buying and urged their American counterparts "to make quicker progress with the stockpiling of essential commodities," especially rubber and tin.[33] In August, when the Senate Appropriations Committee recommended that stockpile officials attempt to buy raw materials first in the United States, the British Treasury countered sharply, arguing that this policy would undermine Western strategy, further disrupt the free world economy, and "have important political consequences, particularly in the Far East."[34] The Attlee government proved willing to take drastic steps to emphasize its concern, especially for tin. When American stockpile purchases diminished, the British Ministry of Supply began buying all Malaya's tin—worth some £8 million— with the hope of selling it eventually to the United States. The British also issued vague threats to sell tin to the Soviet Union, previously proscribed by Anglo-American understanding.[35]

Selling natural rubber to the United States raised special problems. For one thing, some American industrial consumers disparaged the quality of Malayan rubber and preferred the reliability and availability of domestic synthetic. The Colonial Office encouraged Malayan producers to market their rubber vigorously in the United States, and the producers responded enthusiastically; in late 1949 they formed the Natural Rubber Bureau to represent and advertise their shared interests.[36] At the same time, the British were forced to compete in an American market that favored domestic synthetic producers. In 1948 Congress had approved the Rubber Act, which mandated a minimum consumption of 222,000 tons of synthetic rubber per year. This meant, in effect, that no matter how high the price of synthetic rubber rose, natural rubber could be imported only after the synthetic quota had been absorbed. Improved technology in the production of synthetic pushed total consumption to 442,000 tons in 1948, which depressed the price of natural rubber and cost the sterling area an estimated $200 million for the year.[37] British officials lobbied against the Rubber Act, pointing out to the Americans that the mandatory synthetic "floor" sliced into sterling bloc dollar earnings and contradicted the administration's free trade philosophy.[38]

Unlike rubber prices, tin prices had not collapsed by the summer of 1949, but the Attlee government believed a large tin metal surplus was only months away. United States government restrictions on industrial tin consumption, a holdover from the war, were unhelpful. The British also urged the Americans, as well as the Dutch and the Belgians, to accept an international commodity agreement for tin. The agreement would coordinate worldwide production and consumption of tin, preventing sudden shortages or drops in price. The Americans instinctively balked at the notion of trade regulation, but the State Department agreed to consider British proposals during the summer of 1949 under the auspices of the International Tin Study Group.[39]

None of these exertions on behalf of Malayan exports would amount to anything if the colony could not be protected from hostile forces. Rebellion had erupted in Malaya during the spring of 1948. The emergency, as the British called it, was a disjointed uprising led largely by Chinese nationals sympathetic to Chinese communism. The guerrillas' major targets were the rubber plantations and tin mines, and by early 1949 the situation had grown serious. "Production of rubber and tin has not yet fallen in Malaya," observed Anthony Creech Jones, secretary of state for the colonies, in March, "but it [will] fall unless something [can] be done to ease the strain" on European planters and engineers.[40] As a member of Parliament put it, "It is no good talking about closing the dollar gap if we lose Malaya."[41]

The British moved swiftly to suppress the uprising. Malcolm MacDonald, the British commissioner general in Southeast Asia, declared a state of emergency in mid-June 1948 and mandated the death penalty for anyone caught carrying a weapon without authorization. The government mobilized a 20,000-man police force, reinforced by British military units. Periodic raids on Communist party headquarters in Singapore and a government offensive beginning in late 1948 drove the rebels deeper into the jungles. For a time, the guerrilla war degenerated into widespread acts of terrorism. The British created mobile "jungle squads" to go after the enemy in their jungle redoubts. The day before Cripps announced a cut in dollar imports, the British squeezed £6 million from a supplementary budget for the Malayan police force.[42]

Publicly officials maintained a stoic optimism about the emergency. Privately, they grimly acknowledged that the campaign had not gone well. In January 1949, the Foreign Office admitted that "the task of cleaning up some 5,000 determined communist guerrillas . . . is proving a tough one and will take quite a long time."[43] "I confess to being disturbed about the position [in Malaya]," Defense Minister Emanuel Shinwell wrote Attlee in late March. "I am told that matters are improving and they are now taking a firm hold, but I take leave to doubt whether this is so." Other officials expressed similar doubts.[44] At the end of 1949, according to the Malayan annual report, the rebels "were still in a position to maintain their attacks at the same level and even to intensify them in certain areas." The dollar-earning raw materials remained most vulnerable.[45]

The internal rebellion was only part of the threat to Malaya. Since late 1946, the French, in an effort to hold their colony of Indochina, had been at war with Vietnamese guerrillas (the Viet Minh) led by the Communist nationalist Ho Chi Minh. The war had gone badly for the French, and so they had changed tactics. Hopeful of capturing popular support from the Viet Minh, the French encouraged former Vietnamese emperor Bao Dai to accept the presidency of an "associate state" within the French union. On March 8, Bao Dai agreed to this vague arrangement. After lingering on the Riviera for six weeks, he returned to Vietnam and gingerly took his place as head of the French "associate state." The French government submitted the March 8 agreement to Parliament for ratification. The Viet Minh remained unreconciled, and the fighting continued.[46]

From the beginning, the Attlee government had serious doubts about the wisdom of French policy in Vietnam, doubts that did not dissipate after the French chose the diplomacy of the Bao Dai solution. Officials at the British embassy in Paris described the former emperor as "being of a sybaritic nature" and traced his movements from the "flesh pots of Paris" to Cannes, "where the golf courses are better than in Saigon."[47] The signing of the March 8 agreement did not persuade officials that the French had honorable intentions. "Viet Nam independence as defined in [the] proposals . . . is of a very qualified nature," complained one Foreign Office man, and this lament was shared by virtually the entire foreign policy establishment.[48] Ernest Bevin concurred: "I rate the chances of the continuance of French rule and influence in Indo-China very low. I think that France has missed the bus."[49]

Yet while British policymakers were skeptical of French policy and pessimistic about its chances for success, they were so concerned that a victory for Ho Chi Minh in Vietnam would jeopardize the security of all Southeast Asia that they ultimately supported the French position as the best among unpleasant alternatives. If Vietnam fell, its weak neighbors—Laos, Cambodia, Burma and Thailand—might also succumb, placing great pressure on Malaya. A briefing paper for Ernest Bevin, prepared in March 1949, suggested darkly that without help from the West, "eventually the whole of South East Asia will fall a victim to the Communist advance and thus come under Russian domination."[50] Malcolm MacDonald described the most frightening possibility: "When the Chinese Communists had conquered the whole of China, they would probably try immediately to crumble the anti-communist front in South East Asia while the going was good. They could probably seize large parts of Indo China in the next six months: Siam would be unable to resist them without Western assistance . . . . [T]he possibilities of Communist domination in Burma were well known. If these three countries were to fall, Malaya and India would be exposed to a direct Communist threat."[51]

British officials did not necessarily believe Malaya would be invaded or even heavily infiltrated by outside Communist forces. Policymakers, however, were concerned about "contacts" between the Viet Minh and the rebels in Malaya. They were even more worried that Communist victories in the nations just north of Malaya would cut off rice supplies that the colony, a rice importer, needed to survive.[52] Malaya was only part of the British problem. The war in Vietnam placed such an enormous strain on the French military and resources that France was unable to contribute satisfactorily to the defense of Western Europe. After examining estimates of French casualties in Vietnam, a British official wrote, "The figures . . . are really rather staggering! 100,000 to 120,000 French troops lost in three years: no wonder they are not producing much for [the] Western Union."[53] In December 1949, William Hayter, minister at the British embassy in Paris, wrote the Foreign Office, "The fact remains that it is very much in the general interest that France should be free from the heavy burden she is carrying in Indo China, in order to be able to increase her military effort in Europe . . . . This is yet a further reason for giving all the support we can to Bao Dai."[54] Still, perhaps the best argument for supporting Bao Dai was that he was not Ho Chi Minh. "If we accept that the alternative to Bao Dai is something we would heartily dislike," argued a Foreign Office man, "then it seems only sensible to do all we can to encourage him."[55]

The financially strapped British were incapable of providing much more than verbal support for their needy friends. Accordingly, they hoped to convince the Americans to establish a program of economic assistance for the underdeveloped nations of Southeast Asia and sterling nations in that region and elsewhere. British officials welcomed the Point Four proposal, but feared its modest scope and lack of public support made it an inadequate response to the problems of the poor nations. Herbert Morrison, lord president of Council, had in mind a different model: "I have been wondering what new and acceptable outlet might be found to enable the Americans to go on financing the world with dollars as Marshall Plan aid tapers off."[56] The British probed the Americans on this throughout the summer of 1949. In the fall, the British government formed a Committee on U.S. Investment in the Sterling Area. Chaired by the Treasury and made up of representatives from the Foreign and Colonial Offices and the Board of Trade, the committee issued reports emphasizing the need for American investment in the underdeveloped world. "It would seem natural," the committee contended, "that in a healthy expanding world economy capital would flow on a large scale from the United States to less developed countries . . . . The volume of United States foreign investment will certainly affect to a most important extent the magnitude of the dollar problem." The committee concluded that unless substantial investment by the United States was forthcoming, Western Europe's balance of payments would remain unfavorable, and the United States itself would be unable to maintain an export surplus.[57]

The British could lobby in Washington, exhort rubber producers in Singapore, and offer encouragement to Bao Dai through their embassy in Paris. They could not, however, overcome economic problems caused by parsimonious buying of Malayan raw materials, pacify Southeast Asia, or underwrite the development of the Asian sterling area. Only the Americans could do these things. By the middle of 1949, British officials concerned with the strategic and economic importance of Southeast Asia had embarked on a determined effort to make the United States acknowledge the importance of the region. "The problem lies distinctively in persuading the Americans to play the part which they now can play," Malcolm MacDonald told the Foreign Office. "[If] something really reassuring is not done reasonably soon, we may find Indo China and Siam virtually lost to our cause. That would probably tip the scales in favour of the Communists in Burma and bring the front line to the borders of Malaya."[58]

At best, as far as the British were concerned, American policy in the Far East was designed to hold a "strategic perimeter" of nations off the Asian mainland, leaving Southeast Asia itself to the Western Europeans. Frequently it seemed "that the Americans . . . are without any clear policy in regard to the Far East and South East Asia" and because of "having burnt their fingers in China," the Americans were disinclined to increase their commitments in the region.[59] On a visit to Washington in early April 1949, Bevin urged Dean Acheson to explore "the creation of a commitment against Russian expansionism" in Southeast Asia, but the secretary of state was unenthusiastic.[60] Just after this meeting, the British under secretary for Far Eastern affairs, M. Esler Dening, wrote the embassy in Nanking: "One thing which is clear is that a great many minds are thinking on similar lines all over the world, except perhaps in America, where there is little evidence that any serious thinking is being done about Asiatic problems. . . . All this is not very encouraging," Dening admitted, "and it is clear that our task will be long and difficult."[61]

There were indeed great obstacles on the path to American cooperation. Primary, of course, was the administration's ideological objection to colonialism. At best, the problems of Malaya were British concerns. At worst, the British were struggling to maintain an unfree, atavistic system that relied on the suppression of political rights and the retention of discrimination against American exports. For American industrialists, this discrimination was a far more serious matter than it had been before the war, for Great Britain's troubles during and immediately following the war had allowed American exporters to replace the British as the suppliers of the underdeveloped sterling nations, particularly India.[62] Triangular trade, if fully restored, would curtail American exports to the sterling nations. American investments in Malaya amounted to $148 million by 1949, 11 percent of all foreign investment in the colony.[63] It was also unlikely that in mid-1949 the administration or Congress would approve large expenditures, either as inducements for sterling balance holders to reduce Great Britain's sterling debt or to help the British maintain high rubber and tin production in Malaya.[64] Point Four remained during this period a meek request to the private sector, and it had just been introduced to a generally apathetic Congress. The government continued to subsidize synthetic rubber and domestically smelted tin, placating domestic producers but contradicting multilateralist doctrine and frustrating Malayan efforts to sell more to the United States.[65]

Yet by the summer of 1949 the Truman administration, and in particular the State Department, began to understand the relationship between British economic troubles and instability in Southeast Asia. Beyond that, American policymakers concluded that the British could not be forced instantly to abandon all remnants of colonialism and protectionism. The assumption underlying the 1945 British loan—that an immediate return to multilateral trade would restore Western prosperity—was plainly unsound. The assumption on which the Marshall Plan was based—that multilateralism would work if it was combined with an enormous dollar grant—had been challenged by the continued stagnation of the British economy. American policy now began to congeal around a much different idea: that certain elements of British colonialism and protectionism must be preserved if the essential objectives of British recovery and the containment of communism were to be attained.

This new assumption brought with it several changes in American policy toward the British and Malayan economic crisis. For one thing, the United States increasingly sympathized with British difficulties created by the sterling balances. In 1945, the Americans had argued that the balances encouraged discrimination against dollar exports to the sterling creditor nations and urged that they be scaled down. By 1949, two subtle changes had occurred in American thinking. First, though U.S. policymakers still insisted that the balances be reduced, their rationale was no longer that they discouraged American exports, but that they allowed British exporters markets that were comfortably noncompetitive and dissuaded them from contending for dollars in Western markets. Second, several officials recognized the role of the sterling balances in aggravating Great Britain's dollar difficulties and raised the possibility of granting World Bank or Export-Import Bank loans to sterling creditors in exchange for concessions on the balances.[66] This was not, in mid-1949, a well-developed or widespread notion in Washington, but its expression served to prepare policymakers for future British importunities along this line.

Despite their persistent fears that a decline in American exports would invite depression, policymakers accepted with relative equanimity Cripps's decision to limit Great Britain's dollar imports. Willard Thorp, assistant secretary of state for economic affairs, noted that Section 9 of the British loan agreement prohibited discrimination against U.S. exports, and he concluded bluntly: "The British will have to violate Section 9."[67] Days later, Acheson echoed that the United States could not "realistically object" to Great Britain's attempt to curtail dollar imports, though he cautioned that it must be a temporary measure.[68] "We recognize," wrote Under Secretary of State James Webb, "that the U.K. and sterling area must restrict its dollar purchases . . . . We recognize that the need for this is absolute, that it is not a breach of contract, [and] that it is taken in good faith."[69] Even doctrinaire multilateralist John Snyder conceded that although Section 9 should remain in effect, "the time for its rigid enforcement" had passed.[70]

Most encouraging to the British was the increased recognition by

American officials of the importance of triangular trade. This under-standing intensified as the Americans prepared to meet with British and Canadian experts at the Tripartite Economic Conference, to be held, as Snyder, Cripps, and Douglas Abbott, the Canadian finance minister, had agreed, in September 1949. The perception that British economic problems might be addressed through Malaya was natu-rally most vivid among American representatives in Singapore, Kuala Lumpur, and London. William Langdon, consul general in Singa-pore, complained first and most vigorously. In January 1949, he wrote the State Department: "If the fundamental national interest or overall objective of the United States is considered to lie in the recov-ery of Western European nations including Great Britain, and if the economic progress, prosperity and dollar-earning capacity of the Brit-ish Colonies contribute to such recovery, and if moreover one of these colonies, Malaya, is providing us with strategic stockpiles of our tin metal and natural rubber, it would seem logical to give Malaya's two vital productive industries, tin and natural rubber, every support." Langdon concluded, "And yet we seem to be disposed to subject these two industries to uncertainty, fear and even loss for the sake of individual, localized [i.e. domestic] interests."[71] Six months later, as the dollar drain from Great Britain grew critical, Lewis Douglas in London noted the "sharp decline" in the dollar earnings of Malaya and British West Africa.[72]

By the summer of 1949, the emissaries' concerns had started to rub off on policymakers. President Truman, seeming to anticipate the conclusions of the British committee on U.S. Investment in the Ster-ling Area, took his Point Four legislation to Congress with the argu-ment that American aid to underdeveloped nations was needed "to restore the economies of the free European nations" and contribute to "the growing system of world trade which is necessary for Euro-pean recovery."[73] Willard Thorp blamed the British dollar crisis on four factors: an increase in British imports from the dollar nations; the drawing on sterling balances, especially by India; the "decline in dollar earnings of British colonies"; and a decline in British exports to the United States. One of several remedies Thorp suggested was that the United States "take action on rubber" to "help the British balance of payments." Rubber, he continued, was "the largest single dollar earner the U.K. has," and the British had suffered during the first six months of 1949 because of a substantial decline in American con-sumption.[74] In mid-August, the British were cheered by the com-ments of Representative Paul W. Shafer of Michigan, who charged the administration with being unreasonably protective of synthetic rubber. Shafer urged increased rubber purchases by the United States for the strategic stockpile "to bolster the British Empire dollar position" and "to help avoid the spread of Communism in South West [sic] Asia."[75]

This analysis of the British dollar problem suggested several obvious solutions. Douglas, Thorp, and Shafer hoped to use the stockpile to increase Malayan rubber sales, and in early July Acheson promised this idea would be "fully explored" before the tripartite talks began in September.[76] Devaluation of the pound was another possibility. Many economic experts had contended since the end of the war that the pound was overvalued. Devaluation would lower the prices of sterling goods in dollar markets and would, at least in theory, enhance the attractiveness of exports from the sterling area. W. Averell Harriman, the United States special representative in Europe for the Economic Cooperation Administration, declared for devaluation on June 25.[77] Two days later, Acheson instructed Douglas to stress to the British "our conviction that devaluation is probably an essential element in the solution of their problem."[78] Thorp reviewed some of the hazards of devaluation, including the rise in sterling prices of dollar imports, but concluded that devaluation was "probably necessary."[79] George Kennan's Policy Planning Staff stated the case more firmly: a British proposal that did not include devaluation "could not be considered an adequate one."[80] John Snyder agreed.[81]

Those sympathetic with the British position had another opportunity to revise U.S. policy during the summer of 1949: the 1948 Rubber Act was due to expire the following year. In early June, Donald D. Kennedy of the State Department's Office of International Trade Policy recommended the elimination of mandatory consumption of synthetic rubber. Kennedy argued that only the expansion of the dollar market for Far Eastern rubber would offer political and economic stability to the producing nations and Europe and pointed out that Malayan rubber was the "most important item in the dollar income of the whole sterling area." Kennedy later asserted that removing the synthetic quota "would be a most important anti-Communist force in the producing countries of Asia."[82] The recommendation was accepted by the State Department but, as Kennedy anticipated, it soon met opposition from the Munitions Board, the Commerce Department, and the rubber industry. When British officials arrived in Washington in September, the issue had not been resolved, but the State Department provided a sympathetic audience to British pleas for the reduction of synthetic rubber consumption.

The shift in American thinking about British economic problems was captured most comprehensively by a document written in the American embassy in London, circulated at an August 24 briefing session including Acheson, Webb, and Snyder, and eventually incorporated into the background documentation for the approaching financial talks. The paper opened by stressing the seriousness with which the British regarded the upcoming meeting. It reviewed the history of the dollar crisis, which it attributed to seven related factors, the first two being the decline in British and sterling area dollar sales (the result of the American recession and diminished stockpile purchasing) and the "fall in the price of important sterling area dollar earners." The British had reacted quickly, as the crisis demanded, by curtailing dollar imports, but they recognized that this alone would be insufficient to solve the problem. The British would come to Washington, the document said, "in a mood of desperation," aware that they were in technical violation of British loan clauses requiring convertibility and nondiscrimination against dollar imports and knowing that their Marshall Plan appropriation was to be reduced the following spring. British representatives would stress the importance to the world of maintaining the sterling area, point out that many of their best dollar earners—"rubber and tin from Malaya and jute from India"—were threatened by invasive and subversive communism, and would probably resist, for internal political reasons, "any pressure on them to devalue" the pound.

The stakes for the United States were high, the embassy argued. Continued cuts in British dollar imports threatened the American economy. Problems in Great Britain could affect other European nations and jeopardize the objectives of the Marshall Plan. Most of all, cooperation between the United States and Great Britain was "a cornerstone of our general foreign policy" that must not be permitted to crack. United States policymakers would have to act firmly to prevent the spread of Great Britain's problems. They must instruct the British that more direct dollar aid was not a permanent solution to their difficulties and that the "crux of the problem" was the sterling area's diminished ability to export to the dollar area. While the administration should exhort sterling nations to increase production of their most effective dollar earners, the United States also had a responsibility to "behave like a creditor nation." This meant the United States must end its protectionist policies, including those that encouraged domestic tin smelting and production of synthetic rubber. The percentage of required synthetic consumption should be reduced, buying for the stockpile should resume, and the Congress should "give urgent consideration to the President's 'Fourth Point.' " Finally, the situation demanded patience: "We must face the fact that conditions have not yet been created which permit an immediate return to multilateral trade and convertible currencies. For some time other countries will have no alternative except to support themselves by means of agreements which discriminate against the U.S."[83]

It was on the final point that the American way of looking at the world shifted most dramatically during the summer of 1949. Some of the changes in official thinking resulted from a frank reassessment of American policy in light of multilateralist principle. Government subsidies of synthetic rubber and domestically smelted tin violated the free market doctrine that underpinned liberal capitalism. On August 15, Lewis Douglas wrote in a postscript to a memo to Acheson: "We talk a great deal about multi-lateral trade and non-discrimination and we are very critical of other countries on this score. But actually, it seems to me that if we look at ourselves with complete intellectual honesty, we don't enjoy a particularly pure record. We want multilateral trade and we object to discrimination in respect of all things which we do well, but we reserve to ourselves the right to discriminate in those matters which we do inefficiently."[84] What the ambassador had in mind, as he had confided to Roger Makins of the Foreign Office, was synthetic rubber and "the Texas smelter."[85]

But what ultimately mattered more were the compromises the Americans made of liberal capitalist ideology. When they accepted, however ruefully, the British decision to discriminate against dollar imports to the United Kingdom and the colonies, the Americans acknowledged the temporary need for what the British called "the two-world concept," in which various impediments to trade and exchange divided the sterling and dollar areas.[86] In May 1949, the British ambassador to the United States, Sir Oliver Franks, described State Department officials for his colleagues: "They are impregnated with the convertibility and non-discrimination philosophy, but alive to difficulties which prevent a frontal attack on the bilateral practises of the non-dollar area."[87] A month later, Dean Acheson confirmed Franks's judgment. "[We] should be prepared to agree to [British] proposals for . . . the creation of a wide non-dollar trading area," he wrote Douglas. At the same time, the United States "must receive assurances . . . that this action is not a reversal of policy into the line of complete restrictionism," but a temporary measure, permitted to assure British trade "ultimately with hard currency areas."[88]

The American willingness to suspend liberal capitalist ideology took the United States beyond acceptance of economic protectionism. If rubber and tin were to provide the dollars the British needed for economic revival, Great Britain could not allow the Communists to destabilize Malaya. The colonial tie must be strengthened, and the United States would have to permit it. More than that, if the British proved incapable of protecting Malaya themselves, especially from outside forces, the United States might well be asked to help.

4

The United States, Nationalism, and Colonialism in Postwar Southeast Asia

The rebellion in Malaya was part of a larger pattern of anticolonial activity in Southeast Asia, catalyzed by the Second World War and accelerated following the spring of 1948. In the long run, the Japanese occupation proved a beneficial influence on Asian nationalism. The ease with which the Japanese defeated the Europeans erased any remnants of the myth of the invincible white man and emboldened Asians previously intimidated by the colonialists' power. More significant, the occupation gave Southeast Asians an opportunity to participate in governing, either by collaboration, as in Burma and Indonesia, or through organized resistance movements in Malaya, the Philippines, and Indochina. The Atlantic Charter and Franklin Roosevelt's opposition to the return of French rule in Indochina were well publicized in Southeast Asia and were taken to mean that the United States would support Asian nationalism once the Japanese had been defeated.

It thus came as a shock when, following the war, the United States seemed to acquiesce in the reimposition of colonialism in Malaya, Indonesia, and Indochina and offered support to those who had collaborated with the Japanese in Thailand. The British granted independence to Burma, but many Burmese were unhappy with the results of the cession, and the Burmese government was attacked by rebels on the right and the left. To the north, the Chinese drama played before an increasingly attentive Southeast Asian audience. By 1948, rebellions had broken out in each one of the Southeast Asian nations. They soon attracted the interest of statesmen in the hills of north China and in Moscow, in London, Amsterdam, and Paris and, somewhat belatedly, in Washington.

Burma

The Burmese nationalist movement, under the leadership of a group of left-wing intellectuals known as "Thakins" (teachers), had gained valuable experience during the occupation, first by collaborating with the Japanese rulers, then by reversing course in late 1943 to direct armed resistance against the Japanese. When the war ended, the resistance movement, known as the Anti-Fascist People's Freedom League (AFPFL), demanded Burmese independence and declared it would defy any attempt by the British to reimpose colonialism. The British themselves were at first ambivalent. A government white paper, published in May 1945, advised a gradual loosening of the colonial tie, but did not specify when independence might be granted. By late summer, the freshly elected Labour government was receiving conflicting advice from its leading representatives in Burma. Sir Reginald Dorman-Smith, the governor, was sympathetic to Burmese independence but firmly opposed negotiating with the AFPFL, while Lord Mountbatten, the supreme commander of the Southeast Asian theater, regarded the AFPFL as the legitimate mouthpiece of Burmese nationalism. In the spring of 1946, when a wave of strikes threatened to create chaos, Dorman-Smith asked his government for permission to arrest the charismatic nationalist leader, Aung San. Recognizing the possible consequences of that act, the British government instead recalled Dorman-Smith and replaced him with Sir Hubert Rance, an acquaintance of Mountbatten. Soon after arriving in Burma, Rance dismissed the Burmese members of the Governor's Council and replaced them with representatives of AFPFL. Aung San became deputy president.

The colony now moved rapidly toward independence. The Aung San–Attlee Agreement, signed in January 1947, established the machinery for self-government. The election of a constituent assembly in April confirmed that the AFPFL was the most popular party in the country. Most of the individualistic ethnic states near the frontier agreed to join a Burmese federation and willingly took seats in the national assembly. The British government recognized Burmese independence in October, and on January 4, 1948, at 4:20 A.M.—a moment judged propitious by astrologers—the independent Union of Burma was proclaimed.

Sadly, Aung San was not there. He had been assassinated in July on the instructions of former Prime Minister U Saw, the leader of a group of conservative older politicians jealous of the AFPFL's success. The British method of granting independence had alienated a variety of indigenous groups who came to oppose the AFPFL government. Along with the disgruntled conservatives, ethnic Karens renounced the union and rebelled in late 1948, seeking their own state in southern Burma. On the left, the Communists, who drifted in and out of alliances with the AFPFL throughout 1947, ultimately rejected the independence agreement and started an uprising in March 1948. The new Burmese government, intent on creating a socialist economy at home and holding an independent course in foreign affairs, found itself at war with its political opposition.

Burma's untried political institutions and battered economy left it poorly prepared to deal with the Karen and Communist rebellions. Attempts at appeasement failed. In July elements of Aung San's former militia, the People's Volunteer Organization, joined the Communists. The Karens, who had been loyal allies of the British during World War II, were receiving aid from nongovernmental British concerns. By early 1949, the Communists had secured a sizable base in central Burma. The Karens held several cities and threatened others, including Rangoon.

The government sought assistance. Great Britain was perhaps the logical source, but soon after independence the Burmese assembly had voted against remaining in the Commonwealth, dismaying the British and making them reluctant to provide aid. The Socialist government was also intent on nationalizing foreign holdings in Burma. As the internal crisis intensified, however, the government began to retreat from its leftist position. Prime Minister U Nu reorganized his cabinet in September, replacing a number of Socialists with representatives of the conservative faction. In January, U Nu made drastic cuts in the salaries of civil servants and cabinet members, precipitating strikes and, eventually, the resignation of the remaining Socialists from the cabinet. U Nu replaced them and pressed on. Most significantly, the Burmese government abandoned its policy of international neutrality and appealed to the Commonwealth, then to Great Britain alone, and finally to the United States for assistance in fighting the Communists and Karens and rebuilding the economy. The constitutional prohibition on foreign investment was removed in June 1949, and the Burmese government invited foreign enterprise to develop the mining industry. The British were asked to provide arms.

Though the British moved with extreme caution into the volatile situation, they were willing to be asked back. In late April 1949, Ernest Bevin told cabinet members that "the time had come" for the United Kingdom "to state openly" its support for the Burmese regime. The Foreign Office promptly informed the United States that Great Britain's policy toward Burma had "materially changed," and while the British still regarded Burma as something of a "rathole," they felt that without foreign assistance the nation would degenerate into chaos, encouraging the spread of communism.[1] The British were particularly concerned about the effect of the fighting on the emergency in Malaya. Burma was traditionally the world's leading supplier of rice, and of the 500,000 tons of rice imported by Malaya in 1948, two-fifths was Burmese.[2] Before the war, Burma had been a leading Asian exporter of petroleum, tungsten, tin, silver, and lead, and the country was a potential dollar earner for the British if they could regain economic influence there.[3] Stability in Southeast Asia seemed to require stability in Burma. In early June, the Commonwealth granted economic and military aid to Burma. The British provided £8 million for the rehabilitation of the Burmah Oil Company. Arms trickled in for use by the Burmese government.[4]

United States officials showed some concern for events in Burma during early 1949, but their concern was not sufficient to prompt them to provide even modest assistance. Trade between the United States and Burma had never been extensive, and if any Western country were to come to the union's aid, American policymakers thought it should be Great Britain.[5] The Communist victory in China and the subsequent rise in the importance of Southeast Asia during the summer of 1949 did bring a greater regard for the problems of Burma, at least in the State Department. The embassy in Rangoon reported that most of the city's 50,000 Chinese were at least "passive sympathizers" with the Chinese Communists.[6] In July, General Ne Win, the commander-in-chief of the Burmese armed forces, visited Acheson in Washington, and he was followed, in August, by Foreign Minister U E Maung. To Ne Win, the Americans were encouraging about the possibility of Burma's receiving Point Four aid, and U.S. officials noted that the general seemed "quite interested" in this prospect.[7] Acheson and U E Maung discussed the Chinese Communist threat to Burma. The foreign minister felt the Communists would eventually make claims on northern Burmese provinces and would exert pressure both through external force and internal subversion.[8] But Acheson was noncommittal on the issue of U.S. aid. Even in mid-October, a congressional mission recently returned from the Far East recommended that the United States support Karen autonomy.[9] In short, Burma was hardly a matter of much significance in Washington during this period.[10]

Thailand

Thailand was the only Southeast Asian nation without a colonial legacy, and the nation emerged from Japanese occupation with hopes of retaining its independent status. Neither France nor Great Britain was inclined to grant the Thais much latitude. The Thai government had rapidly capitulated to Japan, then declared war on the Allies and used Japanese help to annex tracts in Malaya, Burma, and Indochina. With the defeat of the Japanese, the collaborationist military government of Marshal Phibun Songkhram was replaced by a liberal coalition led by the widely admired leader of the resistance, Pridi Phanomyong. Pridi expressed a willingness to surrender the territory taken from the British colonies and made reassuring statements about the future of democracy in Thailand. This was not quite enough for the British, who demanded a guarantee against the return of military rule, short-term restrictions on Thai exports of rubber, tin, and teak, and 1.5 million tons of free rice for distribution in India, Burma, Malaya, and Singapore. It was far from enough for the French, who claimed, with a good deal of justice, that the 1941 treaty ceding Indochinese land to Thailand was accepted under duress by the illegitimate Vichy government and therefore had no force. Thai liberals thought the British and French demands were unfairly punitive and appealed to the United States for assistance.

American officials were sympathetic to the Thais. They chose to ignore the Thai declaration of war as unrepresentative of Thai popular opinion and pointed to Pridi's base in the resistance as evidence that the new government had effectively liberated the nation from Japanese control. The United States prevailed on the British to conclude a generous peace treaty with the Thais and successfully blunted British demands for a purge of the military and rice donations. Most Americans harbored deep suspicions that the concessions demanded by the Europeans were part of a larger attempt to restore colonial control in southeast Asia, and they invoked the Thais' ostensible love of freedom with great energy during the fall of

1945. Following the signing of the Anglo-Thai peace treaty on the first day of 1946, the United States lent the Thais $10 million for renovation of the transportation system, joined the British in agreements to buy Thai raw materials, and supported Thailand's request for membership in the United Nations, despite strong objections from the French.

American fantasies about Thai independence notwithstanding, republican government had a short and troubled history in Thailand. Pridi was able to produce the trappings of representative democracy—general elections, a westernized constitution, and a bicameral legislature—but he could not generate any enthusiasm for the government within the military. This problem proved fatal. When Pridi's government failed to solve the June, 1946 murder of the Thai King Ananda and dealt ineffectively with the country's imposing economic problems, the military acted. On November 8, 1947, the army staged a bloodless coup and removed the liberals from power. For a time the officers, who were anxious not to antagonize the United States and Great Britain, forged an unsteady alliance with the conservative Democrat party and promised to retain free elections and an independent Parliament. However, when the military's Tharmathipat party made a poor showing during January elections and the conservatives began to perform their constitutional chores with surprising enthusiasm, the officers seized control. Phibun Songkhram, the dictator who had collaborated with the Japanese, was returned to power on April 7, 1948.[11]

American policymakers clearly would have preferred the success of the liberal Thai government to the resumption of military rule under Marshal Phibun. The prospect, however, of a strongly anti-Communist regime in Thailand was not without attraction. Phibun was not the puppet of a foreign power, and his opposition to the Chinese revolution and expressed desire to work closely with the West made him easier to support than the French-sponsored Bao Dai in Vietnam. The United States delayed two weeks, then recognized the new government.[12]

The relative lassitude of U.S. policy toward Thailand during 1948 indicated a general lack of interest in Southeast Asia and American satisfaction with, though perhaps not enthusiasm for, the military government. Marshal Phibun tightened his control following a stillborn army coup in October. Edwin Stanton, the American ambassador, struggled to keep the marshal from dealing harshly with the Chinese community in Thailand.[13] Anomalously, the Laotian and Cambodian resistance movements maintained headquarters in Bangkok, moving at will between the capital and their respective guerrilla wars to the east.[14]

The British were concerned about Thailand because it shared a border with Malaya. After the emergency broke out in 1948, the Attlee government negotiated a "hot pursuit" agreement with the Thais, enabling British forces to enter Thailand after insurgents seeking sanctuary. In January 1949, the British asked the United States to arm five Thai battalions to seal the Malayan border. When the Americans refused, the British provided the arms themselves. Well into the spring, the Americans appeared unyielding. State Department representatives "hinted strongly" that because the Americans "had their fingers burned in China, they are unwilling to risk burning them further in S[outh] E[east] Asia." Thailand was "primarily a British interest." G. H. Thompson, the British ambassador in Bangkok, lamented in April that "it very much looks as though we shall have to try and hold the Siamese baby alone."[15]

In fact, by early spring some officials in the State Department, most notably the embassy in Bangkok, the Policy Planning Staff, and the Far Eastern Office's Division of Southeast Asian Affairs, began to lobby for increased American interest in Thailand. They did so because of the growing threat of Chinese communism, coupled with another attempted coup in Thailand on February 26. This uprising was instigated by the vanquished liberal Pridi Phanomyong and carried out by the Thai navy, which had grown jealous of the perquisites Marshal Phibun heaped on his army followers. The government defeated the rebels after three days of hard fighting, in part because of Phibun's promises to allow the navy a larger role in his government. But many naval officers remained unreconciled, and sporadic violence continued.[16]

On March 29, an important Policy Planning Staff paper, "United States Policy toward Southeast Asia" (known as PPS-51), advised: "We should seek to strengthen Siam [Thailand], help maintain the relative stability which its government [has] achieved, and generally cultivate that nation as a strategically located center of stability . . . in Southeast Asia."[17] The State Department received Ernest Bevin's plea for "a common front against Russian expansionism" in early April.[18] The following month, William S. Lacy, assistant chief of Southeast Asia affairs, wrote a memo for his superior in the division, Charles S. Reed II. Lacy believed the Thai political situation had grown serious in the months since the coup. The army and navy mistrusted each other, and most Chinese in Thailand seemed sympathetic to the Chinese revolution. Lacy claimed that "authoritarian methods" were the only way to stabilize the country and that only Marshal Phibun was capable of asserting the necessary ruthlessness. "Phibun," wrote Lacy, "for all his unsavory past and all his faults of character, is anti-Communist, appears prepared to accommodate himself to the policies of the United States and the United Kingdom, and is eager and as able as anyone to bring the Army and the Navy together again." Lacy concluded that since "diplomacy is the science of the possible, we should move quickly to strengthen Marshal Phibun's government." Reed agreed, and passed Lacy's memo to W. Walton Butterworth, head of the Office of Far Eastern Affairs.[19] A month later, Edwin Stanton urged on Acheson "the judicious extension of modest aid" to Thailand.[20]

During the early summer of 1949, Acheson and the State Department moved slowly toward the Lacy-Stanton position. On June 1, Elliot Thorpe, the military attaché to the embassy in Bangkok, sent to Washington his quarterly military survey of conditions in Thailand. The report made much of Communist Chinese military victories and noted evidence of Chinese "incursions" on behalf of the Viet Minh and Free Laos groups in northern Indochina. These interventions had "grave implications" for poorly armed Thailand. Thorpe concluded that "the potential threat to Thailand's political integrity is much more serious than three months ago."[21] Acheson reacted to this intelligence with surprise and concern, though hardly with haste. He asked Stanton to comment on the attaché's "extraordinary statements" regarding the recent deterioration of Thai political stability and requested specific information on the type and amount of military aid the Thais expected from the United States. Acheson had assumed that Thailand would be grateful for the opportunity to borrow money from the United States. Was it possible that the Thais wanted more?[22]

In the meantime, the Policy Planning Staff had drafted a sequel to its March paper on Southeast Asia. This report, circulated on July 7, was a "Suggested Course of Action in East and South Asia," written by the China hand John P. Davies. Davies' main purpose was to suggest steps the United States might take in the Far East to counter the loss of China. Thailand, with its noncolonial but anti-Communist government, played a pivotal role in Davies' plan to "change the political climate" of Southeast Asia. Davies made four proposals: first, the United States should permit the transfer to Thailand of gold held in Tokyo and claimed by Bangkok; second, the United States should send technical missions to Thailand; third, the Americans should grant the Thais a small amount of military aid; and finally—

"with a real sense of theater"—the United States navy should visit Thailand occasionally.[23]

Policy Planning Staff papers rarely determined U.S. policy, and certainly this one did not. During the late summer and early fall of 1949, however, the State Department moved to implement several of Davies' recommendations. In August, the State Department approved an American mission to survey Thai natural resources.[24] The same month, Truman released to Thailand almost $44 million in gold, held by Japan, as payment for previously unrequited goods and services provided by the Thais during the war.[25] Extensive American purchases of Thai rubber, tin ore, and rice, the latter for use by the Economic Cooperative Administration in Western Europe and China, gave Thailand the only favorable balance of trade in Southeast Asia in 1948.[26] At the same time, American investors grew increasingly interested in Thailand. A journalist noted that "American businessmen, ignoring recent political upheavals which have converted Siam from a shaky democracy to what seems to be a strong military dictatorship cloaked in democratic forms, are invading Siam with the headlong fervor of forty-niners rushing West to hunt gold."[27]

Agreement on supplying military aid to the Phibun government was not as readily achieved. Stanton and the Far Eastern Office were not prepared to recommend the Thais be given a large sum, but they were convinced that a loan would not adequately address the problems faced by the Thai government. During August, Butterworth, Stanton, and Reed separately urged Acheson to endorse "modest gratis military aid" to Thailand. These advocates did not favor the United States taking responsibility for the defense of Thailand, but stressed rather the psychological impact of an offer of aid.[28] Their pleas were in harmony with the State Department's growing concern over Southeast Asia following the publication of the *China White Paper* earlier in the month.

Acheson hesitated. The problems of Thailand had only recently become matters of any importance. The secretary may have felt persistent doubts about Marshal Phibun's rectitude, and the Thais were notoriously unreliable allies, who refused, for example, to take sides in the Indochina war. (The Thai finance minister airily told Butterworth, "Ho Chi Minh is your problem, not ours.")[29] At the same time, Acheson could not be sure that funds were available for military aid for Thailand. If they were, the Office of Far Eastern Affairs (renamed the Bureau of Far Eastern Affairs after a State Department reorganization on October 3) hoped to claim some for Thailand. In the fall of 1949, a bureau memo cast the argument in terms familiar to

Acheson. Thailand was threatened both internally and externally by communism. If Thailand collapsed, it was "unlikely that Malaya could be held. This would mean that from Korea to India there would be no place on the Asian mainland where the United States would have an open friend and ally." There were economic considerations as well: if Thailand and Malaya fell, the United States would be denied strategic raw materials such as tungsten, tin, and rubber. It was clearly "of considerable political and economic importance to the United States to support Thailand in opposition to the forces of communism."[30]

There were several differences between U.S. policies toward Thailand and Indochina during this period, not the smallest of which was the growing disparity in attention the administration gave the two nations. After late 1949, Thailand seldom assumed the significance of Indochina in American planning. Whether or not it was a conscious process, however, U.S. policy toward Thailand served as a prototype for subsequent American policy toward Indochina. Phibun Songkhram was not a colonial puppet, but, like Bao Dai, he was authoritarian, his claim to popular support was dubious, and his regime was threatened by disgruntled elements in the military, liberals, and Communists. Most of all, when the administration argued that U.S. military aid was essential to prevent instability in Thailand, it implicitly acknowledged that Marshal Phibun was incapable of maintaining order and thus muddied the distinction between Bao Dai's dependence on the French and Phibun's need for American support. During the autumn of 1949, as the question of military aid to Thailand became not whether but how, the administration's reluctance to endorse French policy in Indochina seemed increasingly contradictory and even subversive of American objectives in the Far East.

Indonesia

Founded in 1927, the Indonesian National Party (PNI), under the leadership of Sukarno, learned the art of governing in the interstices of colonial rule and Japanese occupation. While the PNI had no monopoly on Indonesian nationalism—the Communists (PKI) and especially the conservative Islamic Masjumi had large followings by the end of 1945—the nationalists had worked both with the Japanese and with the underground during the occupation, and when the Japanese were defeated, the PNI quickly assumed the tasks of leading the nation toward independence. The Dutch had no intention of permitting this, but the war had so weakened them that they were incapable of immediately reoccupying the archipelago. Beginning in September 1945, the British assumed control in the populous western islands of Java and Sumatra. The British were not inclined to disinherit the Dutch, but Lord Mountbatten, who was in charge of the interregnum, had no wish to use British troops to suppress Indonesian nationalists, and he urged the Dutch to negotiate. Hardly in a position to object in late 1945, the Dutch made some tentative overtures to the new Indonesian prime minister, Sutan Sjahrir. In the meantime, the Dutch mobilized their former prisoners of war and reoccupied some of the outlying islands in the eastern half of the archipelago.

The Dutch seem to have been committed to an autonomous Indonesia, but on highly restrictive terms. Immediate independence was unthinkable. The Dutch felt that granting sovereignty must be a slow process, so that the inexperienced Indonesians might learn self-government. The Dutch also hoped to maintain a close relationship with the colony. Believing that an Indonesia united under the PNI would prove headstrong and resistant to continued Dutch control, the Netherlands planned to create an Indonesian federation rather than a republic. The Dutch assumed a federation would be approved by Indonesian local leaders, who would appreciate the greater autonomy fostered by the system and would allow the Dutch to play various Indonesian factions against each other. Between 1946 and 1949, the Dutch negotiated with republican leaders, but strictly for the eventual independence of an Indonesian federation. When each attempt to negotiate reached an impasse, the Dutch used force to achieve their objectives. Thus the Linggadjati agreement (November 12, 1946) which achieved a cease fire and de facto Indonesian control of some areas, was followed by the Dutch "police action" of July 1947; the Renville agreement (January 19, 1948), full of Dutch assurances of fair plebiscites in recently conquered areas, was followed by the second police action in December 1948.

Each of these attacks against the Java-based republican government of Sukarno, Sjahrir, and Mohammed Hatta (prime minister after January 1948) brought misery and death to the East Indies and widespread condemnation of the Dutch. In fact, Dutch aggression in Indonesia was one of the few events of the period that united the Communist, non-Communist, and nonaligned nations. There were several reasons the Dutch were willing to incur this vilification. One was psychological. The Second World War had traumatized the Dutch public, and the acceptance by the Netherlands government of Indonesian independence following such profound national humiliation might have destroyed public confidence. Connected to this issue was a political one. The Dutch Catholic party attracted a good deal of support for its conservative views on the Indonesian issue. Before 1948, the Catholics restrained more accommodating parties from acting more speedily, and in elections in July 1948 the Catholics showed enough strength to ensure the appointment of one of their own, L. J. M. Beel, to the post of high commissioner for the East Indies.

Most important was the Dutch economic stake in Indonesia. Before the war, Indonesia had been the Netherlands' fourth largest market and fifth greatest source of imports, supplying such essential products as rubber, tin, and petroleum.[31] During the war, the Dutch prime minister warned that "if the bonds which attach the Netherlands to the Indies are severed there will be a permanent reduction in the national income of the Netherlands which will lead to the country's pauperization."[32] Following the first Dutch police action, the manager of the Netherlands Bank argued that his country needed to retain Indonesia because one-fifth of the Dutch people were dependent on the colony for their incomes.[33] The Dutch worried that the complete loss of political control in Indonesia would jeopardize their postwar economic recovery, already a tenuous prospect.

During the period 1945–49, U.S. policy toward the Dutch East Indies moved from "studied noninvolvement" to distress and then intense displeasure with the Dutch.[34] After the second police action in December 1948, the new toughness in American policy angered the Dutch, enheartened the Indonesian Republicans, and ultimately increased the possibility of a negotiated solution to the crisis. The administration delayed only a few days before suspending ECA aid for Indonesia.[35] During the first three months of 1949, through the United Nations and the State Department, both publicly and privately, U.S. policymakers sternly lectured the Dutch on their international responsibilities.[36] The Senate threatened to cut off military and economic aid to the Netherlands; in late March Acheson bluntly informed Dutch officials that the anger of the American public over events in Indonesia "gravely jeopardizes the continuation of ECA assistance to the Netherlands."[37]

It is worth noting that these measures were never taken with the French in Indochina. There were several reasons for this distinction in U.S. policy. First, following the first police action in July 1947, the United States had allowed the United Nations to take up the Indonesian question, and in August the United States took the initiative in creating a three-member U.N. Good Offices Committee (GOC), formed to go to Indonesia and mediate the dispute. Because the United States was one of the members of the committee, good will for the United States in Indonesia and throughout the underdeveloped world came to rely on the success of the mediation. The GOC effort was also a test of legitimacy for the U.N. itself.[38]

Second, the Indonesian Republican leadership was anti-Communist and, at least by the fall of 1948, American policymakers acknowledged this. In May of that year, a Soviet announcement that the USSR and Indonesia were about to exchange consular representatives caused alarm in Washington, but Hatta hastily reassured the United States that no such exchange was planned.[39] In September the Communists revolted on Java. The republic responded with force, and by October it had stifled the rebellion. Robert Lovett, the under secretary of state, had exhorted the Republicans to take "firm action" against the Communists to ensure the government a "clean bill of health" in the West. By December, Lovett was convinced the Republicans had proven their opposition to communism and felt Dutch claims that they were holding the line against Soviet expansionism were false and self-serving.[40]

In confronting European colonialism in Southeast Asia, U.S. officials felt they had to choose between supporting Asian independence movements and holding the line against perceived Communist expansionism to rebuild or maintain the strength of the Western European nations. In Indonesia, the absence of a potent Communist movement after October 1948 tilted the scales toward favoring the nationalists. Nearly as important in the American decision was the relative insignificance of the Netherlands to the revitalization of Western Europe. Compared to Great Britain or France, the Netherlands had only a minor role in the future security and prosperity of Western Europe. Dutch threats to subvert the emerging political and economic order in the North Atlantic community simply were not credible. Similar threats by the French were. At the same time, unlike France, the Netherlands enjoyed a high degree of political stability. The United States could afford to push the Dutch harder than the French because there was less at stake in Western Europe.[41]

Although it is undeniable that there were clear differences between U.S. policy toward the Dutch in Indonesia and the French in Indochina, common to both policies was the refusal by the United States to take the final, critical step toward compelling the European power to relinquish its colonial possession: in neither case did the United States actually cut off ECA funds for the European nation. Despite the administration's policy of openly castigating the Dutch and encouraging negotiations, there remained in Washington a deep ambivalence toward the conflict between nationalism and colonialism in Indonesia, an indecisiveness that served as a brake on any determination to push too hard or move too fast. In the last analysis, Southeast Asia mattered to U.S. officials in 1949 largely because of its importance to the stability and prosperity of Japan and Western Europe. Though American policymakers regarded the Netherlands as less vital than France to European recovery and security, and though they believed that a negotiated settlement between the Dutch and Indonesian Republicans would best serve these objectives, they were finally unwilling to force the Dutch to relent in Indonesia at the cost of U.S.–Netherlands relations. The administration tried to persuade the Dutch to grant independence in Indonesia, but it never coerced them.

American ambivalence toward Dutch policy in Indonesia was reflected in the careful language with which policymakers expressed their displeasure. In early 1948, State Department officials advised the Dutch to show "more than average restraint" in Indonesia and urged "a far greater than halfway effort" to reach a negotiated settlement.[42] What these words meant precisely was left for the Dutch to discern. A desire to lend legitimacy to the United Nations might have contributed to the United States' determined pursuit of negotiations through the U.N., but the United States itself did not first bring the Indonesian matter to the Security Council and watered down an Australian proposal that called for the withdrawal of Dutch troops from Republican territory, as recognized by the Linggadjati agreement.[43]

Most revealing was U.S. policy following the second police action in December 1948. While the administration suspended ECA aid to Indonesia and mounted a spirited attack on the Dutch in the United Nations, U.S. officials privately hedged their bets. Dean Rusk, head of the State Department's Office of United Nations Affairs, wrote Philip Jessup, then acting U.S. representative at the U.N., that the "U.S. has no intention [of] bringing about [a] general break with [the] Dutch over [the] Indonesian question. For us to insist upon full compliance with [the] highest standard of conduct as [the] price of our association with other gov[ernmen]ts and peoples would lead us quickly into [a] position of not too splendid isolation."[44] When the Indian government urged U.S. officials to suspend ECA aid to the Netherlands, Joseph C. Satterthwaite, director of the State Department's Office of Near Eastern and African Affairs, countered archly that he was sure the Indians did not want the United States to practice "economic imperialism" against the Dutch.[45] In late January, Acheson expressed hope that the U.N. Commission for Indonesia, a new version of the Good Offices Committee, would "not press matters" with the Dutch.[46] Though the secretary of state menacingly raised the Senate resolution to cut ECA aid for the Netherlands in his talks with Dutch officials, the department itself viewed the resolution as "untimely and inappropriate."[47] Despite impatience with the Dutch in Congress and among American representatives in Indonesia, the administration's policy remained cautious.

The ambivalence in U.S. policy toward the Netherlands in Indonesia anticipated the American response to the French war in Indochina. The Dutch got out of Indonesia, and U.S. pressure was a factor in their withdrawal. But the central dilemma of U.S. policy—freedom for Asians or stability and prosperity for Western Europeans—remained unresolved. In August 1949, Dean Acheson wrote: "Of critical importance is our concern over the stability of Southeast Asia and the development of friendly, peace-loving and economically sound governments in that area. It is of equal importance, in the context of United States world policy, that the adjustment in Indonesia be accomplished in a fashion which will not vitiate the Netherlands' position as a leading democratic nation."[48] At that moment, the secretary could have substituted "Indochina" for "Indonesia" and replaced "the Netherlands" with "France," and no one in the administration would have noticed the difference.

Indochina

As the problems in China, Japan, and Western Europe intensified during 1949, drawing attention to Southeast Asia, U.S. policymakers came to regard Indochina, and especially Vietnam, as the key to the resolution of regional and international crises. Officials saw stability and prosperity in Indochina as necessary for the achievement of similar results in Burma, Thailand, Malaya, and Indonesia and, more and more, as a prerequisite to the political and economic success of the developed, non-Communist world.

Vietnam attracted special concern for several reasons. For one thing, the war there was the most violent and widespread of those in Southeast Asia. Only the Dutch-Indonesian war approached the intensity of the Indochina conflict, and by early 1949 the former seemed destined for negotiated resolution. The French and the nationalist-Communist Viet Minh fought on, each determined to defeat the other militarily. Unlike the opposition in Malaya and Thailand, the Viet Minh were not politically isolated, and the genuine appeal of Vietnamese nationalism, coupled with French brutality, swelled the ranks of the anticolonialists.

A second reason American policymakers were particularly concerned with Vietnam was the communism of the Vietnamese nationalist leadership. The Indonesian nationalists had proved their anticommunism during the autumn of 1948. The head of the Viet Minh, Ho Chi Minh, freely professed his communism, though he permitted other parties to participate in governing the organization. The possibility that the United States might negotiate with Ho was raised by some in the Far Eastern Office of the State Department—their arguments were similar to those used by the China negotiators—but this possibility was decidedly less probable than extending diplomatic recognition to the Chinese Communists. While Ho himself compromised and twisted uncomfortably to avoid dependence on Communist China, the United States viewed Ho as an agent of world communism and refused him any encouragement.

Third, the war in Indochina involved France, the United States' most important ally on the European continent. American policymakers considered the political and economic freedom of France a vital postwar objective, and the active French left and economic stagnation continued to threaten these goals in 1949. Their diversion of resources to Indochina prevented the French from effectively confronting their problems at home. In addition, the United States hoped to mitigate French objections to the rearmament of West Germany by pursuing this goal through the newborn institutions of the North Atlantic Treaty. American policymakers ultimately regarded a rearmed West Germany as essential to restore a sense of psychological security to Europeans who feared Soviet invasion or subversion, but the French were wary of their historically bellicose neighbor and would not countenance German rearmament, even within an Atlantic community, while their own forces and equipment were committed in Indochina. A strong French presence in Europe was necessary to make the North Atlantic Treaty credible. Such a presence was unlikely without a significant change in the Southeast Asian situation.

Finally, Indochina was strategically the most important area in Southeast Asia. Because it shared a border with China, Western officials viewed it as a potential corridor between the People's Republic and all of Southeast Asia. This view rested on two assumptions: first, that the Chinese Communists were interested in expanding into Southeast Asia, either directly or by arming their indigenous surrogates and, second, that if Indochina went Communist, all of South-east Asia would be imperiled. As the State Department reviewed its Far Eastern policy during the summer of 1949, these assumptions were most important in the formulation of new responses. They ensured top priority consideration for the dilemma posed by the French war in Indochina.

At the Potsdam conference in July 1945, the Allies had divided Vietnam into two zones of reoccupation split at the sixteenth parallel, with the British moving into the south and the Chinese taking the north. American policymakers acknowledged then that the joint custodianship would lead to the return of French authority. For reasons of their own, neither the British nor the Chinese were inclined to obstruct the French. As they had in Indonesia, the British—and Lord Mountbatten again—doubted the wisdom of reimposing colonial political control, but they believed the French were entitled to discover this for themselves in Indochina. The commander of British forces in Cochin China, General Douglas Gracey, believed his mandate to restore order in Vietnam permitted him to assist the French in overcoming the resistance of Vietnamese nationalists. In the north, the Chinese hoped to exchange their withdrawal for French concessions on Vietnamese trade, but the pressure of the Chinese Communists and the firm Vietnamese dislike for the Chinese led ultimately to French-Chinese negotiations. Both Great Britain and China began to remove their troops in March 1946.

The decision to restore French rule in Vietnam came as a shocking blow to the Vietnamese nationalists. The nationalist movement centered around the Viet Minh, organized in May 1941 to resist the Japanese. While most of the Viet Minh hierarchy, including Ho Chi Minh, was Communist, the organization had as its major aim the unity and independence of Vietnam, and the leadership was willing to put aside temporarily its radical social goals to attract domestic and international support. In early 1945, the Japanese eliminated the collaborationist French Vichy government and established a nominally independent Vietnamese government under emperor Bao Dai. With the Japanese surrender, the Bao Dai regime collapsed under the weight of its own identification with the oppressor and the enormous popularity of the Viet Minh, the acknowledged leaders of Vietnamese nationalism. In Tonkin and Annam, the northern and central provinces of Vietnam, the Viet Minh took control of the government within a week of the Japanese surrender. In Cochin China in the south, the Bao Dai government was succeeded by a coalition of diverse nationalists and religious sects that was rapidly infiltrated and soon dominated by representatives of the Viet Minh.

The nationalists' hopes for unity and independence clashed with French plans to maintain control over a divided Vietnam. As the British and Chinese gave way to the French, conflict became inevitable. In the south, the French, with British assistance, seized control of Saigon during the early morning hours of September 22, 1945. The Vietnamese government was removed from power, and French citizens, emboldened by the coup, physically attacked any Vietnamese they could find. The Vietnamese retaliated, then retreated into rural Cochin China, and the war in the south began.

In the north, the French inability to mobilize a force capable of dislodging the Viet Minh government brought an uneasy truce between the two sides throughout much of 1946. In the meantime, the government held elections (they resulted largely in the validation of Viet Minh control) and struggled to foster economic recovery despite the depradations of the occupying Chinese. Ho made a genuine effort to reach an understanding with the French, signing two treaties: the Ho-Saintény agreement of March 6, 1946, which allowed a French military presence in the north for five years in return for a nebulous assurance to make Vietnam a "free state within the French Union," and the Fontainebleau "modus vivendi" of September 14, 1946, which proposed an Indochinese customs union but deferred agreement on all the important issues. Ho pleaded for more; the French, he begged, must give him "a weapon against the extremists."[49] The French refused, and Viet Minh radicals harshly criticized Ho for his apparent willingness to compromise.[50]

In retrospect, the radicals seem to have been more realistic about French intentions than was Ho Chi Minh. On June 1, 1946, as the Vietnamese delegation left for Fontainebleau, the high commissioner for Indochina, Admiral Georges Thierry d'Argenlieu, suddenly declared Cochin China a "free republic," a member of the French Union but not a part of Vietnam. The announcement shocked and angered even moderate Vietnamese. The situation disintegrated in late November, when a series of clashes led to a French demand that the Viet Minh evacuate certain neighborhoods in the northern port of Haiphong within two hours. When the Vietnamese did not immediately comply, the French opened fire with heavy artillery, killing at least 6,000 Vietnamese. Subsequent pleas by Ho for calm left both sides unmoved, and on December 19 the Vietnamese attacked the French in Hanoi. War now engulfed all of Vietnam.

To the west, in Laos and Cambodia, the French had less difficulty reimposing colonial rule. The nationalists who had assumed power in the late stages of the Japanese occupation were arrested or expelled, and the French installed in their places governments responsible to the high commissioner in Saigon. Disillusioned nationalists in both countries fled to the hills or the cafés of Bangkok, there to plot the overthrow of colonial authority. In Cambodia, enough nationalists subsequently returned to the political arena to force the supple king, Norodom Sihanouk, to undertake certain democratic reforms. By May 1947, both Cambodia and Laos had new constitutions, the former creating a parliamentary democracy, the latter a constitutional monarchy. France retained control of every important aspect of Cambodian and Laotian public policy.

There were a number of reasons the French were willing to fight to reestablish their control of Indochina. Like the Dutch in Indonesia, the French had an important economic stake in Indochina. Before the war, Indochina had supplied France with rubber and minerals and had served as a market for French light industry. The market was plainly expanding by 1946. As one of the few colonies in the French empire with a positive balance of trade, Indochina was an important source of foreign exchange for France. French investment in the colony was enormous: $2 billion in the early fifties, when the French still owned "all the rubber plantations . . . , two-thirds of the rice, all the mines, all the shipping, virtually all the industry, and nearly all the banks." A sudden rupture of this lucrative relationship would have been disastrous for key sectors in the French economy.[51]

As important as economic considerations were in France's decision to remain in Vietnam, they did not by themselves make the critical difference. By 1948, the French were spending for military operations in Vietnam nearly three times as much as they received in exports from all Indochina.[52] Even more than in the Dutch case, the factor of national pride was a major reason for the attempt by France to reconstruct its empire. France had been humiliated during the Second World War to a far greater degree than the Dutch had been. The Netherlands had not been expected to withstand the German blitzkrieg, but the rapid capitulation of France, allegedly the military equal of Germany, raised questions about the French will to fight. The collaboration of the Vichy government further increased French shame. Vietnam thus became a proving ground for the Fourth Republic, an opportunity to exhibit a readiness to do battle and a chance to regain France's status as a great power.

This psychological factor was enhanced by the prominence of the French military in Indochina. Jean Lartéguy, the journalist-novelist who chronicled the trials of the French army in Vietnam, described the thoughts of an officer whose post was about to be overrun by the Viet Minh. He held a grenade in his hand: " 'All I need do,' he reflected, 'is drop it at my feet just as the Viets are on top of me and count to five; then we'll all leave this world together, them at the same time as me. I shall have died in the true tradition, like Uncle Joseph in 1940, like my father in Morocco, and my grandfather at Chemin des Dames. Claude will go and join the black battalion of officers' widows. She'll be welcome there, she'll be in good company. My sons will go to La Flèche, my daughters to the Legion d'Honneur.' "[53] This sense of heroic nobility may have been behind the decision of d'Argenlieu to declare Cochin China a "free republic." It was also a military man—d'Argenlieu's deputy, General Jean Valluy—who ordered the artillery barrage against the Vietnamese in Haiphong.

All the same, though military officials readily took initiatives in Indochinese policymaking, French civilians were ultimately responsible for Indochina policy. D'Argenlieu's Cochin Chinese republic was embraced by civilian authorities in Paris. Valluy's order to use force against Haiphong fell within the range of responses permitted d'Argenlieu by French Premier Georges Bidault.[54] The civilians, for their part, were susceptible to political pressure. The French majority party, the moderate Mouvement Republicain Populaire (MRP), felt no significant political necessity to withdraw from Indochina and saw grave political liabilities in a decision to pull out. The parties on the French left, the Socialists and Communists, usually subordinated their anticolonialist ideologies to the more practical pursuit of political power and rarely made Indochina a central issue in their campaigns.[55] On the right, Charles de Gaulle stood ready to exploit any sign of MRP vacillation on the interventionist policy. Moreover, it is likely that by 1948 French policymakers recognized that withdrawal from Indochina would nullify their strongest reason for opposing American plans for German rearmament. If the core of the French army returned to Europe, French policymakers could not object to a restored German force because it would be counterbalanced, within a North Atlantic organization, by the enlarged French army. The French recognized that the North Atlantic Treaty implied the eventual rearmament of Germany and privately conceded to American officials that this was necessary for the security of Western Europe.[56]

To have consented to this publicly, however, would have enraged French public opinion and assured the political destruction of the MRP. The war in Vietnam kept the issue submerged. For the French, the economic and psychological reasons for fighting were thus effectively reinforced by political factors.

Following the Viet Minh attack on Hanoi in December 1946, the French decided that negotiations were futile and took the offensive. In February 1947, after hard fighting, the French reclaimed Hanoi. The Viet Minh prepared for a long war. Ho was not sanguine about the outcome and again proposed negotiations. He appealed for Western support by reorganizing his cabinet to include several non-Communists. The French rebuffed these conciliatory gestures. By the early spring of 1947, however, it became apparent to the French that they would not win a quick victory. A revolt in the colony of Madagascar reduced the number of troops available for Vietnam, and the superior tactics of the Viet Minh confined French military successes to the cities, and then only during the day. This discouraging state of affairs drove the French back to the possibility of negotiation. Ho Chi Minh's demands for unity and independence were clearly unacceptable, and so the French cast about for a more tractable alternative.

In March 1947, Emile Bollaert, who had replaced d'Argenlieu as high commissioner in February, turned to the former Vietnamese emperor Bao Dai, then living in Hong Kong. Bollaert may have hoped that the former emperor would become a mediator between the French and Viet Minh. From the first, however, the military and colonial administration in Vietnam saw Bao Dai as an alternative to Ho, someone whose personal prestige and ties to the Vietnamese monarchy could win for him the support of moderate nationalists and Catholics chary of Viet Minh radicalism. Following several quiet overtures to Bao Dai during the spring of 1947, Bollaert went to Hong Kong in June to try to persuade the ex-emperor to reenter Vietnamese politics.

Bao Dai was ambivalent about the French requests. On the one hand, he was a nationalist, convinced that the time had come for French withdrawal from Indochina. Bao Dai was anti-Communist, but he was not unsympathetic to the Viet Minh, who also recognized his personal prestige and continued to woo him ardently. Yet, Bao Dai's experience with political power under the French before the war and under the Japanese during the war's late stages now provided a strong temptation to govern once more. The deep antagonism that characterized Ho's relationship with the French did not exist between the French and Bao Dai, who fancied himself a civilized man, capable of achieving understandings with other civilized men. In the face of increased attention and superficially conciliatory gestures by the French, Bao Dai initially wavered between remonstrance and cooperation.

On September 10, 1947, Bollaert announced at Ha Dong that the French had agreed to accept the unification of Tonkin, Annam, and Cochin China "within the French Union." Bollaert had wanted to offer more in the hope of renewing contact with the Viet Minh, but officials in Paris had purged the word "independence" from a draft of Bollaert's speech to prevent this possibility. Predictably, it was not Ho Chi Minh but Bao Dai who rose to the bait. A week after the Ha Dong speech, Bao Dai announced his willingness to negotiate with the French on behalf of Vietnamese nationalists who opposed the Viet Minh. These negotiations led to the signing, on December 6, of a joint declaration in which the French recognized Vietnam's right to unity and independence and a secret protocol that placed strict limitations on this promise. Bao Dai signed both documents, but when he returned to Hong Kong, his supporters discovered the protocol and demanded that he repudiate it. Bao Dai subsequently qualified his promises, but the French had gotten what they needed. On December 23, the French cabinet told Bollaert "to carry on, outside the Ho Chi Minh government, all activities and negotiations necessary for the restoration of peace and freedom in the Vietnamese countries."[57] Bao Dai now personified the French hope for maintaining their influence in Vietnam.

An elaborately choreographed courtship now ensued. Bao Dai, pressed by his advisers, continued to insist the French government grant him generous concessions on unity and independence so that he might challenge Ho Chi Minh for nationalist support. The French offered tantalizing morsels—a shadow "central" government under General Nguyen Van Xuan, then the Baie d'Along agreement of June 1948, which recognized Vietnam's unity as "an Associate State within the French Union"—but did not promise independence. These offers were ultimately sufficient for Bao Dai. Although negotiations between Bao Dai and French officials were reportedly acrimonious, privately the French acknowledged that the alleged difficulties were invented as a "smoke screen" to restrain rumors that Bao Dai was a "French stooge."[58] Agreement was reached in the spring of 1949. The Elysée, or March 8, agreement established Bao Dai as the head of a unified Vietnam within the French Union, and four days later the French Parliament voted to allow Cochin China, still operating as a nominally independent "free state," to join Vietnam with the consent of the Cochin Chinese. An absurd turnout of 700 Cochin Chinese and nearly 500 French elected a territorial assembly that voted to join Vietnam as long as the country remained in the French Union. Satisfied, Bao Dai returned to his country on April 28, ending three years of self-imposed exile. He went first to the resort city of Dalat, his favorite site for practicing his hobby of hunting tigers.

The Bao Dai solution immediately ran into trouble. To begin with, the French felt they had made sufficient concessions to the non-Communist nationalists, and they implemented the agreements they had made in a most conservative fashion. The French retained control of Vietnam's economic and foreign policies; the Vietnamese, one analyst has written, "were given offices but no authority, titles but no power."[59] As a consequence, most prominent nationalists hesitated to commit themselves to Bao Dai's government. Bao Dai's cabinet was filled with neophytes, sycophants, and small-time operators, and the former emperor finally appointed himself prime minister when no one of any standing sought the job. Bao Dai was an earnest but colorless leader whose return to government "aroused no popular enthusiasm" among the Vietnamese.[60] The British consul general in Saigon described Bao Dai's arrival in the capital in June 1949: "The band of Vietnamese guards were dressed in white, and with their peculiar shape of beret, strangely resembled a detachment of cooks." The official noted that "in spite of some hard-working cheerleaders among the crowd, little enthusiasm was shown."[61] A French journalist depicted the same scene: "A dreary ceremony took place at the inevitable town hall, with the inevitable Vietnamese and French notables. Not a scrap of color in the streets, in spite of the order to hang out flags. Not a moving creature either, nothing but an emptiness and a silence that meant contempt."[62]

The divisions the French had hoped the new government would create among the Viet Minh did not occur. The Viet Minh retained both the political and military initiative, and their intensified guerrilla activity in the spring of 1949 frustrated French pacification efforts.[63] Workers deserted the rubber plantations in droves to join the Viet Minh.[64] The Communists were sweeping to victory in China. In the face of these events, the French turned, with increasing desperation, to the United States. In January 1949, before the March 8 agreement had been signed, French officials "intimated" that once Bao Dai had returned to Vietnam the United States would be asked to extend him economic assistance.[65] On April 13, Jean Daridan, counselor of the French embassy in Washington, sounded out State Department officials on the matter of aid for Bao Dai. Walton Butterworth of the

Office of Far Eastern Affairs replied cautiously that circumstances would dictate American policy and wondered whether Bao Dai would succeed in uniting Vietnamese nationalists. Butterworth felt he had given the French "no encouragement" on the issue of economic aid.[66]

The American attitude toward the French return to Indochina was characterized by an ambivalence more profound than that which marked U.S. policy on Indonesia. On one side was a genuine opposition to colonialism. This belief included not only a moral antipathy for the lack of freedom under colonial rule, but also a reflexive sympathy for nationalism and a suspicion that colonialism could not succeed and would ultimately radicalize the opposition. On the other side, some American policymakers argued that French friendship and cooperation in Western Europe were more important than the immediate success of Vietnamese nationalism, which was in any case tainted by its Communist leadership and associations. The French would leave eventually, ran the argument, but for the time being liberal capitalism and anticommunism could best be served by supporting the French efforts to grant independence gradually, while excluding the Communists from the negotiating process. Between 1945 and 1948, the American position oscillated between these two poles.

Throughout the Second World War, Franklin Roosevelt had sought to deny the French their former colony by advocating a postwar Chinese trusteeship over Indochina. Under pressure from military officials, members of the State Department's European Office, the British, and the French, Roosevelt gradually softened his anticolonial position. At Yalta in February 1945, the Allies agreed that only colonies surrendered "voluntarily" by the colonial powers would be subject to the trusteeship plan.[67] In mid-March, the president confided to a State Department official that he would agree to allow the French to return to Indochina if they promised eventual independence, and days later he reluctantly authorized American air support for the French fighting the Japanese in Indochina.[68] If FDR had not totally abandoned his hopes for an end to colonialism in Indochina by the time of his death, the legacy he left for his successor was at best ambiguous.[69]

Partly because the situation in Vietnam was not a matter of great importance to the United States in 1945, the Truman administration's policy soon settled into the same uneasy ambivalence.[70] The Truman foreign policy demanded a strong, democratic France, and no one in the administration contemplated denying Marshall Plan aid to the

French because of their policy in Indochina. The administration, however, did rebuff requests for direct economic and military aid for Indochina,* and officials repeatedly lectured the French on the need for concessions to the demands of the non-Communist Vietnamese nationalists. Colonialism plainly offended the administration's liberal capitalism. From Saigon, American officials warned that the French were quietly restoring the agencies of "economic exclusivism which prevailed before the war."[71] The French colonial administration supported itself in part through the sale of opium, on which it held a monopoly. French plans to transfer opium revenues to the Bao Dai government angered the State Department.[72] And, beginning in early 1949, there was Bao Dai himself.

At the root of the United States' persistent doubts about French sincerity in Vietnam was the perception, shared with the British, that Bao Dai was a lascivious Chiang Kai-shek, without Chiang's acknowledged organizational abilities. Bao Dai's personal habits and his obvious reliance on the French made the United States reluctant to dignify him with direct assistance. When Bao Dai lingered in France during early 1949, speculation on both sides of the Atlantic had it that the delay had little to do with patriotism, but with the fact that Bao Dai had recently "come into some money" and was "reluctant to move from the Riviera fleshpots at this juncture." The French were curious but not greatly concerned because Bao Dai had always been dependent on them for money, and they assumed he would be again soon.[73] In February, Charles Reed warned Butterworth against precipitate recognition of the Bao Dai government lest "we lay ourselves open to the charge of supporting a French-inspired and French-dominated political zero."[74] Even the French businessmen in Vietnam regarded the Bao Dai solution as "part *deus ex machina* and part comic opera."[75]

Following his return to Vietnam, Bao Dai continued to plead with the French for further concessions, but his behavior subverted the apparent seriousness of his public posture. Bao Dai holed up in Dalat with a flashy bleached blonde, there ostensibly to make a film of the former emperor's life. When officials delicately suggested to Bao Dai that the masquerade was fooling no one—neither the woman nor

---

*This policy had little actual impact on the French because the United States sent arms to France and did not prohibit their reshipment to Indochina. This obvious abrogation of anticolonialist principles left the State Department troubled but unwilling to consider broader sanctions against the French. See "Department of State Policy Statement on Indochina," Sept. 27, 1948, in *FRUS* (1948), vol. 6, *The Far East and Australia*, pp. 43–49.

members of her entourage could handle a camera—Bao Dai replied, "Yes. I know. But really that girl is quite extraordinary in bed." Then he added, "She is only plying her trade. Of the two I am the real whore."[76] The view of Bao Dai as a playboy persisted into late 1949, at least in the private discourse of American officials. A report from Hanoi recounted a British view that Bao Dai's entire "loyal following probably comprised some half-dozen Hong Kong concubines."[77] When a French official diplomatically characterized Bao Dai as "shy," someone in the State Department penciled next to this description, "He doesn't want to get shot!"[78]

Cynicism about Bao Dai was characteristic of those in the State Department who advocated a cautious, wait-and-see policy toward the Bao Dai experiment. Suspicious of the French and lacking confidence in Bao Dai's statesmanship, advocates of this position recommended that the United States withhold diplomatic recognition of the Bao Dai government and deny economic and military assistance to Indochina until the French indicated their intention to move toward Vietnamese independence and Bao Dai demonstrated an ability to attract nationalist support. Most of the exponents of the wait-and-see policy were associated with the State Department's Office of Far Eastern Affairs: the office director, Butterworth; Charles Reed, Kenneth P. Landon, and Charlton Ogburn, Jr., of the Division of Southeast Asian Affairs; Cora DuBois, an analyst in the Division of Intelligence Research for the Far East; and Edwin Stanton, the ambassador to Thailand.

For the first five months of 1949, Dean Acheson stood with these cautious officers. The secretary expressed American doubts about the Bao Dai solution in a telegram to the embassy in Paris on February 25, 1949. The French government, wrote Acheson, had forsaken serious negotiations with the Vietnamese, had refused to press the matter of Vietnam's unification in the French assembly, and had generally "shown no impressively sincere intention or desire [to] make concessions which seem necessary [to] solve [the] Indochina question." Acheson was vague about the concessions he had in mind, but he insisted the French must provide Bao Dai with the "means to succeed" in attracting popular support. A reconsideration of the U.S. ban on ECA aid to Indochina, "intimated" by the French the previous month, must "await developments."[79]

Not everyone agreed with the wait-and-see policy. In mid-March, Ambassador to France Jefferson Caffery replied to Acheson's February 25 telegram, taking issue with the secretary's firm policy toward the French. Bao Dai, he argued, represented the only hope for an "anti-communist nationalist solution" in Vietnam. The ambassador urged that the United States study the text of the March 8 agreement with the thought of extending to Bao Dai some "moral and perhaps some economic support." Caffery acknowledged the riskiness of his proposal, but felt the alternative—waiting for Bao Dai to establish broad support before sending him aid—was far more dangerous. Caffery hoped American aid would enhance Bao Dai's prestige when it mattered most: before he undertook the difficult task of uniting Vietnam's non-Communist nationalists.[80]

The Acheson-Caffery exchange occurred as the signing of the March 8 agreement and oblique requests for aid from Paris caused in the State Department an upsurge of interest in the Vietnam problem. In late March, the Policy Planning Staff produced its report, PPS-51, on U.S. policy toward Southeast Asia. For Indochina, the document recommended neither "full support of . . . French imperialism" nor "unlimited support of militant nationalism."[81] The solution to this dilemma, according to a revised draft of the paper, had three parts: "1. We should frankly tell the French what we think about Southeast Asia. 2. We should consult with the British and Indians on a cooperative approach to the impasse in Indochina. 3. We should attempt to have the French transfer sovereignty in Indochina to a noncommunist indigenous regime." Colonialism threatened U.S. objectives in Southeast Asia: "The good effects of enlightened U.S. and British policies in SEA have been seriously compromised by French and Dutch colonialism in Indochina and Indonesia. Dutch and French policies are an economic drain on them, on Western European strength and on the U.S.; they contribute to the spread of communism in SEA, and they cannot succeed." The stakes were high, for "not until the political problems of SEA are well on their way to a solution can the region begin to fulfill its major function as a source of raw materials and a market for Japan and Western Europe." The document was silent on the issue of U.S. aid for the Bao Dai government. It was approved, with some reservations, by all relevant agencies in the department, including the Office of European Affairs.[82]

Bolstered by PPS-51, the advocates of a wait-and-see approach for a time successfully urged caution in the department's treatment of Bao Dai. On April 14, Reed warned Butterworth that premature support for Bao Dai would lead the United States "blindly down a dead-end alley" for a cause that might well prove "hopeless."[83] A week later, Charlton Ogburn compared the Bao Dai government to a potential "little Kuomintang," and Reed later told a British representative that any American aid for Indochina should be conditional on the willingness of the non-Communist nationalists to rally around the new regime.[84] Cora DuBois saw a "high likelihood" that Bao Dai would fail because of "inadequate concessions from France" and proposed national elections that would include Ho Chi Minh and his followers. (This was too much even for Reed.)[85] Within the Far Eastern Office the only dissenter was William Lacy, who in mid-May urged American support for Phibun Songkhram and Bao Dai.[86]

Acheson stayed in the fold, though he did hold open the possibility that, if circumstances changed, the United States might yet support Bao Dai. The secretary offered no encouragement to Caffery in Paris. In three May telegrams to George Abbott, the consul general in Saigon whose own view was similar to that of Caffery, Acheson reiterated American policy to make no promises to the French. He made his position clear in a May 15 cable: If the French proved to be offering "too little too late," the United States would not go *rushing into [the] breach to support [the] Baodai agreements at [the] cost [of] its own remaining prestige [in] Asia"* (emphasis in original). Instead, the United States would work toward a common stance with its allies who, as Acheson surely recognized, would approach the Bao Dai solution at least as warily as the Americans.[87] On May 20, Acheson left for a foreign ministers' meeting in Paris.

David K. E. Bruce had on May 9 replaced Caffery as ambassador to France. Bruce was the former chief of the ECA mission in France, and Acheson thought highly of him.[88] Bruce shared Caffery's sympathy for the French position on Indochina, and it is likely that Bruce attempted to convince Acheson of French sincerity while the secretary was in Paris. Bruce certainly pressed the issue with the State Department during this period. In telegrams to Washington on May 30 and June 2, Bruce emphasized the concessions offered by the French in the March 8 agreement, arguing that they afforded "as much room for satisfying Vietnamese aspirations . . . as [the] Vietnamese themselves are now able to cope with." The ambassador did not endorse U.S. recognition of the Bao Dai government, but thought the State Department should offer a general statement of support for the Vietnamese state. From Saigon, George Abbott, no doubt frustrated by Acheson's cautious attitude, chimed in with a cable supporting Bruce's proposal.[89]

On June 6, Bruce received from the State Department a memorandum for the French detailing the department's views on the March 8 agreement. The statement was carefully worded, but it reflected the views of PPS-51, criticizing French colonialism and urging the French to add to the Elysée agreement "assurances that Vietnam is to exercise control of its own destinies." Convinced that the message would infuriate the French, Bruce requested that he be allowed to withhold the memo in favor of a less prickly oral summary of its contents. On June 16, James Webb, the acting secretary of state, agreed. Bruce had turned aside the department's attempts to force concessions from the French.[90]

Meanwhile, Webb himself, presumably with permission from Acheson, endorsed Bruce's proposed statement of support for Bao Dai. On the morning of June 14, he authorized Abbott to speak with Bao Dai, and that evening Webb sent to the relevant embassies a draft statement that pronounced the formation of the Bao Dai government a "gratifying" development.* Edwin Stanton, in Bangkok, quickly protested, but he was overruled, and the statement was released to the press on June 21. To be sure, the statement was restrained in its praise of the March 8 agreement, and it contained no promise of future recognition or aid. Still, the larger implications of a unilateral expression of support plainly outweighed the relative caution of its words, and both French and Vietnamese authorities were profuse in their thanks.[91]

This apparent policy shift brought despair to one advocate of the wait-and-see policy. On June 28, Charlton Ogburn summarized the conflict between the West European and Far Eastern Offices (as he saw it) in the department. Bruce had first blunted the department's memo of June 6, then had taken advantage of Acheson's presence in Paris and "forced us to issue a statement welcoming the Bao Dai Government." What has happened, complained Ogburn, "is that SEA's policy has been junked, nothing effective is being done to promote a non-Communist solution in Indochina, and FE is being put in an extremely vulnerable position." He concluded, "I think we are heading into a very bad mess in the policy we are now following toward Indochina."[92]

Ogburn's judgment was a few months premature. Having offered its expression of support, the State Department now awaited developments in Vietnam. Signs were inauspicious and warranted caution. In Saigon, George Abbott actually read the March 8 agreement and had second thoughts: "There did not seem to be a single right accorded Vietnam which was not limited [in] some way [by] requirements for approval or consultation with [the] French."[93] Bao Dai seemed to indulge in "petty politics," and the American consul gen-

*This was subsequently changed to an expression of "welcome."

eral in Hanoi reported a "general conviction" that Bao Dai's government had "been thrown together hastily in [a] desperate last minute effort."[94] Bruce himself told Bao Dai's advisers that the United States could not contemplate diplomatic recognition of the Vietnamese government until it had "attracted widespread popular support" and "demonstrated its ability to govern effectively."[95] Officials had hoped to coordinate Southeast Asian policy with sympathetic Asian nations, but even such firmly pro-Western bastions as Thailand and the Philippines refused to make any but the meekest statements of support.[96] The State Department also stayed "aloof" from a plan for an anti-Communist Pacific Union devised by Syngman Rhee of South Korea, Elpidio Quirino, president of the Philippines, and the increasingly desperate Chiang Kai-shek.[97]

But this was a critical summer in Asia and Europe. The Communists neared total victory in China, and the white paper was published the first week of August. The British suffered through their economic crisis. And in March 1949, the United States and many Western European nations had pledged themselves to mutual military assistance through the North Atlantic Treaty. United States objectives in shaping the treaty were various, but all of them depended on a strong French presence on the Continent. American policymakers soon recognized that the war in Indochina demanded the diversion of French resources to Southeast Asia and thus prevented the revival of French power in Europe.

Like the Marshall Plan, the North Atlantic Treaty responded to problems on a variety of levels. Article 2 of the treaty obligated the parties to "seek to eliminate conflict in their international economic policies," a phrase that was later used by American officials to promote the economic integration of Western Europe. According to Article 4, member nations would consult whenever "the territorial integrity, political independence or security of any of the Parties" was threatened. This meant troops from member nations could be used to suppress uprisings within other member states. Article 5 declared that an attack on one of the member nations "shall be considered an armed attack against them all." This phrase pledged the signatories to mutual defense against invasion. The treaty was signed on April 4, 1949, by representatives of twelve nations.[98]

The treaty's military potentialities had their most serious implications for the French. The treaty had originated early in 1948 when the Americans, with fortuitous assistance from the Czech coup, had convinced the French and British to expand their anti-German military alliance (the Dunkirk Treaty, March 4, 1947) to a pact directed against any possible aggressor (the Brussels Treaty, March 17, 1948). The elimination of Germany as the object of the alliance reflected two American positions: first, that the Soviet Union, not Germany, was the real threat to European security and, second, that West Germany could not permanently be isolated from Western Europe but must be enlisted on the side of anticommunism in the Cold War. This second view meant not only that the United States would seek West German economic recovery and political stability, but raised the prospect of a rearmed West Germany participating in the NAT.

In France, the press, military officials, and left-wing politicians warned of this possibility during the spring and summer of 1949.[99] This concern may have been premature, but it was not paranoid, for American officials anticipated the need for German rearmament and saw a multilateral agreement such as the NAT as the logical means of pursuing it.[100] By the fall of 1949 neither Truman nor Acheson successfully effaced the rampant rumors that West Germany would be rearmed.[101] Whether German rearmament would prove acceptable to France depended on American assurances that any restored German force would be so tightly supervised or numerically overmatched within the NAT that the Germans could never begin military operations unilaterally. During the early months of 1950, policymakers would confront what West German rearmament meant precisely for the French war in Indochina.

Of more immediate importance in the summer of 1949 was the growing conviction of many policymakers that the French were fighting the expansion of world communism in Indochina. To be sure, not all American officials believed this. Evidence concerning Ho Chi Minh's ideology and loyalties was mixed. At the end of the Second World War and for some time later, Ho Chi Minh was encouraged by the friendly attitude of several officers in the Office of Strategic Services, and he appealed to the United States for help in blocking the restoration of French rule. Between October 1945 and February 1946, Ho sent at least eight messages to the United States asking for assistance, and he pursued a conciliatory policy toward the French.[102] Even in 1949, Cora DuBois described Ho's attitude toward the Marshall Plan and the North Atlantic Treaty as "astoundingly moderate . . . quite un-Kremlinish." Ho also seemed interested in the Point Four proposal.[103] Chronically wary of the Chinese, regardless of their ideological predilection, Ho maintained that "China's New Democracy is Chinese, ours Vietnamese," and his Vietnamese government was the last Communist regime to recognize the PRC in late 1949.[104]

But U.S. policy was never officially receptive to Ho Chi Minh. No

U.S. official ever acknowledged any of Ho's entreaties.[105] The Truman administration correctly gauged Ho's communism, but incorrectly assumed that it attached him to the monolithic forces of world revolution, even in the face of contradictory or sparse evidence. In October 1946, Acheson saw great significance in the flag selected by the Viet Minh government—a gold star on a red field.[106] Four months later, Secretary Marshall insisted that "Ho Chi Minh has direct Communist connections, and it should be obvious that we are not interested in seeing colonial administrations supplanted by . . . political organizations emanating from and controlled by the Kremlin."[107]

Despite Marshall's certainty, policymakers had a difficult time proving the existence of these connections and strained for explanations. Questioned by Butterworth in March 1948, a British official admitted that intelligence had found no link between the Kremlin and Ho—Radio Moscow's reception was weak in Indochina—but argued that a "trained communist" did not need direct guidance because he instinctively followed the party line.[108] An Office of Intelligence Research survey concluded in the fall of 1948 that "if there is a Moscow-directed conspiracy in Southeast Asia, Indochina is an anomoly [sic] so far." The survey offered four possible explanations for this, but did not include the possibility that Ho might be acting on his own.[109] In early 1949, George Abbott admitted from Saigon that there was little information available on Ho's relationship with Moscow, and found it "peculiar" that the Viet Minh did not indulge in much anti-American propaganda.[110]

Any doubts about how to interpret these contradictions were put aside by Acheson on May 20, 1949, just as he departed for the pivotal foreign ministers' meetings in Paris. Having apparently received a disappointing reply to his query of late 1946—and having remembered it—he wrote stiffly, "U.S. not impressed by nationalist character red flag with yellow stars." Then: "Question whether Ho as much nationalist as Commie is irrelevant. All Stalinists in colonial areas are nationalists." Only France, through concessions to the non-Communist nationalists, could solve the problems of Indochina. Ho Chi Minh had no place in American plans for a peaceful settlement.[111]

By the summer of 1949, American policymakers had become concerned with the fate of Southeast Asia in light of the Communist victory in China. Policymakers saw Indochina as the next Far Eastern battleground in the war against communism. But the problem of Communist expansion was not confined to Indochina. By the late summer of 1949, instability gripped Southeast Asia from Tonkin to the outskirts of Kuala Lumpur, and the presence of large Chinese communities in most Southeast Asian countries created what one American official called "Trojan horses" throughout the region.[112] United States policymakers were concerned about not only the fate of the French in Indochina, but about the spread of communism to all of Southeast Asia and its implications for the recovery of Japan and Great Britain. Vietnam was increasingly important not simply or even primarily for its own sake, but because it held the key strategic position between China and the rest of Southeast Asia. As Dean Rusk wrote Acheson in mid-July, it was now essential to "broaden the present China problem into the larger problem of Asia."[113] The American attitude toward Indochina was part of a larger tapestry, one aspect of a policy that by the summer of 1949 had become regional and even global in scope.

While the United States hesitated in the summer of 1949 to extend full-scale support to the Bao Dai solution in Vietnam, the growing urgency of the situations in Western Europe and the Far East forced policymakers to confront the potentially ominous implications of indecisiveness. The moment during which the United States might have provided an inspiration for Vietnamese nationalism had passed, and now there was only disillusionment and antagonism. Policymakers still refused to extend diplomatic recognition to Bao Dai and denied the French economic and military aid for Indochina, but a report approved by the State Department in late May noted that if political conditions improved in Indochina, American assistance "would greatly contribute to the attainment of . . . U.S. objectives."[114] More startling and prophetic was a memo by Charlton Ogburn, written three days after his indictment of the department's statement of support for Bao Dai. To Charles Reed, Ogburn wrote: "The one eventuality we must on no account allow to come to pass is the crumbling away of Asia into the Communist abyss for lack of sufficient military and economic assistance which we have never tried to obtain. I do not think we should ever be able to explain why, when it was generally accepted that the United States would have to put out 20 billion dollars to save Europe, we planned to save Indochina, Siam, Indonesia, Burma, Ceylon, India and Pakistan on a pittance."[115] During the final months of 1949, Ogburn's determination rubbed off on the State Department. The stakes in Indochina, and by extension in all of Southeast Asia, had gone higher.

5

Shifts in United States Policy toward the Far East and the World, Autumn 1949

George F. Kennan had global interests by the summer of 1949. On August 22, the author of the containment policy and the architect of the State Department's crank-up program for Japan addressed the American people over the CBS radio network on a characteristically ambitious topic. "The international situation at the present time," Kennan began, "is primarily one of transition. It is a transition from the immediate posthostilities era, with its short-term problems and demands, to a new state of affairs which may endure for a long time." After surveying conditions in Western Europe and the Near East, Kennan moved on to China, where, he thought, political and economic instability would prevail for many years. "Meanwhile," he continued, "in China and throughout the Far East we will have to guard our own proper interests, and the interests of international peace, as best we can, facing frankly the fact that there are forces at large which are dangerously antagonistic to both."[1] The world was changing again, and American foreign policymakers would have to adjust their responses accordingly.

The late summer and fall of 1949 was a period of transition for U.S. foreign policy, as the Truman administration struggled with the problems of a new and dangerous phase of the Cold War. The Communist victory in China was the critical event contributing to the charged international situation because of what it implied for China, the recovery of Japan, and the future of Southeast Asia. As we have seen, the problems of Western Europe also became more acute during the second half of 1949. The British financial crisis, the domestic and foreign difficulties of France, and the continued weakness of West

Germany threatened the unity and strength of the developed, non-Communist world. A terrifying new blow struck the West in September, when Truman announced that the Soviet Union had recently exploded its first atomic weapon. "This is now a different world," wrote a solemn Senator Arthur Vandenberg. "The new problems are appalling. Where do we go from here and what do we do about it?"[2]

The administration had already initiated a serious reappraisal of its Far Eastern policy. Acheson had hoped the *China White Paper* would muffle the domestic debate over the failure of the administration's China policy, but he acknowledged the need to move beyond the China debacle to explore fresh alternatives for U.S. policy toward the entire Far East. On July 18, the secretary authorized Philip Jessup, the ambassador-at-large, to make proposals for American action in the non-Communist nations of Asia. "You will please take as your assumption," wrote Acheson, "that it is a fundamental decision of American policy that the United States does not intend to permit further extension of Communist domination on the Continent of Asia or in the Southeast Asia area." Acheson recognized that the administration might not be able to implement all Jessup's proposals, but nevertheless directed the ambassador "to make absolutely certain that we are neglecting no opportunity that would be within our capabilities to achieve the purpose of halting the spread of totalitarian Communism in Asia."[3] Jessup knew this would be a formidable task, and he suggested that Acheson appoint "two outsiders" to assist the State Department with its reformulation of Far Eastern policy. The secretary concurred. On the day the white paper was issued, Acheson signaled a new beginning in U.S. policy toward the Far East by announcing the appointment of Raymond Fosdick, former president of the Rockefeller Foundation, and Everett Case, president of Colgate University, as consultants to the administration on Far East policy.[4]

Part of the consultants' mandate required them to examine the future of American relations with the People's Republic of China (PRC). On this issue Jessup, Fosdick, and Case at first formed an alliance with the advocates of negotiation with Communist China. The consultants affirmed the need for maintaining the open door in China.[5] For Jessup, at least, this included the possibility of extending diplomatic recognition to the Communist government.[6] Jessup's views were reinforced by most of the thirty Far East specialists he had invited to comment on the recognition question and by a round table conference sponsored by the State Department in early October, during which only Harold Stassen, president of the University of Pennsylvania, dissented from the prorecognition view.[7] Fosdick urged that business, educational, and philanthropic contacts in China be maintained: "It must not be we who draw down an iron curtain." Case, though less ardent, agreed.[8]

The consultants were Acheson's creation, and they now became his liberal conscience. There was an affinity between the secretary and those who advised him: Jessup, the Columbia professor who had loyally come to the service of his government; Fosdick, with his Rockefeller connections—these were Acheson's sort of men, public-spirited and bright. For a time during the autumn of 1949, Acheson wavered between the consultants' position and a hard-line posture that demanded conciliatory behavior by the Chinese Communists before the United States would even consider recognition. Certainly Acheson found persuasive the argument that the United States should "attempt to detach [China] from subservience to Moscow," and he emphasized this alternative in a conversation with Truman on November 17.[9] The secretary agreed that trade with China should continue.[10] In discussing the question of recognition with the British, who had resolved by November 1949 to recognize the PRC, he stressed that the administration objected to early recognition and did not specifically rule out the possibility that the United States might someday recognize the People's Republic.[11]

Despite these intellectual sympathies, Chinese Communist behavior, American ideology, and political pressures made it unlikely that Acheson would press for U.S. recognition of the PRC. In China, Communist party radicals had gained influence when repeated overtures to the United States had proven fruitless. On July 1, 1949, Mao Tse-tung issued his famous declaration "On People's Democratic Dictatorship," in which he excoriated American imperialism and announced the policy of "leaning to one side"—the Soviet Union.[12] Communist harassment of Americans, which had occurred sporadically and often without official sanction, now increased.[13] In July, William Olive, the American vice-consul in Shanghai, was arrested and beaten up by police. In October, the American consul-general in Mukden, Angus Ward, was jailed after a year of house arrest. Ward was deported in November. The final blow came in January 1950, when authorities in Peking seized the American consulate, prompting the administration to withdraw all remaining U.S. personnel from China.[14] This action by the Chinese shocked even the stalwart China negotiator Roger Lapham, who now lapsed into perplexed silence.[15]

Ideology was a two-way street. For Acheson to have overcome his rigid anticommunism to advocate the recognition of the PRC would have required some breathtaking mental gymnastics, and there is little evidence that Acheson was prepared to do more than approach the mat. In May 1949, he wrote John Leighton Stuart in Nanking, that "we sh[ou]ld strongly oppose hasty recognition Commies," and he presented three conditions the PRC would have to satisfy to gain American recognition. First, the government must control all of China; second, the People's Republic "should establish some form of acquiescence by the Chinese people"; and third, the government was to honor its "international obligations."[16] Acheson reiterated these conditions the following October.[17]

All of these conditions meant what Acheson construed them to mean. It is unlikely, for example, that Acheson would have regarded any Communist state as capable of obtaining even popular "acquiescence." As long as there was "any opposition to the Communist regime," he told the British and French in mid-November, "it would be a stab in the back for this opposition if we were to accord the Communist Government recognition."[18] The secretary also pointed out that the declaration establishing the PRC on October 1 contained no assurances that the Communists were willing to assume their "international obligations," which, of course, included the agreements the Kuomintang had negotiated with the United States.[19] The Communists would not honor these, as Acheson well knew. No member of the administration ever softened this condition.[20] Meeting with the consultants in late October, Acheson explained that the administration's position on recognition was "not to be eager. We do not regard U.S. recognition of the Chinese Communists as a major instrument for showing interest in the Chinese people or for winning concessions from the Communist Government."[21] In January 1950, the secretary told members of the Senate Foreign Relations Committee that "nobody will gain any advantage by going on and recognizing the Communists" since they would "act entirely in accordance with their own interests" and would not be influenced by conciliatory gestures from the West.[22] By mid-October, Acheson's resistance to recognition had begun to rub off on Jessup, who told senators that while China might follow the example of Yugoslavia, "we do not think it is safe to bank on it."[23] The administration would not act, but it would wait and see if tensions developed between Moscow and Peking.

The political situation in the United States also contributed to the acrimony that characterized Sino-American relations in late 1949. The publication of the white paper triggered a new and more vociferous round of criticism of the administration. China lobbyists scornfully dismissed Acheson's claim that the United States had done all it could to save Chiang Kai-shek's regime and demanded that the administration supply military aid to the new Kuomintang government on Taiwan, something Acheson and Truman resolutely refused to do.[24] To conservative representatives in Congress, recognition of the PRC was inconceivable, and Truman, who was keenly sensitive to the limits on diplomacy imposed by party politics, was not inclined to defy the China lobby for a position of which he was not himself enamored.

In China, Mao leaned to one side without apparent enthusiasm. Stalin had always dealt cautiously, even disparagingly, with the Chinese Communists, and only after the CCP had established its military supremacy on the mainland did the Soviets express their unqualified satisfaction with the party's ideology. The American refusal to negotiate with the CCP left the party little alternative but to ask the Soviets for the assistance it needed to rebuild the shattered country. Still, to most Americans, the signing of Sino-Soviet pact in February 1950 (following a month of strenuous bargaining) confirmed the PRC's subservience to the Kremlin. At the same time, the Soviet Union and China recognized Ho Chi Minh's Viet Minh as the legitimate government of Vietnam. This step was anticipated by the administration, but in the minds of policymakers, its announcement effectively annealed the representatives of Asian communism.[25] The appearance of Chinese Communist troops just north of the Tonkinese border raised fears that Southeast Asia would be next on the agenda of Communist expansionism. Along with the seizure of the U.S. consulate in Peking, these events destroyed what remained of the negotiation option.

Beyond the loss of China, there was in Washington during the autumn of 1949 a feeling that the United States had surrendered the initiative to the Soviet Union in the Cold War. The Marshall Plan and the North Atlantic Treaty had represented American and Western victories at the moments they were promulgated—bold thrusts in the diplomatic offensive against the Communists. Now these initiatives seemed stale. The British financial crisis exposed the inadequacies of the Marshall Plan. No one knew exactly what to do with the North Atlantic Treaty. The Americans hoped to use it to rearm Germany, but there would be no German rearmament without French consent, and that would not be forthcoming until resources then committed to the war in Indochina could be returned for use in Western Europe. For U.S. policymakers, these were very serious matters. American foreign policy needed to get moving again.

Both the sense of crisis and the determination to confront it with renewed vigor were revealed in the U.S. response to the Soviet explosion of an atomic bomb late in August. The explosion deeply troubled policymakers, who had expected the United States would maintain its nuclear monopoly for a few more years, and it represented another Cold War triumph for the Soviets. United States Ambassador Alan G. Kirk found the Russians "rather cocky over their successes in China, elsewhere and their own atomic bomb; I would not say truculent but still quite self-satisfied with [the] year's progress— and perhaps with reason."[26] Policymakers moved with dispatch and firmness to counter the new threat. The administration accepted the view of the deputy assistant secretary of state for European Affairs, Llewellyn Thompson, who advised that as a result of the Soviet atomic explosion it was "particularly important that we avoid any actions which might be interpreted as . . . appeasement of the Soviet Union."[27] The president's first reaction was to speed the development of the hydrogen bomb.[28] A second response by the administration, one that was to have serious implications for the French, was increased interest in Western European rearmament. This coincided with the administration's heightened expectation that West Germany would have to be included in a Western Europe integrated politically, economically, and militarily.[29]

Doubts lingered about American resolve in the Far East. If the Soviet A-bomb had brought parity to the arms race, Mao's victory in China had tipped the balance of power in Asia toward the Communist side. The administration judged it essential to respond, but it was not yet clear which tactics would prove most effective, least dangerous, and relatively inexpensive. Yet something forceful, something positive had to be tried. In mid-October, a House subcommittee recently returned from a tour of the Far East warned that a "negative" American policy toward the Far East, "designed merely to 'check Communism' by military means, is not likely to accomplish its purposes." The United States needed a reaffirmation of its principles: "If we remain true to our heritage of freedom . . . and with missionary zeal dedicate our policies in the Far East to the principles of the advancement of human freedom and the uplift of the level of material well-being and human dignity, we shall not only check communism but place it decisively on the defensive."[30] "Incidentally," Raymond Fosdick wrote Jessup in early December, "it seems to me that too much of the thinking in the [State] Department is negative . . . . We are *against* communism, but what are we *for*?"[31] To redefine American objectives in the Far East and to design and implement policies to achieve them were the tasks the State Department set for itself in the fall of 1949. The United States was "for" the attainment of a free world system linked together by liberalism and capitalism. At the same time, the gravity and urgency of Far Eastern problems seemed to demand solutions—regionalism, protectionism, despotism, and colonialism—that subverted the United States' quest for an ideal world. Each of these solutions required a corresponding shift in U.S. policy toward Southeast Asia.

The first shift moved the United States toward an appreciation of regional solutions for the problems of the Far East. With the communization of China, the focus of U.S. concern in the Far East no longer rested on a solitary nation, but was diffused over a number of nations, including those in Southeast Asia. The destinies of the Southeast Asian nations were connected because instability or communism in any one of these countries threatened the others. The American perception that the economic recovery of Japan rested in large measure on Southeast Asia also suggested a need to strengthen regional commercial ties. These views led some U.S. policymakers to contend that Southeast Asia and the Far East must be treated as a region, a group of nations with similar problems, somehow distinct from other areas in the world.

The consultants, following Dean Rusk's urging to "broaden the . . . China problem into the larger problem of Asia,"[32] endorsed the regionalization of Southeast Asia and the need to coordinate U.S. policies toward the area. On October 27, at a meeting of the consultants, Acheson, and representatives of the State Department's Far Eastern Bureau, Jessup pointed out that the consultants had been asked to consider "the whole area lying between and including Japan and Pakistan," and that they had concluded that the nations concerned should be approached as a unit. Anchored in the west by India and in the east by Japan, the Southeast Asian nations could best confront their problems as common problems solvable through a division of labor involving Japanese industrial production and expertise and the natural resources of other nations. Jessup's aide Walter Wilds argued that "if the United States wrapped up in a single package its resources, interests, and obligations in the area the effect would be to mobilize and electrify both Asian and American opinion." Fosdick was convinced that a centralized administration of programs for Southeast Asia was essential "if disaaray and confusion were to be avoided." "The point was," added Case, "that the Consultants saw a common feeling arising in Asia which we would be unwise to neglect."[33]

Many of the State Department's Far Eastern experts believed the Southeast Asian nations were so diverse that a coordinated policy for them could not succeed. Charles Reed made this argument, and it was accepted by his superior, Walton Butterworth, who pointed out at the October 27 meeting that some nations in Southeast Asia plainly needed more attention than others.[34] Others questioned regionalism not by advocating particularism, but by arguing that even regionalism was too narrowly conceived to represent adequately Southeast Asia's role in U.S. foreign policy. Southeast Asia could not by itself, or even with Japan, hope to raise its standard of living through a closed, intraregional system, for it depended on the West for trade and capital, just as the West relied on it to supply strategic raw materials and to balance world trade. "This region must live and certainly can only develop by means of its vital trade and investment arrangements with the rest of the world," cautioned Charles J. Shohan of the department's Office of International Trade Policy. Southeast Asian membership in the International Trade Organization, or something like it, was "necessary for the satisfactory development of these countries, for their integration in a world order of the type we like, and for the satisfactory development of our relations with these countries."[35]

The consultants disagreed with the Reed-Butterworth argument that regionalism represented an excessively broad approach to the problems of Southeast Asia. Acheson's view of this debate was Delphic. He told the participants in the October 27 meeting that "the proposal for a unified treatment of the area perhaps required further development and clarification" and added that "the responsibility for pulling our policies toward the component countries together rested with Mr. Butterworth." This seemed both a concession to Butterworth's view and an implicit acknowledgment of the merits of a coordinated policy.[36] Charles Shohan's disagreement with the consultants was a matter of emphasis rather than substance. Though the consultants magnified the need for Far Eastern regionalism to put the argument across, they believed regionalism was simply a first step toward linking the area to the political economy of the developed, non-Communist world. First, the consultants argued, intraregional bonds must be forged, with the Southeast Asian nations sending rice and raw materials to Japan for textiles and light industrial goods. Then they assumed the Asian perspective would broaden further, moving from intra- to interregionalism, and that the Far East would become an essential building block in the reconstruction of the world economy. British and French commercial claims in Southeast Asia would be respected; an integrated Western Europe would trade with an integrated Far East. As the consultants told Acheson, "Asia and the Far East present a single problem and should be covered by a single policy. This regional policy should be part of a global national policy."[37]

The growth of regionalist thinking among U.S. Far Eastern policymakers corresponded to their increasing acceptance of economic protectionism by other countries, and this was the second key shift in U.S. thinking. Protectionism—preferential trade agreements, high tariffs, spheres of predominant influence, and so forth—obviously violated free trade doctrine and was thus in principle anathema to U.S. officials. By 1949, however, enormous problems in the Far East and Western Europe forced policymakers to endorse economic protectionism.

The administration had slackened its emphasis on political reform and now stressed the economic recovery of Japan, and had concluded that Mao's victory in China raised the possibility of reviving Japan through trade with Southeast Asia. This objective frankly suggested the need for Far Eastern economic regionalism, and despite the sanguine notions of the consultants, the success of extensive bilateral trade between Japan and Southeast Asian nations depended on preferential arrangements that discriminated against other nations seeking commercial access to the Far East. If pursued to its logical extreme, the United States' plan to tie Japan to Southeast Asia through trade would result in the bloodless imposition of an East Asian co-prosperity sphere and would thereby complete what the Japanese themselves had failed to accomplish through war. This idea naturally compromised the administration's multilateralist aspirations and also threatened its nascent commitment to include underdeveloped Southeast Asia in the global political economy.

American policymakers began to change their thinking about British protectionism in the summer of 1949. Great Britain's financial crisis temporarily halted American efforts to destroy the remnants of imperial preference. The administration acquiesced in British Chancellor of the Exchequer Stafford Cripps's decision to limit imports from the dollar area and began to study sympathetically British pleas for policies designed to restimulate British-Malayan-American trade. These policies would mean, ironically, that the United States would favor British over American protectionism because greater imports of Malayan rubber and tin would mean fewer purchases of American-made synthetic rubber and American smelted tin. It might also portend discrimination against smelted tin from Western Hemisphere sources. As the September Tripartite Economic Conference [United States, Great Britain, and Canada] approached, the administration considered the possibility of showing preference for Malayan exports, a policy designed to assure the recovery of the United States' most important ally.

The administration remained ambivalent about the French war in Indochina down to the autumn of 1949. Some State Department members were doubtful that the Bao Dai government could succeed in uniting the country, and these officials urged that the United States withhold further support of the French experiment until France promised independence for Indochina at some specified time. But while the department had extended neither diplomatic recognition nor direct assistance to the Bao Dai regime by the fall of 1949, policymakers had acknowledged French commercial privileges in the colony. American objections to French policy centered on France's unwillingness to grant political concessions to the Vietnamese, and not on French economic protectionism. In fact, the unratified March 8 agreement, viewed with cautious favor by the United States, permitted the continuation of the French-Vietnamese economic relationship. United States policymakers were too concerned about the serious condition of the French economy to worry about the retention of exclusive commercial ties between France and Vietnam.

Finally,—and here was the third important shift—by 1949 the Truman administration had grudgingly agreed to accept despotism and colonialism in Southeast Asia as alternatives to the advance of communism and the ongoing economic difficulties of the developed, non-Communist nations. Despotism and colonialism did not always correspond. Thailand's Marshal Phibun was a despot, but Thailand itself was free of outside control. On the other hand, British Malaya was part of the empire, but it was not despotically ruled. The disjunction of these two evils may have made it easier for American policymakers to justify their backing of both governments. In any case, the United States did support them.

Once more, Vietnam was the Southeast Asian state that most starkly challenged American ideology. It offered the worst of several worlds: a colonial nation attempting to bolster an unpopular indigenous regime, both of them stubbornly resistant to reform and ineffective in their fight against Communist nationalism. Liberal capitalism dictated a strong stand against colonialism, but when officials identified Ho Chi Minh as an agent of international communism, the Americans inclined toward the French as the lesser of two evils. The obvious liabilities of the Bao Dai government, not the slightest of which was its dubious chance for success, were beginning to submerge in late 1949. Although the administration continued to urge the French to offer concessions to the non-Communist nationalists in Vietnam, it simultaneously moved to provide economic and military support for the client of French colonialism.

This shift proved the most difficult to make. As we will see, the China consultants in particular debated the issue during the fall of 1949. But at an October 26 meeting including the consultants and leading members of State Department, Dean Rusk resolved this dilemma. "We must," he said, "support against aggressive pressure from the outside even states which we regard unfavorably. We must preserve them merely as states . . . . Our first concern is not with the internal structure of states but with their safety from aggression."[38] In ensuing months this view was increasingly expressed in U.S. foreign policy. The developing American policy toward Southeast Asia, and by extension Japan, Great Britain, and France, required the suspension of liberal capitalism and the acceptance of the previously forbidden principles of regionalism, economic protectionism, despotism, and colonialism.

There was one other important conceptual change in the administration's foreign policy thinking at this time. The fall of 1949 marked the height of congressional discussion of Truman's Point Four program. The proposal rested uncertainly on the twin pillars of technical assistance and investment by the private sector, embodied in the two bills the president had sent to Capitol Hill the previous June. Most congressional representatives, unsure of the intent and scope of the program, continued to regard it with something between mild curiousity and studied indifference.

The most resolute analyst of Point Four was Walter Salant, who continued to insist the program would be most effective if it included extensive capital investment in the underdeveloped world by the U.S. government.[39] During the year Salant's position gained support from several organizations and important individuals. In June, the United Nations Food and Agriculture Organization (FAO) reported that the Far East required $1.5 billion per year for ten years for recovery and development.[40] In October, a combined Economic Cooperation Administration (ECA)–Commerce mission to Western Europe concluded, following months of study, "that the present critical lack of balance in world trade should be corrected *primarily by stimulating an expansion of exports . . . from other countries to the United States, accompanied by an expansion, as far as feasible, of United States foreign investment*" (emphasis in original).[41] Under secretary of Commerce Cornelius Vanderbilt Whitney and Assistant to the President John R. Steelman emphasized the virtues of foreign investment by the government. As Steelman pointed out, "stamping out yellow fever and malaria has been good business."[42]

In late 1949 two other economists with academic and government experience expressed their agreement with Salant. Seymour E. Harris (Harvard and the FAO) and Charles Kindleberger (MIT and the ECA) agreed that U.S. foreign investment was necessary to encourage economic development and revive triangular trade, thereby eliminating the dollar shortage. Harris, who acknowledged Salant's assistance in preparing his booklet *Foreign Aid and Our Economy,* urged the administration to go "beyond the relatively small sums" proposed by Point Four because underdeveloped nations needed not only technical assistance but dollars with which to buy equipment and consumer goods. Many of these products could be purchased from Western European nations that badly needed the dollars. The U.S. development program could serve as a substitute for declining European Recovery Program appropriations: *A gradual transfer of aid from Western Europe to the underdeveloped areas will contribute towards a solution of the dollar problem of both Europe and the underdeveloped areas"* (emphasis in original). A "vigorous foreign aid program," Harris concluded, was "a necessary condition for a prosperous America."[43]

Kindleberger cited Salant and acknowledged the help of Harris in his book *The Dollar Shortage,* in which he argued that the shortage was at least in part due to the United States' reluctance to invest in the underdeveloped countries. Neither technical assistance nor investment by private enterprise was sufficient to alleviate the dollar shortage. Ample "external financing" of development was required to increase the ability of the poor nations to purchase European products.[44] Though it is difficult to say whether Harris and Kindleberger had any impact on policymaking, they were part of an influential group of "international Keynesians" who fought stubbornly against less sophisticated economic thinking in the administration and Congress.[45]

By autumn American policymakers increasingly acknowledged the important of U.S. investment in the underdeveloped world and its role in vitiating the dollar shortage. Presidential adviser David Lloyd, who had been enthusiastic about Salant's ideas since December 1948, was still the conduit between Salant and the Oval Office. On December 1, Lloyd wrote George Elsey that, with "the national interest . . . at stake," the United States could not afford to rely on the possibility that the private sector might provide investment capital. For Lloyd, it was "essential that capital be provided in steadily increasing amounts." If private capital was "reluctant to take the risks, the Government will have to supplement it until this reluctance is over-come."[46] Two days later, Lloyd warned the other presidential assistants that the State Department was dangerously "under-playing the role of foreign investment."[47]

In fact, although the State Department was less optimistic than Lloyd about the effects of capital investment, it too came to regard government investment in the underdeveloped nations as a partial solution to the economic problems of the developed, non-Communist world. James Webb told congressional representatives in late September that investment would stimulate production, which in turn would encourage the expansion of world trade.[48] More significant was a portion of the joint communiqué issued in mid-September, following the Tripartite Economic Conference. The foreign ministers agreed that a "fundamental" approach to the dollar gap involved an "increase [in] the flow of investment from the North American Continent to the rest of the world, including the sterling area." A high level of investment, particularly in the underdeveloped nations, "could make an important contribution toward reducing the sterling-dollar disequilibrium." After the communiqué was released, Truman asked the President's Committee on Financing Foreign Trade, established in 1946, to study the investment problem and consult with British and Canadian business representatives.[49]

The administration had agreed that the dollar gap could be addressed in part by investment in the underdeveloped world and had now taken a step toward involving the U.S. government in the investment process. This was a conceptual change that in itself had no specific implications for Southeast Asia. But the turmoil in Southeast Asia acted like a lightning rod to draw to the region the policy shift implicit in this change. Direct aid to the nations of Southeast Asia now entered the range of possible American responses to increasingly urgent problems there, especially the growth of Chinese and Vietnamese communism. The nations of Southeast Asia were important members of a regional and global system. Japanese, British, and especially French exclusivism in Southeast Asia no longer seriously troubled most U.S. policymakers, who recognized that the recovery of the developed, non-Communist world was of greater moment than the success of Southeast Asian nationalism and simultaneously acknowledged that radical nationalism jeopardized the emerging world order. Southeast Asia could be a fulcrum for Japanese and Western European recovery, and the United States evidently had the economic power to shape the destiny of Southeast Asia.

There were two possible sources of American economic aid for the

Far East. One, of course, was Point Four, which remained lodged in Congress in late 1949. A second was the China Aid Act, originally passed with the Marshall Plan in 1948 and also overseen by the ECA. As its name indicated, the China Aid Act was designed to assist China only, but Nationalist losses had prevented the administration from spending the appropriation as rapidly as expected and raised the possibility that the allocation, of which roughly $100 million remained, might be directed elsewhere in the Far East. (The China Aid program was to expire on Feb. 15, 1950, but Congress acted in early February to extend the program's life until June 30.) The chief prospective source of military assistance for Southeast Asia was Section 303 of the Mutual Defense Assistance Act of 1949, passed by Congress on September 28.The section gave the president the power to spend $75 million from the Military Assistance Program (MAP) "in the general area of China," a phrase widely understood to mean Southeast Asia.[50]

By late 1949, there were several discernible hallmarks of the administration's new Far Eastern policy. One of these was the presence and continued deliberations of "Phil Jessup's boys," the Far East consultants. As already noted, Case, Fosdick, and Jessup himself took a negotiator's view of U.S. policy toward the PRC and emphasized a unified approach to the Far East in general. On China their influence was limited, as they may have suspected; they pricked Dean Acheson's conscience, but they could not fully sway him. Their opportunities to affect Far Eastern policy were far greater. As Acheson told Fosdick in early October, "he had not yet formulated a policy" toward the Far East. It was "a blank sheet of paper, a white page on which the future [was] to be written."[51] The consultants increasingly concentrated their efforts on nations outside China, especially those in Southeast Asia, and in particular on Indochina, the "most festering problem in the Far East."[52]

Three major issues unified the consultants' discussions, memoranda, and position papers on the Far East. The first was whether American interests required support of Far Eastern governments that failed to meet the most elementary standards of independence and democracy. For a time during the fall, the consultants were divided on the matter. In a September 2 memo to Acheson, the consultants first pronounced the United States' "long-range" goal of helping nations move gradually toward independence, but they also declared it unnecessary that these nations have " 'democratic' governments in the Western sense of the term."[53] During top-level conversations in late October, however, Jessup cautioned against repeating the mistake the administration had made in China when it failed to insist that Chiang undertake reforms. Acheson indicated his persistent ambivalence on the issue by suggesting that the administration "might have to push the French harder" in Indochina and surprisingly hinted that the United States might take "a closer look at Ho Chi Minh," though he did not say why.[54]

These tantalizing possibilities may have emboldened Raymond Fosdick to attack proposals for unconditional support of Bao Dai. On November 1, Charles Yost, the consultants' aide and consistently the principal advocate of immediate support for the Bao Dai government, wrote Jessup, Case, and Fosdick that the administration must announce that it "mean[t] business" in Indochina because it could not "accept the loss of Indochina without having thoroughly explored every possible expedient to prevent it."[55] Fosdick responded swiftly and sharply to this open-ended proposal. He believed the Bao Dai government was "doomed" and that even French implementation of the still unratified March 8 agreement would be insufficient to prevent Bao Dai's failure. The agreement was not a genuine concession to Vietnamese nationalism, but a "shabby business" that was merely a "cheap substitute" for French colonialism. Fosdick recommended that the United States reserve action on Indochina. He concluded: "Certainly we should not play our cards in such a way that once again, as in China, we seem to be allied with reaction. Whether the French like it or not, independence is coming to Indochina. Why, therefore, do we tie ourselves to the tail of their battered kite?"[56] Jessup passed Fosdick's memo to Butterworth with his mild endorsement.[57]

Yost responded three days later. "What troubles me," he wrote, "is the possibility that, in our distaste for French colonialism and Bao Dai as its 'running dog' and in our wholly sound desire to be on the side of the angels in the Far East, we should slip involuntarily into a position in which we would implicitly accept Ho as an angel and allow him (to mix metaphors) to lead us up the garden path in the same way as he has led the majority of his countrymen."[58] Everett Case sided with Yost, and the ambivalent Jessup later wrote that the Yost memos "revealed our attitude toward Communist expansion and our conviction that Ho Chi Minh was a tool of Moscow."[59] Butterworth, though less optimistic than Yost, informed Fosdick that the Far Eastern Office did not agree that Bao Dai was necessarily doomed and that while the United States must refrain from unrestricted support for France, it also "must allow Bao Dai his opportunity to succeed."[60] The decision was neither unanimous nor especially enthusiastic, but it came close to permitting U.S. support for nations prior to (or simultaneous with) requiring internal reforms.

Whatever ambivalence was reflected by Fosdick's dissent on American support for Bao Dai was undercut by the consultants'—and particularly Fosdick's own—position on the second and related issue of economic and military aid for Southeast Asia. From the time of their appointment in August, the consultants planned for the possibility that the United States would provide assistance to Southeast Asia, and they identified potential sources of funding for a broadly based, though modestly financed, coordinated aid program.[61] Everett Case had the grandiose notion of an "Acheson Plan" for the Far East, and he persisted in this vision even after Jessup openly derided a similar scheme of Harold Stassen's.[62] The consultants agreed that some assistance would be useful in order to "expand our markets and assure the availability of raw materials at fair prices" and produce "conditions of stability" in Southeast Asia.[63] Fosdick hoped the administration would press Congress to permit expenditure of the $100 million ECA China fund in Indonesia, Burma, Thailand, Indochina, and "probably" in India and Pakistan and urged Livingston Merchant, the deputy assistant secretary of state for far eastern affairs, to organize a program "relatively soon" to "underscore American interest in this general area."[64] By early December, Fosdick's timetable had accelerated: while the State Department lobbied to get congressional approval to broaden the scope of the China fund, other programs "could be *started at once*" with the remaining $75 million in MAP money.[65] Evidently Fosdick believed the administration should provide aid to the Bao Dai government while nevertheless regarding it as "doomed."

The third major issue considered by the consultants was the role of Southeast Asia and other Far Eastern nations in the economic recovery of Japan. The consultants discussed this matter less than they did the other two because Japan was still in the military's bailiwick, but a section on Japan found its way into most of the group's comprehensive memos during the period. Jessup wanted Japan to "increase its influence in Asia through the expansion of its trade," and together the consultants urged the "development of [the] Japanese economy and foreign trade in order to relieve the present burden on the U.S. and to enable Japan to contribute effectively to the economic progress of the [Far Eastern] area as a whole."[66] Their efforts closely paralleled and reinforced the State Department and SCAP initiatives for Japanese economic recovery and a peace treaty.

Even as the consultants and the administration formulated policies toward the Far East during the transition autumn, policymakers agreed on the importance of a gesture to dramatize American concern for the area. In his "Suggested Course of Action in East and South Asia," a paper drafted in early July, John P. Davies recommended that Jessup take a tour of the region, with stops in Manila, Bangkok, Singapore, Batavia, Rangoon, New Delhi, Colombo, and Karachi to consult with Asian leaders on topics of "mutual interest."[67] Davies' suggestion was later taken up by Harlan Cleveland of the China ECA and Charles Yost, among others, and the administration sent Jessup off in mid-December.[68] The tour was more ambitious than the one suggested by Davies, for to the stops he recommended were added Tokyo, Seoul, Okinawa, Taipei, Hong Kong, and Saigon.[69] Jessup spent six weeks in the Far East during late 1949 and early 1950. The progress and results of his trip are considered in Chapter 8.

Another important hallmark of American foreign policy during this period was the application of a rudimentary domino theory to the Far East. To American postwar policymakers, the principal lesson of Munich was that an aggressor is not by nature satisfied with one conquest, but will expand its area of control beyond its first victim unless resisted. In the early stages of the Cold War, policymakers transferred this interpretation of Hitler's expansionism to Soviet behavior in Eastern Europe. Though it was not yet called the domino theory, the American fear of limitless contiguous military or political expansion by the Communists emerged in 1947 as one of reasons for the Truman Doctrine.[70] The debacle in China led the administration to apply the same interpretation to events in the Far East. The nations of Southeast Asia, already gripped by instability and harboring large and potentially disloyal Chinese communities, were immediately threatened.[71] Indochina seemed to be the most vulnerable area in Southeast Asia, and by the fall of 1949 policymakers stressed its importance as the gateway to the entire region. In September, Butterworth told Esler Dening of the British Foreign Office that if Bao Dai failed, "a Communist-dominated Indochina would expose Siam and Malaya to immediate Communist pressure."[72] The implications of a Communist victory in Indochina were explored in an October 19 report by the CIA. An Indochinese government controlled by Ho Chi Minh, "in conjunction with pressures from Communist China, would almost certainly greatly strengthen an existing tendency in Thailand, Burma and Malaya to seek accommodation with Communist China. Since Indochina may prove to be the key to control of the whole Southeast Asia peninsula, it might also be the critical breach in the non-Communist crescent around China."[73]

The application of the domino theory to Southeast Asia suggests that while the administration was most concerned about Indochina, policymakers also regarded as vulnerable the neighboring nations that would be threatened if Indochina succumbed to communism. Just as Southeast Asia was significant mainly for its role in the recovery of the developed, non-Communist world, so was Indochina, on a smaller level, important because of its effect on all Southeast Asia. The acceptance of the domino theory and its regional implications appeared most strikingly during late December 1949 in NSC-48, the most important statement of U.S. policy toward Southeast Asia issued to that date.

On June 10, 1949, Secretary of Defense Louis Johnson, "increasingly concerned at the course of events in Asia" and determined to increase the influence of the military in Far East decision making, asked the National Security Council for a comprehensive study of U.S. policy toward the Far East.[74] The NSC set to work, collecting information from the various departments within the government. The State Department's first contribution was PPS-51 (later NSC-51), the March 29 paper that urged, among other things, that the United States eschew total support for French "imperialism" in Indochina.[75] The military, for its part, attempted to reopen the issue of aid for Taiwan and ultimately tried to remove from the study recommendations on Japan. In general, however, Acheson and the State Department managed to keep control of the document.[76] The thirty-page report submitted to the NSC on December 23, 1949, as NSC-48/1—"The Position of the United States with Respect to Asia"—largely reflected the thinking of the State Department and captured the new urgency in U.S. policy toward the Far East.

The document characterized Asia as a continent of "poverty, nationalism, and revolution," a land of majestic strategic and economic potential. Asia was threatened by the Soviet Union, which sought to dominate the continent "through the complementary instruments of communist conspiracy and diplomatic pressure, supported by military strength." It was the task of the United States to contain Soviet expansionism in Asia and to reduce the strength of Soviet influence where it already existed. Revolutionary Asia was particularly susceptible to communism, but even Japan, India, and Pakistan were threatened by the Soviets. Communist subversion operated according to the domino theory: "The political offensive of the Kremlin or its protégés . . . tends to gather additional momentum as each new success increases the vulnerability of the next target." In China, the Soviets had achieved their first goal, and it was "now clear that southeast Asia [was] the target of a coordinated offensive directed by the Kremlin." The victory of communism in China was a "grievous political defeat" for the United States, and "if southeast Asia also is swept by communism we shall have suffered a major political rout the repercussions of which will be felt throughout the rest of the world." It was essential that the United States react.

These were strong words, but they were not strong enough for the joint chiefs, who met on December 29 to consider NSC-48/1. While the chiefs agreed with the paper's analysis of Far Eastern problems, they felt its conclusions were vague and overcautious. "The situation in Asia," they wrote Louis Johnson, "has developed to the point where concrete action is required." They offered six pages (to the NSC's single page) of precise recommendations designed to encourage the "development of sufficient military power in selected non-Communist nations of Asia to maintain internal security and to prevent further encroachment by communism." The joint chiefs' conclusions, accepted by the NSC as paper number 48/2, in fact echoed those proposed sporadically by the State Department and Far Eastern consultants during the previous several months. Together, NSC-48/1 and NSC-48/2 offered potent prescriptions for Southeast Asian problems.

Politically, NSC-48/2 in part reflected the administration's continued ambivalence on the conflict between colonialism and nationalism in Southeast Asia. The document recommended that "action should be taken to bring home to the French the urgency of removing the barriers to the obtaining by Bao Dai or other non-Communist nationalist leaders of the support of a substantial proportion of the Vietnamese." There was to be no military support for Taiwan. However, the joint chiefs also concluded bluntly that the United States "should support non-Communist forces in taking the initiative in Asia." Strategically, NSC-48/1 urged that the United States maintain a military presence "at least" along the Asian offshore island chain, including Japan, the Ryukyus, and the Philippines.

Here caution ended. The NSC had no doubt that the United States must help the Asian nations obtain "peace, national independence and stability." This idea applied with particular force in Southeast Asia, where these conditions either did not exist or were at best fragile. The United States should provide "political, economic, and military assistance" in order to check Communist aggression, "direct or indirect," in the Far East. NSC-48/1 urged the nations of Southeast

Asia to increase their production of agricultural goods and especially raw materials in order to supply the United States with strategic materials, provide a "market for the processed goods of industrialized states," and once again offer Western Europe "a rich source of revenue from investments and other invisible earnings." Most important was the Japanese trade. Japan could sustain itself only if it was "able to secure a greater proportion of its needed food and raw material . . . imports from the Asiatic area, where its natural markets lie, rather than from the U.S., in which its export market is small. In view of the desirability of avoiding preponderant dependence on Chinese sources, and the limited availability of supplies from pre-war sources in Korea and Formosa, this will require a considerable increase in Southern Asiatic food and raw material exports."

Finally, NSC-48/1 and its conclusions specified some of the forms U.S. assistance might take. Besides offering moral support to anti-Communists, the administration could introduce legislation to increase the stockpile of Southeast Asian raw materials, including tin, fibers, and natural rubber, providing "an important source of dollars for use by Asiatic countries in and outside the sterling area." The Point Four program should be implemented vigorously in the Far East and would supplement a general "revival of trade along multilateral, non-discriminatory lines." Finally, the joint chiefs added that the $75 million remaining of the MAP allocation for "the general area of China" should be rapidly dispatched to the region. On December 30, Truman directed that all but one of the conclusions of NSC-48/2 be implemented by the appropriate agencies. On the matter of the $75 million MAP appropriation, the president reserved judgment. "A program will be all right," he said, "but whether we implement it depends on circumstances." Quickly moving events over the next several months would persuade the president to take the next step.[77]

NSC-48 was not, of course, a published document, and Congress and the American public saw little visible evidence that the State Department was moving on Asian policy in late 1949. What congressional conservatives did see they did not like. During the December debate over NSC-48, Acheson had beaten back an attempt by the joint chiefs to enlist the United States in the defense of Taiwan. On January 5, 1950, Truman rejected a request by Senators H. Alexander Smith, William F. Knowland, and Robert Taft and former President Herbert Hoover to provide naval protection to Chiang Kai-shek's government. It was Acheson who followed Truman's statement with a press conference emphasizing the hands-off policy, and it was he who took the brunt of right-wing criticism that amplified throughout the month. Acheson had already decided to give a public address on the Far East in which to announce "the limitation of our power" and "the direction of our purpose," and his decision was reinforced by his desire to respond to his detractors.[78] The secretary delivered the speech a week later, before the National Press Club in Washington.

The Press Club speech is best remembered for its emphasis on "the limitation of our power." Repeating, almost word for word, what Douglas MacArthur, Dean Rusk, and the NSC had all said previously,[79] Acheson described an American "defensive perimeter" that ran from the Aleutians through Japan and to the Ryukyus and the Philippines. Inside the perimeter, Acheson said, no one could guarantee the Far Eastern nations against an attack, and, in general, it was a mistake to think that the problems of the Far East could be solved militarily. In China, Chiang's incompetent government had simply collapsed, and the Communists had harnessed the "revolutionary spirit" and ridden it to victory. The United States could not be blamed for losing China, and Acheson implied that there was little the U.S. could do about it now. In southern Asia, the United States was merely "one of many nations who can do no more than help" find solutions to postwar problems. These cautious views were consistent with what Acheson had told the Senate Foreign Relations Committee two days earlier and corresponded to the secretary's recollection that one of his purposes in making the speech was to discredit the "silly" idea of a Far Eastern Marshall Plan.[80]

This Acheson certainly did. In elaborating on "the direction of our purpose," however, the secretary also indicated that American economic aid might stand in for unilateral military assistance in Southeast Asia. The United States was already helping Japan restore its disrupted Far Eastern trade, including its commercial relations with Southeast Asia. For Southeast Asia itself, Acheson stressed that the United States could only "help where we are wanted." But the U.S. was "organizing the machinery through which we can make effective help possible." The United States and other Western countries knew "techniques" of administration and ways of improving agricultural production and would be willing to supply aid where it represented "the missing component" for economic success. Significantly, Acheson expressed satisfaction with the "noticeable signs of progress" in Indochina, where the French, "although moving slowly, are moving," and he flatly offered assistance to the new Indonesian government.[81]

It was possible to draw divergent conclusions from these remarks. Acheson's stress on "techniques" strongly suggested Point Four, and nowhere in the speech did the secretary allude to a need for the "large amounts of capital" the president had called for in his state of the union address eight days before.[82] On the other hand, Acheson's mention of U.S. help as a possible "missing component" in the Far East and his statement of support for French policy in Indochina publicly signaled the widening American interest in Far Eastern problems, a concern expressed in private by the NSC two weeks earlier.

It is perhaps too much to argue, as Charles Wolf has, that the beginning of U.S. economic aid to Southern Asia in May 1950 "was a direct outgrowth of the policy set forth in Acheson's January statement."[83] But as a hallmark of the gradually evolving American posture toward the Far East and especially Southeast Asia, the Press Club speech expressed the countervailing forces of caution and commitment still struggling for custody of U.S. policy. Acheson told the Press Club that it was important to understand U.S. policy toward the Far East "not as a mere[ly] negative reaction to communism but as the most positive affirmation of the most affirmative truth that we hold, which is the dignity and right of every nation, of every people, and of every individual to develop in their own way, making their own mistakes, reaching their own triumphs but acting under their own responsibility."[84] By early 1950, U.S. policy toward Southeast Asia and related U.S. policies toward Japan, Great Britain, and France remained in transition, but the administration had in fact moved away from a positive expression of American ideology in a way that would ultimately demand a victory for the forces of commitment.

PART **III**

THE SOLUTIONS AND
THEIR AFTERMATH,
1949–1950 AND BEYOND

6

The Reconstruction of Japan:
The Southeast Asia Connection

The new regional scope of the administration's Far Eastern policy had its most obvious effect on the occupation of Japan. By early 1948, the United States had jettisoned political reform in favor of the economic reconstruction of Japan, and American policymakers had recognized that Japanese recovery would occur only with domestic austerity and a vigorous foreign trade, especially with other nations in the Far East. This chapter documents the crystallization of this perception during the early months of 1950, reports in some detail on the methods the administration employed to promote economic regionalism in the Far East, and finally discusses the bureaucratic and international obstacles to the realization of officials' boldest schemes for accomplishing the goal. Despite these impediments, policymakers ultimately reached a consensus on the importance of Southeast Asia to the containment of communism and the restoration of Japan.

In the early months of 1950, despite the hostility between the United States and the new government of China, the State Department continued to permit both West Germany and Japan to trade with the People's Republic in accordance with the recommendation of NSC-41.[1] The document had warned, however, against the establishment of a "preponderant dependence" by Japan on the China trade, and the events of 1949 deepened the pessimism about China within the administration. By February 1950, SCAP's chief economic adviser observed that "any substantial revival" of Sino-Japanese trade seemed to be "blocked indefinitely," and prospects were "now much less favorable than they appeared to be in the summer of 1949."[2] The unreliability of the China market made it imperative that the administration take Philip Jessup's advice and widen the search for Japanese markets to include "alternative outlets" throughout the Far East.

The halting initiatives taken in this direction during the fall of 1949 were accelerated during the first three months of 1950. In Japan itself, steady postwar growth and the astringent medicine of the Dodge plan to stabilize the Japanese economy [see Chapter 2] raised production by early 1950 nearly to prewar levels.[3] This increased production prompted Dodge to warn that "the danger for the U.S. [in Japan] lies in the progressive drying up of foreign trade while domestic production . . . steadily increases and the need for exports grows."[4] Acheson acknowledged in the Press Club speech that the Japanese had to find Far Eastern markets, nations with which to exchange its manufactures for the food Japan required to maintain its increased productivity. SCAP's chief economic adviser concluded that Japanese "self-support cannot be attained either in a Far East economic vacuum or by integration of Japan's economy with that of the United States. With her colonies lost and with her special relations with China severed, Japan perforce must look to other nearby Asian areas for foodstuffs and raw materials, for which she is prepared to export capital and consumer goods."[5] "I have a feeling," wrote Ralph W. E. Reid, economic adviser to the Department of the Army, "that the best way to spur action [on] this matter [Japanese trade] . . . may eventually turn out to be to issue a U.S. interim directive requiring General MacArthur to take all necessary steps . . . to maximize Japanese exports."[6]

Officials hoped all the Far Eastern nations other than China would conduct mutually profitable trade with Japan. India and especially Pakistan produced raw cotton that could be shipped to Japan and returned as textiles.[7] In the first three months of 1950, half of Taiwan's trade was conducted with Japan.[8] An ECA mission to Korea estimated that "at least 70 percent of the industrial and consumer goods which Korea will need in the future will have to come from Japan" and that many of these goods would be bought with Korean rice.[9] But most of the administration's attention fastened on Southeast Asia. The nations in this area were potential exporters of food and raw materials, and they required finished goods to stimulate economic development and, as a consequence, reduce political instability.[10] Japan, as Dodge put it, "complemented" Southeast Asia economically; it was "the natural workshop of the East," and to get the Japanese "off our shoulders, we must build up their trade."[11] "The problem may be stated as follows," wrote Edward M. Doherty of the Far Eastern Bureau's Office of Northeast Asian Affairs. "How can we utilize idle labor and capital in Japan to furnish needed economic assistance to the countries of South Asia now threatened by communism and at the same time help Japan balance its international accounts and become independent of U.S. assistance?"[12] This was the challenging question the administration pondered in the spring of 1950.

American occupation officials tried a number of ways to encourage Japanese–Southeast Asian trade. Like the Dodge plan, several initiatives required structural changes in the Japanese economy. In October 1949, MacArthur removed the minimum price limits he had earlier imposed on Japanese exports, allowing the Japanese to undercut their competitors in foreign markets.[13] On December 1, SCAP stripped itself of the authority to license all Japanese exports and returned export trade to the Japanese private sector. Though it left a few exceptions, SCAP did the same for Japan's imports a month later.[14] MacArthur also progressively loosened the restrictions on foreign business activity in Japan. SCAP permitted the reintroduction of foreign investment in January 1949 and in early 1950 responded to the complaints of Western businessmen by granting tax exemptions to foreign investors in Japan.[15] The intended effect of these measures was to sustain the growth in Japanese industrial production by attracting foreign capital and increasing the flow of Japanese exports through the removal of various impediments.

MacArthur also negotiated on behalf of the Japanese trade agreements with nations in South and Southeast Asia. Japan had concluded a trade agreement with several sterling area nations in late 1948. This agreement was subsequently expanded and a new pact, announced in November 1949, authorized $400 million in Japan–sterling area trade through June 1950. Because the British objected to Japan's drawing dollars out of the sterling area, SCAP devised an elaborate plan through which the Japanese sold textiles for sterling, then used the pounds to buy food. The food was then "sold" to the United States for dollars, and the United States promptly handed both the food and the appropriated dollars over to the Japanese with the stipulation that the money be used to purchase American cotton. The success of this shell game was limited by the short supply of food available in the underdeveloped sterling area, but the arrangement nonetheless encouraged trade between Japan and India, Pakistan, Ceylon, and, to some extent, Malaya.[16]

SCAP negotiated directly with two Southeast Asian nations in late 1949. One of these was Burma. Here, by late 1949, the political situation had deteriorated. Civil war had halted production in the lumber, mining, and oil industries, and the rice crop, once the most abundant in Southeast Asia, had been sharply reduced. In early 1950, several thousand Kuomintang troops crossed the border into northern Burma and refused to disarm. The Burmese government proved incapable of removing them, and the Chinese established a base in the west, from which they helped direct Karen military operations. The Burmese Chamber of Commerce reported dolefully, "one after another, all the major industries of the country have been brought to a standstill . . . . There can be no permanent improvement of the country's economic situation until the strangleholds on the country's main arteries . . . have been removed."[17]

These conditions seemed to make Burma an unlikely trade partner for Japan, but occupation officials recognized the potential compatibility of the two nations' economies—Japan had been Burma's third largest source of imports before the war—and hoped that a trade agreement would inspire confidence in the struggling Burmese government. A SCAP trade delegation and Burmese representatives opened negotiations in November 1949 and met for a ten-day trade conference in mid-January to discuss a formal arrangement. On March 21, officials signed an agreement calling for the exchange of $50 million worth of goods. Almost all the Burmese exports were to be rice or rice products, while the Japanese promised $9 million in textiles. The agreement immediately raised buyer confidence in the future Burmese rice market. Shortly after it was signed, Ceylon contracted for 90,000 tons of rice and Indonesia agreed to buy 12,000 more. As U.S. officials had hoped, Japan's agreement with Burma had a ripple effect throughout the region.[18]

SCAP also sought an extensive Thai–Japanese trade agreement. At first the Thais were reluctant to cooperate fully with SCAP. In a September 1949 conversation with State Department officials, Prince Wiwat, the Thai finance minister who had earlier told the Americans that Ho Chi Minh was not his problem, argued that the Japanese preferred glutinous rice to the nonglutinous strain that was grown in Thailand and complained that the Japanese did not produce the sort of manufactured goods in which the Thais were interested. Willard Thorp, assistant secretary of state for economic affairs, replied that "the Japanese prefer[red] any kind of rice to the wheat they [were] receiving from the United States" and added that if the Thais would tell SCAP what sort of manufactures they wanted, the Japanese could probably provide them.[19] The Thai government reluctantly agreed to barter agreements with Japan in December 1948 and December 1949, the latter calling for trade of $90 million. In exchange for rice, the

Thais received rolling stock and other railway equipment, machinery, and some textiles. As it did in Burma, the announcement of the second Thai–Japanese trade agreement inspired purchases of Thai rice throughout the Far East. It strengthened a Southeast Asian government friendly to the West and assured Japan access to food and a market for its finished goods.[20]

By the fall of 1949, the State Department and SCAP had concluded independently that the time had come to sign a peace treaty with Japan and thus end the U.S. military occupation. American officials argued that no government under foreign control could win the confidence necessary to restore its domestic and international credibility. William Sebald, MacArthur's political adviser, urged the restoration of Japanese independence in international affairs. "Not until the Japanese are able to maintain their own establishments abroad," Sebald argued, ". . . will the people of the world begin to accept the Japanese, and their trade, on an unequivocal basis." Sebald also pointed out that the occupation had instigated Japanese leftist hostility and concluded that the immediate source of friction could be eliminated without seriously compromising American influence in Japan. Occupied Japan was a parasite, a hindrance and not an asset to the strategy of containment.[21] Japan's friendship could not be "compelled," explained Walton Butterworth, and the Japanese were "unlikely to display requisite responsibility and initiative and otherwise to work with maximum effectiveness for the solution of their nation's pressing economic problems until restored to treaty status."[22] The peace treaty, wrote Philip Jessup, "would be one of the dramatic steps by which we could recapture from the Russians the initiative" in world affairs.[23]

The fall of Chiang Kai-shek and the apparently increased aggressiveness of the Soviets persuaded most policymakers that the Chinese and the Russians should be excluded from treaty negotiations. In mid-September, Acheson told Bevin, "We cannot have a treaty written for us which we have to sign or which goes into effect anyway if we don't like it" and proposed that instead of negotiating in the Council of Foreign Ministers, the United States and the Commonwealth countries should draw up a treaty on their own.[24] Surprisingly, MacArthur did not agree that the Soviets should be denied a voice in treaty negotiations and thought that if the Soviets consented to "an absolute guarantee of non-aggression" against Japan, the United States could remove its troops.[25] On the other side, the joint chiefs, led by Defense Secretary Johnson, regarded any talk of a peace treaty as "premature," an attitude that exasperated Acheson and paralyzed his efforts to achieve an agreement within the policy-making establishment.[26]

MacArthur's disquieting generosity and especially the military's reluctance to consider a treaty also prompted the State Department to seek an early end to the occupation. Despite the general agreement between SCAP and department officials, the joint chiefs' balky behavior on the treaty reminded the State Department that the military wielded great influence in Japan and would continue to do so until control of the government was returned to the Japanese. Relations between Louis Johnson and State Department officials deteriorated during early 1950. Johnson charged the department with leaks on the peace treaty negotiations and frequently upbraided department personnel. Ultimately, Acheson sought the president's intercession to end the bureaucratic stalemate and break the military's hold on Japanese policy.[27]

But progress on the treaty remained slow that spring. Prolonged exposure to Sebald and others in agreement with the State Department's position brought MacArthur around, but the joint chiefs remained unreconciled. State maneuvered by suggesting that the United States might maintain military bases in Japan, and in early April Acheson persuaded Truman to appoint John Foster Dulles as an adviser to the department on Japan.[28] A Republican who supported the peace treaty initiative, Dulles proved a happy choice. But when the Korean War broke out on June 25, Dulles's presence had not yet moved the military to acquiesce in the State Department's intended policy.

Along with Louis Johnson, one of the most forceful opponents of an early peace treaty was Tracy S. Voorhees, who had succeeded William Draper as under secretary of the army. While Johnson was outspoken and direct in his opposition, Voorhees tried to outflank his adversaries by proposing an alternative to the peace treaty, while at the same time incorporating State Department ideas on shoring up Japan through trade with East Asia. The Voorhees scheme, reflected in his NSC-61 of January 27, 1950, and fully articulated in several memorandums in February and March, was a plan to use U.S. dollar aid for Japan to encourage or require Japanese trade with other Far Eastern nations. State Department officials labeled Voorhees's scheme "The Greater East Asia Co-Prosperity Sphere," and the plan was earnestly debated among policymakers responsible for the occupation.

Actually, Voorhees's "co-prosperity sphere" was the more far-reaching of two variants that emerged in early 1950 as tactics that could be used to promote the intraregional strategy. The less ambitious of the two plans, sponsored by officials in the State Department, sought the extension of credit by Japan, or some agency on behalf of Japan, to Far Eastern nations for the development of agricultural or raw materials exports or the direct purchase of Japanese exports. In an August 22, 1949 report to Jessup, State's Roswell H. Whitman argued that U.S. posture toward the Far East should be "built upon the concept of regional policy," which demanded "the maximization of Japanese trade with Southern Asia." Whitman suggested that the World Bank tie loan money for Southern Asia to purchases in Japan "where this would be economic" and urged SCAP to sell Japanese exports on credit to southern Asian countries, "which could use these goods to produce exports with which to repay Japan."[29] This proposal was given sharper form in early 1950. On February 28, a report by a State Department research group recommended that the United States require that Japan pay in yen for American aid. The U.S. would then give or lend these yen to underdeveloped Far Eastern nations to purchase Japanese exports. This plan had advantages for Japan and for other Far Eastern countries. For Japan it offered an opportunity to achieve self-support without the frustration of dependence on the United States. For the rest of the Far East, the yen would appear to be reparations from Japan and would act like economic assistance, thus strengthening these countries' resistance to communism and increasing their production of food and raw materials exports for Japan. In addition, the use of Japanese yen rather than American dollars for Far Eastern aid circumvented the need to ask Congress to fund a new aid program and blunted possible charges of American economic imperialism in the underdeveloped world.[30]

The "yen fund" proposal gained the support of the State Department's Office of Northeast Asian Affairs, which prepared the most comprehensive analysis of the need for Japanese–Far Eastern trade during the spring of 1950. The report, "Possible Methods of Increasing Intra-Regional Trade and Commerce among Countries of South and East Asia," opened with the prolix premise that "the expansion of intra-regional trade between the 'free' countries of south and east Asia is generally recognized as the most practical method of . . . employing the people and plants of industrial Japan and providing the people of Southeast Asia with a nearby market for their primary export products and source of inexpensive consumer goods and much needed capital equipment for economic development." There remained formidable obstacles to the attainment of increased trade.

Some Southeast Asian nations continued to fear the Japanese, while others hoped to retain preferential trade arrangements with Western nations. Food production in Southeast Asia remained depressed, creating the most nearly insurmountable obstacle of all: though the "goods and industrial equipment" that could help increase agricultural production were available in Japan, Southeast Asia lacked the foreign exchange with which to purchase these exports. The missing component was credit, to be extended by the Japanese to Southeast Asian countries for purchases in Japan. The report concluded by citing the "possibilities" for using "United States assistance to countries of the Far East to finance intra-regional trade."[31] The yen fund approach proved attractive to officials in the State Department and SCAP. By mid-June, it had been "tentatively" approved by the State Department.[32]

Meanwhile, Tracy Voorhees's "co-prosperity sphere" plan progressed on a parallel, though rather more stratospheric course. Voorhees's plan differed from the yen fund proposal in two important respects. First, opposed to the peace treaty but sensitive to civilian fears of continued SCAP control in Japan, Voorhees recommended the appointment of a single coordinator of all Far Eastern economic programs, who would be superior to SCAP on matters concerning intraregional trade. Second, Voorhees urged that any U.S. loan or grant to a Far Eastern nation be explicitly tied to Japan. In other words, if a nation wanted American aid, it could have it only to purchase Japanese exports. Furthermore, any U.S. purchases of Far Eastern raw materials would be routed through Japan, even if this raised the product's cost. Much like the co-prosperity system created by the Japanese themselves during the early 1940s, the Voorhees scheme required that the Far Eastern nations trade with Japan.[33]

Officials saw major differences between the State Department and Voorhees plans for increasing Japanese trade.[34] In general, however, the two proposals shared the same assumptions. They agreed, of course, that more Japanese trade with other Far Eastern nations was necessary for the security, political stability, and economic welfare of the region. They also granted that Japan was an economic burden on the United States, one that Congress in particular was increasingly reluctant to support. Both plans involved shifting existing appropriations rather than soliciting new funds or cloaking relatively modest new outlays in the flashy garb of complex trade arrangements. Though Voorhees's proposal to place all Far Eastern aid under a single agency went beyond anything envisioned by the State Department, the yen fund plan reflected the recognition that economic intraregionalism required coordination, and Truman's appointment of Dulles was a concession to this view.

Finally, neither of the plans showed much immediate concern for possible U.S. exports to the Far East or the larger goal of economic multilateralism. Both proposals clearly favored Japan over other industrial nations seeking commercial inroads in East Asia. Edward Doherty noted objections that the yen fund "scheme would unduly concentrate trade in the area with Japan." His response to this was "simply that the export capacity exists in Japan; shall it go unutilized?"[35] The Office of Northeast Asian Affairs paper on "Intra-Regional Trade" declared it necessary that Japan fight trade discrimination with preferential devices of its own because, in the Far East, "the elimination of preferences must for the present be regarded as a long run objective."[36]

The final tactic for reviving Far Eastern trade considered by occupation officials during early 1950 involved dispensing with the yen fund shell game and offering economic and military aid directly to the Far Eastern nations judged most essential to the reconstruction of Japan. Through SCAP, the United States freely adjusted the Japanese economy, but had no comparable authority to manipulate conditions elsewhere in the region. Yet here was the crux of the matter. Japan may not have been seriously threatened by communism, but the same could not be said for Korea and the Southeast Asian nations bordering China or Indochina and torn by internal conflict. While Japanese production had increased so much that the need to export became critical, Southeast Asian food and raw materials production had fallen drastically, particularly in Burma and Indochina.[37] United States military and economic aid was the most direct way to protect and augment production in the underdeveloped nations of the Far East, especially those in Southeast Asia. The administration could consider this alternative in light of the new diplomatic context, in which, as Acheson told MacArthur, "problems of our policy in the Far East are taking a large part of our thought"[38] and because of the administration's implicit acceptance of Walter Salant's international economic theory of capital investment over technical aid.

The security of Southeast Asia was the first requirement for any possible aid program. As the Alsop brothers put it: "Talking about trade between Japan and Southeast Asia before Burma and Indo-China have been made safe is like planning the garden while the house is burning down."[39] Military aid, including vehicles, weapons, and communications equipment, could be made available for Southeast Asia from the $75 million remaining to the Military Assistance

Program for use in "the general area of China." The State Department energetically sought military assistance for Southeast Asia, but it viewed economic aid as a more permanent solution to problems of production and security. In early April 1950, a State Department paper acknowledged that even if SCAP assured the Southern Asian nations that Japan would provide an expanding market for their exports, these nations would still "find themselves handicapped in expanding production for export . . . by their lack of . . . foreign exchange."[40] The underdeveloped Far Eastern nations needed money.

The administration was most interested in restoring Japanese trade with Burma and Thailand, the two nations with which SCAP had negotiated trade agreements. The escalating chaos in Burma pushed the Thakin Nu government further away from its resolute socialism of previous years and deeper into the Western camp. The Burmese begged for British and American aid, and their pleas grew more shrill as government forces lost ground to both the Karens and the Communists in early 1950.[41]

Burma's departure from socialism pleased the administration. On October 25, 1949, the China consultants recommended the "unstinted application" of measures designed to bolster Thakin Nu's government, including "administrative, economic and security help."[42] A State Department report in mid-December advised "as a matter of urgency" the use of MAP funds for Burma,[43] and in late January George McGhee, the assistant secretary of state for Near Eastern, South Asian, and African affairs, wrote Rusk and Acheson that "the U.S. should take positive steps to complement British and Commonwealth effort with such needed assistance as we may be better able than they to provide" for Burma.[44] Three weeks later, on February 13, 1950, Acheson accepted in principle a policy granting economic and military aid to Burma, as long as it only supplemented British assistance programs.[45] In early April, the R. Allen Griffin mission to Southeast Asia recommended that the U.S. give Burma more than $12 million in economic aid.[46]

United States aid for Thailand was approved in principle with less qualification. Acheson ultimately accepted the judgment of the Southeast Asia Office that the Thais be granted, not sold, military equipment, and on March 10, 1950, Truman approved the State Department's request for $10 million, to be taken from the $75 million MAP fund.[47] The Griffin mission asked $11.4 million in economic aid for Thailand, aimed largely at the "maintenance and increase of Thailand's exportable agricultural surpluses."[48] In the meantime, Phibun Songkhram's government expelled the Viet Minh from their agency in Bangkok and extended diplomatic recognition to the Bao Dai government.[49] Thailand had secured its niche in the non-Communist world as a key primary producer in the Far East.

Despite the Truman administration's remarkable interest in encouraging Japanese–Southeast Asian trade, not all of the tactics it proposed were rapidly adopted and smoothly implemented. Several of the tactics were blocked by a combination of domestic and foreign obstacles that arose in late 1949 and early 1950. Despite the administration's acceptance of the importance of the Far East, despite policymakers' commitment to reviving Japan by increasing its trade with Southeast Asia, the demands of Far Eastern regionalism frequently collided with plans for the recovery of Western Europe and with the persistent belief of some officials that the world would never return to multilateralism if its principles were too deeply corrupted. When the Korean War broke out in June 1950, the regional policy had been incompletely realized. Japan's trade with Burma and Thailand had increased considerably as a result of the trade agreements and the new American interest in pacification and production in these Southeast Asian countries.[50] Programs of military and economic aid for Southeast Asia had been approved by Congress and the president, but assistance had just begun to flow in June. No peace treaty had been signed with Japan. Finally, despite the tentative approval of the State Department, the yen fund credit scheme had not been effected, and Voorhees's co-prosperity sphere had been consigned to oblivion. The arguments used by opponents of these plans provide an instructive glimpse at bureaucratic rivalry and the limits of intraregionalism in U.S. foreign policy on the eve of the Korean War.

The Voorhees plan was most easily dispatched. It was apparent to the State Department that Voorhees was promoting his scheme with the hope of preventing a peace treaty, and the department regarded it with skepticism from the outset. In a conversation with Butterworth in early February, MacArthur "refer[red] disparagingly to Mr. Voorhees, and said that he understood that Mr. Voorhees now had a fantastic scheme for Asiatic trade which no doubt he conceived he would lead."[51] Charles Shohan and William Lacy pointed out that tying credits to Japanese exports would create "maximum ill will" in Southeast Asia and concluded bluntly: "We cannot require trade with Japan."[52] Voorhees's superiors agreed. Following an acrimonious meeting between Acheson and the joint chiefs in April, Frank Pace, the recently appointed secretary of the army, eased Voorhees aside by becoming more directly involved in occupation decision making and in early June removed the under secretary from office.[53]

The yen fund plan had a larger constituency, and it was not so readily dismissed. Its sponsors did not seek to appoint a White House "czar" for Far Eastern programs, nor did they insist that all U.S. aid dollars to the Far East be used to buy Japanese exports. The plan's opponents raised several carefully constructed objections to the scheme. First, they argued that the plan would be inflationary, undoing the delicate work of the Dodge plan by compelling massive Japanese exports on credit while fueling labor demands for higher wages.[54] Second, opponents in the cautious Treasury Department claimed that the credit plan did not confront the real reasons for the low level of Japanese–Far Eastern trade. W. W. Diehl, financial attaché at the mission in Tokyo, attacked the yen fund as too narrowly focused and listed eleven reasons other than retarded production and the shortage of foreign exchange for the inability of Far Eastern nations to trade with Japan.[55]

Finally, and most significant, opponents of the yen fund contended that the plan represented the overzealous application of protectionist principles. Department officials agreed that some commercial favoritism was necessary for the reconstruction of Japan and the pacification of underdeveloped Asia. The yen fund plan, however, simply went too far. The scheme appeared too restrictive and discriminated too openly against other nations interested in exporting to the Far East in exchange for food and raw materials. The Japanese trade was significant, Shohan wrote in early January, but "what is more important to the countries of the region . . . is their dependence on trade with the rest of the world."[56] The Northeast Asia Office's avid promotion of regionalism encountered strong opposition from Commerce Department officials, who were "suspicious that State [would] go too far in promoting intra-regional trade."[57] Even NSC-61/1, the ironic offspring of Tracy Voorhees's co-prosperity sphere, pointed out: "U.S. assistance programs in the Far East are but one phase of the worldwide problem of providing economic stability and raising living standards[,] and efforts to coordinate such programs must be consistent with actions on the larger problem. Accordingly, a global approach rather than a narrow regional approach is required."[58]

The strongest protest came from the Economic Cooperation Administration, which favored assistance for the underdeveloped Far East but was particularly sensitive to the need of Western Europe for triangular trade. An ECA report of April 22, 1950, drafted by ECA official John D. Sumner, charged that the yen fund proposal revealed "inadequate recognition of the close economic ties that exist between parts of the Far East with Europe and the Western Hemisphere. The natural trade interests of certain Far Eastern areas, especially in exports, are much less importantly with Japan than with the West and will continue to be so in the predictable future." The yen scheme placed "a disturbing emphasis on the importance of bilateral trade between the Far Eastern countries and areas, and extending U.S. support to the further development of such trading on the basis of local currencies." Sumner presumed supporters of the yen fund understood that "U.S. support of bilateral trading arrangements" was "only a temporary device to meet the exigencies of the immediate post-war period," but worried they did not "sufficiently recognize the dangers of . . . the further and continued use of bilateral trading arrangements in the region." As an antidote to this narrow formulation, Sumner urged that "vigorous and prompt efforts should be made to broaden the geographic scope of coordinated activities to include U.S. assistance in Europe and elsewhere, especially in view of the close economic relations between certain Far Eastern areas and countries in Europe and the Western Hemisphere."[59]

The Sumner memorandum brought into the open the previously latent tension between intra- and interregionalism. Yet it is essential to emphasize once more that bureaucratic disagreements over tactics never threatened the larger American strategy in the Far East. Even Charles Shohan, a self-confessed "agnostic" on the matter of American-sponsored trade arrangements in the region, agreed forcefully with the administration's strategy. "As I recognize them," he wrote on April 14, "our principal relevant objectives are the economic development of Southeast Asia, with the relations between the areas characterized by a large and growing volume of trade involving Japanese capital goods, in exchange for Southeast Asian rice, vegetable oils and industrial raw materials."[60] Officials could squabble over means, but the objective remained in plain sight.

Here it is worth recalling the opposition by certain Far Eastern countries and by Great Britain and other Commonwealth nations to the revival of Japanese and Far Eastern trade. This opposition waned but had not expired entirely by the spring of 1950, and it constituted a serious obstacle to the realization of U.S. policy. The Philippines, Indochina, Malaya, and Indonesia remained hostile to the establishment of trade contacts with the Japanese.[61] The British professed to accept Japanese competition, but protested SCAP's subsidizing of Japanese industry and remained generally apprehensive about increased Japanese exports to Southeast Asia.[62] In the spring of 1950, a small crisis arose when the Japanese trade agreements with Burma and Thailand threatened to limit the rice purchases of the rice-deficient Southeast Asian nations, especially Malaya. On March 16, the British complained that it was "unreasonable that Japan . . . should now be allowed to take more than her fair share of the limited rice supplies available."[63] An American expert warned the State Department that because of increased Japanese purchases and the continuing confusion in Burma, "we are now facing the grave possibility that there will be insufficient rice to meet even the minimum needs of British territories in Southeast Asia."[64] *The Economist* noted that the Japanese were competing for "rice surpluses that are barely sufficient to feed Malaya and neighbouring countries." Prophetically the journal added: "If food shortages are created by this growing Japanese demand, the Americans will find themselves pumping into underfed and discontented South-east Asia the very aid that they have tried to cut down in Japan."[65]

Once again, this time in the international context, the contradictions in American Far Eastern policy came into focus. Could the United States revive Japan through intraregional trade and preserve multilateralist values? More to the immediate point, was it possible to reconcile this policy toward Japan with one that would rescue Western Europe, and especially Great Britain? The answers, as *The Economist* shrewdly forecast, involved the application of American capital, through economic and military aid, to the underdeveloped Far East. This aid benefited both Western Europe and Japan. On behalf of the British, however, the United States could and did take other measures.

7

The Reconstruction of Great Britain: Triangular Trade and the Limits of American Commitment

The British economy was in a dismal state in the late summer of 1949. Great Britain remained in debt to the other sterling nations. The sterling-dollar gap had widened: despite the Marshall Plan, which would in any event end in 1952, the sterling area's balance of trade with the United States continued to suffer from the failure of America's sterling imports to keep pace with its exports to the sterling area. By late August, the State Department agreed that the restoration of the prewar pattern of triangular trade, in which the British dollar deficit was partially offset by a British trade surplus with Malaya and a Malayan surplus with the United States, provided the best hope for alleviating the British economic crisis. The apparent threat of communism overhung the process of trade reconstruction. As Will Clayton, under secretary of state for economic affairs, explained, it was not important how the British had gotten into economic trouble "because the patient little man in the Kremlin sits rubbing his hands and waiting for the free world to collapse in a sea of economic chaos."[1] By the fall of 1949, the department and the British were working in tandem to prevent such a collapse.

British officials and the State Department agreed that the crisis could be solved only if the United States suspended its premature efforts to dismantle the sterling bloc by imposing on the West the ideology of liberal capitalism. British economic problems required that the Truman administration acquiesce in the British decision to reduce dollar imports by the United Kingdom itself and throughout the Commonwealth. The crisis also silenced administration critics of European colonialism in Asia. If British economic recovery required

British control of Malaya, so it must be. If the security of Malaya demanded support for the French-sponsored, anti-Communist government in Vietnam, the United States would offer its support. The ideal of liberal capitalism would be sacrificed temporarily to the more urgent objective of Great Britain's economic revival.

This was the view of the State Department, but it was not universally shared within the administration. In late 1949 and early 1950 the department was able to make substantial progress in putting across its solutions for the dollar gap problem. Its major victory was the increased importation of Malayan rubber and tin by the United States. The department also argued that U.S. military and economic aid for South and Southeast Asia would contribute to the solution of the British economic problem, and this argument was a factor in Truman's decision to approve aid programs in the spring of 1950. Yet some of the State Department's boldest initiatives were blunted by bureaucratic resistance within the administration, which reinforced the president's persistent political and economic caution. The story of American efforts to solve the British economic crisis is in good part a chronicle of the State Department's search for a solution to the problems threatening Southeast Asia.

Other than a cool statement noting a "frank exchange of views," the only positive resolution to emerge from Treasury Secretary John Snyder's discussions with British officials in early July was the decision to continue the talks at the ministerial level in Washington in September. Throughout July and August, the British avidly planned for these meetings, hoping the State Department's reassuring posture during the summer would be translated into American action on the dollar problem. Preliminary discussions between British, American, and Canadian representatives ran from August 27 to September 2. Ernest Bevin and Stafford Cripps departed London on September 5 with the solemn pronouncement that they had embarked upon "one of the most important missions in history."[2] Talks began at the ministerial level on September 7.[3]

As they prepared for the economic conference, British officials worried that their efforts would be frustrated if Snyder's Treasury Department was put in charge of the American delegation. Snyder continued to insist that the British could go far toward solving the dollar problem if they would abandon state economic planning. British representatives in the United States naturally found Snyder's views discouraging. "Snyder was cautious and he was not always at the big canvas of the world," recalled Oliver Franks, British ambassador to the United States.[4] Embassy Minister F. R. Hoyer Millar wrote the Foreign Office: "The general atmosphere here is, I am afraid, pretty depressing. However anxious the State Department may be to help us, the attitude of Treasury . . . is far from encouraging."[5] The British hoped Dean Acheson would lead the discussions from the American side. When word reached London in mid-August that Snyder would be in charge, the gloom at the Foreign Office was palpable.

The British underestimated the State Department's commitment to economic recovery and its bureaucratic resourcefulness. Although the department failed to convince Snyder to surrender leadership of the delegation, the treasury secretary allowed Under Secretary of State James Webb to chair the preliminary discussion sessions, which were to produce the conference agenda.[6] George Kennan, who had a major role in planning the American position for the talks, several times reassured the Foreign Office that the State Department was sympathetic toward the British and disclosed that Snyder had been given the chair largely for reasons of political expediency.[7] In July, John Strachey, at the Ministry of Food, had a gratifying conversation with Norris Dodd, director of the Food and Agriculture Organization of the United Nations and a personal friend of President Truman. Dodd deplored the "Treasury campaign against the pound," implied that few in the administration agreed with Snyder, and told Strachey that the solution to the dollar problem was increased purchases by the United States of rubber, tin, and wool.[8] Truman himself greeted the British with "a most helpful speech" to the American Legion in Philadelphia on August 29, in which he stressed the need for patience and cooperation in Anglo-American relations.[9] At the conference itself, Webb quietly circulated a conciliatory memo by Kennan that Snyder had previously ordered withdrawn, and Kennan's recommendations were "followed with greatest fidelity" by the American delegation.[10] Snyder's attempt to include in the conference's final communiqué a stipulation that the British reassess state planning was successfully resisted by the State Department.[11]

That the tripartite conference was judged a success by the British was due in no small part to State Department cooperativeness, but the British themselves could claim a good deal of responsibility for the concord that characterized the talks. The day the conference opened, Cripps announced in confidence to a small group of American and Canadian officials that the pound would be devaluated. Officials in the State Department, who had encouraged the British to take the step, warmly greeted Cripps's statement. Critics of British economic policy, like Snyder and Paul Hoffman of the ECA, were disarmed. The reason for the British decision was clear. Devaluation would lower the prices of sterling goods in dollar markets and would, at least in theory, enhance the attractiveness of exports from the sterling area.[12]

The decision to devalue had not come easily. Cripps had opposed it from the start, arguing that the economic and political costs of more expensive dollar imports in Great Britain offset any possible advantage gained by sterling bloc exports to the dollar area. The mere "suggestion [of devaluation] . . . makes the Treasury see red from the Chancellor downward," observed Deputy Under Secretary of State Roger Makins in April. For Cripps, the four-dollar pound (a pound was actually worth $4.03) was "the ark of the Covenant."[13] By the end of the difficult June, Cripps began to come around. He allowed to John Snyder on July 8 that the British "would consider the revaluation of sterling, though he doubted its efficacy."[14] Throughout the summer, the British position grew worse. On August 29, the cabinet decided to devalue. The tripartite ministers were told of the decision the morning of September 7 and were informed of the extent of the devaluation—from $4.03 to $2.80 the pound—on the thirteenth. "The Government have come to this decision," the Foreign Office explained, "chiefly because they believe that, in present circumstances, devaluation gives us the most effective immediate opportunity of increasing our dollar earnings." The British hoped that competitively priced raw materials exports would take the lead in this enterprise.[15]

The British devaluation would have no effect unless the dollar area, led by the United States, would accept the view that increased imports from the sterling area, not the constant expansion of unrequited exports, was essential to restore the strength of the non-Communist world. The Marshall Plan had partially bridged the trade gap by supplying Great Britain and the rest of Western Europe with dollars to buy American products, but the $2.8 billion worth of purchases made by Western Europeans in the United States during 1949 had not prevented an increase in the sterling area's dollar deficit.[16] The Tripartite Economic Conference marked the inauguration of an American (and Canadian) effort to ensure British recovery by accepting more imports from the sterling area. The tripartite ministers agreed that "the United States and Canada should reduce obstacles to the entry of goods and services from debtor countries, in order to provide as wide an opportunity as possible for those countries to earn dollars."[17] The British had taken the agonizing step of drastically devaluating the pound, and now it was up to the dollar countries to make the step worthwhile.

Many Western Europeans and some American policymakers had long understood that the United States must increase its imports of all Western European products. Most strident among the Americans was Paul Hoffman, head of the ECA. Hoffman often antagonized European officials with blunt statements blaming the dollar gap on indolent British exporters, but he clearly had sympathy for the British position.[18] For every exhortation he made to European statesmen, Hoffman delivered an equally firm appeal to his own country. "Europe must earn the dollars she needs and she must earn most of them by selling her products in the American market. We must buy if we intend to sell," he wrote in the introduction to an ECA–Commerce Department report.[19] In October 1949, Hoffman's ECA warned that the United States had to buy at least $2 billion more in European goods each year or see its exports "dwindle to a mere trickle."[20] Hoffman repeated and expanded on this theme in a much-quoted article in the Sunday *New York Times* on November 13, and in February 1950 he told the Senate Foreign Relations Committee that "we must sell less and buy more from Europe." There was, Hoffman knew, "little appeal in such a program," but if it was not undertaken, "we must either continue our aid or see the European economy placed in grave danger."[21]

During and after the tripartite conference, leading American policymakers came to share Hoffman's view. Acheson became a vocal advocate of increased purchases for the stockpile and lower tariffs "so that the British, the French, the Dutch, and others would not find that their efforts to earn dollars were blocked" by protective legislation.[22] Following the conference, Acheson embarked on what Ernest Bevin described as "an educational campaign to inform the U.S. public of [the United States'] responsibilities as . . . a creditor nation."[23] On November 2, Acheson carried this message openly to a potentially hostile audience of National Foreign Trade Council representatives. Acheson noted that the large American trade surplus was described by many as a "favorable" balance of trade. "I get impatient with this talk about our 'favorable' trade balance," Acheson said. "The bald fact is, though many people don't seem to realize it, that we are in real balance of payments difficulties." Exports had far outstripped imports, leaving other nations dependent on extraordinary dollar assistance from the United States to pay for essential goods and services from the dollar area. The solution was a large increase in imports by the United States. Throughout the winter of 1949–50, Acheson continued to make this point within the administration and in public.[24]

Harry Truman also emphasized the need for more American imports. In his August 29, 1949 speech to the American Legion, the president said flatly, "We must increase our buying abroad if we are to achieve a balanced world trade."[25] Truman left no doubt that he considered balanced trade a significant free world objective when he delivered his annual economic message to Congress on January 6, 1950. "We need to move vigorously toward a world-wide increase of international trade," he said. "This will result in larger imports into our country, which will assist other countries to earn the dollars they need, and will at the same time increase our own standard of living."[26] By the end of 1949, the administration was pressing Congress for legislation that would increase the efficiency of the customs service, enlist the United States in the International Trade Organization, and lower tariffs.[27]

Meanwhile, the State Department, inspired to act by the tripartite deliberations, began to study possible remedies for the dollar gap. On December 12, the Economic Affairs Division and the Policy Planning Staff produced a paper on the subject, which Acheson subsequently used as a basis for his own memorandum to the president, dated February 16, 1950. "The problem I should like to submit for your consideration," Acheson began, "is how to develop an Administration policy for adjusting the balance of payments of the United States." The United States had an export surplus of $6 billion, and most American goods were purchased with "extraordinary foreign assistance," especially Marshall Plan dollars. But the European Recovery Program would expire in 1952. Unless something took its place, enabling Western Europeans to finance American exports, "the key commodities on which our most efficient agricultural and manufacturing industries are heavily dependent, will be sharply reduced, with serious repercussions on our domestic economy." In addition, the Western European nations, along with "friendly areas in the Far East and elsewhere, will be unable to obtain basic necessities which we now supply, to an extent that will threaten their political stability." After 1952, Western Europe and the rest of the world would be unable to procure the dollars needed to buy in abundance from the United States. Acheson called this "the problem of the 'dollar gap' in world trade."

To bridge the dollar gap, the United States had to increase its imports and offer economic assistance and investment to potential customers. These measures were imperative to prevent "a substantial shift of power from the democratic to the Soviet sphere." Because finding a solution to the dollar gap required "a far higher degree of coordination between our domestic and foreign economic policies than heretofore," Acheson urged Truman to take personal charge of the matter. Attached to Acheson's memo was a department paper on the same topic. "When all is said and done," it observed, "it is evident that if exports are to be maintained and there is to be curtailment in extraordinary assistance, the main burden of adjustment in our balance of payments must be accomplished by an increase in our imports."[28]

The president responded on March 31 by appointing Gordon Gray, recently retired as secretary of the army, as special assistant to the president to study the balance of payments problem and propose solutions to it. In his letter of appointment to Gray, Truman wrote: "Our basic purpose had been, and must continue to be, to help build a structure of international economic relationships which will permit each country, through the free flow of goods and capital, to achieve sound economic growth without the necessity for special financial aid. We cannot continue to sell our goods abroad, or receive a return on our public and private investments abroad, unless foreign countries can obtain the necessary dollars to make their payments."[29] The Gray Commission began in mid-April to determine how the United States would reconstruct the international economic system following the expiration of the Marshall Plan.

The most vital U.S. imports were raw materials from underdeveloped nations. Policymakers often singled out the Far Eastern countries—the "have-nots" of Asia, as Kennan put it—as sources of many of these products.[30] This perception both resulted from and reinforced the State Department's increased understanding of the need to restore British, Malayan, and American triangular trade, and in the weeks following the tripartite talks, this perception took hold within the administration. Paul Hoffman described in the *New York Times* the disruption of triangular trade and the resulting "sharp loss of dollar income to Europe" because of reduced "American purchases of rubber, silk, tin, jute and other raw materials from the Far East."[31] David Lloyd attributed the persistent European dollar shortage to the breakdown of triangular trade and told White House aide George Elsey that "one of the lessons of 1949 is that the recovery of Europe is bound up with the economic position of the underdeveloped areas of the world."[32] Dean Acheson, whom Oliver Franks praised for his recognition that the "British balance of payments was the balance of payments and reserve of the whole sterling area rolled into one," scribbled notes to himself in late 1949: "The area—S[outh] E[ast] A[sia] M[iddle] E[ast] & Africa. West has most important strategic, economic and political interests. Essential to keep area in our economic system."[33]

President Truman's inkling that Point Four had a role in the restoration of triangular trade had deepened considerably. Truman acknowledged that the international economy was built on the "prosaic" foundations of rubber agreements and the value of currencies. The underdeveloped nations, he argued, had to be included in the process of reconstruction; they must "double and redouble their production" in order to make "an increased contribution to an expanding world economy and a balanced world trade." The United States would help the underdeveloped countries by extending them economic aid. This would not be a handout from a sympathetic observer interested solely in the welfare of poor people, for the United States was most concerned with "trying to expand the exchange of goods and services among nations." "We are not," Truman stressed, "engaged in a charitable enterprise."[34]

Policymakers promoted the import drive as a way of solving international economic problems generally, but the policy had specific implications for the British dollar shortage. Of course, the devaluation of the pound by itself provided immediate relief. In the months following devaluation, exports from the sterling area to the dollar area increased dramatically, checking the run on British reserves and bringing more dollars to the sterling nations, especially the primary producers. "The general picture [has] of course changed substantially as the result of devaluation," a British Treasury official reported in early January.[35] "Devaluation has done the main job in making a large increase in exports possible," added another.[36] During the first quarter of the new year, the gold and dollar reserves of the sterling area rose by nearly $300 million.[37] The National City Bank of New York announced that, because of devaluation, "American exporters have faced more effective price competition abroad" and "foreign goods, offered in large quantities and more attractively priced, have had a good reception in American markets."[38] Paul Nitze, who succeeded Kennan as head of the Policy Planning Staff in January 1950, later admitted that "the devaluation worked much better than any of us had really thought it was going to work" and implied it was largely responsible for the success of sterling area exports during early 1950.[39]

148

Along with the pound devaluation, the American willingness to buy more Malayan rubber and tin contributed to the closing of the dollar gap. Throughout the summer of 1949, British officials made it clear that increased purchases of these products by the United States were essential to the revival of the British economy.[40] By the time the tripartite talks opened, the State Department had decided the British were right. It was time, Acheson told his leading advisers, "to take some real action" on stockpiling policy and rubber legislation.[41] On September 10, Commerce Secretary Charles Sawyer, at Acheson's urging, told a meeting of the conference's Working Group on Commodities and Stockpiling that the United States planned to "undertake a reconsideration of synthetic rubber policy" and "explore steps" toward increased stockpiling of Malayan tin.[42] Roughly equal parts of caution and commitment were reflected in the language of the conference's communiqué: "The United States Government was prepared to open to natural rubber a substantial area of competition, including a modification of the Government order relating to the consumption of synthetic rubber. The United States would review its stockpiling program, with particular reference to rubber and tin."[43] The vagueness of this language properly anticipated the difficulties of convincing agencies other than the State Department that these policies were sound.

Certainly the British were convinced of the State Department's good intentions. British representatives at the conference reported that "the meetings were very friendly and both sides were able to speak freely . . . . On the whole United States officials appeared to be sympathetic about our points . . . . They explained the domestic issues involved but gave the impression that they were hopeful that these might be overcome."[44] Oliver Franks was more enthusiastic: "[We have seen] the creation of an entirely new spring of goodwill and confidence towards us on the American and Canadian sides and a corresponding enhanced degree of readiness to help. The previous crisis of confidence was resolved. The precise value of this in dollars is incalculable but is possibly very great."[45]

There were several ways for the Americans to increase their purchases of Malayan natural rubber. One possibility, raised by Lewis Douglas (American ambassador in London), Acheson, and others during the summer and fall of 1949, was to buy more rubber for the strategic stockpile. Unfortunately, the stockpile quota for rubber had been met by late 1949, and the Munitions Board, the agency with direct responsibility for stockpile purchasing, saw no reason to haggle with Congress over an additional appropriation it considered unnecessary for national security. The State Department assessed the odds of overruling the board and wisely decided not to fight.[46]

Instead, the department chose to concentrate its efforts on an attempt to remove the minimum synthetic rubber consumption level mandated by the 1948 Rubber Act. In late September, Charles Sawyer, prodded by the State Department, cut the amount of mandatory synthetic rubber required for use in the United States to one-fourth of the natural rubber consumed, stating: "By this action we hope to strengthen the world-wide security of the United States by assisting the stabilization of the economy of Europe and the Far East rubber producing countries."[47] This was a start, but the State Department, and particularly Donald Kennedy, did not consider the reduction sufficient. Kennedy now worked to write a new law that would eliminate or substantially reduce the synthetic minimum.

The Commerce Department grudgingly went along with the September reduction, but, with the Munitions Board, it resisted State Department attempts to go further. Commerce was especially concerned about the impact elimination of the requirement would have on the domestic synthetic industry. The Munitions Board generally argued that the reduction of synthetic use would make the United States too reliant on imported natural rubber, endangering national security. Kennedy grappled with both these arguments. He argued, first, that technological improvements in synthetic rubber production removed the need to protect the industry, since it could now compete, on its merits, with the natural product. Kennedy responded to the Munitions Board argument by insisting that national security was affected by destabilizing events occurring throughout the world. The State Department's "proposed suspension of mandatory usage," argued Kennedy, "would further national security by lessening economic and political tensions abroad, while at the same time stimulating the more rapid development of a free, competitive industry at home." Kennedy also argued that the administration's position on mandatory usage "should rest on the broadest of policy considerations, which include political, strategic, and economic factors in the Far East situation, as well as dollar assistance to the U.K."[48]

These decisions were not entirely Kennedy's to make. Truman gave responsibility for drafting the new rubber legislation to the National Security Resources Board (NSRB), an interagency committee chaired by White House adviser John Steelman. The board, in turn, appointed a committee to work exclusively on the law. At this level, Kennedy's presence was clearly felt. When early drafts of the proposed law suggested a synthetic consumption quota of 200,000 tons a year, Kennedy remonstrated vigorously, and Steelman sided with him. The rubber bill the NSRB submitted—the one Truman took to Congress on January 15, 1950—gave the president the authority to set a mandatory usage requirement for synthetic, without recommending any amount or percentage. The State Department believed Truman would keep the synthetic minimum very low or not require one at all. On this issue, thus far, the State Department had won.[49]

The imminent end of the American recession, the devaluation of the pound, and the September reduction of the synthetic quota combined with the promise of the proposed new rubber bill prompted a rapid rise in Malayan natural rubber imports to the United States. By late September, American business was contracting for more natural rubber.[50] Monthly consumption of natural rubber rose from 44,000 tons in September 1949 to more than 51,000 in October and nearly 60,000 in January 1950, while synthetic consumption remained at the same level.[51] As American demand for Malayan rubber rose, the price of rubber soared to its highest level in twenty-five years. The deputy chairman of Great Britain's Rubber Development Board reported confidently that "there need be little fear of Communist inroads [in Malaya] if the demand for rubber continues to expand."[52] And it did. As late as May, natural rubber prices continued to climb.[53]

By late 1949, world smelted tin production had surpassed its highest prewar levels, and the vast supply forced prices steadily downward.[54] The slack market most affected Malayan smelters, who continued to produce 40 percent of the world's total of pig tin, and the British pleaded with the United States to honor the commitment it had made in the tripartite communiqué.[55] The administration was sympathetic. In late November, American officials told the British that the Commerce Department had removed all government restrictions on domestic tin consumption, impediments that had been in place since the war. The tangle of restrictions, substitutions, and prohibitions surrounding tin had been appropriate during the days of scarcity of the immediate postwar period, but by 1949, with the changed conditions in the Far East and Great Britain, they were irrelevant. For the first time in almost ten years, tin entered an unrestricted American market. Malayan tin exports to the United States rose almost immediately.[56]

The State Department also decided to accept some sort of international commodity agreement for tin. A commodity agreement would control production or distribution of smelted tin, guaranteeing suppliers a stable market at a reasonably high price. Great Britain, the

Netherlands, and Belgium—the Western European nations hoping to persuade the United States to raise its tin consumption—lobbied intensively within the International Tin Study Group for some sort of arrangement. At four meetings of the group between 1947 and 1949, the tin-producing nations had been unable to overcome the opposition of the American representatives, who regarded with suspicion all schemes urging government control of prices and supplies. Following a meeting of the Study Group's "Working Party" in November 1949, however, the department decided it could accept a tin control agreement in principle as long as the completion of the American stockpile remained the first priority. The European participants in the Tin Study Group approached their fifth meeting, scheduled for March 1950, confident that a commodity agreement for tin would at last be achieved.[57]

Finally, the tripartite conference and congressional approval of the stockpile allocation budget in October inspired the department to expand and accelerate purchases of smelted tin for the strategic stockpile. Unlike natural rubber, stockpiled tin lagged far behind its quota, and the stockpile program offered the department an opportunity to serve the interests of national security and the needs of the British by increasing the flow of American dollars to Malaya. At an early November meeting, representatives of the Reconstruction Finance Corporation, the Munitions Board, and the State Department agreed to purchase 107,000 long tons of tin for the stockpile over the next two years. Of this total, 22,000 tons would come from the Texas City smelter, 14,000 from the Belgian congo, 27,000 from Indonesia, and 45,000 from Malaya. At prevailing prices, the proposal would bring $72 million to Malaya before the end of 1951.[58] The State Department subsequently moved to speed stockpile purchases, and in December it recommended that the tin quota be raised by another 60,000 tons.[59] Even before these cheerful figures were reported to the British, the American business recovery, the pound devaluation, and the removal of government restrictions on tin consumption elevated American imports. Between the third quarter of 1949 and the first quarter of 1950, U.S. imports of Malayan tin rose in value by $10 million.[60]

By the end of 1949, the British could not doubt that the State Department, at least, had taken the language of the tripartite communiqué seriously. The $300 million increase in the sterling area's gold and dollar reserves during the first quarter of 1950 had little to do with exports from Great Britain; it was inspired primarily by increased sterling area exports of cocoa, wool, tin, and rubber. Of these, only tin and rubber promised to remain attractive to dollar area buyers following the winter. As a result of British restrictions, U.S. exports to Malaya dwindled, while Malayan sales to the United States rose to a level approximating the successful triangular pattern of the prewar years. Between the late summer of 1949 and June 1950, Malaya had a trade surplus with the United States of $185.7 million, $142 million more than the next largest contributor to the sterling area dollar pool.[61]

Not all of the State Department's proposals regarding rubber and tin imports from Malaya were implemented. In fact, in this realm the State Department lost as many battles as it won. The proposals to remove the mandatory consumption quota for synthetic rubber and to accept a commodity agreement on tin were highly controversial and attracted strong opposition from government agencies and private concerns that felt, for various reasons, that these suggestions threatened bureaucratic or pecuniary interests. The setbacks suffered by the State Department on British and Malayan policy are a reminder that U.S. policy toward the Far East and the world in late 1949 and early 1950 was not a confident, linear thrust, but a series of often uncoordinated and occasionally contradictory responses to a complex set of problems upon which not everyone in the administration agreed. That the British economic problem was important and demanded a solution that included Malaya was a universally accepted truth that winter in Washington. Precisely how the administration should confront these problems was a matter for some debate.

Serious difficulties arose over rubber policy. While the State Department had won the bureaucratic battle over the language of the new rubber law, interest now turned to a special subcommittee of the House Armed Services Committee, which opened hearings on the bill February 20. Along with the controversial clause granting presidential discretion on the synthetic consumption minimum, the bill also contained proposals to expedite the release of the synthetic plants to the private sector and to make the new bill law for ten years. Both these proposals encountered immediate opposition from subcommittee members, who felt the synthetic industry was still too vital to national security to remove it from government control and who resented the administration's attempt to protect the issue from congressional scrutiny for a decade.

But the possible elimination of the synthetic quota drew most of the fire, not only from congressional representatives but from industry spokespersons invited to testify. W. J. Sears of the Rubber Manufacturers Association, R. S. Wilson of Goodyear, and Harvey S. Firestone, Jr., appeared before the subcommittee to argue, as Firestone put it, that the American synthetic rubber industry was "the best paid-up insurance policy our country ever had."[62] Subcommittee Chairman Carl Vinson made it known from the beginning of the hearings that he resented the administration's attempt to circumvent Congress by leaving the synthetic consumption level to presidential discretion. John R. Blandford, the subcommittee's professional staff member, forced Charles Sawyer to admit that a statutory minimum level of synthetic consumption would better protect national security than no minimum at all.[63]

Acheson later observed that the synthetic minimum question had "got Charlie Sawyer all tangled up,"[64] and in fact Sawyer found himself torn between his responsibilities as the bill's defender to Congress and his belief in the need for a strong domestic rubber industry. Ultimately, he backed down and returned to the position that a 200,000-ton synthetic minimum was not unreasonable.[65] Because Commerce continued to bear chief responsibility for guiding the bill through Congress, it had no chance of passing. On March 14, the House subcommittee rejected the bill and reported instead a proposal to extend the 1948 Rubber Act, with its synthetic quota intact, for another three years.[66] The administration's hope that Congress would reject the subcommittee's recommendation was destroyed by the outbreak of the Korean War in June.

At the same time, the British discovered that their promotion of Malayan rubber in the United States had been too successful. The increased demand for the Malayan product after September 1949 caused the price of rubber to rise sharply. Synthetic sold in the United States for the fixed price of $18\frac{1}{2}$¢ per pound, and for the first eight months of 1949 natural rubber stayed at least 3¢ per pound less. By early 1950, however, natural had risen to about 21¢ per pound, more than enough to compensate for the devaluation. By the end of May, a pound of natural rubber cost twice as much as a pound of synthetic, and the price was still climbing.[67]

Leading American rubber consumers and some administration officials recognized that rubber prices could be driven down if recently deactivated synthetics plants could be brought back into production. When several warnings to the British about high rubber prices failed to bring results, the administration, at the urging of the Defense Department, decided to act. On July 7, officials announced the reopening of three synthetic rubber factories. Maxwell Elliot, general counsel for the General Services Administration, told congressional representatives that the purpose of reopening the plants was to "get the price of natural rubber down."[68] The production of synthetic, which had fallen off in September 1949, was expected to increase by at least 75 percent through the rest of 1950.[69]

State Department officials were uncomfortable with this decision and acknowledged that it might postpone further improvement in the British balance of payments. Yet the Americans convinced themselves that the decision would work to the ultimate good of the rubber producers and, by extension, Great Britain. Both Maxwell Elliot and Charles Shohan argued that once natural prices were reduced to a more reasonable level by the increased competition, the United States would purchase more natural rubber than it had even in the halcyon days of the nine preceding months.[70] Ultimately, not because of but in spite of the price, it did; war in Korea would send purchases skyrocketing.

There were problems with tin, too. The administration, and particularly the State Department, had committed itself to the quick resumption of tin purchasing for the stockpile. These plans hit a snag in January 1950, when Commerce Department officials proposed that Malayan producers offer the United States a discount of three cents per pound from the average market price for the first three months of 1950 in exchange for the American promise to buy 45,000 tons during the next two years. Dismayed, British negotiators pointed out that the discount would reduce what was already a very low price and could well negate the benefits of sterling devaluation. The State Department agreed with the British, but once again it was unwilling to confront those directly responsible for stockpile purchasing. The Foreign Office considered offering a smaller discount, but ultimately refused any special terms, and negotiations reached an impasse. On February 19, the British government announced that "substantial difficulties" had prevented the conclusion of a long-term contract for American stockpiling of Malayan tin. The United States agreed to resume stockpile buying in any case, but the absence of a long-term contract for Malayan tin meant that the Americans might seek to fill the stockpile quota by purchasing smelted tin from Indonesia or raw tin concentrates from Thailand or Bolivia. Within weeks, tin prices, which had at last shown signs of recovery, plunged once again.[71]

Equally frustrating for the British was the Americans' reluctance to approve a commodity agreement for tin. While the State Department was prepared to accept in principle a tin agreement, the department was constrained by the opposition of other agencies, the administration's insistence that prices be kept low enough to ensure that the stockpile quota could be achieved within the budget, and, not incidentally, the limits of official ideology. Averell Harriman recalled that

Cripps raised the issue of commodity agreements at the tripartite conference, "but he put it up in such a socialistic way that we all got scared of it, because it sounded like world socialism."[72] Even during a period of ideological elasticity, that was going too far.

In late 1949, the Tin Study Group's Working Party produced a draft agreement that proposed the creation of an International Tin Council to include representatives from tin-producing and tin-consuming nations. The council would have the authority to collect from the producers a "buffer stock" of tin metal. When tin prices rose to an established ceiling price, the council would release tin from the stock. When prices fell, the council would purchase tin for the buffer stock. The price of tin would thus remain partly insensitive to fluctuations in production and demand.

When the buffer stock plan was announced at the Tin Study Group meeting at Paris in March 1950, the American delegates raised a series of objections to it. They offered amendments, but these were rejected by the producers and their allies. The meeting reached a stalemate. In the end, the producers managed to pass a resolution asking the United Nations to consider the buffer stock proposal, but all the delegates recognized that no plan could be effected over the opposition of the United States. The producers, including British Malaya, would have to survive without a commodity agreement.[73]

It is worth pointing out that neither the breakdown of tin stockpile contract talks nor the failure to secure a commodity plan demoralized the British. They had hoped to obtain American support for their position on tin, and they had captured the sympathy of the State Department. They had also sought assurances that the United States would resume buying tin for the stockpile. Despite the absence of a contract, by early 1950 British officials were confident that tin sales to the United States would continue to increase. In late February, following the miscarriage of the contract discussions, one of the chief negotiators for the British wrote the Foreign Office: "We . . . were quite reasonably satisfied with the outcome, in the sense that though we may lose a bit of money by not making a formal contract, we don't expect to lose as much as we should have if we had accepted a discount of £10 a ton; and we don't expect to lose much anyway."[74] The official was right. Within six months, Malayan tin sales to the United States would exceed Whitehall's fondest expectations.

The dollar gap was not the only source of British economic troubles. During the last quarter of 1949, while production in Great Britain itself increased, most exporters continued to sell principally to nations holding the United Kingdom's sterling balances. At the end of 1949, these balances totaled roughly £2.8 billion, or almost exactly what they had been in 1945.[75] British and American policymakers recognized that each British sale to a sterling creditor meant one less potential sale to the dollar area and prevented any narrowing of the dollar gap.[76] Prior to the tripartite talks, the British asked the United States to consider offering dollar aid to the underdeveloped sterling creditor nations in return for a reduction of the sterling balances. By late August, Oliver Franks detected American interest in this plan, and Under Secretary Webb, claiming to represent Acheson, acknowledged the "common responsibility" of the United States and Great Britain for solving the sterling balance problem.[77] The conference comuniqué was characteristically imprecise on the issue, concluding that the problem "concerned other countries and would require further study." Still, the State Department took the matter seriously. In November, following consultations within the department and after several meetings with British authorities, officials began to formulate "a departmental position" on the sterling balances.[78]

Acheson was at first unwilling to embrace openly the possibility of trading U.S. aid for scaled-down sterling balances, but he spoke to the British with evident sympathy. The indications given by the secretary during two meetings with British officials in January 1950, if ambiguous, were nonetheless tantalizing. On January 6, Acheson discussed the sterling balance problem with Oliver Franks. Though he made no commitments, Acheson "observed that the time might come when the British would have to tell the Indians [India was the leading holder of the balances] that 'the party is over'; the Indians might then ask the British what the next step was; the British might then probably say 'We had better go across the street to see our rich friend.' "[79]

What did the secretary mean by this cryptic statement? Franks tried on January 24 to get a clarification. Acheson commented that the sterling balances were "primarily British problems." Franks asked if the United States was contemplating an aid program for Asia. Acheson replied "that we were not working on any such program at present. [The secretary] suggested the possibility of pressures for some such program. If this should happen, the matter of dealing with certain of the sterling balances might be related to such a program." Acheson concluded: "We should have some definite ideas of what possible measures the British had in mind with respect to the sterling balances—and the sooner the better."[80] What began as a discouraging statement about the prospect for United States assistance for Asia ended as a strong hint that British recommendations for an aid program were urgently needed.

The British responded by preparing a proposal, which they submitted to Acheson on April 17. The paper, titled "Sterling Balances and South East Asia," made a strong case for buying off the sterling balances with American dollar aid. The British attempted to connect the balance issue with the plight of South and Southeast Asia and argued that reduction of the balances was vital for the solution of Great Britain's economic problems. If drawing on the balances by the creditor nations was reduced to a level the British could afford, the Asian sterling nations would be unable to maintain even modest rates of development. There was, therefore, "no prospect of a satisfactory settlement of the sterling balance problem consistent with a continuous economic development in South and South East Asia unless new money can be found for development (or settlement of the sterling balances) from outside the Sterling Area. On any realistic assessment," the paper concluded, "this can only mean dollars."[81] The solutions to the problems of the sterling balances and underdevelopment in Asia, to the economic dilemmas of Great Britain and the poverty and instability in the Far East, were coterminous.

By May 5, when Acheson summoned the minister of the British embassy to respond to the paper, President Truman had approved a program of military and economic assistance for a number of nations of the Far East. The Americans, Acheson said, thus agreed with the British on "the great strategic importance" of South and Southeast Asia. Acheson, however, made no promises on funding the sterling balances. If the American aid program for the Far East had the effect of helping the British, the United States "would be very glad," but the secretary did not explicitly link the program with the sterling balance question, as the British hoped he would.[82]

Acheson's refusal to make promises discouraged the British, but it did not defeat them. Analysts of Acheson's May 5 response concluded, no doubt correctly, that the secretary had been constrained once more by John Snyder. British officials also took solace in Acheson's qualification that his comments were his "first thoughts" on the matter of funding the sterling balances, though they clearly were not.[83] In any case, of more immediate concern was the United States' larger commitment to Southeast Asia. The sterling balances were a lingering annoyance. The protection of Malaya from Communist influence was the matter of paramount concern to the British government by early 1950, and American help was critical if Southeast Asia was to be fortified.

The British therefore hoped the United States could be enlisted actively in the struggle against communism in Southeast Asia. The British claimed they could handle the emergency in Malaya, but the task of defeating the revolutionaries continued to prove far more difficult than the British had first thought. Communist attacks increased during December 1949 and January 1950. In early February the colonial government announced the inauguration of "Anti-Bandit Month," an attempt to mobilize thousands of loyal Malayans for a final, all-out strike against the guerrillas. The campaign failed. One body count, probably optimistic, put the toll for the month at seventy-seven members of the security force killed to only thirty-eight guerrillas, and, as one member of Parliament pointed out, the fighting had "immobilized a division of troops which ought to be in Western Europe." In the House of Lords, L. D. Gammans charged that "the situation is getting worse instead of better." Another MP, Oliver Stanley, "beg[ged] the Government to regard this whole question of Malaya as priority number one, not only in foreign and defense policy but in our economic policy, because all will come crashing to the ground if we lose this war in Malaya."[84] The British refrained from asking the United States for help in Malaya, but their limited resources were stretched very thin. In mid-April an American reporter concluded, "It has become apparent that despite nearly two years of combat against the Malaya Communist rebellion, the insurgents are a greater menace than ever to the security of Malaya."[85]

But the emergency remained only part of the Malayan security problem. The British hoped the Americans would help in the region's most vulnerable spot: Indochina. Even before their American counterparts, key British officials accepted a version of the domino theory for Southeast Asia and agreed that the preservation of a non-Communist Indochina was essential to the security of all Southeast Asia, including, of course, Malaya. Through late 1949 and into early 1950, the British tried to persuade U.S. policymakers to extend diplomatic recognition and material assistance to the government of Vietnam.

The most persistent British advocate of American support for the Bao Dai government was Malcolm MacDonald, commissioner general in Southeast Asia. MacDonald had long urged Western help for the beleaguered French puppet and had even called for "Asian equivalents of the Marshall Plan and the Atlantic Pact."[86] In November 1949,

MacDonald held a series of meetings with Foreign Office officials and Far East diplomats and visited with French authorities and Bao Dai in Vietnam. He increasingly sympathized with the French. MacDonald believed the West should offer "every possible assistance" to the French in Indochina, and he urged his government and that of the United States to extend "maximum recognition" to the Bao Dai government on the day the French Parliament ratified the March 8 agreement, or perhaps earlier. MacDonald liked and trusted Léon Pignon, his French counterpart in Indochina, and was, to his surprise, "impressed" with Bao Dai. Despite the general impression that the former emperor was "a dull dog," MacDonald found him "talkative, intelligent and charming." Bao Dai was "not (repeat not) a genius" and was inclined to be "a bit diffident," but he also possessed "physical courage," "independence," and "a sound grasp of the political problems in his country and a good judgement about their handling." "I do not think he is given sufficient credit for his actions over the last year," MacDonald argued. "[He] is our friend, and his Government offers the only chance of Indo-China being saved from Communist capture."[87]

By early December, the State Department was persuaded that MacDonald was "taking [the] ball" on Southeast Asian matters.[88] There were good reasons for this belief. R. H. Scott, head of the Foreign Office's South East Asia Department, came to agree with MacDonald that something should be "done quickly by the British Government" to encourage the Bao Dai regime.[89] The logical thing was to extend diplomatic recognition to Bao Dai. The British previously had agreed with the Americans that recognition could only follow the ratification of the March 8 agreement by the French Parliament, but at MacDonald's urging the Foreign Office accelerated the process unilaterally.[90] "The situation in Indo-China is serious," Scott wrote Attlee on December 29, "and it has grave implications for the whole of our position in South East Asia. Anything we can do to prevent Communist domination of Indo-China is worth doing."[91]

The next day, Attlee agreed to offer de facto diplomatic recognition to Vietnam. The French were informed of the move in secrecy and asked not to announce it, but they were permitted to pass word of the démarche to Bao Dai.[92] The Americans were told on January 6. The British averred that Bao Dai commanded "a considerable measure of popular support" and therefore had "a reasonable chance of establishing a stable administration in Viet Nam."[93] Announcement of the de facto recognition, the British decided, should come only at the end of the Commonwealth conference to be held at Colombo,

Ceylon in mid-January. At Colombo, the British tried to use conference sessions to convince other members of the Commonwealth to recognize Bao Dai, but a strong plea from Ernest Bevin—Malcolm MacDonald, he said, "had allayed his suspicions"—fell on deaf ears. The British made their announcement anyway, and planned to drop the de facto qualification when the French parliament ratified the March 8 pact. On February 7, following ratification, Great Britain recognized the Bao Dai government without restriction.[94]

British officials did not believe Western diplomatic recognition was enough to prevent communism from spreading throughout Southeast Asia. The French, the British knew, needed military equipment to fight Ho Chi Minh. Just after the British and American recognition announcements, the French submitted a request for arms to the Attlee government. After receiving this request, the military let its enthusiasm for anti-Communist combat get the better of it. General Harding, commander-in-chief of the Far East land forces, implied to French authorities that Great Britain might intervene in Indochina. (This possibility was hastily denied by the Foreign Office.)[95] Civilian officials, however, were willing to help the French with more modest designs. Though Great Britain was using most of its jungle warfare material in Malaya, the British chiefs of staff offered the French "any equipment which is surplus to our own requirements" and promised to sell France, "at the minimum replacement value," equipment from British war reserves.[96]

The British knew it would not be enough. Only American military and economic assistance, in far greater magnitude than Great Britain could supply, could save Southeast Asia. This was the principal conclusion of the Colombo conference, held January 12–17, 1950. According to his private secretary, Ernest Bevin "was very keen that something practical should come out of the conference . . . . His primary objective was to find some way to raise the standard of living in the countries of South and Southeast Asia."[97] On January 10, before the conference had actually begun, Percy Spender, the Australian minister for external affairs, anticipated Bevin's interest when he circulated a memorandum recommending a coordinated program of economic aid for the region.[98] Spender urged the developed Commonwealth and Western non-Commonwealth nations to supply economic aid to Southeast Asian states. The purpose of assistance, said Spender, was to "help the countries of South East Asia to develop their own democratic institutions and their own economies and thus protect them against those opportunists and subversive elements which take advantage of changing political situations and low living standards." Spender also noted the enormous "economic benefits to the rest of the world, and particularly the United Kingdom and Continental Europe, from the restoration and development of the output of food and raw materials" in South and Southeast Asia. A revived and protected Southeast Asia could make "a substantial contribution towards solutions of the dollar problem by way either of direct dollar earnings or replacement of supplies on which the sterling area and Western Europe are dependent." The Spender, or Colombo Plan, emerged from this memorandum.[99]

There was never any question that Spender's plan would flourish or perish at the whim of the United States. While the Commonwealth welcomed private investment in Southeast Asia, many dollars were needed instantly, and only the United States government could supply them. Spender and British officials made this point repeatedly. Spender's January 10 memo acknowledged that "the economic progress of South and South-East Asia depends very much on the willingness of the United States so to conduct its domestic and foreign economic policies as to provide stable markets for the area's exports, and to supply the predominating share of the capital equipment and consumption goods which the area needs to increase its production."[100] It was "almost an article of faith with me" that the United States would be the major contributor to Southeast Asia's development, Spender confessed.[101] Oliver Franks had suggested to Acheson that "the main hope of maintaining a strong democratic force in South and Southeast Asia would be for the U.S. not only to inject some dollars into that area but to maintain both a military and political interest as well."[102] Lord Strang, the permanent under secretary in the British Foreign Office, spoke of the need for "concerted" policy with the United States "since American resources would be indispensable" to the recovery and protection of the Far East.[103]

When the conference ended, the Australians and the British approached the Americans for funds. This matter was a delicate one on both sides. When American officials offered to send an observer to a Commonwealth meeting at Sydney in May, the Commonwealth Relations Office protested that "outside" nations had never attended such gatherings, and the Foreign Office, in the interest of bureaucratic amity, stood behind the CRO.[104] The obstacles in the path of American cooperation were even greater. Any sign by the United States that it was interested in the plan might bring what Esler Dening of the British Foreign Office had called "a staggering bill," something the administration sought to avoid. In fact, Bevin disclosed privately that he envisioned an "initial" American commitment of "two or three hundred million dollars a year."[105] Moreover, the Colombo Plan was still very new. Membership in the organization created by the plan had to that point been confined to Commonwealth states, leaving out the key domino—Indochina. The procedures for supplying economic aid under the plan had not been worked out, and so the structure of the organization was substantially unfinished. On June 21, 1950, Merrill Gay of the Far Eastern Division recommended against "interjecting ourselves too strongly into this matter at this time."[106] Until late 1950, the United States maintained a detached interest in the Colombo Plan.

This is not to say that the administration was unsympathetic toward the Commonwealth's effort. A week after the Colombo Conference, Assistant Secretary of State George McGhee warmly greeted the Spender proposal and promised that the United States was "ready to adapt [its] own efforts in furtherance of this endeavor."[107] By early March, according to the Foreign Office, American officials had "shown great interest" in the Colombo Plan.[108] James Plimsoll of the Australian embassy got a friendly reception when he discussed the plan with State Department officials later that month.[109] Dean Acheson affirmed that the United States was "willing as far as possible [to] adapt and coordinate [its] own projects [in] this area with projects undertaken by [the] Commonwealth."[110]

Here was the crux of the matter. The United States certainly welcomed the Colombo Plan, but in many ways it ran parallel to the administration's own projects that were taking shape that spring. Politically, the United States had, with the British, recognized the Bao Dai government in Vietnam. Economically, Point Four was finally moving in Congress, and the recommendations of the R. Allen Griffin mission targeted unspent ECA funds for the Far East. On the question of military aid, the State and Defense Departments agreed to send unallocated Military Assistance Program funds to certain Southeast Asian nations. These initiatives had as their objectives the stability, economic recovery, and security of Southeast Asia, and these objectives were in turn meant to ensure the permanent revival of Japan, Great Britain, France, and the rest of continental Western Europe.

By the spring of 1950, the British could claim they had strongly influenced American policy toward Southeast Asia during the previous nine months. The Americans had long ignored the region. They had been disdainful of colonialism, insensitive to the fragility of the British economy, and narrow-minded in their insistence on an early return to multilateral trade. American policy had changed during 1949. The British had educated U.S. policymakers and persuaded them finally that the sterling area required protection against the flood of exports from the dollar nations. Multilateral trade, the State Department concluded, must temporarily give way to such artificial devices as British import quotas and American purchases of Malayan rubber and tin, with little regard for price and strategic necessity. The connection between British economic recovery and the pacification of British Malaya was plain, and so United States officials were virtually wordless in their acceptance of British colonialism in Malaya. Because Malaya was vital to Western interests, it must be protected from hostile outside forces. If the Bao Dai government collapsed, as Walton Butterworth told Esler Dening in September 1949, Malayan security would be jeopardized.[111] The lesson had taken. Once American policymakers had accepted protectionism and colonialism by the British, it became difficult to demand their eradication by the French. The United States would find it had been easier to oppose colonialism in all its forms than it was to make distinctions between the relatively successful British example in Malaya and the increasingly ugly version practiced by the French in Indochina.

8

The Reconstruction of Western Europe and the Beginning of United States Aid to Southeast Asia

By the middle of 1950, the United States had reshaped its policy toward Southeast Asia on behalf of the Japanese and the British. American policymakers no longer regarded Southeast Asia as a disparate jumble of unrelated states, but as a region that had to be tied to the most important industrialized nations in the Far East and Western Europe. American officials had simultaneously suspended their hopes for an anti-Communist bloc joined by liberalism and capitalism and endorsed despotic or protectionist policies practiced by Thailand, Japan, and Great Britain. Finally, Harry Truman's request for "large amounts of capital from . . . the United States" in January 1950 signaled the end of the modest economic philosophy that underlay the Point Four proposal and indicated the administration's willingness to provide government capital for underdeveloped nations on the principle, though not the magnitude, of the Marshall Plan. It remained only to extend the new policy to French Indochina.

In early 1950, following the administration's acceptance of the assumptions of NSC-48, Indochina—especially Vietnam—was regarded by policymakers as the key to Southeast Asia. As Livingston Merchant wrote in early 1950, "it can be assumed that Thailand would change sides promptly if French Indochina goes Communist. Burma would be outflanked. The position of the British in Malaya would be gravely prejudiced and the opening up to the Communist coalition of the raw materials of . . . Indonesia would be accelerated."[1] A Communist takeover in Southeast Asia would make slaves of the region's peoples, deny important raw materials to the non-Communist world, and tip the balance of power in favor of the Soviet Union and its puppets.

Policymakers argued that the security of Indochina was important also because of its relationship with France. The continuation of the war against the Viet Minh drained France financially, making the still precarious nation more vulnerable to Communist subversion. In addition, both American and French officials regarded a strong France as a prerequisite to an integrated Western Europe that included West Germany. The Americans pursued the objective of Western European integration with increasing vigor during the spring of 1950, but it quickly became clear to them that this goal was incompatible with the continuation of France's enormous military effort in Indochina. The French, who had cautiously sounded out the Americans on the matter of political and economic support for Bao Dai in the spring of 1949, renewed their plea in the fall, this time through the highest channels.[2] At the time of Acheson's National Press Club speech, the administration contemplated the possibility of preserving Southeast Asia and reconstructing Western Europe by helping the French in Indochina.

American support for Bao Dai, and incidentally for the monarchies in Laos and Cambodia, could take political, economic, and military forms. First, the United States could extend diplomatic recognition to the three governments. Second, on the basis of either Point Four or Walter Salant's theory of foreign aid, the administration might offer technical or capital assistance to the Asian states. Finally, although almost no one in the administration envisioned sending American troops to defend Indochina, the United States could supply arms and other military equipment to the French or directly to the native armies the French were supposed to be constructing. These options were often considered simultaneously by American policymakers, who believed the initiatives complemented one another. Because the decisions for diplomatic recognition, economic assistance, and military aid were made separately, however, and simply to clarify what would otherwise be a confusing, overlapping narrative, I will consider these decisions one at a time, in the order in which they were made.

Diplomatic Recognition of the Indochinese Governments

Irked by French unwillingness to grant political concessions to Indochina and largely unimpressed with the Bao Dai government in Vietnam, American policymakers did not immediately follow their expression of support for Bao Dai in June 1949 with diplomatic recognition. In the fall, when French officials insisted that U.S. recognition would give Bao Dai the stamp of legitimacy he needed to attract widespread support among the Vietnamese, the State Department countered with several conditions the French would have to satisfy before the administration would take that step. First, although French Premier Georges Bidault and Bao Dai had signed the March 8 agreement, the French Parliament had not yet ratified it. The administration was aware of serious objections to the agreement in the assembly, and it demanded assurance that the French would at minimum promise the Indochinese states "independence within the French Union," as the agreement stipulated, before it ventured to recognize.[3] Second, the administration hoped to convince both the United Kingdom and potentially sympathetic Far Eastern nations, such as India, the Philippines, and Thailand, to recognize the Bao Dai government along with the United States. In the autumn of 1949, the prospect that the Asian nations would agree to this was not promising.[4] Third, the administration deplored the French practice of handling Indochinese affairs through the Ministry of Overseas Areas—the Colonial Office—and urged the French to substantiate their claim that Indochina was largely independent by dealing with it through their Foreign Office.[5]

Finally, the Office of Philippines and Southeast Asian Affairs (PSA)* and Dean Acheson himself were troubled by indications that the French viewed ratification of the March 8 agreement as their final concession to the independence of Indochina. This was not at all what the PSA officers had in mind. They argued that the March 8 pact represented only a small victory for the Vietnamese and that it must be regarded merely as a first step in an evolutionary process leading to the full independence of Indochina.[6] On November 28, the PSA office agreed that the French should follow the ratification of the March 8 agreement with the announcement of a timetable for granting the Indochinese full independence. Three days later, Acheson cabled David Bruce in Paris that he feared the agreement "may well be . . . another instance of too little and too late" and endorsed PSA's timetable suggestion.[7] The American demand for a French "evolutionary statement" on Indochina inspired among the French more indignation than any other condition for American recognition of Bao Dai. The French government was struggling to gain the assembly votes necessary for the ratification of the March 8 agree-

---

*As a result of the department reorganization of Oct. 3, 1949, the Divisions of Southeast Asian (SEA) and Philippines (PI) Affairs were merged to form the Office of Philippines and Southeast Asian Affairs (PSA).

ment, and there was no chance it would risk further antagonizing the undecided by interjecting an "evolutionary statement." In late 1949, this issue alone threatened Franco-American cooperation on Indochina policy.

But by late 1949 the tide of events pressed hard against the advocates of caution toward Indochina. The new urgency of the problems of Southeast Asia, the Soviet atomic explosion, and the Communist victory in China had persuaded the Far East consultants to endorse aid to Bao Dai and had induced the National Security Council to invoke the domino theory as justification for American assistance to Southeast Asia. These events increased the number of State Department officials who were willing to relent on one or more of the conditions for U.S. diplomatic recognition. W. Walton Butterworth told British officials in September that the department believed there was "no alternative to the recognition and support of Bao Dai."[8] James O'Sullivan of PSA warned that Bao Dai needed more popular support in Vietnam and that recognition by Asian nations should precede British and American recognition, but he was silent on the matters of the Colonial-to-Foreign Office transfer and the evolutionary statement.[9] Reports from the American consulates in Hanoi and Saigon radiated optimism over French political and military progress.[10]

David Bruce, American ambassador to France, remained the most persistent and influential advocate of U.S. recognition and aid for the Bao Dai government. By October, Bruce had decided, as he told a group of U.S. ambassadors in Europe, that Bao Dai "was doing better than anticipated" in Vietnam, and that "the French, too, had been playing squarer than we had hoped." Bruce admitted that Bao Dai's connections with French colonialism presented difficulties for U.S. policy. "But [can] we afford to be purists and perfectionists?" he asked. The question was rhetorical, for Bruce believed "a more pragmatic approach was essential if we were to get out of the woods." There were, after all, only two choices for Vietnam: Bao Dai, "with his imperfections," or Ho Chi Minh, who was clearly identified with "Stalinist Communism."[11]

Bruce again stressed the need for "pragmatism" on December 11, when he responded to Acheson's suggestion that the French set a timetable for withdrawal from Indochina. According to Bruce, French politics and the military situation in Indochina made the timetable proposal unthinkable. Instead, the United States had to reconcile itself to certain "practical measures" that would "further our objective of halting Communist expansion at the Tonkinese border. If that is not done," Bruce warned, "Burma and Siam will fall like over-ripe apples and the British . . . will be forced to reconsider the tenability of their position in Malaya." Bruce anticipated French ratification of the March 8 agreement, and he recommended transfer of Indochinese affairs out of the Ministry of Overseas Areas and an evolutionary statement, but he significantly qualified this last recommendation by allowing that the French could announce it after ratification had taken place. The United States, in turn, should recognize the Bao Dai government and offer Indochina both economic and military assistance. It was vital, Bruce concluded, that the United States act "courageously and speedily" to support the anti-Communists in Indochina.[12]

These arguments ultimately prevailed with Acheson and Truman. Throughout December 1949 and January 1950, the secretary of state gave ground. At dinner with Oliver Franks and Canadian Ambassador Hume Wrong on December 17, Acheson "interpolated a paean of praise about French achievements in Indochina" and reported that the United States, "in distinction from its earlier views," would recognize and aid the Bao Dai government once the French had ratified the March 8 agreement.[13] On January 5, Butterworth told Dean Rusk, then the deputy under secretary for political affairs, that the Far Eastern Bureau favored the "de facto" recognition of Vietnam, the sort the British had already offered privately.[14] Two days later, Acheson informed the London, Paris, and Far Eastern embassies and consulates that the administration planned to extend Vietnam "some form [of] recognition" following ratification of the March 8 agreement and the expected British announcement of de facto recognition. Acheson hoped U.S. recognition would be "preceded by or synchronized with a 'spontaneous' " evolutionary statement by the French and recognition by "as many south Asian and other nations as possible," but he did not say that these were conditions for U.S. recognition.[15] Acheson further softened his position on January 20, when he closed a telegram detailing Bao Dai's liabilities with the hint that the administration might eliminate the de facto stage of recognition for all three Indochinese states. Acheson also authorized Philip Jessup, who was then touring Southeast Asia, to inform Bao Dai that the United States "looks forward to establishing a closer relationship with Vietnam."[16]

The French assembly ratified the March 8 agreement on January 29. The following day the Soviet Union announced its recognition of Ho Chi Minh as the legitimate leader of Vietnam. That evening, Acheson informed the embassy in London that the State Department now believed straightforward recognition, without the de facto qualification, would best serve U.S. interests. When the Parliament's upper house accepted the March 8 pact on February 2, Acheson recommended immediate recognition to Truman. The next morning the full cabinet, then the president, accepted the secretary's recommendation. On February 7, 1950, the United States, like Great Britain, extended diplomatic recognition to Vietnam, Laos, and Cambodia.[17]

As of February 7, only one-and-a-half of the four original conditions for U.S. recognition had been met. The French had ratified the March 8 agreement, and the British had embraced Malcolm MacDonald's views on Southeast Asia and recognized the Indochinese governments. Great Britain, however, was the only nation to join the United States. Not even such devoted Asian allies as the Philippines or Thailand consented immediately to recognize, and in India Prime Minister Nehru continued to insist that the Bao Dai government was a French shadow play. Although French Foreign Minister Robert Schuman agreed that the Overseas Ministry was no longer the most appropriate agency for managing Indochinese affairs, the French had not yet moved their relations with the Indochinese states to a different department. The French refused to make an "evolutionary statement" on Indochina. As Alexandre Parodi, the secretary-general of the French Ministry of Foreign Affairs, told Bruce, "we cannot afford to kindle unrealistic nationalist appetites whose necessary disappointment by us would have retrograde rather than progressive effects out there."[18] Despite this discouraging record, there were several reasons the administration decided to recognize the Indochinese governments in early February.

Certainly the timing of the British decision to recognize Bao Dai influenced American policymakers. State Department officials who had hoped to make Western diplomatic recognition contingent on a French evolutionary statement found themselves undercut by the British decision.[19] British decisiveness in late December and early January forced the department to consider the possible consequences of inaction, especially for the Western alliance. By late January, the United States was following the British lead throughout the region. "We want to carry the Americans with us in South East Asia," Esler Dening wrote on January 26.[20] Five days later, the State Department informed His Majesty's government that it intended to recognize Bao Dai in early February.[21] P. F. Kinna of the Foreign Office was exultant. "We have worked hard for a long time to stimulate American interest in Indo-China," he wrote the embassy in Paris, "and I think we can take some of the credit for the Americans' views" on recognition.[22]

A second reason the United States abandoned most of its conditions for recognition was the burden placed on the French treasury by the war in Indochina. Expenditure for the war, wrote Bruce in a summary of an embassy memo on the issue, had become "an important obstacle to the success of the whole French recovery and stabilization effort." The French had spent 167 million francs in Indochina in 1949, an amount equivalent to more than two-thirds of American aid for France during the period, and the drain plainly jeopardized the success of the European Recovery Program. Bruce argued that the United States could help solve this problem by following the advice he had offered in his December 11 telegram: the administration should recognize Bao Dai and provide him with economic and military aid. The United States had "a double opportunity to resist Communist expansion in Asia at one of its most dangerous points while contributing directly to the maintenance of French economic stability." A generous U.S. policy toward French Indochina would thus serve two important functions.[23]

Another factor that pushed Acheson closer to Bruce's position on Indochina was the increasingly vociferous attack by right-wing Republicans on the administration's Far Eastern policy. Congressional Republicans were incensed about the administration's refusal to offer military support to Taiwan. Acheson's January 12 Press Club speech did not mollify most conservatives, who still contended that the administration should act to salvage what remained of non-Communist China. On January 21, Alger Hiss, the former State Department official accused of being a Communist spy, was convicted of perjury. At a press conference following Hiss's sentencing on January 25, Acheson bravely declared, "I do not intend to turn my back on Alger Hiss." That statement, the secretary later reflected, "absolutely took the roof off everything." Key congressional representatives, enraged, called for Acheson's resignation.[24] On February 2, the day before the cabinet met to decide on recognition for Indochina, Klaus Fuchs was arrested in London. The furor over China, the Hiss conviction and Acheson's subsequent statement, and the arrest of Fuchs created a political atmosphere that made caution a liability and anti-Communist commitment in the Far East an asset. If nearly unconditional recognition of the Indochinese governments was for Acheson a close call, the attacks from the right tipped the balance in favor of the French.

The most important reason for Acheson's new willingness to jettison a majority of the conditions for recognition was the public establishment of an alliance between both Peking and Moscow and Ho Chi Minh's guerrillas. As late as Labor Day, 1949, Edwin Stanton, American ambassador to Thailand, quoted a reliable source who reported that the decision whether to accept Chinese Communist aid remained "a tremendous problem for the Ho Chi Minh Government."[25] By late 1949, however, the Communists had assumed control in China, and the French showed no indication of negotiating an end to the war. The first firm step toward Peking by the Viet Minh occurred in December, when they convened the first National Conference of Vietnam Trade Unions in northern Tonkin. The conference, which was lavishly publicized over Viet Minh radio, aligned itself firmly with China and the Soviet Union in the global struggle against imperialism. In early January, Viet Minh Commander-in-Chief Vo Nguyen Giap held secret meetings with PRC officials in southern China, and several days later Ho requested the establishment of diplomatic relations. On January 18, the PRC recognized the Viet Minh government and announced the conclusion of a military trade agreement between the two "nations." The Soviet Union recognized Ho on January 30.[26]

American policymakers immediately denounced both the Chinese and Soviet moves. Acheson responded to the PRC recognition of Ho by virtually eliminating the de facto stage of U.S. recognition of the Bao Dai government. The department's attack on the Soviet Union after January 30 was thunderous. The department's press officer told the media that Ho had been revealed as "an agent of world Communism," a nationalist *poseur* who preached "Indo-China for the Kremlin and not Indo-China for the Indo-Chinese."[27] Charles Yost, recently promoted to director of the Office of Eastern European Affairs, saw Soviet recognition as evidence that the Soviets intended "to accelerate the revolutionary process in South East Asia" and believed it "confirm[ed] the conclusion that Indo-China may now be the focal point of the most intensive and determined Communist pressure."[28] For Philip Jessup, this was proof "that Ho Chi Minh [was] a Communist agent trained in Moscow," and Acheson argued that Soviet recognition "reveal[ed] Ho in his true colors as the mortal enemy of native independence in Indo-China."[29] The secretary recommended immediate U.S. recognition of Bao Dai three days after the Soviets recognized Ho.

The Decision for Aid

Most American policymakers agreed that diplomatic recognition was the first of several steps toward a deeper commitment to the French. The State Department had already indicated some sympathy for French requests for American aid, and by February 7 the administration was considering proposals for both economic and military assistance. At this juncture, a number of officers in the Bureau of Far Eastern Affairs made a last attempt to separate the issues of recognition and material assistance for Indochina. These officers, led by Bureau Chief Butterworth (an early supporter of recognition), hoped to force the French to fulfill the conditions that had earlier been considered prerequisites to American recognition. Despite Schuman's assurances, the French continued to procrastinate on the transfer of Indochinese affairs to the Foreign Ministry, and this inaction drew the fire of Livingston Merchant, deputy assistant secretary of state for Far Eastern affairs, and William Lacy, after February 17 the head of the PSA Office, among others.[30] Officials also pointed out that by March 1 only Thailand among the friendly South Asian states had recognized Bao Dai and that Thai recognition had triggered a cabinet crisis that led to the resignation of the Thai foreign minister.[31]

Most of the opponents of aid for Indochina worked to elicit an evolutionary statement from the French. A week after American recognition of the Indochinese governments had been announced, Lacy wrote Merchant of his concern over the French refusal to make an evolutionary statement. After reviewing the history of French obstructionism on the issue, Lacy contended: "In view of the imminence of the receipt of request for both economic and military aid for Indochina, I believe that now is a suitable time for us to insist upon an evolutionary statement as a prerequisite to United States aid." The administration would never again have a better opportunity "to force, if necessary, a statement from the French." If the French needed aid, it seemed to Lacy "that we have every right to insist on an act which they should have made long ago." The demand for a quid pro quo would also teach the French that the United States was not "indulgent [or] dumb."[32]

The official French request for aid came two days later, delivered to Acheson by Ambassador Henri Bonnet. Lacy had asked Merchant to discuss his February 14 memo with the secretary, and though it is not clear whether Merchant actually did, he was present at the Bonnet-Acheson meeting. The secretary accepted the French *aide-mémoire* on economic and military aid, then raised with Bonnet the matter of an evolutionary statement. Acheson attributed the reluctance of South Asian nations to recognize the Indochinese governments to the widely held belief that Vietnam, Laos, and Cambodia "did not in fact enjoy independence." The United States had "brushed aside this question" in deciding to recognize, but Acheson was "extremely fearful, in the absence of some expression of intent or further action on the part of the French, [that] the reluctance of the

Asiatic powers to come forward . . . would persist." After Bonnet left, having agreed to report the secretary's views to his government, Acheson observed to Merchant "that our bargaining position disappears the moment we agree to give them aid."[33] Once again, as in early December, Acheson was flirting with a stern line toward the French.

Merchant now encouraged the Bureau of Far Eastern Affairs to draft a sharply worded memo that would pointedly reserve judgment on the question of aid until the French had made their evolutionary statement. On March 7, PSA sent Merchant a draft telegram for the French. The telegram's authors, Lacy and Elim O'Shaughnessy of the Western Europe Office, argued that "it behooves the French Government to do what it can to quote sell unquote Bao Dai" and that the best way for the French to do this was "to make a statement showing the evolutionary character" of their intentions in Indochina. This was not strong enough for Merchant, who suggested that because the telegram failed to make the statement a condition for United States aid, it was an initiative containing "mostly milk and water."[34] Merchant hoped to incorporate into the memo an earlier recommendation by Butterworth "that no ECA or military aid be committed to French Indochina" until an evolutionary statement had been made.[35]

Philip Jessup saw both the draft telegram and Butterworth's recommendation when he returned from his tour of the Far East and Western Europe on March 15. The trip had been most enlightening for the ambassador-at-large and, as we will see, had transformed Jessup from a mild advocate of some sort of American initiative in the Far East to a strong supporter of immediate U.S. aid for Southeast Asia. On March 20, Jessup wrote to Butterworth and attempted to discourage him from insisting on an evolutionary statement prior to extending aid. The French, Jessup wrote, seemed to him "strongly on the defensive" over U.S. pressure, and even the mildly worded draft telegram might so antagonize the government that it would "reduce the likelihood of the French acting." "I am interested in results," Jessup finished, "and frankly doubt . . . whether the approach indicated in the draft telegram would be the most fruitful."[36]

Butterworth responded to Jessup's letter the next day. He had passed it on to PSA, he wrote, but he continued to stand by his quid pro quo position of the previous month. "My experience," he noted, "is that the moment of maximum persuasion is before the carrot goes into the donkey's mouth and not afterwards."[37] But Butterworth, Merchant, and the others were fighting a losing battle, for by March 21 essential aspects of an aid program for Indochina had already been approved at the highest levels. The watery March 7 PSA draft was further diluted by O'Shaughnessy and was sent to Bruce with instructions to give Schuman an oral summary of its contents. Even this demarche, really a timid representation transmitted through a source known to be sympathetic to the French, was frustrated by the protests of Edmund Gullion, the new American consul in Saigon. Bruce informed the State Department that, in light of Gullion's arguments, he would not speak to Schuman until he received further word from Washington. There is no evidence that the meeting was ever held.[38]

The administration rejected the advice of the Far Eastern experts because it was inconsistent with the assertive policy toward Southeast Asia formulated over the previous months. The advocates of the evolutionary statement prior to assistance argued that diplomatic recognition of Bao Dai need not lead to aid for his government. To others within the administration, however, it was impossible to separate the two issues. By the early spring of 1950, both conceptual and practical precedents existed for the extension of U.S. aid to Southeast Asian nations.

The conceptual precedent for American aid to Southeast Asia occurred with the Truman administration's implicit acceptance of Walter Salant's view of foreign aid. By the fall of 1949 the administration acknowledged that American aid to Southeast Asia could have a positive effect on Great Britain's dollar problem if it were used to protect the Malayan extractive industries. Officials' statements indicated that it was not only Great Britain, but all of Western Europe that would benefit from the production and protection of Southeast Asia. The president, undoubtedly helped by David Lloyd, had come to recognize that U.S. aid to underdeveloped nations was necessary for "an expanding world economy."[39] The second report of the Organization for European Economic Cooperation (OEEC), released in February 1950, contended that prospects for Western Europe's recovery "would be greatly enhanced if there were substantial United States investment in, and assistance to countries outside Europe" and judged it "essential that, in a healthy, expanding world economy, capital should flow on a large scale from the United States to less developed countries."[40]

In late March, Lieutenant Colonel Charles H. (Tick) Bonesteel, the executive director of the European Coordinating Committee of the Mutual Defense Assistance Program, summarized the reasons for the continued economic difficulties of Western Europe: "The 'dollar problem,' disruption of triangular trade, the rise of nationalism in Southeast Asia and sub-Asia with the inevitable concomitant of desires for national self-sufficiency, the problem of industrialized Japan—not to mention Communism, the loss of China, and possible subversion of more of free Asia—all tend to leave Western Europe with an industrial production potential which will require positive action if it is to be sustained unaided." One type of action Bonesteel recommended was the "development of underdeveloped areas in many parts of the world."[41] Salant himself continued to stress the need for the transmutation of Point Four into a program of government investment.[42] Acheson told the Foreign Relations Committee that economic development would bring "certain practical material benefits" to the United States and especially to "our friends in Europe, who depend far more than we do on foreign goods and markets."[43] Clearly by this time a conceptual framework that permitted consideration of government aid for underdeveloped nations had taken hold with the administration, setting a precedent for honoring French requests for assistance in Indochina.

The practical precedent for United States aid to Indochina was the American decision, in late 1949 and early 1950, to offer economic and military assistance to Sukarno's new government in Indonesia. Of course, the decision to help Sukarno, who was a fervent nationalist and an enormously popular figure in his country, was far simpler than the American choice to back Bao Dai, who owed most of his modest political standing to the French. Still, by February 1950 the United States had inaugurated a program of economic and military aid for a Southeast Asian country that was formerly a colony of a Western European nation, a country that remained an integral part of Western Europe's economy and a potential trade partner for Japan.

The administration stood watchfully on the perimeter as the Dutch and Indonesians argued over the terms of independence at The Hague during the fall of 1949. The United States had helped convince the Dutch to permit independence in Indonesia, but the Americans refused to risk a permanent split with the Dutch on the issue and continued to seek a middle path between nationalism and colonialism. By late 1949, when independence was a foregone conclusion, the United States and the Netherlands found that their hope for the future of Indonesia in many ways coincided. Both nations wanted the Dutch to retain a naval base at the Java port of Surabaya. Under Secretary of State James Webb informed the embassy in the Netherlands that the department regarded as important the incorporation into The Hague agreements of "specific safeguards against confiscatory taxation, etc., for foreign including Amer[ican] investments" in Indonesia.[44] The U.S. representative on the United Nations Committee on Indonesia, A. Merle Cochran, pressured the Indonesians to assume a significant portion of the Dutch debt in the islands, a debt largely incurred as a result of the Dutch "police actions."[45] Cochran also persuaded the Indonesians to accept at least temporary Dutch control of West Irian, part of the East Indian archipelago.[46]

Part of the reason for this sympathy for the Dutch position was the American desire to mend fences with its ally; as Selden Chapin, the American ambassador in the Netherlands, put it, "The Dutch are sore and we fear that this resentment will be aimed at us."[47] More important, the United States wanted for Indonesia generally what the Dutch did: a secure, non-Communist nation, open to penetration by Western goods and capital, and an abundant source of primary products. These goals were again connected to the recovery of Western Europe, still the top priority.

Despite deeply felt mutual suspicions between Dutch and Indonesian officials, The Hague negotiations concluded successfully in early November, and the Netherlands legislature approved sovereignty for the United States of Indonesia on December 22, 1949. With the official declaration of independence scheduled for December 27, the ECA rushed to Indonesia $37.5 million in funds that had been appropriated for the Dutch colony, then suspended following the police action in December 1948. The United States recognized the Sukarno government promptly on December 27.[48]

Prior to independence, the Indonesians had made persistent overtures to the United States for aid, and with the Communists apparently threatening the stability of the new republic, the administration acted quickly and favorably on the requests. From the $75 million remaining from the Military Assistance Program appropriation for use "in the general area of China," Acheson recommended, on January 9, 1950, a grant of $5 million to provide police equipment for the Indonesian constabulary. The funds were needed, Acheson told Truman, because "the loss of Indonesia to the Communists would deprive the United States of an area of the highest political, economic and strategic importance and would doubtless result in economic difficulties in the Netherlands which would be unable to retain its beneficial interests in Indonesia." Truman approved the request that day.[49] Philip Jessup talked with Sukarno on the Indonesian leg of his Far Eastern tour and afterwards cabled the State Department that Indonesia had a "real chance to achieve stability and withstand Communism" if U.S. economic aid were forthcoming. Acheson cabled his agreement.[50] Three days later, on February 10, the Export-Import Bank authorized a $100 million loan for Indonesia, to be used to purchase capital goods from the United States.[51] In late April, R. Allen Griffin, who had been sent to Southeast Asia to recommend economic assistance projects, recommended $14.5 million in economic and technical assistance for Indonesia. Griffin hoped that revived production and export of Indonesia's primary commodities would "help Europe, and particularly the Netherlands, achieve a viable economy" through triangular trade.[52]

Meanwhile, the United States missed no opportunity to cultivate the East Indian market itself and resolved that the Dutch would also have to share the Indonesian trade with Japan. The Indonesians were eager for commerce with developed nations other than the Netherlands, for, as one Indonesian official put it, "the Dutch managed us well, but they managed us."[53] In early 1950, the Reconstruction Finance Corporation (RFC) agreed to buy 50,000 tons of Indonesian tin ore and smelted metal over the ensuing two years, on terms more favorable than the agency was able to obtain from Malaya.[54] In mid-May, Cochran reported that Indonesians preferred "Japan and United States textiles to higher priced products from Netherlands, France and Belgium" and thought that the "Indonesia market fit well into United States plans for marketing its own cotton and for supporting [the] Japanese economy."[55] For the most part, though, the United States assisted Indonesia to increase the new nation's production and to make the Indonesian market lucrative to all the developed, non-Communist nations. This was not the purely Europe-centered policy the administration pursued toward British Malaya, but it was similar to American policy in Indochina, the success of which was essential to the recovery of Japan and Western Europe. Because of that, the American willingness to assist Indonesia in early 1950 provided an example for those debating the question of aid for Indochina. After Truman approved the $5 million MAP aid in early January, the precedent existed; the United States could assist Indochina if the situation warranted.

In contrast, however, to the relatively placid beginning of Sukarno's government, Bao Dai's Vietnam was gravely troubled. French authorities in Vietnam routinely offered optimistic assessments of the progress of the war against the Viet Minh, and these evaluations were too often received uncritically by American diplomats in the field. Yet enough disquieting information slipped through—after all, a certain amount of distress was necessary if the French were to justify their requests for American aid—to alarm American policymakers. In December 1949, for example, Vietnamese workers in Saigon organized a series of strikes aimed primarily at French enterprises. By the middle of the month, the strikes, according to Consul General George Abbott, had "assum[ed] serious proportions," with 30,000 workers out and another 17,000 threatening to stop work.[56]

The Chinese-Vietnamese rapprochement in January created a crisis both perceived and real. On February 21, the increasingly confident Viet Minh government called for a general mobilization and began consolidating its widely scattered forces. Eyewitnesses reported that Viet Minh troops pursued by the French were taking refuge in southern China, and in late March William Lacy acknowledged "pretty clear evidence" that the Chinese Communists were supplying the Viet Minh with small arms, possibly mortars and 75 mm guns. Ho also denounced Tito and placed himself more openly at Stalin's side.[57] Bao Dai's government was afflicted with instability. In late March the defense and foreign ministers resigned, charging that the government had no political program and no popular authority. The premier himself flew about the country in his private plane, sometimes followed by a second plane carrying one of his mistresses and, perhaps, her poodle.[58]

A second event in the spring of 1950 seemed to increase the threat to Indochina. When Chinese Nationalist forces had abandoned the mainland, they had retreated not only to Taiwan but to the island of Hainan, south of Kwangtung and across the Gulf of Tonkin from Vietnam. In early January the Chinese Communists established a beachhead there, but by March they still had not moved, and General Hsueh Yueh, commander of the island's Nationalist army, confidently declared that Hainan's defenses were too strong for the Communists to overcome. The general was mistaken. In mid-April, the Communists mounted a powerful amphibious assault on Hainan and, after linking up with guerrilla forces operating in the interior, swept across the island. On April 23, Chiang Kai-shek ordered Hainan evacuated; the Kuomintang armies, ordered to fight a rearguard action, were left to their fate. The *Far Eastern Economic Review* noted that the Communists were "now in a position to exert strong pressure on Indochina."[59] Truman allocated $10 million in military aid for Indochina on May 1. The timing was not coincidental.[60]

Indochina was not the only trouble spot, and it was not the most important. American policymakers also sensed a crisis in Western Europe during the first months of 1950. The problems on the continent were fundamentally those of France, whose difficulties in turn resulted in good part from the war in Indochina. For all the fresh concern the Truman administration showed for underdeveloped Asia, American foreign policy in early 1950 remained principally committed to the success of the developed, non-Communist nations, most of which were in Western Europe. United States aid for Indochina would support this commitment in several ways. American assistance would in part stanch the drain on French funds for the war. It would allow France to use Marshall Plan aid for desperately needed economic recovery at home and thereby deflect leftist attacks on the French Mouvement Republicain Populaire (MRP) government. United States policymakers also hoped for the economic and military integration of Western Europe, recognized that a rejuvenated West Germany was essential to its attainment, and knew that the French would not permit German recovery, especially military recovery, while France remained weakened by the diversion of its resources to Indochina. Perhaps the United States could barter aid to Indochina for a French agreement to work diligently toward a Western European union that would include West Germany. Finally, once more, policymakers considered Indochina the first domino in the path of Communist expansionism. Victory for Ho in Indochina would trip the dominoes, and the recovery of Japan, Great Britain, and the Netherlands would be threatened if the Communists poured into Burma, Thailand, Malaya, and Indonesia.

American policymakers had no doubt that French economic and political stability, tenuous in any event, were seriously jeopardized by the fighting in Indochina. A series of strikes in late 1949 and threats by Communist assembly representatives to block the loading of military supplies for Vietnam gave urgency to the situation. In late January, following the Soviet recognition of Ho Chi Minh, Bruce warned from Paris that France "may soon be faced with [a] situation similar to that formerly prevailing in Greece and even in Spain."[61] Anne O'Hare McCormick, the influential writer for the *New York Times*, also compared France to Greece and added, "Ho Chi Minh's guerrillas are more potent than the Greeks because they keep the French army on the other side of the world and at the same time stir up serious trouble between Communist workers and the gendarmerie at home."[62] The Bureau of Far Eastern Affairs claimed in February that U.S. aid for Indochina would increase "economic stability" there and would "assist in the rehabilitation of metropolitan France and therefore contribute directly toward a lessening of United States aid" to the country.[63] R. Allen Griffin advised Acheson that the drain of French Marshall Plan funds to Indochina "powerfully affects the [French] Government's capacity to deal with labor, social and educational exigencies at home."[64] American policymakers decided that aid to Indochina was a step worth taking to prevent a French political crisis.

Officials also understood the relationship between aid to Indochina and the integration of Western Europe. Policymakers believed France was destined to be the hub of a Western European economic community. There was a theoretical difference between economic and military integration, and because talk of Western European union inevitably came around to the sensitive topic of Germany, the Americans and the British went to some lengths to reassure the French that they understood the distinction. At the London Foreign Ministers conference in May 1950, Acheson and Bevin explicitly denied any intention of rearming Germany, at least in the immediate future.[65]

In fact, although there was no attempt to deceive the French with these assurances, in practice the rearmament of West Germany became increasingly difficult to separate from plans for German reconstruction and economic integration with Western Europe, which United States policymakers had long contemplated.[66] Back in February 1949, when Acheson was attempting to convince Senators Tom Connally and Arthur Vandenberg to support the North Atlantic Treaty, he argued "that a pact of this nature would give France a greater sense of security against Germany" and that "it was doubtful that, without some such pact, the French would ever be reconciled to the diminution of direct allied control over Germany."[67] The possibility of German rearmament was never completely submerged during 1949, and the growing difficulties late in the year brought it closer to the surface. Within six weeks after the announcement of the Soviet atomic explosion, the army had drafted a plan for the rearmament of Germany which was subsequently approved by John J. McCloy, the high commissioner in Germany, and the joint chiefs. The State Department and Truman refused to accept the plan, and it was shelved.[68] Yet Truman later admitted that "without Germany, the defense of Europe was a rearguard action on the shores of the Atlantic Ocean. With Germany, there could be a defense in depth, powerful enough to offer effective resistance to aggression from the East."[69] And in early 1950 John Foster Dulles asked a series of questions: "Can Germany be held against the Soviet Union, except perhaps by German troops? Does that mean the rearmament of Germany? Will France consent, and what dependence can be placed on rearmed Germans? Can we be sure that they will shoot in what we think is the right direction?"[70]

During the first months of 1950, German rearmament moved into the realm of the ponderable. On January 31, when Truman authorized continued work on the hydrogen bomb, the president also asked the Defense and State Departments to reevaluate "our objectives in peace and war" and "the effect of these objectives on our strategic plans."[71] For the next two months a combined committee met to formulate a new strategic position that confronted the fall of China, the Sino-Soviet pact, the Communist diplomatic recognition of Ho Chi Minh, the disintegration of bipartisanship in foreign policymaking at home, and the continued crisis in Western Europe, recently aggravated by the Soviet atomic explosion. The report, which Truman first received on April 7, became known as NSC-68. Though the president did not approve the document until September, its conclusions were accepted in April by the State Department, the joint chiefs, and a reluctant Louis Johnson, secretary of defense. The paper captured the contemporary sense of crisis and emphatically stated the need for strong action to regain the initiative in the Cold War.

NSC-68 has been capably analyzed elsewhere, and a brief summary of its contents will serve here.[72] The paper defined Soviet motives as "the complete subversion or forcible destruction of the machinery of government and structure of society in the countries of the non-Soviet world and their replacement by an apparatus and structure subservient to and controlled from the Kremlin." The Soviets were willing to use military force to gain their objectives, and the size of their army in Europe, combined with their recently acquired ability to "attack selected targets using atomic weapons," menaced world peace. In the face of this threat, the authors of NSC-68 argued that the United States must oversee the build-up of the free world's political, economic, and military strength: "We must organize and enlist the energies and resources of the free world in a positive program for peace which will frustrate the Kremlin design for world domination." The "program for peace" would be expensive, but according to NSC-68 the United States could, if necessary, devote 60 percent of its gross national product ($255 billion in 1949) to "direct and indirect military purposes and foreign assistance." A vigorous show of force was the only way to prevent war with the Soviets. The American people must be convinced "that the cold war is in fact a real war in which the survival of the free world is at stake."[73]

The document contained only two references to Southeast Asia—China was now a "springboard" for Communist expansion into the region—and two passing references to West Germany. The authors of NSC-68 were unprepared in April 1950 to proclaim the need for the remilitarization of West Germany. In fact, however, no other conclusion could be drawn from NSC-68's prescription for containment. Because the United States was determined that a productive West Germany should be a vital part of an economically integrated Western Europe, there was no way to guarantee the security of this arrangement unless West Germany were prepared to defend itself. As the authors of NSC-68 put it: "Unless the military strength of the Western European nations is increased on a much larger scale than under current programs and at an accelerated rate, it is more than likely that those nations will not be able to oppose even by 1960 the Soviet armed forces in war with any degree of effectiveness." This was strong stuff, and, as Acheson later said, the authors of the document made it "clearer than truth."[74] The conclusion of NSC-68 imposed no limit on the militarization of the West. Despite policymakers' public denials that they contemplated the rearmament of Germany, the principles they adopted to guide American foreign policy led relentlessly to that strategy.[75]

The French continued to speculate that German rearmament was, as *Le Monde* had put it during the genesis of the North Atlantic Treaty, contained in the pact "like the yolk in an egg."[76] While Foreign Minister Robert Schuman insisted that France would never admit Germany to the North Atlantic Treaty,[77] Premier Georges Bidault appeared increasingly willing to comply with what he perceived as the direction of U.S. policy toward Germany. In late April, he announced a plan to create a "High Atlantic Council of Peace," which would provide the basis for Western European unity on political and economic matters. Privately, he told Bruce he hoped that through the council, "Germany [could] be associated as closely as is practicable with the interests of other European nations." Bidault then raised the question of rearming Germany,. He did not regard it as "politically possible" for the French to countenance rearmament at that moment, but "if weapons become more plentiful and it seems safe to rearm the Germans, that is a matter which can be considered at a later date." Bidault was "not one who would say that Germany should never be rearmed. Long ago he learned never to say 'never.' "[78] On May 7, Bidault told an audience in Dunkirk that the North Atlantic Treaty was open to "suitable enlargements."[79]

What the Americans pursued by indirection the British sought frankly. British officials had long recognized that West European integration must include the remilitarization of West Germany and that this in turn demanded that the French be relieved in part of their military burden in Vietnam.[80] The British ambassador in Japan reported on a conversation with his French counterpart: "Thousands of Frenchmen were being killed annually in Indochina; this could not possibly continue, for France would not be able to fulfill her military responsibilities under the Western Union."[81] On April 25, Deputy Under Secretary of State Gladwyn Jebb and Ivone Kirkpatrick, Great Britain's high commissioner in Germany, told American delegates to the upcoming Foreign Ministers Conference that it was "impossible to speak of [the] incorporation of Germany in [the] North Atlantic community on [a] partnership basis without considering rearmament, and conversely that strengthening [the] North Atlantic Treaty had to be [the] forerunner of German rearmament."[82] Two weeks later, the British cabinet resolved that "France should be persuaded to adopt a realistic view of the future place of Western Germany in Europe." More specifically, it would soon be "necessary to consider how Germany could best contribute towards the defence of Western Europe."[83]

American and British hopes aside, there would be no rearmament in France, much less in West Germany, unless the French were assisted in Indochina. Indochina was a factor in the future of Germany because the war there absorbed French troops and matériel that could otherwise be used to counterbalance a rearmed West Germany. While France had started to receive the largest single grant of U.S. military aid under the North Atlantic Treaty, in early 1950 more than half of the French army was using 35 percent of France's military budget in Indochina.[84] Without the divisions and weapons in France to protect against a recurrence of German militarism, the French publicly resisted even veiled suggestions that Germany be rearmed. As Schuman explained to American officials in mid-March, the drain caused by the war "prevented France from doing its part in the defense of Europe."[85] Hervé Alphand, France's deputy representative to the North Atlantic Council, was even more explicit when he listed three "grave French concerns" for the immediate future: "1. Rearmament program threatened to wipe out economic and financial successes of recent years . . . . 2. Indo-China continued to be a great drain both financially and militarily, and France's efforts there conflicted with her obligations under ECA bilateral and North Atlantic and Brussels Pacts. . . . 3. The dollar gap was most threatening and present statistical projections indicated that in spite [of the] best French efforts it might not be bridged [by 1952]." Alphand solicited American help with all three problems.[86]

And the Americans responded. Acheson told his subordinates that NATO should consider not only problems within the Atlantic community "but might cover such things as Southeast Asia and the Far East as they bore upon the situation of the member countries."[87] On April 3, Charles Bohlen, minister at the embassy in France, made a statement before an army committee charged with the study of Western Europe's defense problem. France, Bohlen believed, eagerly sought the rearmament of Western Europe, for it feared "being mashed up in the beginning of a war while the United States gains time to win it." Bohlen worried that "the Kremlin may be getting ready for some big operation this spring," and he did not "detect the slightest influence on Russian policy resulting from our possession of the A bomb." Rather, the Soviet Union respected American production, reflected in the number of conventional weapons the United States gave its friends in Europe. This was what the French wanted: a forward strategy, not a defensive one, buttressed by American-made "anti-tank and jet fighter protection."

On the French side, Bohlen saw two obstacles to the implementation of this strategy. The first was France's opposition to rearming West Germany. Bohlen believed French security was incompatible with a permanently weakened central Europe: "The doubt as to the future success of our policy is not due to Russian successes so far but to the need for clarification of the relation between Western Europe and the rest of the Atlantic community, including particularly German integration with the Western European nations." The second problem was the enormous French commitment to Indochina. Not only was a large percentage of France's military potential being spent in Indochina, but the French officers there were "badly needed in France to train the 16 divisions which France has promised for the defense of Europe." Bohlen stated the problem concisely near the end of his talk: "As to Indo-China, if the current war there continues for two or three years, we will get very little of sound military development in France. On the other hand, if we can help France to get out of the existing stalemate in Indo-China, France can do something effective in Western Europe."[88]

This was the key: the United States must help France in Indochina. As Hervé Alphand put it, "Without outside help the future of Indo-China [is] black."[89] But more than Indochina's future was at stake, for France would be secure and prosperous only if its burden in Indochina could be reduced. A secure, productive France was, in turn, a prerequisite to a politically, economically, and militarily integrated Western Europe, with a reconstructed and rearmed West Germany anchoring its eastern border. The heightened confidence provided Bao Dai by U.S. recognition soon dissipated, and the French experiment in Indochina became increasingly vulnerable to the potent Viet Minh. Policymakers decided it was necessary to deepen the American commitment.

Economic Aid for Southeast Asia

The Jessup Mission: December 15, 1949–March 15, 1950. Ambassador-at-Large Philip Jessup left Washington in mid-December 1949 for an extended tour of the Far East and a return by way of Paris. The official purpose of the Jessup mission was "fact finding," but as one of the architects of the policy reorientation toward the Far East in late 1949, Jessup was aware of greater possibilities. During discussions with Bevin and Schuman following the Tripartite Economic Conference in September, Acheson had held out the prospect of modest economic and military aid for Thailand and Vietnam.[90] At a meeting on September 20, officials in the Far Eastern Division decided that the $75 million remaining to the Military Assistance Program for "the general area of China" should be used in "contiguous areas such as Indochina or Burma or other countries in the area," and should not be confined to military projects but could be used to start economic programs as well.[91]

As Jessup began his trip, indications continued to surface that the United States was contemplating economic and perhaps military aid for some of the nations he was scheduled to visit. In mid-December, Acheson, referring to the MAP fund, confided to British Ambassador Oliver Franks and Canadian Ambassador Hume Wrong that "he had been scratching together what dollars he could" for Southeast Asia. From now on, Acheson said, the Americans "would look after" Indonesia, the Philippines, and Indochina, "with a little to spare" for Thailand.[92] On January 5, Butterworth wrote Dean Rusk that Bao Dai would require strengthening following U.S. recognition, and that the administration would consider "economic support [Point Four and ECA aid] . . . , military items, and political moves."[93] This idea was still tentative, and apparently none of it was spelled out to Jessup until late in January. But from the outset, the Jessup mission was given poignancy by the ambassador's close relationship with Acheson, his immersion in Far Eastern affairs beginning the previous spring with the *China White Paper*, and the question posed to Jessup by Raymond Fosdick just prior to the ambassador's departure: "We are *against* Communism, but what are we *for*?"

Jessup's journey began in Japan, where he met with MacArthur and learned of the general's disgust over the joint chiefs' refusal to allow a peace treaty with Japan.[94] Jessup told a group of Japanese businessmen that Japan should expect to provide machinery and technicians to Southeast Asia and, in an interview with British Ambassador Alvary Gascoigne, gave the impression "that the United States should take more interest in South East Asia and furnish such aid as might be possible."[95] On January 11, Jessup borrowed William Sebald, MacArthur's political adviser, and flew to Seoul. South Korean president Syngman Rhee "stressed the familiar pleas for planes, ships and tanks" and exchanged views with Sebald on ways to increase Korean–Japanese trade. Jessup also witnessed the interrogation of a North Korean infiltrator and discussed civil liberties with the vice minister of home affairs, whose English, Jessup dryly observed, was "not very good and when he found it convenient he was unable to understand what I said."[96] Then it was on to Taiwan for two days. Jessup talked with Chiang Kai-shek, who denounced the British recognition of the People's Republic and suggested that war between the free and Communist worlds would come "in a few years." Jessup carefully refrained from being dragged into a discussion about future U.S. aid for the Nationalist government.[97] From Taipei Jessup flew to Manila, and then, on January 24, to Saigon.

Jessup's arrival in Vietnam coincided with the culmination of debate within the administration over whether to recognize Bao Dai. Two cables from Acheson were waiting for Jessup when he arrived: the January 20 message that the United States would consider bypassing the de facto stage and the January 21 telegram instructing the ambassador to inform Bao Dai of American hopes for "a closer relationship" between the two governments. The message proved impossible to deliver immediately, for the French had taken the Norodom Palace in Saigon for their government offices and Bao Dai, refusing to accept the city's second palace for his headquarters, instead located in Hanoi.

The French officials—High Commissioner Léon Pignon and General Marcel Carpentier—approached Jessup with a mixture of cajolery and veiled threats. Pignon argued that the French war in Indochina was really the free world's battle against communism, and Carpentier added that because the French army was bogged down in Indochina it could not contribute to the defense of Western Europe. Both intimated that unless assistance were forthcoming, increasing casualties, costs, and dissatisfaction with the war among the French public would eventually force France out of Indochina. "Indochina is not the Rhine," said Pignon. "We've had it." Jessup countered by asking about ratification of the March 8 agreement, an evolutionary statement, and the French refusal to surrender the Norodom Palace to Bao Dai. All the same, the French were encouraged when the ambassador referred to the problems of Indochina as "our problems," and the British consul general in Saigon thought it now "clear" that Jessup was "convinced of the urgency and importance of helping the French and Bao Dai . . . achieve stability in Vietnam."[98]

Jessup flew to Hanoi on January 26. He was greeted by stringent security precautions and the usual "spontaneous" welcoming demonstration. ("Actually," noted Jessup, "the population was ordered by the Vietnam Government to hand out the American flags which were manufactured and distributed by the Government itself free of charge.") He met Bao Dai the following afternoon. Jessup was impressed with the premier's intelligence, sincerity, and "amazing[ly] detailed knowledge of economic statistics," but he wrote Acheson that Bao Dai was not a man of "great force or great strength." Bao Dai presented Jessup with a 108-page memo requesting economic and military assistance.[99]

Jessup left the following day for Djakarta. On January 29, the French assembly ratified the March 8 agreement. Two days later, as Jessup held the first of several fruitful discussions with Indonesian officials, word came that the Soviet Union had recognized the Viet Minh.

The remainder of Jessup's trip was shaped by his experience in Vietnam, and his public and private statements henceforth reflected the contradictory impressions he had acquired there. In press conferences at Singapore (February 6), Rangoon (February 10), and New Delhi (February 25), Jessup explained that the United States had recognized the Indochinese governments because they had been established as independent states. Because Jessup (as he put it) "omitted" reference to the states remaining part of the French Union, French officials became extremely concerned that Jessup would demand an evolutionary statement when he arrived in Paris in mid-March.[100]

But Jessup proved willing to discuss an increased American commitment to the Indochinese and other Southeast Asian governments. In Malaya, Jessup heard British Commissioner General Malcolm MacDonald's view that Indochina was the "key area" in Southeast Asia, and issued a statement stressing the "urgent" need to save the region from communism and noting that "quicker action may be necessary than the Point Four program."[101] (The grateful MacDonald saw this as "a significant advance in the American attitude" since Acheson's National Press Club speech, and he later wrote Jessup, "We all owe you a debt."[102]) From Singapore Jessup flew to Rangoon, where he talked with Thakin Nu, the prime minister. Thakin Nu contended that conditions in Burma were "very much improved over a year ago . . . when it was my candid opinion that the Burmese Union would go to pieces." The prime minister hinted strongly that his country needed U.S. aid. Jessup's response was non-committal, but he did not rule out the possibility of assistance.[103]

On February 10, Jessup arrived in Bangkok for discussions with Thai officials and a conference of U.S. chiefs of mission in the Far East. The Bangkok conference, attended by Butterworth, Abbott, Gullion, and Sebald, among others, considered the problem of communism in the Far East and how the United States might best confront it. Jessup observed that all the diplomats accepted the "strategic importance of the whole Southeastern Asia area," but agreed that Indochina, Burma, and Thailand faced particular danger. In his remarks to the final session of the conference, Jessup expressed his conviction that Southeast Asia was "vitally important" to the United States, though he quickly added that the United States should maintain its "special emphasis" on the problems of Europe. Officials at the conference agreed that the "United States must support friendly Asian governments and cannot afford [to] withhold such moral, economic [and] military aid [that is] in our power to give."[104] Following the conference, Jessup continued his journey to India, Ceylon, Pakistan, and Afghanistan; he reached Paris on March 13.

The ambassador had experienced quite a bit of the Far East since the late summer of 1949, when he had been ambivalent about recognizing Communist China. In many ways, Jessup's evolution mirrored the movement in U.S. Far Eastern policy. The work with the consultants had sensitized Jessup to the importance of Southeast Asia and especially Indochina in the struggle against communism and the success of liberal capitalism in the underdeveloped and developed worlds. The Asian tour brought the ambassador face to face with the nations the United States hoped to save, and exposed him to the importunities of tough anti-Communists like Abbott, MacDonald, and Phibun Songkhram. The United States recognized the Indochinese governments. The Bangkok conference produced unanimity on the crucial issue of American aid for Southeast Asia.

These events were followed by a series of occurrences that intruded on Jessup's trip and pushed him further toward a position favoring a deeper U.S. commitment to Southeast Asia. On February 22, Bruce reported that a French official had told him flatly that unless the United States offered a "long-term program of assistance" for Indochina, France might find it necessary to "cut her losses and withdraw from Indochina." Schuman quickly denied that the French intended this, but the threat had touched a nerve.[105] In Karachi in early March, Jessup learned that he had been attacked by Joseph McCarthy for being "soft on communism." The ambassador continued his trip, but decided to shorten his stay in Paris and fly, rather than sail, back to Washington.[106]

Finally, Jessup's failure to mention the French Union in his press conferences and ensuing complaints by French officials earned Jessup a mild reprimand from Washington. "I was instructed to make a clarification," Jessup wrote. At a press conference held following a meeting with Schuman on March 13, Jessup did.[107] President Vincent Auriol told Jessup the next day he was pleased the ambassador had accepted the need for Indochina to remain within the French Union and stated his opposition to any further mention of an evolutionary statement. Jessup let the matter drop and even apparently told the French that American arms for Vietnam would soon be forthcoming. On March 15, he flew home.[108]

Jessup delivered a summary of his impressions to top officials in the State Department, including Acheson, on March 23. He counted both the strengths and weaknesses of the countries he had visited. He stressed the regional scope of the major problems in the Far East and urged the coordination of Western efforts on behalf of Southeast Asia. Jessup and the Far Eastern chiefs of mission agreed with the conclusion of a recent NSC study that "all measures should be taken to prevent Communist expansion in Southeast Asia." Jessup concluded that "the situation in the East is bad but not desperate. The area cannot be written off. We are committed."[109] Jessup explained what he meant to the Foreign Relations Committee the following week: the United States, he thought, should begin a number of "economic, information and small-arms programs" in Southeast Asia.[110]

The Griffin Mission: February 27–April 22, 1950. When Jessup left Washington in mid-December, proposals for assistance to Southeast Asia were being formulated in the Far Eastern Bureau and the Pentagon. By the middle of January, following NSC-48, these proposals had started to receive serious consideration from policymakers. Military aid became a distinct possibility. Truman tapped the unvouchered Section 303 of the Military Assistance Program fund for $5 million for Indonesia on January 9, and on the twentieth the joint chiefs requested additional MAP money for Indochina, Thailand, Burma, and Malaya.[111] Proposals for economic aid also moved forward, although they were at first less precisely articulated because the funds for economic programs were not yet fully available. But by January 27, following up his earlier promise to Oliver Franks and Hume Wrong, Acheson had determined that an economic aid program of some kind would be implemented. He wrote the Southeast Asian consulates that the department, "having in mind [the] objectives stated [in the] Secretary's speech January 12," was anxious to "accelerate feasible econ[omic] activities in Southeast Asia" as soon as possible. In order to shape these initiatives, the department might send a small mission to the region "to determine by spot surveys and discussions [with] United States missions" the type of projects that were most urgent. The Jessup mission was fact-finding; the one Acheson had in mind would make specific proposals for economic aid.[112]

The mission was put together rather hastily during the first two weeks of February. The administration selected R. Allen Griffin, formerly Roger Lapham's deputy with the ECA in China, to lead the group. Griffin, who had left the ECA and returned to publishing a Monterey newspaper, was a Republican and close friend of Senator William Knowland, the China lobbyist.[113] To assist Griffin, the State Department chose Samuel P. Hayes, special assistant to Willard Thorp and executive secretary of the Point Four ACTA, William McAfee of the Far Eastern Bureau, Henry Tarring, Jr., an engineer from the J. G. White Engineering Company, and a handful of technicians. Griffin was also accompanied by two military representatives. Truman approved the mission on February 20.[114]

The purpose of the Griffin mission was to analyze conditions in Southeast Asian nations and recommend economic assistance projects that could be initiated by small amounts of U.S. aid. Publicly, the State Department confined the mission's mandate to the application of Point Four funds in the region, once the technical assistance legislation had been approved by Congress.[115] In diplomatic channels, both the sources of funding and the purposes of the mission were more freely described. Truman told Acheson he would agree to economic aid allocations from the $75 million leftover MAP fund, and the secretary and James Webb so informed Griffin and the Southeast Asian consulates. Acheson also suggested that residual ECA-China funds might be tapped and supplemented with Export-Import Bank loans.[116] The instructions to Griffin from Webb included the order to investigate "the possibilities of a regional approach to the implementation of programs to meet regional needs." Dean Rusk's assistant Merrill C. Gay sent a memo instructing Griffin to keep in mind "particularly the possibilities of developing an expanded trade between the countries visited and Japan." That the mission was attentive to this matter was later confirmed by Samuel Hayes.[117]

Deputy Chief Hayes also recalled that the "United States wanted more than simply the containment of Communism in Southeast Asia. It wanted free intercourse with the nations there—economic, cultural and political." The United States was interested in "stable, self-reliant, responsible and responsive governments" in the region and the abundant natural resources of the Far East. In addition, Hayes recalled that the mission was sensitive to Western Europe's economic and political interests in Southeast Asia. While the United States hoped to buy more raw materials from Southeast Asia, these exports were even more important "in the great triangular pattern of international trade involving primarily the United States, Western Europe, and Southeast Asia." Because of the "yawning 'dollar gap,' " the region was vital to Europe "as a source of raw materials that would be purchased for currencies other than dollars, as a market for its European industrial products, and as a big earner of the much-needed dollars that tended to flow from Asia to Europe."[118]

Griffin had an additional impression of his mission's objectives:

> The purpose . . . , so far as I was concerned, was altruistic to a point—after all, they were in a hell of a shape. Also, I felt—as I think the State Department, a little more cynical than I, felt—that if you put the foot in the door, you could extend American influences a little bit further, and have on your side the . . . ruling classes of those countries. You can't get anyone else on your side. You never see them . . . . You have nothing to do with the masses.[119]

The Griffin group followed a course similar to that taken by Jessup. After a day-long briefing with Asia experts at Stanford University, the Griffin mission left San Francisco on February 27 and arrived in Japan on March 2. In Tokyo the mission met with MacArthur and Major General Charles A. Willoughby, chief of SCAP's intelligence section, who told the group, according to Hayes, that "Vietnam was the strategic key to Southeast Asia." With W. F. Marquat, head of the Economic and Scientific Section of SCAP, Griffin discussed the possible sale of Japanese agricultural implements and capital goods to the Southeast Asians.[120]

The mission's next stop was Indochina. Griffin began his stay on March 6 in Saigon, where he conferred with the same French and Vietnamese officials Jessup had met. General Carpentier warned that the Chinese could attack Tonkin "any day" and that U.S. arms for the French were necessary in order to protect Malaya. The Viet Minh greeted the mission with a grenade attack on Griffin's hotel. The Americans escaped injury, but ten French soldiers were wounded.[121] Along with the meetings, the attack was apparently persuasive to Griffin, who cabled Washington March 9 that Vietnamese expectations for American aid were high, and the "early arrival of United States aid, even if token aid, might contribute to the rallying of popular support about Bao Dai." (Griffin had not yet met Bao Dai.) The mission chief concluded, "We emphasize now that all red tape must be ruthlessly cut, and the program be put underway with dramatic speed following the recommendations which will be cabled next week." This also applied to military aid, "since the problem of security must also be met in connection with economic aid."[122] Four days later, after Griffin had visited Bao Dai in Dalat, he repeated to Acheson that it was "extremely urgent to prepare and initiate [an aid] program at earliest date or political benefit will be vitiated." Griffin also affirmed that Cambodia and Laos would welcome American aid and that ECA-China funds should be used to finance all the Indochina projects because the French showed no enthusiasm for Point Four.[123]

Griffin made his preliminary recommendations on March 16, the day the mission left Indochina for Singapore, and he later transmitted them in detail as Report No. 1 of the Economic Survey Mission, "Needs for United States Economic and Technical Aid in Cambodia, Laos and Vietnam (1950)." The mission asked for $23.5 million to begin a fifteen-month program of economic aid for Indochina. This request followed logically from the survey's assessment of conditions in Vietnam. Bao Dai was not a French "puppet," but led "an intensely nationalist Govt. struggling to secure more control and authority from Fr[ance]." With the prestige of U.S. aid behind him, Bao Dai could win over the non-Communist members of the Viet Minh and the *attentistes*—fence-sitters. If some Vietnamese remained unconvinced, U.S. assistance would help the French and loyal Vietnamese "checkmate" a possible Chinese invasion "and sterilize areas of Vietminh infection which might link up" with the invaders. Indochina was important economically, as a potential food exporter in the Far East and as an important contributor to France's balance of payments, and vital strategically, "for it provides a natural invasion route into the rice bowl of Southeast Asia." American aid, as long as it was "bold, quick and generous," would become "[a] major contributing factor" to the stability and success of the Bao

Dai government. Consul General Gullion concurred with the mission's recommendations.[124]

The Griffin mission's departure from Indochina was timed to coincide with the visit to Vietnamese waters of two U.S. destroyers and the aircraft carrier *Boxer*. After careful publicity, the carrier sent forty-two planes screaming over Annam, and the destroyer *Stickwell* offered a twenty-one-gun salute to the French Union and the state of Vietnam. Vice Admiral Russell S. Berkey welcomed Bao Dai on board the *Stickwell*, then joined the premier and Edmund Gullion on shore for a tiger hunt. Gullion wrote Robert Hoey at PSA that the navy visit was "having a grand effect." The only problem was "that it may be too good," creating so much excitement among the Vietnamese "that they are a little difficult to hold." Indeed they were. Protest strikes in the cities crippled Standard Oil and Shell. On March 20, Vietnamese demonstrators incinerated the Saigon marketplace, ripped down American and French flags, burned vehicles, and "shoved around" American sailors on shore leave. The police counterattacked, killing three and wounding more than sixty of the demonstrators. Students at all Saigon schools promptly went on strike to protest police brutality.[125]

The mission was in Singapore and Malaya the week of March 16. Griffin and the others met with colony officials and American and foreign businessmen with interests in the oil, tin, and rubber industries and toured a rubber estate and a tin dredge. Griffin found Malcolm MacDonald enormously solicitous—"no man could have tried more earnestly and honestly to give us a little help and guidance"— and throughout the trip Griffin found that the British "were the only good advisers I had . . . the greatest possible help." MacDonald also asked Griffin for American aid to Malaya, adding that the amount of aid the United States could provide was less important than the "fact [of] American participation." Griffin's report noted that "law and order do not obtain in Malaya" and emphasized the colony's significance as a producer of strategic raw materials. Malaya's dollar-attractive exports, "especially rubber and tin," were "of critical importance in the effort to achieve a balance of payments between the sterling area and the dollar area." Without Malaya's dollar earnings, Great Britain would require more direct aid from the United States "or face a noticeable reduction in its already austere standard of living." And Malaya provided a market for British manufacturers, "helping the United Kingdom maintain its arduously achieved overall balance of payments." Griffin agreed with MacDonald that the fact of United States aid mattered more than its magnitude. He proposed a program of $4.5 million, most of it for a police radio network, patrol cars, and jungle equipment.[126]

Griffin found the situation in Burma, where the mission stayed from March 23 to April 4, "not . . . as bad as [he] had expected it to be." The many armed opponents of the Thakin Nu government remained active, but Griffin agreed with U Hla Maung, the Burmese finance minister, that the government's pacification program had "turned the corner" in early 1950 and suggested that U.S. economic aid "might well prove to be the necessary element which would lead to rapid improvement in whole situation in Burma." The mission recommended $12.2 million in assistance, more than a third of it targeted for agriculture, mostly for rice growing.[127]

Thailand, the next stop, was described by Griffin as the "oldest free independent country" in Southeast Asia. The Thai government had little internal opposition, but like the rest of Southeast Asia was "threatened by Communist imperialism controlled from China" and the fifth column of the large Chinese community. Truman had already approved $10 million in military aid for Thailand, and on April 12 Griffin proposed $11.4 million in economic assistance to supplement the military appropriation. Four and a half million was slated for Thai industry, especially for the extraction of exportable raw materials.[128]

Griffin's final Southeast Asian visit was to Indonesia. It was a sobering ten-day sojourn. The Indonesians, Griffin warned, were not ready for self-government. The Dutch who remained in the country as "advisers" were even worse, and they refused to consider any specific projects for the economic redemption of Indonesia "until 'law and order' had been established." Little had been done to create projects to be funded by the $100 million Export-Import Bank loan. Yet, the mission considered Indonesian raw materials and potential agricultural production an important contribution to the "reestablishment of triangular world trade" and added that "to have Indonesia as a full political and economic partner in a free world would be of prime importance to the free world and to other like-minded nations." The mission urged the rapid dispatch of $14.4 million in economic aid.[129] Then, after stopping in Paris to confer with Averell Harriman, the members of the Griffin mission returned to Washington.

The View from Washington. The Griffin mission recommendations were received by Washington officials who were now almost universally sympathetic to plans for aid to Indochina and other Southeast Asian nations. The objections of those Far Eastern experts who sought to detach diplomatic recognition from economic and military support had been beaten back by Bruce, Gullion, and Jessup. Within a three-week period encompassing late February and mid-March, coincident with the early part of the Griffin mission, two major declarations of policy, one top secret and the other a public speech, signaled the administration's willingness to assist Indochina.

The first of these declarations was yet another National Security Council document, this one number 64, sent to the State Department for study on February 27. Unlike NSC-48, its ideological predecessor, NSC-64—"The Position of the United States with Respect to Indochina"—was not a sweeping survey of conditions, but a terse prescription for American policy toward Indochina. The document began with the domino theory: "It is recognized that the threat of Communist aggression against Indochina is only one phase of anticipated Communist plans to seize all of Southeast Asia." Thailand and Burma "could be expected to fall under Communist domination" if Indochina, the "key area of Southeast Asia," was itself overtaken by communism. Therefore, the NSC urged that "the Departments of State and Defense should prepare as a matter of priority a program of all practicable measures designed to protect United States security interests in Indochina." Planning accelerated in both departments. Truman approved NSC-64 on April 24.[130]

The public declaration of commitment to Indochina came on March 15, when Acheson spoke to the California Commonwealth Club in San Francisco on U.S. policy toward Asia. The secretary referred several times to his Press Club speech two months earlier and made no effort to conceal the crucial differences between the two talks. In the January speech, Acheson had emphasized the limits of American commitment in the Far East by describing the "defense perimeter" and by offering only vague solace to the nations on the Southeast Asian mainland. At San Francisco, Acheson noted that since January 12, the Soviet Union and China had concluded a mutual assistance treaty, which exposed the Chinese government as a tool of Soviet imperialism. The secretary now warned the Chinese against "aggressive or subversive adventures beyond their borders" and contended that in Southeast Asia "American help may be the indispensable element required" to reinforce the fledgling governments against communism. Acheson told his audience that the administration had in mind military, economic, and technical assistance, and he spoke approvingly of the Griffin mission. Finally, Acheson cautioned against the belief that U.S. policy was designed solely to prevent the expansion of communism. "That is far too negative a way of putting it," he said. "We are for something positive, for the most fundamental urges of the human spirit."[131] The next day, Charles Ross, the presidential press secretary, told reporters that Truman thought Acheson had made "a fine speech."[132] Oliver Franks was also well satisfied.[133] By the early spring of 1950, the administration was prepared to go beyond Point Four and offer economic aid to Indochina and Southeast Asia.

Despite this commitment, it was not clear in mid-March whether the funds necessary to begin the program were available. Nearly $75 million remained from Section 303 of the MAP, but the Defense Department was reluctant to permit the use of a military appropriation for an economic aid program. Roughly $100 million remained of the 1948 ECA-China appropriation. In early March, Acheson appealed to the Senate to extend the "general area of China" formula to this fund, thereby releasing the money for Southeast Asian aid projects. The Senate's response was cautiously favorable, but China lobby senators recognized that the department's proposal would divert funds from Taiwan, a move they promised to resist.[134]

These bureaucratic and legislative obstacles were gradually overcome. In early April, Defense Secretary Johnson grudgingly authorized the MAP appropriation for use in a Southeast Asian economic program. Acheson recommended that $5 million of the appropriation be allocated for this purpose, but the president, wary of stretching the budget and solicitous of the sensitive Johnson, refused to go that far. On May 1, he approved "in principle" a program of economic aid for Southeast Asia and allocated $750,000 from the MAP for medical supplies in Indochina.[135] Meanwhile, Congress went to work on an extension of ECA aid for China. China lobbyists were mollified by a formula that continued the program through June 1951 and reserved $40 million for China (Taiwan) "so long as the President deems it practicable." Forty-four million dollars were authorized for use "in the general area of China," the Section 303 phrase that meant Southeast Asia. This aid was attached to the Foreign Economic Assistance Act, approved by Congress on June 5, 1950.[136]

The president's decision on May 1 allowed the State Department to assure the French that some aid for the Bao Dai government would soon be forthcoming. On May 7, just before the foreign ministers and NATO council meetings in London, Acheson stopped in Paris for two days of "friendly talks" with the French. That day, in utmost secrecy, Schuman disclosed to Acheson and Bruce a plan he and Jean Monnet—commissioner general for the French Modernization Plan—had developed to place all French and German coal and steel production under a single authority. The Schuman Plan, as it came to be known, was a step toward the economic integration of Western Europe and a sign that French officials had acknowledged the need for an economically vigorous West Germany. John Foster Dulles called the plan "brilliantly creative" and argued that it "could go far to solve the most dangerous problem of our time"—how West Germany's vast industrial potential could be linked to the Atlantic community. Acheson and Truman were equally enthusiastic.[137]

The following day, Acheson talked with Schuman about Indochina. The French foreign minister proved, by Acheson's definition, flexible on several important issues. Schuman declared that the March 8 agreement was "not the last word" on Indochina and added ambiguously that "obviously after [the] war [the] agreements probably will be modified." Schuman also revealed plans to create a new ministry to handle the affairs of the associated states and promised that France would construct national armies in Indochina that would eventually relieve all the French troops. Acheson replied by thanking Schuman for his "wise and progressive statement" and asserted that "we are all agreed on [the] strategic importance of Indo-China: if it goes, Southeast Asia goes." He confided that the "aid question" could be worked out satisfactorily. That afternoon, Acheson announced publicly that the United States would send economic aid and military equipment to Indochina and France.[138]

The disclosure to Acheson of the coal and steel plan and Schuman's timid concessions on Vietnam, while not in themselves crucial to the United States' decision to aid Southeast Asia, did provide a symbolic terminus to the administration's debate over assistance. Commitment had conquered caution because a strong France was needed to offset German recrudescence in Europe, and U.S. policymakers felt that a resilient, non-Communist Indochina was necessary for the protection of all Southeast Asia. A satisfied David Bruce captured these twin themes in his May 16 cable to Acheson: "May 8 talks resulted in recognition by U.S. that Indochina was essential to defense of SEA and that defense of SEA was closely connected with defense of western world."[139] American economic aid confirmed this understanding.

Even before the residual ECA-China funds were extended and made available for Southeast Asia by Congress, the administration began to inform recipients and build the mechanisms through which the aid would be distributed. On May 15, the State Department alerted the Saigon legation and other Southeast Asian consulates that the Griffin recommendations had been approved "in principle," and

Acheson on the twenty-fourth informed the Indochinese governments of the emerging aid program. Two days later the ECA announced the creation of a Special Technical and Economic Mission (STEM) to administer American aid in Saigon and promised that STEMs would soon be organized in Burma, Thailand, and Indonesia. (Griffin's recommendations for Malaya were temporarily shelved.) Robert Blum of the ECA was chosen to direct the STEM in Saigon.[140]

Military Aid for Southeast Asia

On September 29, 1949, the day after Congress passed the Mutual Defense Assistance Act, Livingston Merchant, deputy assistant secretary of state for Far Eastern affairs, asked the division chiefs in the Far Eastern Office to estimate the amounts of the $75 million Section 303 fund that might be spent on military projects in Southeast Asia. The chiefs responded in early October with reports for Thailand and Vietnam calling for reimbursable military aid "at the very minimum."[141] On October 24, Butterworth sent to Acheson recommendations for other Southeast Asian nations. The Far Eastern Bureau sought about $16 million for Southeast Asian nations outside of Indochina.[142] In late December came NSC-48's advice that the $75 million fund "be programmed as a matter of urgency" for Southeast Asia, and following consultations between State and Defense representatives in early January, Louis Johnson asked the joint chiefs of staff for their opinion on how the funds should be spent. The joint chiefs recommended grants of $15 million for Indochina, $10 million for Thailand, and $5 million for Indonesia "for direct and immediate usage" and an additional "contingency reserve" allocation of $30 million for Taiwan and Tibet, $10 million for Burma, and $5 million for Malaya. The State Department ultimately endorsed these recommendations.[143]

At this point, both the Vietnamese and French submitted requests for U.S. military aid. On January 27, Bao Dai handed Jessup his long manuscript detailing his government's needs. The French asked for equipment on February 16 and forwarded lists of what they wanted on February 22, March 22, and March 31. The requests were calculatedly extravagant, and each plaintiff sought to keep the other from gaining control over the donated supplies. Despite these annoyances, the State Department was persuaded that military aid complemented economic help and was urgently required in endangered Indochina. On March 9, Acheson asked Truman to approve $10 million for Thailand and $15 million for Indochina in military aid. "The choice confronting the United States," noted a document accompanying Acheson's request, "is to support the legal governments in Indochina or to face the extension of communism over the remainder of the continental area of Southeast Asia and possibly farther westward." Truman approved the request on March 10. The aid was allocated May 1, when the president, along with his approval of $750,000 for Indochina from the ECA China fund, granted $10 million for Indochina and added $3 million for Indonesia. Thailand, which proved reluctant to crack down on arms smuggling by Thai nationals to the Viet Minh, had to wait until July before its $10 million was allocated.[144]

The debate over who should actually receive the equipment in Indochina—the French or their Vietnamese allies—had not yet been resolved. Administration officials were sympathetic to the Vietnamese. After his talks with Bao Dai in late March, Vice Admiral Berkey reported that it was "highly desirable for reasons of prestige that a certain amount of direct aid be given to the Vietnamese for specific projects and operations."[145] The State Department pressed the French to form a "quadripartite body" with the three Indochinese governments to which American military aid could be consigned, and planned to provide nearly $6 million to arm twelve Indochinese infantry battalions "as separate from [French] Union forces."[146] The problem, wrote Robert Hoey, PSA's Indochina expert, "is to extend aid, to support those [Indochinese] governments, and to prevent Communist aggression but without at the same time appearing to support the continuation of French colonialism in Indochina." Hoey concluded, "This is a continuing problem whose final solution is not yet apparent."[147]

The administration's equivocation on the issue of who should receive the equipment predictably enraged the French. Ultimately, the Americans' reluctance to antagonize France proved decisive, as it had so often during the previous six months. Officials decided to ignore Bao Dai's expensive request for assistance in favor of the French proposal, which included only those items of use to French forces in Vietnam. The administration gave top priority to fighter and transport planes requested by the French and relegated supplies for the Vietnamese armed forces to third-level priority, just behind a half million dollar allocation for army cranes and tractors. State recognized that the top priority items "could obviously not be used by the armies of the three [Indochinese] states" and continued to hope that the quadripartite body would be established by the time the equipment arrived in Indochina. The department acknowledged, however, that even then "political and military requirements" might demand consignment to the French. Acheson wrote Bruce that it would be necessary, "for purely practical reasons," to extend aid through France, while maintaining Bao Dai as the "publicized recipient." According to a French journalist, the first shipments arrived at Saigon in mid-June, in the form of several old DC-3s. American and French pilots exchanged salutes, "then soldiers appeared, carrying pots of paint, and they painted the red, white and blue rings of France over the star of the American Air Force."[148]

For those in the State Department who had questioned the U.S. commitment in the absence of an evolutionary statement by the French, there was one final indignity: PSA was apparently not informed that the priority level of the Vietnamese infantry supplies had been lowered. On June 2, Philip Jessup urged the department to supply the Vietnamese battalions with "some of the newest stuff." Lacy replied that the equipment would be "turned over directly to the Vietnamese at dock side with appropriate ceremonies." But in the next month, only planes appeared in Vietnam. On June 28, Lacy complained to Rusk that Defense Department officials were dragging their feet on the "politically important infantry battalion equipment for [the] Vietnam Army."[149] Lacy would get no satisfaction. The administrative debate over aid to Indochina had by June 1950 degenerated into a mostly trivial squabble about whose finger to place on the trigger.

Truman had allocated $10 million to begin the military aid program in Indochina, but by June 25 the American commitment had increased. On June 1, the president asked Congress for an additional $75 million for military aid to "the general area of China" during the 1951 fiscal year.[150] Following the advice of the joint chiefs,[151] the administration moved forward in other areas as well. The Southeast Asia Aid Policy Committee was established and charged with responsibility for formulating a "general policy for political-military-economic aid from the United States to Southeast Asia."[152] Truman approved '$6.5 million for covert military operations in Indochina.[153] The administration also resolved to send a mission to survey the military needs of Southeast Asia and to set up organizations of American military personnel to help implement military aid programs in Indochina, Thailand, Indonesia, and Burma. The ECA had its STEMs; now the military would have MAAGs—Military Assistance Advisory Groups. The Indochina MAAG, the first to be formed, existed only on paper when the Korean War broke out.[154]

In early March 1950, Acheson received a personal, five-page letter from Brigadier General Carlos P. Romulo, the Philippines permanent representative to the United Nations. Romulo delicately criticized the United States' growing support for French policy in Indochina. Romulo objected to the recognition of Bao Dai: it looked "to the rest of Asia that the United States, in fighting Communism, may have unwittingly espoused . . . the demonstrated iniquity of colonial imperialism." Bao Dai was not even "pseudo-independent" because he was "helpless without the French." Only a major military effort by the French could extend the area of Bao Dai's control, and Romulo doubted the French were capable of mounting such a campaign. "In such an event," Romulo asked pointedly, "would the United States be willing to commit itself to extending the armed assistance which the French would require to achieve victory against the stubborn guerrilla resistance which they have failed in the last five years to overcome?" Even with American help, Romulo doubted the French could achieve the total "reconquest" of Indochina, but only that would defeat Ho Chi Minh.[155]

Romulo followed up his letter by calling on Acheson for an off-the-record meeting March 10, the day the president approved military aid for Indochina. Acheson agreed with Romulo that an evolutionary statement by the French "would be desirable," but added that "we have to be careful here that the French did not get discouraged by . . . difficulties at home and withdraw from Indo China." When Romulo denied that he advocated either the recognition of Ho Chi Minh or a Bao Dai–Ho Chi Minh coalition, the exasperated secretary asked him what policy he recommended. Romulo replied that the United States should attempt to determine whether Ho might be induced to lay down arms if France and the United States promised Vietnam its independence. According to his memorandum of the conversation, Acheson said that he "would think it over."[156]

Romulo's prescient warning and advice went unheeded. Harry S Truman's decision on May 1, 1950 to provide $750,000 in economic aid and $10 million in military assistance to Indochina was not made with the benefit of hindsight, and at the time no one in the administration regarded this small allocation as particularly ominous. As the author of the *Pentagon Papers* later pointed out, no one involved with the decision for aid believed that any "significant *commitment threshold* was being crossed." But as the same author thoughtfully observed: "The importance of the decision was that when the U.S. was faced with an unambiguous choice between a policy of anti-colonialism and a policy of anti-communism, it chose the latter. And, although this decision was not *perceived* as getting the U.S. more deeply 'involved' in Indochina, it did mark a tangible first step in that direction."[157]

9

The Korean Intervention and After

North Korean troops attacked the South on June 25, 1950, in an attempt to unite the nation under Communist rule. The Truman administration responded promptly and forcefully to the attack. American arms were funneled to South Korea, the Seventh Fleet was ordered to the Straits of Formosa, and after a brief delay Truman sent American ground forces into the battle. On the night of June 25, Dean Acheson urged that American aid for Indochina be increased.[1] There were no local wars in Asia anymore, and there was no island perimeter. It was as if the United States had stretched a drumhead across the non-Communist nations of the continent; a blow to one part of the drum sent reverberations from one end to the other.

Alongside the evident surprise the attack elicited from U.S. policymakers, there was also a perverse feeling of satisfaction accompanying the crisis that so many officials had long anticipated. Joseph Dodge was at an ECA meeting the morning of June 27 when ECA Deputy Administrator William Foster walked in with a draft of a tough Truman statement to be delivered that noon. "A wholesome sigh of relief seemed to prevail," recalled Joseph Dodge, the Detroit banker in charge of Japanese economic recovery, "because a firm stand finally had been taken and we are no longer running away while being nibbled to death."[2] With this sense of relief came a fresh determination to halt the expansion of communism in the Far East.

For Southeast Asia, this meant that the restrained American commitments of the previous months now assumed a far greater importance. Korea confirmed policymakers' beliefs that the Communists would use direct military means to expand in the Far East, and they suspected that the next blow would be struck at Southeast Asia. The Korean War did not change American policy toward Southeast Asia, for the major conceptual and practical shifts had occurred over the foregoing nine months.[3] Korea, however, accelerated everything. Now that the non-Communist world was under military attack, the salvation of Japan, Britain, and Western Europe seemed more urgent, and the revival and protection of Southeast Asia were imperative.

Korea and Japan

The extraordinary American effort to revive Japan's trade with mainland Asia was well under way by the spring of 1950, but U.S. policies had not fully taken effect when the Korean War broke out. In April, Japanese official H. Kano complained to his friend Joseph Dodge that although Japanese exports were increasing, the rise was far from enough to overcome the balance of payments deficit. "Export is not good," Kano lamented.[4] American officials were certain that conditions would improve eventually, but for a time, they felt, the Japanese would have to continue to live frugally.

The Korean War changed things. After June 25, Japan became the base for the United Nations force in Korea. Millions of dollars in procurement contracts were placed with Japanese industry. Japan also took principal responsibility for supplying the troops with consumer goods. Spurred by the heavy demand and foreign exchange windfall, Japanese production leaped ahead during July and continued to climb throughout the rest of the year; by late 1950, Japanese export totals were breaking records every month. At the end of 1949, Japan had a trade deficit of $300 million. By December 1950, Japan's international accounts were $40 million in the black. For the first time since the end of the war, Japanese industrial production exceeded the lofty levels attained during the mid-1930s.[5]

Japanese exports were stimulated by the infusion of Western (especially American) capital into the Far East. Mobilization for war demanded extensive purchases of raw materials, many in Southeast Asia. The massive stockpiling the Truman administration would not implement during peacetime proceeded at an almost frantic pace during the last six months of 1950, flooding the Far East with dollars. The American representatives in Southeast Asia did what they could to direct these dollars toward purchases in Japan. In time, the Japanese found themselves competing with their Western allies for Asian raw materials, and the escalating demand forced prices steadily upward. But for nearly a year, the Japanese were the major beneficiaries of the United States' sudden willingness to route capital to the Far East.

Well before that, the Japanese acknowledged that the Korean War had brought prosperity. On September 7, precisely five months after he had fretted to Dodge about the slow growth of the Japanese economy, Kano wrote his friend: "Export is vital importance to Japan's economy. Now export is good, particularly after the Korean War."[6]

Korea, Malaya, and Great Britain

The sellers' market in raw materials resulted in the vastly increased prosperity of the Southeast Asian nations. Throughout the region, underdeveloped nations benefited from improved terms of trade, higher incomes, and balance of payments surpluses. "The blunt and grimly paradoxical fact is," wrote the executive secretary of the U.N.'s Economic Commission for Asia and the Far East, "that these improvements were based primarily on the impact of the Korean War."[7] The world dollar shortage, already reduced by the devaluation of the pound the previous autumn, now declined even more dramatically. Burma, Thailand, and Indonesia were major beneficiaries of this economic shift.[8]

But the Korean War was especially profitable for British Malaya, and thus in some measure Great Britain. The United States was primarily responsible for this situation. The reactivation of the synthetic rubber plants, approved by the State Department just prior to the war, distressed the British only temporarily, because the administration almost immediately stated its intention to stockpile as much natural rubber as it could obtain. The war also pushed American-British disagreements over tin prices into the background. In fact, the major difficulty in tin after June 25 was the inability of the Malayan smelters to keep up with American demand.

In late August, Acheson announced that the United States would simultaneously increase its production of synthetic rubber and its purchases of natural rubber for the stockpile. State Department planners had concluded that, after the end of the year, access to Southeast Asian raw materials might well be severely restricted by Communist military gains. Though State Department personnel continued to haggle over high prices with their British counterparts, any notion of holding out until prices dropped was plainly inconsistent with the urgency suggested by State's conclusion. On January 5,

1951, the Munitions Board directed the General Services Administration to buy "all the rubber and other materials on the [stockpile] purchase program originating in Indonesia, Malaya, Thailand and French Indo China that you can find. The matter of price should be of no consequence in your re-doubled efforts to acquire the maximum amount of these materials." The GSA hastily complied.[9] United States purchases of natural rubber quadrupled between 1949 and 1951, making the product America's second most valuable import. Tin purchases, by contrast, declined, though not for lack of effort by the United States. Malayan tin smelters suddenly found the demand for their product so high that they simply could not keep up. Prices, of course, skyrocketed. By early 1951, Malaya's export surplus was more than $1.1 billion and climbing. American dollars were now more accessible to the British, who needed only to sell more extensively to their colony to reestablish the final, critical leg of the trade triangle.[10]

American assistance to Great Britain following the outbreak of the Korean War also took more direct forms. In early June, the administration authorized a Mutual Defense Assistance Program survey mission to Southeast Asia, led by John Melby, who was special assistant to Dean Rusk (as of March the assistant secretary of state for Far Eastern affairs), and Major General Graves B. Erskine, commander of the First Marine Division. The mission met with British officials, including Malcolm MacDonald, in Singapore that August. Melby told the British that "United States interest in [Southeast Asia] had increased and was increasing, and the Mission's purpose was to determine how the United States could help to secure common British and American objectives." General Erskine put in "that the Mission's main objective was to stop Communism in Asia." With what was doubtless an air of satisfaction, MacDonald responded that the British "would naturally prefer to defend Malaya by defending Indo-China."[11]

In mid-November 1950, Special Assistant to the President Gordon Gray's "Report on Foreign Economic Policies" was released. Consistent with the administration's policy over the previous year, the study stressed the need for Western Europe to bridge the dollar gap by exporting more to the United States. Great Britain and the sterling area had the key roles in this effort: "Not only is the sterling area an indispensable source of raw materials, but the position of Britain as banker and trading center of the world's largest currency area makes Britain's trading and currency policies of great importance to the realization of United States foreign economic objectives." Because the

British economy had not yet fully responded to the Marshall Plan and the devaluation of the pound, the Gray report recommended that the United States continue supplying economic aid to Great Britain and Western Europe "for another 3 or 4 years." This assistance would be administered in a way that would encourage the economic integration of Western Europe.[12]

Finally, the administration decided to declare its support for the coordinated development of Southeast Asia through the use of Western capital. The United States had begun to assist the Southeast Asian nations during the spring of 1950, but the administration had refused to attach itself formally to the Commonwealth's "Colombo Plan" organization. The Korean War strengthened British and Australian claims that a united effort by the West would have greater impact on the Far East than separate efforts by individual countries. The ECA acknowledged the validity of this approach in August, when Administrator Harlan Cleveland wrote that "the West" was prepare to provide "development capital" to the Southeast Asian nations. "The economy of the United States and Western Europe is complementary to that of the countries of Southeast Asia," Cleveland continued. "Each needs the others. Each is able, through the normal processes of trade and investment, to enrich the others."[13] Following a determined lobbying effort by Percy Spender, Australian minister for external affairs, and Ambassador Lewis Douglas in London, the United States consented in November 1950 to join the Colombo Plan's Consultative Committee and agreed to distribute a large portion of its aid to Southeast Asia through the plan's offices.[14] American cooperation underscored the administration's concern that the West respond to the Communist invasion of South Korea with unity and vigor.

The Korean War was hardly an unqualified success for the British economy. The United States, through NATO, demanded the acceleration and expansion of Western European rearmament programs, and this demand diverted British resources from the pressing business of economic recovery. The British continued to worry about Japanese economic competition in Southeast Asia. On the other hand, like the Japanese, the British were forced to compete with their allies for increasingly expensive Far Eastern raw materials.[15] Finally, R. Allen Griffin's recommendation that the United States offer modest economic and military aid to Malaya was never approved. The proposal was first lowered to the status of a $6 million loan, and then even this limited offer was withdrawn when Congress discovered that the

Malayans had been quietly shipping rubber to China and the Soviet Union.[16]

Despite these problems and disappointments, the British had reason to be satisfied with the evolution of American policy between September 1949 and the end of 1950. The Truman administration had accepted the need for British protectionism, had moved to restore British prosperity by reinvigorating triangular trade, and had committed itself to a coordinated program of economic aid for Southeast Asia.

Korea, Indochina, and Western Europe

Before the Korean War, Indochina had been the focus of American interest in the Far East, and to a surprising extent this situation did not change. When the North Korean invasion was first reported in Vietnam, French and Vietnamese officials worried that Indochina might be next, but when the United States intervened in Korea, the British consul general in Saigon detected "a marked change to a feeling of optimism, with the conviction that they could rely on United States aid" if Indochina were attacked.[17] Indochina nevertheless remained the most vulnerable to Communist attack and the key to the recovery of France and the reintegration of West Germany. The administration gave serious attention to the problems of Indochina after June 25, with important consequences for Southeast Asia, Western Europe, and the United States itself.

To the chagrin of the State Department, Griffin's recommendation for aid to Southeast Asia had been trimmed by Congress. With the beginning of the war, the legislators' frugality seemed foolish. "These cuts could be tolerated last week," William Lacy, chief of the PSA office, wrote Dean Rusk on June 30. "They are now increasingly obnoxious in view of the changed political situation." With his position strengthened by Acheson's June 25 request for more money for Indochina, Rusk decided to implement the full Griffin recommendations immediately and ask Congress to make up the deficiency later.[18] Walter Salant rejoiced that the massive outlays for the Korean War meant that Congress could no longer insist that economic aid must come largely in the form of private capital. The "pretense" of Point Four was over, Salant thought; the idea of substantial economic aid for the underdeveloped nations could "be sold to Congress as economic warfare."[19]

At last, Salant was a prophet with honor. Finally approved in June as part of the Foreign Economic Assistance Act, the technical assistance portion of Point Four limped home a loser in the late summer of 1950. By the time Congress finished with it, the technical aid appropriation contained only $22.5 million. The administration had previously earmarked $2 million of this for the Far East, but in light of the far more ambitious ECA programs already under way in the region, the Point Four contribution seemed pitifully small. The State Department decided to divert most of the $2 million to technical assistance programs in other underdeveloped areas.[20] David Lloyd wrote in late November that the ECA operations were now "a more complete realization of the Point Four concept than the attenuated technical assistance program which now goes by that name."[21] By the end of 1950, both private investment and technical assistance had been supplanted in the Far East by capital assistance from the U.S. government.

The French and their Vietnamese allies were more interested in military assistance. Supplies were slow in arriving, and at first the American decision to furnish equipment only the French could use prompted one exasperated Vietnamese to ask, "When [the] Viet-Minh comes what do we do, throw DDT?"[22] Although the United States continued to send mostly sophisticated matériel, the Korean War immediately boosted the amount of military assistance the Americans were willing to provide Indochina. Along with the $10 million he approved on May 1, Truman allocated $5 million for military assistance on June 27 and an additional $16 million on July 8; Thailand finally got its $10 million on July 10. In October, Congress appropriated half a billion dollars for military aid to the Far East, with "a major part of this sum" earmarked for Indochina.[23] In the meantime, the Melby-Erskine mission toured Vietnam and reported that American assistance requested by the French was insufficient to have a significant impact on the war. Erskine criticized the French for their "Maginot Line" mentality in Vietnam and argued that the American Military Assistance Advisory Group had to be expanded and empowered to advise the French military more actively. By the end of 1950, there were seventy American officers assigned to the Saigon MAAG.[24]

The increased American concern for Indochina after June 25 was a result of some officials' conviction during the summer of 1950 that the Chinese planned to invade Vietnam. That the Americans expected Chinese intervention in Southeast Asia, rather than in Korea where it ultimately came, testifies to the importance of Southeast

Asia in American policy. William Lacy asserted that U.S. military aid must prepare the French "to meet an attack in force from China," and the joint chiefs, though less confident in the prediction, agreed.[25] In late July, the French received reports from intelligence in Taipei and Shanghai that the Chinese Communists planned to attack Indochina "on July 29" or "during the first days of August." As August arrived without the Chinese, the French pushed the invasion date back, first to the end of the rainy season in mid-September, then to early October. Their reports from Vietnam were confirmed by American intelligence sources and were passed along uncriticized by Lacy, David Bruce in Paris, and W. W. Blancké, consul at Hanoi.[26]

The attack in Vietnam came in early October, but the Chinese did not openly participate. The Viet Minh alone attacked a series of French forts strung out near the Chinese border and captured or destroyed them. "When the smoke had cleared," wrote Bernard Fall, "the French had suffered their greatest colonial defeat since Montcalm had died at Quebec."[27] Soon afterward, the French high commissioner for Indochina, Léon Pignon, was replaced by General Jean de Lattre de Tassigny, a hero of the French Resistance during World War II. For a time de Lattre checked the Viet Minh, but American anxiety grew. Following Chinese intervention in Korea in late November, the British consul general reported from Saigon that "official circles," presumably including Americans, believed the Chinese move was "the prelude to the beginning of [the] third world war" and noted their "firm belief" that Chinese intervention in Tonkin was "imminent." On December 4, Truman told Prime Minister Attlee that the Chinese Communists were "satellites of Russia." "The only way to meet communism," he said, "is to eliminate it. After Korea, it would be Indochina, then Hong Kong, then Malaya." The dominoes, the president feared, had started to fall.[28]

United States policymakers also feared a Soviet probe into Western Europe. They therefore felt it was imperative to strengthen and unify continental Western Europe, including West Germany. The Truman administration pressed for European unity under NATO's aegis and now frankly discussed the need for German participation in the military organization. As one analyst observed, "the outbreak of the Korean War . . . brought the German rearmament issue to the forefront of alliance politics."[29] French officials countered that German rearmament remained unthinkable until French troops could return from Indochina to participate in the Western European force.[30] William Lacy acknowledged this necessity. "The deteriorating international situation and the increased danger of the outbreak of a world war makes the early return to Europe . . . of the crack French troops now in Indochina a matter of high priority," wrote Lacy. The first problem was to convince the French to build native armies in Vietnam. "The second task," Lacy concluded, "is for us to obtain funds to equip these new troops."[31] The United States should thus take substantial responsibility for helping loyal Vietnamese in the war against communism, releasing the French for the European theater that policymakers—even Asianists—judged more critical.

By the late summer of 1950, the handful of American advisers who had arrived in Vietnam had managed to antagonize the French far out of proportion to their strength in numbers. The French had mixed feelings about U.S. aid. Although on balance they welcomed it, they worried the Americans might seek undue influence in Vietnam, perhaps by depicting the French as stubborn colonialists and themselves as avatars of freedom. Even before any aid arrived, Pignon complained to the British consul general in Saigon that while the French fought the war, "the United States with a few million dollars played the role of Santa Claus."[32] The Americans who came to Indochina to oversee the aid program often rubbed the French the wrong way. The minister—later ambassador—was Donald Heath, formerly the minister to Bulgaria. Heath loathed the Vietnamese and feared poisoning or assassination. He got along fairly well with the French. Edmund Gullion, the consul general, arrived in Vietnam a strong supporter of French policy, but soon concluded that the French were not very interested in Vietnamese independence. He said so in an abrupt and abrasive way that irritated Heath and enraged the French.

The man the French most disliked was Robert Blum, the head of the ECA mission in Vietnam. Blum was an academic and an idealist, and de Lattre particularly distrusted him. The two men quarreled repeatedly over the autonomy of American officials and the role of the Vietnamese in receiving military aid. De Lattre charged Blum with "fanning the flames of extreme nationalism" and called him, apparently without irony, "the most dangerous man in Indochina." The Americans accused the French of "holding out" on them. The French delayed a bilateral economic agreement between the United States and the Indochinese states because they objected to the use of the phrase "high contracting parties." The Indochinese, they argued, were not "high." The agreement was not signed until September 1951.[33]

There was disharmony in the American camp as well. The State Department's Office of Philippines and Southeast Asian Affairs, long a haven for those who questioned the uncritical acceptance of the French position, became the principal champion of the French after the Korean War erupted. William Lacy ordinarily had the ear of Dean Rusk and struggled (with good success) against the ECA and the Defense Department, some of whose representatives urged that the effort to elicit French concessions on Indochina not be abandoned.[34] There were also a few out-and-out dissenters to the growing U.S. intervention. Most were minor bureaucrats or people outside the government, and most found their way to the office of Charlton Ogburn, who in 1950 became the public information officer for the Far Eastern bureau. Reporter Harold Isaacs argued that the best the United States could hope for in Indochina was a military occupation of a "devastated" Indochina, full of "bitterly hostile and vengeful" people.[35] H. A. Osborn of PSA wrote, "We tried our present method in China with the KMT and learned, the hard way, that it won't work. Here we go again in Indochina!"[36] William E. Palmer, a businessman with interests in Southeast Asia, complained that policy seemed to be dictated by the "European-minded elements" in the administration.[37] All of this was apparently too much for Ogburn, who had moved toward a pro-French position during the early months of 1950. On January 15, 1951, he sent a frustrated memo to Rusk. It ended this way: "Can we not stop taking the lead everywhere and making what seems to me a display of ourselves? Can we not start being the judge of other peoples and stop being the one who is judged? Can we not be a little harder to get, and let the favor of the United States be what other peoples aspire to? Darn it, they are the ones who are threatened with a fate worse than death—not we."[38]

After Korea

The production and export boom instigated by the Korean War did not last. By late 1951, it was clear to Japanese and American economic planners that the war itself had not provided sufficient impetus to assure the permanent stability of Japan's economy. Many Japanese, including Prime Minister Yoshida, concluded that trade with mainland China was essential for Japan despite its potential strategic liabilities. Dulles and Dodge saw this attitude developing and worked to head it off. Dulles pressed ahead with negotiations toward a peace treaty that would end the occupation. The Americans presented their draft of the treaty to Japan at an international conference in San Francisco in September 1951. While the terms of the draft were generous to the Japanese, several conditions attached to the treaty, formally or not, sharply circumscribed Japanese behavior: Japan (and the other nations present) could not amend the document, Japan had to accept some rearmament and the presence of American forces on Japanese soil, and Yoshida was forced to renounce any interest in trade and diplomatic relations with the PRC. Yoshida, with some reluctance, accepted these terms. At the same time, Dodge redoubled his efforts to link Japan and Southeast Asia economically. With the belligerents in Korea drifting toward a truce and the China market seemingly closed once and for all, the integration of non-Communist Asia seemed the only chance to secure Japan's economic success.[39]

To an extent, the regional strategy worked. Japan's exports to Southeast Asia increased substantially during the 1950s, from a value of just over 100 million yen in 1950 to nearly 360 million by 1960. But this commerce did not fully discourage Japanese trade with China. Despite Yoshida's promise to abjure the China market, the traditional relationship between the two nations proved too much to resist. From 1956 to 1958, for example, Japanese exports to China averaged 21.5 million yen in value each year. Policymakers may have been even more distressed if they had hoped to end Japan's economic dependency on the United States. Japan's economic success was assured in the late 1950s, when the United States began to buy supplies in Japan for Southeast Asia. By the mid-1960s, the growing U.S. military involvement in Vietnam led to even greater procurement in Japan; between 1964 and 1969, the United States spent $2.6 billion in Japan for war-related supplies. A final irony, of course, was the Japanese discovery that the United States itself was a lucrative market, if properly approached. Japanese products, once scorned in the States as "cheap imitations of our own goods," found increasing favor with Americans, and beginning in 1958 the United States itself bought more each year from Japan than all the nations of Southeast Asia combined.[40]

After 1950, changed circumstances and new personalities somewhat altered the course of Great Britain's policy toward Southeast Asia. The war in Korea was a sobering experience. American hints that the United States might use the atomic bomb in Korea suggested that Britain's powerful ally might behave recklessly, without benefit of British counsel. Ernest Bevin and Dean Acheson, who had liked and admired each other, were gone from the scene by early 1953: Bevin had died, and Acheson had retired following the 1952 election that brought Dwight Eisenhower to the White House. In their places were Anthony Eden, a career diplomat representing Winston Churchill's Conservative government, and John Foster Dulles, the doctrinaire conservative. The Eden-Dulles relationship lacked the spirit of cooperation that had characterized the Bevin-Acheson partnership.[41] This difference emerged most clearly on the issue of French policy in Vietnam.

Though at first inclined to sympathize with the problems of France, Eden was by early 1954 largely out of patience with his neighbor's behavior in Southeast Asia. The French still refused to promise eventual independence to Vietnam. Bao Dai, never a favorite of the Foreign Office, had failed to grasp control of the government and earned from Eden yet another epithet: "the baccarat king." With General de Lattre's death in early 1952, the French command structure had dissolved once more into confusion. French military strategy, designed in part to impress the Americans with its boldness, instead produced a disaster. Late in 1953, the French commander, General Henri Navarre, dispatched 12,000 French troops to Dienbienphu, a village in northwest Vietnam. The French, who had been unnerved by the enemy's guerrilla tactics, hoped to entice the Viet Minh into fighting a pitched battle, in which superior French training and firepower would surely prevail. The French miscalculated. By early 1954 the improvised fortress was under siege, subjected to daily bombardments and cut off from help.[42]

The siege of Dienbienphu brought the Vietnam crisis to a head. The French government concluded that the time had come for greatpower negotiation and put the issue on the agenda of the upcoming Geneva "East-West" conference. But Secretary Dulles resisted the kind of negotiated solution to the Vietnam question he felt Geneva would produce. Dulles instead sought congressional and international support for what he called "united action" to help the French, some kind of collective military intervention in Vietnam against the Communists. Key congressional representatives balked at this plan; the British were even more adamant in their opposition. Eden and Churchill endorsed the Geneva negotiations and urged "some form of partition" of Vietnam.[43] Although partition would acknowledge Viet Minh control of at least northern Vietnam, the British would then be willing to guarantee the protection of the rest of Southeast Asia through a treaty organization resembling NATO.[44]

Dulles nevertheless lobbied furiously to gain British support for "united action." When he failed to do so, he became bitter, charging that Eden was "playing a cagey game" in hopes of succeeding Churchill as prime minister.[45] Eden had more exalted reasons for favoring negotiation to intervention. He, Churchill, and the British chiefs of staff agreed that military action in Vietnam would not work. It would become, Eden told Dulles, "a bigger affair than Korea, which could get us nowhere." British public opinion would not countenance another Asian war, especially one undertaken on behalf of French colonialism. The views of the Asian Commonwealth nations were also important, and Eden was skeptical that India in particular would approve a Western intervention in Southeast Asia. Finally, Eden and other British officials believed a negotiated settlement in Vietnam would best provide for the security of Malaya. This, Eden recalled, was his "chief concern" in early 1954: "I wanted to ensure an effective barrier as far to the north of [Malaya] as possible." Indochina remained for the British a means to an end; an insulated and productive Malaya was by itself evidence of a successful policy elsewhere in the region.[46]

British views carried weight in Geneva, and in July 1954 the full participants in the conference agreed to divide Vietnam at the seventeenth parallel, with the country to be reunited through a national election in 1956. While it is impossible to know what would have happened if the British had consented to "united action," it is worth noting that neither the Geneva agreements nor their abrogation by southern Vietnam damaged Great Britain's standing in Malaya. The emergency began to taper off in 1954. The growth of the United Malays' National Organization (UMNO), under Tunku Abdul Rahman, gave the British a popular and respectable political party to which to pass power. Malaya became independent on August 31, 1957, and the Greater Federation of Malaya was created in 1963.

These military and political successes gave way to mixed economic results. Commodity agreements for tin and rubber were at last achieved. These two products remained Malaya's chief exports to the dollar area. After the Korean War boom and bust periods, the Malaya–Great Britain–United States trade triangle continued to help the British with their dollar accounts, although modestly. The British did increasingly better selling their own goods in the United States, and heavy American expenditures for the rearmament program in Western Europe supported the British economy in a style to which it had become accustomed during the Marshall Plan years. By the late 1950s, the British had terminated restrictions on dollar area imports and returned to sterling-dollar convertibility. Malaya was safe; the economy was sound; there were no British soldiers fighting in Asia.[47]

There were Americans in Vietnam, more and more of them as the 1950s wore on. They replaced the weary French, for whom the obligations of an Asian empire had become too much. The disaster at Dienbienphu hastened the collapse of the government of Prime Minister Joseph Laniel, who was replaced, on June 17, 1954, by Pierre Mendès-France. The new premier pledged to bring peace in Vietnam or tender his resignation within a month, and it was this commitment that led the French to accept the Geneva agreements in July. Thereafter, the French found ample reason to extricate themselves from Indochina. The war remained a terrible economic burden and a human catastrophe. Officials finally lost patience with Bao Dai, so that by August 1954 they were seeking ways to keep him on the Riviera rather than have him return to his country, where he was "totally discredited."[48] The man who replaced Bao Dai was Ngo Dinh Diem, a Catholic, an apparent patriot, but a difficult man to work with and ultimately something of a cipher. Diem and the French discovered they could not stand each other, and by the spring of 1955 the French were pulling out.

For nearly ten years American policymakers had tried to convince the French to fight on in Vietnam; in that way, the departure of the French and the breathtaking ease with which the United States assumed the burdens of battle suggested that the policy had failed and foretold grave danger. But the Eisenhower administration, like its predecessor, understood that the approach of French withdrawal created at last an opportunity to rearm West Germany. This had been impossible as long as thousands of French soldiers were tied down in Vietnam; the "financial and manpower drain" of the Indochina war, concluded a national intelligence estimate [NIE] in 1952, "seriously reduce[d] France's ability to meet its NATO obligations and to maintain the power position on the continent which it considers necessary to balance a rearmed Germany."[49] As the Americans moved into the breach in Vietnam, they demanded that the French accede to German rearmament.

From the onset of U.S. aid for Indochina, moderate French governments had been moving slowly toward acceptance of a revitalized Germany. In the fall of 1950, Prime Minister René Pleven had outlined a scheme for a Western European army, under NATO, that would include German troops. The Pleven plan evolved into the European Defense Community (EDC), a solely Western European body that would nevertheless be attached to NATO. The EDC organization was established in Paris in May 1952, but the treaty creating it required ratification by national legislatures. In France, this requirement proved fatal. Placed before the assembly in August, 1954, by an unenthusiastic Mendès-France, the EDC was convincingly rejected.

The prime minister immediately came under pressure from the Americans, Germans, and British to get the assembly to reconsider. Dulles threatened the French with an "agonizing reappraisal" of U.S. defense policy in Europe. West German Chancellor Konrad Adenauer was indignant over what he considered an insult to the German people. The British behaved most constructively. Anthony Eden consulted with key European and American officials, convened a conference in London in late September, and there proposed to commit four British divisions and a tactical air force to the defense of the continent, under the auspices of the Western European Union of 1948. West Germany would join the WEU and NATO, but German armaments, Eden promised, would remain limited. The following day, September 29, Dulles told Mendès-France that the United States intended to begin supplying Vietnamese troops, and not their French officers, with arms. The Eden and Dulles statements had a catalytic effect. Eden's announcement reassured the French that the British would stand with them in Western Europe. Dulles's declaration confirmed what Geneva had already implied: that the United States had replaced France as the guarantor of Western interests in Vietnam. Satisfied that France would now be able to counterbalance a rearmed West Germany, Mendès-France shepherded the WEU proposal through the assembly on December 24, 1954. West Germany joined NATO in May, 1955.[50]

It remained only for the Vietnamese to make official the end of French control. Early in 1956, Diem, heady from lavish American support and recent military successes against the powerful Vietnamese sects, formally expelled the French military from Vietnam. The soldiers were all out by April, leaving as a permanent legacy only their floppy-brimmed military caps, which the Vietnamese stubbornly preferred to the straight-brimmed American versions.[51]

The Americans had gotten most of what they wanted. Western Europe was united militarily, and British involvement in continental defense was an unexpected bonus. The high-handed French no longer stood in the way of plans to strengthen the Vietnamese army, to perfect Vietnamese democracy, to cleanse Vietnam of corruption, or to rebuild the economy and open the country to Western European and Japanese trade. To be sure, there was reason to be concerned about the security of Vietnam and about what might happen if the national election, called for 1956, went ahead as planned. The Eisenhower administration vigorously confronted these threats. Dulles carried out his intention to create a NATO in Southeast Asia, forging the Southeast Asia Treaty Organization—SEATO—in September 1954.

Through SEATO, South Vietnam was brought formally under American protection.[52] When Diem canceled the 1956 reunification election, the United States stood behind him. At the same time, the Americans urged Diem to extend his political base. Officials thought southern Vietnam would thrive if Diem could win the support of the uncommitted Vietnamese liberals, the *attentistes*; Under Secretary of State Walter Bedell Smith had argued at Geneva that "1/3 of the Vietnamese people supported Bai Dai, 1/3 supported Ho Chi Minh, and 2/3 [sic] were on the fence."[53] The CIA increased its covert operations, known as the "black psywar," against the Viet Minh.[54] United States aid to the Diem government increased dramatically. Between 1955 and 1961, the United States gave South Vietnam over $1 billion in economic and military aid. By the end of the decade, there were more than 1,500 American "advisers" working in South Vietnam.[55]

Since Harry Truman's announcement of the Point Four program in 1949, the importance of the underdeveloped world, and especially Southeast Asia, had grown considerably. Policymakers believed that if containment was to be something more than an empty concept, the United States would have to be engaged in some manner in Southeast Asia to arrest the flow of Communist expansionism, which had made China its most recent victim. More significantly, in 1949 and 1950, American officials recognized that Southeast Asia was not merely another piece of property in the geopolitical struggle with the Soviet bloc. Instead, the preservation of the region was essential for the recovery of the non-Communist developed nations of Japan, Great Britain, France, and, indirectly, West Germany. United States policymakers agreed that the future success of liberalism and capitalism depended on the development of extensive, unfettered trade between the primary producers of Southeast Asia and the industrial nations of the East and West. Communist control of the Far East would disrupt these commercial linkages, damage the West psychologically, enslave millions of Asians, and bring enormous economic and strategic benefits to the Soviets. The United States resolved that this must be prevented.

This resolution carried with it a host of ironies that were reflected in shifts in American policy. Because of apparent Soviet and Chinese malevolence, U.S. officials judged it necessary to ensure the rearmament of West Germany and the reconstruction of Japan, two recent enemies. Truman, an adamant fiscal conservative, moved away from the reliance on the private sector suggested by Point Four and came to accept, at least implicitly, Walter Salant's idea of using government

aid to underdeveloped countries to reinvigorate world trade and assure the prosperity of Japan and the West. Most ironic was the American determination that the production and protection of Southeast
Asia were of such paramount importance to the ultimate success of
liberal capitalism that the tactics temporarily used to attain these
goals might themselves be illiberal or protectionist. Policymakers
tried to strengthen regional ties between Japan and Southeast Asia,
even while acknowledging that bilateral trade and preferential commercial agreements might discourage the region's global orientation.
United States officials permitted Great Britain and the sterling area to
discriminate against American exports and agreed to disregard the
design of the marketplace in favor of accepting more natural rubber
and smelted tin from British Malaya. Finally, to protect Japanese and
British interests in Southeast Asia and to speed the return of French
resources to continental Western Europe, the United States agreed to
send economic aid and military equipment to the French-sponsored
government of Vietnam. This, as Charlton Ogburn and others at least
faintly understood, was support for colonialism, and it represented
most starkly the suspension of liberal capitalism. Once suspended,
this ideology proved most difficult to reinstate.

There is a quality of innocence about the earliest American intervention in Vietnam—a quality, one should add, that is lost on the
Vietnamese and the Americans who experienced the horrors of the
1960s and 1970s. The Americans in Vietnam were absolutely earnest,
convinced of the righteousness of their mission and their own moral
rectitude. Graham Greene, the British writer who spent some time in
Vietnam during the early 1950s, described in his novel *The Quiet
American* a conversation between an English journalist and Pyle, a
young American recently assigned to the economic mission in Saigon. The journalist has broken off, and addresses the reader: "He
didn't even hear what I said; he was absorbed already in the dilemmas of democracy and the responsibilities of the West; he was
determined—I learned that very soon—to do good, not to any individual person, but to a country, a continent, a world."[56] Or take Philip
Jessup, not a character in a novel but a leading architect of U.S. policy
toward Southeast Asia. Following his journey to the Far East in early
1950, Jessup told British officials "that in the long run the best results
could be obtained in Indochina by winning over the followers of Ho
Chi Minh rather than by shooting them."[57]

But the last word belonged to Dean Acheson. The secretary of state
moved more cautiously toward an interventionist position than did
many of his subordinates. He did not instantly rule out continued

contact with China in October 1949, and for a time he held out against the argument of David Bruce and others that the United States should support the French in Indochina even in the absence of significant political concessions. Finally, in the spring of 1950, Acheson succumbed. Containment in Asia, the success of Japan, Great Britain, and France, the unification of Western Europe, political survival at home—all these desirable objectives, necessary for the success of liberalism and capitalism, came to depend on support for the French in Indochina. Were there limits to the American commitment of May 1950? Perhaps not. As Acheson reflected in 1954, "I don't believe that in precise, difficult situations great spiritual values triumph if you don't have . . . common sense and a little organization and a gun or two around in a critical moment."[58] That statement provides a link between the policies of the late 1940s and early 1950s and the catastrophe of Vietnam.

Abbreviations Used in the Notes

BT 11: Records of the Board of Trade, Public Record Office, Kew, England
CAB 128: Cabinet minutes and conclusions, Public Record Office, Kew, England
CAB 129: Cabinet papers or memoranda, Public Record Office, Kew, England
CAB 134: Minutes of meetings of Cabinet's China and South East Asia Committee [SAC], Public Record Office, Kew, England
CFM: Council of Foreign Ministers records, Lot Files, National Archives, Washington, D.C.
CO 717, CO 852: Colonial Office records, Public Record Office, Kew, England
DDRS: Declassified Documents Reference System, microfiche, Government Documents Library, University of California, Berkeley. The three-digit number and letter suffix refer to the page numbers and item letter of the document in *Declassified Documents Retrospective Collection: Catalog of Abstracts* (Carrollton, Kentucky, Carrollton Press, 1979).
DOS: U.S. Department of State
DSB: Department of State Bulletin
ECA: U.S. Economic Cooperative Administration, Department of State
ECAFE: Economic Commission for Asia and the Far East, United Nations
FEER: Far Eastern Economic Review
FO 371: Foreign Office records, Public Record Office, Kew, England
FRUS: U.S. Department of State, *Foreign Relations of the United States*
H. C. Deb. 5s.: Great Britain, Parliament, *Parliamentary Debates* (Commons), 5th series.
HSTL: Harry S Truman Library, Independence, Mo.
NSC: National Security Council
NYT: New York Times
OES: Office of the Executive Secretariat records, Lot Files, National Archives, Washington, D.C.
Pentagon Papers: U.S. Congress, House Committee on Armed Services, *United States–Vietnam Relations, 1945–1967: A Study Prepared by the Department of Defense*, 12 vols. (Washington, 1971). (Other editions cited as noted.)
PPS: Policy Planning Staff, DOS

PREM 8: Papers of the prime minister's private office, Public Record Office, Kew, England

PSA: Records of the Philippines and Southeast Asia Division, DOS, National Archives, Washington, D.C.

PSF: President's secretary's files, Harry S Truman Papers, HSTL

RG 59: U.S. Department of State Decimal Files, Record Group 59, National Archives Washington, D.C.

T 188, T 236, T 238: Treasury records, Public Record Office, Kew, England

WSJ: Wall Street Journal

Notes

Introduction

1. William Appleman Williams, *The Tragedy of American Diplomacy,* 2d rev. ed. (New York, 1972); Robert A. Packenham, *Liberal America and the Third World: Political Development Ideas in Foreign Aid and Social Science* (Princeton, 1973) p. xv; Gabriel Kolko, *The Roots of American Foreign Policy* (Boston, 1969); Alexander L. George, "The 'Operational Code': A Neglected Approach to the Study of Political Decisionmaking," *International Studies Quarterly,* 12 [1969]: 190–222; John Lewis Gaddis, *Strategies of Containment: A Critical Appraisal of Postwar American National Security Policy* (New York, 1982) pp. viii–ix.

2. N. Gordon Levin, *Woodrow Wilson and World Politics* (New York, 1968).

3. Truman to Michael J. Kirwan, Aug. 13, 1962, in Robert H. Ferrell, ed., *Off the Record: The Private Papers of Harry S Truman* (New York, 1980), pp. 403–4.

4. Robert M. Blum, *Drawing the Line: The Origin of the American Containment Policy in East Asia* (New York, 1982).

1. The Domestic and Foreign Contexts of the United States' Southeast Asian Policy, 1948–1949

1. British Memo of conversation, n.d., FRUS (1947), vol. 2, *Council of Foreign Ministers: Germany and Austria,* p. 815.

2. Quoted in Cabell Phillips, *The Truman Presidency* (New York, 1966), p. 253.

3. Rupert Emerson, *Africa and United States Policy* (Englewood Cliffs, N.J., 1967), p. 21.

4. Stephen G. Rabe, "The Elusive Conference: United States Economic Relations with Latin America, 1945–1952," *Diplomatic History,* 2 (1978): 279; J. Lloyd Mecham, *A Survey of United States–Latin American Relations* (Boston, 1965), p. 170; Gordon Connell-Smith, *The Inter-American System* (London, 1966), pp. 151–54; Connell-Smith, *The United States and Latin America* (London, 1974), p. 205.

5. Quotations in Francis H. Russell to Edwin S. Costrell, Dec. 16, 1966, FW800.50TA/1–2849, Box 4120, RG 59. See also Memos by Benjamin Hardy, Nov. 23 and Dec. 15, 1948, George M. Elsey Papers, Speech File, Box 36, HSTL.

6. Russell to Costrell, Dec. 16, 1966.

7. Elsey to William Tate, July 22, 1952, Elsey Papers, Speech File, Box 36; interview with Raymond W. Miller, Oral History Interview Collection, HSTL; Russell to Costrell, Dec. 16, 1966; Elsey, handwritten notes, Nov. 16, 1949, Elsey Papers, Speech File, Box 36.

8. First quotation from Clifford to Herbert Feis, July 16, 1963, Elsey Papers, Speech File, Box 36; others from Phillips, *The Truman Presidency*, pp. 272–73.

9. Inaugural address, Jan. 20, 1949, *Public Papers of the Presidents of the United States, Harry S Truman, 1949* (Washington, 1964), pp. 114–15.

10. Ibid., p. 115.

11. Truman to chairman of House Foreign Affairs Committee, Mar. 25, 1950, *Public Papers*, Truman, 1950 (Washington, 1965), p. 228; Harry S Truman, *Memoirs*, vol. 2, *Years of Trial and Hope* (Garden City, 1956), p. 232.

12. Statement by Acting Secretary of State James Webb, Sept. 27, 1949, U.S. Congress, House Committee on Foreign Affairs, *International Technical Cooperation Act Hearings:* 81st Cong., 1st sess., 1950, p. 6; memo by Technical Assistance Working Group, Mar. 14, 1949, 800.50TA/2–1849, Box 4121, RG 59.

13. Memo by Hardy, Sept. 12, 1949, Elsey Papers, Subject File, Box 61; U.S. Congress, House Committee on Foreign Affairs, *Point Four: Background and Program* (Washington, D.C., July 1949), p. 12; statement by James Webb, *International Technical Cooperation Act Hearings*, Sept. 27, 1949, p. 5.

14. Truman, *Memoirs*, 2:238. Secretary of state to Truman, Mar. 14, 1949, *FRUS* (1949), vol. 1, *National Security Affairs: Foreign Economic Policy*, pp. 774–83.

15. Quotation in House Committee on Foreign Affairs, *Point Four*, p. 3. See also memo by Technical Assistance Working Group, Mar. 14, 1949; Willard R. Thorp, *Trade, Aid, or What?* (Baltimore, 1954), p. 29. One policymaker explained to British officials "that the needed priority for food production projects precluded any appreciable progress toward industrialization in South East Asia for many years." Hubert Graves to R. H. Scott, regarding conversation with Mr. Brodie, chief of U.S. Division of Research for the Far East, Oct. 26, 1949, FO 371, F16368/1102/61.

16. Dean Acheson, *Present at the Creation: My Years in the State Department* (New York, 1969), p. 337.

17. Ibid., p. 351.

18. *DSB*, Feb. 6, 1949, p. 155.

19. Acheson, *Present at the Creation*, p. 351; *DSB*, Mar. 27, 1949, p. 373; June 12, 1949, p. 762; Aug. 29, 1949, p. 306; *NYT*, Jan. 23, Mar. 2, 1949.

20. Memo of conversation, Winthrop G. Brown and Mr. Swingle, Feb. 18, 1949, 800.50TA/2–1849, Box 4121, RG 59.

21. *DSB*, July 4, 1949, pp. 862, 864.

22. William Adams Brown, Jr., and Redvers Opie, *American Foreign Assistance* (Washington, 1953), p. 392.

23. Raymond F. Mikesell, *United States Economic Policy and International Relations* (New York, 1952), p. 226; editorial note, *FRUS* (1949), 1: 787–788; memo from Elsey to Truman, Apr. 24, 1950, Elsey Papers, Subject File, Box 61; *NYT*, June 13, 14, 18, 1950; statement by Truman, Sept. 8, 1950, Harry S Truman Papers, Charles S. Murphy Files, Correspondence and General File, Box 26, HSTL.

24. Quotations in Francis H. Heller, ed., *The Truman White House: The Administration of the Presidency, 1945–1953* (Lawrence, Kans., 1980), pp. 198–99. See also Interview with Salant, Oral History Interview Collection, HSTL, p. 15, 112; letter from Salant to author, Aug. 10, 1983.

25. Salant to Jerry N. Hess, May 7, 1973, Walter S. Salant Papers, Box 2, HSTL; Heller, *Truman White House*, pp. 199–200.

26. Draft by Salant of proposed letter from Truman to Acheson, Apr. 6, 1949, Salant Papers, Box 2.

27. Memo by Salant, "The Point Four Program and the Domestic Economy," Apr. 22, 1949, Salant Papers, Box 2.

28. Memo from Salant to the Council of Economic Advisers, July 20, 1949, Salant Papers, Box 2; Salant to the Council of Economic Advisers, Sept. 26, 1949, Truman Papers, David D. Lloyd Files, Box 19, HSTL; speech by Salant before Washington chapter of Americans for Democratic Action, Jan. 18, 1950, Salant Papers, Box 2.

29. Salant to Lloyd, Nov. 17, 1949, Truman Papers, Lloyd Files, Box 19.

30. Salant to the Council of Economic Advisers, Sept. 26, 1949, Truman Papers, Lloyd Files, Box 19.

31. Salant to the Council of Economic Advisers, July 20, 1949.

32. Salant to Hess, May 7, 1973; William S. Borden, *The Pacific Alliance: United States Foreign Economic Policy and Japanese Trade Recovery, 1947-1955* (Madison, Wis., 1984), pp. 28, 40-42.

33. Lloyd to Salant, Sept. 30, 1949; Lloyd's handwritten note on Salant memo, Sept. 30, 1949, Truman Papers, Lloyd Files, Box 19.

34. Thomas G. Paterson, "Foreign Aid under Wraps: The Point Four Program," *Wisconsin Magazine of History*, 56 (1972-73): 121. The State Department's tepid interest in Point Four can be traced to a variety of factors, including persistent uncertainty about the program's objectives and the opposition or apathy Point Four encountered on Capitol Hill.

35. State of the union address, Jan. 4, 1950, *Public Papers of the Presidents of the United States*, Harry S Truman, 1950 (Washington, 1965), p. 5.

36. Lionel Max Chassin, *The Communist Conquest of China* (Cambridge, 1965), pp. 183-99.

37. Stuart to the secretary of state, Nov. 6, 1948, FRUS (1948), vol. 7, *The Far East: China*, p. 543.

38. John F. Melby, *The Mandate of Heaven: Record of a Civil War, China, 1945-1949* (Toronto, 1967), p. 289.

39. Nancy Bernkopf Tucker, *Patterns in the Dust: Chinese-American Relations and the Recognition Controversy 1949-1950* (New York, 1983), ch. 6-9.

40. *Marshall's Mission to China, December 1945-January 1947*, intro. by Lyman P. Van Slyke, 2 vols., (Arlington, Va., 1976), 2:520.

41. Memo of Truman's press and radio news conference, Mar. 11, 1948 (extract), FRUS (1948), 7:142.

42. Daniel Yergin, *Shattered Peace: the Origins of the Cold War and the National Security State* (Boston, 1978), pp. 69-86.

43. Memo of conversation between Truman and the under secretary of state, Dec. 14, 1945, FRUS (1945), vol. 7, *The Far East: China*, p. 770.

44. Memo of Truman's news conference, Mar. 11, 1948, FRUS, 1948, 7:141.

45. Marshall to Stuart, Aug. 12, 1948, *ibid.*, p. 415.

46. DOS, *Transcript of Round Table Discussion on American Policy toward China*, Oct. 6, 7, and 8, 1949, p. 412.

47. Policy Planning Staff memo by Davies, Sept. 7, 1948, FRUS (1948), vol. 8, *The Far East: China*, p. 155.

48. R. Allen Griffin to Harlan Cleveland, Nov. 1948, R. Allen Griffin Papers, Box 1, Hoover Institution on War, Revolution, and Peace, Stanford University, Stanford, California.

49. In FRUS (1949), vol. 9, *The Far East: China*, see Clubb to Acheson, Apr. 30 (pp. 974-77), Oct. 8 (pp. 112-13), Oct. 11 (pp. 121-22), Oct. 27 (p. 148), Dec. 24

(pp. 243–44), and Stuart to Acheson, May 27 (pp. 30–31). In Griffin Papers, Box 1, see also Griffin to Cleveland, Nov. 1948; Roger Lapham to Paul Hoffman, July 13, 1949; Lapham and Griffin to Philip Jessup, Sept. 14, 1949.

50. Lovett to Marshall, Nov. 7, 1948, *FRUS*, 1948, 8:194.

51. NSC-22/1, Aug. 6, 1948, *FRUS* (1948), 8:134.

52. Marshall quotation in DOS, *The China White Paper, August 1949*, reissued with a new introduction by Lyman P. Van Slyke, 2 vols. (Stanford, 1967), 1:372. For Acheson quotation see U.S. Congress, Senate Committee on Armed Services and Committee on Foreign Relations, *Military Situation in the Far East*, 82d Cong., 1st sess. (Washington, 1951), p. 1766; see also Acheson, *Present at the Creation*, p. 402.

53. Policy Planning Staff, "U.S. Policy toward China in Light of the Current Situation," Nov. 26, 1948, *FRUS* (1948), 8:214.

54. Joint chiefs of staff to secretary of defense, Dec. 16, 1948, Truman Papers, PSF, NSC Meetings, Box 205.

55. Memo of conversation with Truman, Feb. 24, 1949, Acheson Papers, Memos of Conversation, 1949, Box 64, HSTL.

56. DOS, *China White Paper*, 1:340.

57. Notes prepared by Acheson for meeting with Republican members of House Ways and Means Committee, Feb. 24, 1949, Acheson Papers, Memos of Conversation, 1949, Box 64.

58. DOS, *China White Paper*, 1:intro.

59. See Ross Koen, *The China Lobby in American Politics* (New York, 1960), p. 55.

60. DOS, *China White Paper*, 1:xvi. Acheson remained ambivalent about U.S. policy toward the Chinese Communists, but still endorsed efforts to contain the People's Republic. See Chapter 5, below.

61. Memo of conversation by Butterworth, Sept. 9, 1949, *FRUS* (1949), vol. 7, *The Far East and Australasia*, p. 78.

62. Tucker, *Patterns in the Dust*, pp. 173–194; Warren I. Cohen, "Acheson, His Advisers, and China, 1949–1950," in Dorothy Borg and Waldo Heinrichs, eds., *Uncertain Years: Chinese-American Relations, 1947–1950* (New York, 1980), pp. 13–52. See also Chapter 5, below.

2. Japan: The New Urgency of Reconstruction

1. Dean Acheson, *Present at the Creation: My Years in the State Department* (New York, 1969), p. 554.

2. Joyce and Gabriel Kolko, *The Limits of Power: The World and United States Foreign Policy, 1945–1954* (New York, 1972), p. 304.

3. Kazuo Kawai, *Japan's American Interlude* (Chicago, 1960), p. 17.

4. *DSB*, Sept. 23, 1945, p. 424.

5. See Robert A. Fearey, *The Occupation of Japan: Second Phase, 1948–50* (New York, 1950), p. 7.

6. First two quotations in Harry Emerson Wildes, *Typhoon in Tokyo: The Occupation and Its Aftermath* (New York, 1954), p. 40. Third quotation in William J. Sebald to John M. Allison, June 26, 1948, *FRUS* (1948), vol. 6, *The Far East and Australasia*, pp. 825–26.

7. Harold M. Vinacke, *History of the Far East in Modern Times*, 6th ed. (New York, 1959), pp. 745–46; Kawai, *Japan's American Interlude*, p. 27; William S. Borden, *The Pacific Alliance: United States Foreign Economic Policy and Japanese Trade Recovery, 1947–*

1955 (Madison, Wis., 1984), ch. 2. John Dower notes that Japanese premier Yoshida Shigeru believed that SCAP reversed course in early 1947, under threat of a general strike by workers. See Dower, *Empire and Aftermath: Yoshida Shigeru and the Japanese Experience, 1878-1954* (Cambridge, Mass., 1979), p. 313.

8. John Dower, "Occupied Japan and the American Lake," in Edward Friedman and Mark Selden, eds., *America's Asia: Dissenting Essays on Asian-American Relations* (New York, 1969), p. 175.

9. Michael Schaller, "Securing the Great Crescent: Occupied Japan and the Origins of Containment in Southeast Asia," *Journal of American History,* 69 (1982): 392-414.

10. Statement to be made to Far Eastern Commission by U.S. member, Jan. 22, 1948, *FRUS* (1948), 6:654-55.

11. CIA, "Strategic Importance of Japan," May 24, 1948, Office of Regional Estimates (ORE) 43-48, HSTL.

12. Jerome B. Cohen, *Japan's Postwar Economy* (Bloomington, Ind., 1958), pp. 14-15.

13. Fearey, *Occupation of Japan*, p. 124.

14. Quotation in memo of conversation by Marshall Green, Div. of Northeast Asian Affairs, May 28, 1948, *FRUS* (1948) 6:788-94. See also John Dower, "The Eye of the Beholder," *Bulletin of Concerned Asian Scholars,* 2 (October 1969); speech by Acheson in Cleveland, Miss., May 8, 1947, in *DSB,* May 18, 1947, pp. 991-94; Michael Schaller, *The American Occupation of Japan: The Origins of the Cold War in Asia* (New York, 1985), ch. 4.

15. Sebald to Robert Lovett, Jan. 3, 1949, *FRUS,* 1949, vol. 7, *The Far East and Australasia,* pp. 601-3. MacArthur had conveyed similar thoughts to Kennan and Sebald in early 1948. See "General MacArthur's Remarks at Lunch, March 1, 1948," in *FRUS* (1948), 6:697-99; and William J. Sebald, *With MacArthur in Japan: A Personal History of the Occupation* (New York, 1965), p. 92. Officials in Washington were less sanguine about the Communist threat, but Acheson and Kennan, at least, eventually admitted that MacArthur was right: see Acheson, *Present at the Creation,* p. 556, and George F. Kennan, *Memoirs: 1925-1950* (Boston, 1967), p. 394. On the other hand, the erratic MacArthur later found cause to red-bait the Japanese labor movement. See Schaller, *American Occupation,* pp. 134-36.

16. Interview with Barnett, Oral History Interview Collection, HSTL.

17. Dodge to Cleveland Thurber, Dec. 13, 1948, Joseph M. Dodge Papers, Japan, 1949, Box 1, Burton Historical Collection, Detroit Public Library.

18. Kolko and Kolko, *Limits of Power,* p. 512.

19. DOS, *Round Table Discussion on American Policy toward China,* Oct. 7, 1949, p. 345.

20. Eleanor M. Hadley, *Antitrust in Japan* (Princeton, 1970), p. 6.

21. Ibid., pp. 26, 107, 112, 125, 495-514.

22. James Lee Kauffman, "A Lawyer's Report on Japan," *Newsweek,* Dec. 1, 1947, p. 36.

23. Knowland speech excerpted in Jon Livingston, Joe Moore, and Felicia Oldfather, eds., *The Japan Reader,* vol. 2, *Postwar Japan: 1945 to the Present* (New York, 1973), p. 115.

24. Kawai, *Japan's American Interlude,* p. 146.

25. Royall's speech in Livingston et al., *Japan Reader,* 2:118.

26. Frank Wisner to Frank McCoy, Mar. 2, 1948, *FRUS* (1948), 6:953-54. It was Kennan who demanded this course of action. See Schaller, *American Occupation,* p. 123.

27. Hadley, *Antitrust,* pp. 141-43.

28. Ibid., p. 113.

29. Kennan, *Memoirs,* p. 404.

30. Memo of conversation between Kennan and MacArthur, Mar. 5, 1948, *FRUS* (1948), 6:699-706; Kennan, *Memoirs,* p. 407.

31. Sebald to Lovett, Mar. 23, 1948, *FRUS* (1948), 6:689-90.

32. See PPS-28/2, May 26, 1948, *FRUS* (1948), 6:775–81.

33. Hadley, *Antitrust*, pp. 166–67, 180; Dower, *Empire and Aftermath*, pp. 341–46.

34. *DSB*, Sept. 23, 1945, pp. 424–25.

35. Sebald to Marshall, Nov. 23, 1948, *FRUS* (1948), 6:898–907.

36. Fearey, *Occupation of Japan*, p. 27.

37. Butterworth to Saltzman, Jan. 16; Saltzman to Butterworth, Jan. 22, 1948, *FRUS* (1948), 6:649–53.

38. Memo of conversation between Kennan and MacArthur, Mar. 5, 1948.

39. Sebald to Marshall, May 27, 1948, *FRUS* (1948), 6:785–88.

40. Memo of conversation between Kennan and Canadian officials, June 3, 1948, *FRUS* (1948), 6:801–7.

41. Hans H. Baerwald, *The Purge of Japanese Leaders under the Occupation* (Berkeley, 1959), pp. 78–79.

42. Dower, *Empire and Aftermath*, p. 333.

43. Kolko and Kolko, *Limits of Power*, p. 512; Johnston report in W. MacMahon Ball, *Japan: Enemy or Ally?* (New York, 1949), p. 214.

44. NSC-13/3, May 6; Acheson to London embassy, May 8, 1949, *FRUS* (1949), 7:730–37.

45. Schaller, *American Occupation*, p. 132.

46. Statement of U.S. government, "Economic Stabilization in Japan," Dec. 10, 1948, *FRUS* (1948), 6:1059–60.

47. Dodge to Thurber, Dec. 13, 1948.

48. Fearey, *Occupation of Japan*, p. 127.

49. Ibid., p. 135.

50. Speech by Major General William Marquat, Jan. 27, 1949, *Contemporary Japan*, 18 (Jan.–Mar. 1949):146; Ball, *Japan*, p. 212; Schaller, *American Occupation*, pp. 80–81.

51. Ball, *Japan*, p. 220; handwritten notes by Joseph Dodge, n.d., Dodge Papers, Japan, 1949, Box 4; report of Rep. Charles B. Deane, member of the Special Subcommittee of House Committee on Expenditures in the Executive Departments, on trip to the Far East, Oct. 19, 1949, Truman Papers, PSF, Box 177.

52. Report in the *Baltimore Sun*, Aug. 1947, cited by Dower, "Occupied Japan," p. 190.

53. Kennan quoted in DOS, *Round Table Discussion*, Oct. 6, 1949, pp. 4–5. Johnston report in Ball, *Japan*, p. 220.

54. Marshall to diplomatic and consular offices, Aug. 2, 1948, *FRUS* (1948), 6:993–94.

55. Schaller, "Securing the Great Crescent," p. 397.

56. NSC-41, Feb. 28, 1949, *FRUS* (1949), vol. 9, *The Far East: China*, pp. 826–34.

57. In *FRUS* (1949), vol. 9, see two telegrams from Clubb to Acheson, both Apr. 30, 1949 (pp. 974–77); Robert West to MacArthur, May 7, 1949 (pp. 977–79); Acheson to Clubb, May 8, 1949 (p. 980); Livingston Merchant to Acheson, Nov. 16, 1949 (pp. 996–98).

58. W. W. Stuart, "China," Dec. 7, 1949, PSA, Box 6.

59. See *NYT*, Feb. 4, 1950; *The Economist*, June 17, 1950, p. 1316; Nancy Bernkopf Tucker, "American Policy toward Sino-Japanese Trade in the Postwar Years: Politics and Prosperity," *Diplomatic History*, 8 (1984):183–208. In *FRUS* (1950), vol. 6, *East Asia and the Pacific*, see Dept. of the Army to MacArthur, Jan. 13 (pp. 619–20); John Foster Dulles to Acheson, June 7 (pp. 1207–12).

60. NSC-41, Feb. 28, 1949.

61. James Webb to John J. Mucio, June 17, 1949, *FRUS* (1949), 9:834–37; Charles Yost to Philip Jessup, Sept. 1, 1949, 359E, DDRS.

62. Acheson to Clubb, May 8, 1949. See also Chapter 1, above.

63. Stuart to Acheson, May 12, 1949, *FRUS* (1949), 9:984–85.

64. Memo by Jessup, Nov. 3, 1949, 890.00/11-849, Box C-846, RG 59. On the administration's reluctance to promote Sino-Japanese trade generally, see Yoko Yasuhara, "Japan, Communist China, and Export Controls in Asia, 1948-1952," *Diplomatic History*, 10(1986):75-89.

65. Harold Vinacke, *The United States and the Far East, 1945-1951* (Stanford, Calif., 1952), p. 76; *The Economist*, July 9, 1949, p. 60.

66. Oral History Interview with Barnett; E. Stuart Kirby, "Japan in Asia," *FEER*, Sept. 15, 1949, p. 322.

67. Quoted in Schaller, "Securing the Great Crescent," p. 399.

68. Acheson to certain diplomatic and consular offices, May 8, 1949, *FRUS*, (1949), 7:736-37.

69. Sebald to Marshall, June 22, 1948, *FRUS* (1948), 6:981-82.

70. CIA, "Strategic Importance of Japan"; J. F. Shaw to John M. Allison, Nov. 18, 1949, PSA, Box 2.

71. DOS, *Round Table Discussion*, Oct. 7, 1949, p. 217; Ada V. Espenshade, "Present Conditions and Future Outlook of Japan's Foreign Trade," *FEER*, Jan. 19, 1950, p. 76; "secret" report by U. A. Johnson, n.d., PSA, Box 6. For the genesis of U.S. interest in linking Japan and Southeast Asia economically, see Borden, *Pacific Alliance*, pp. 104-12.

72. Memo of conversation by Warren S. Hunsberger Mar. 2, 1948, *FRUS* (1948), 6:954-58.

73. Memo of conversation on Far East between American, British, and French officials, Sept. 17, 1949, *FRUS* (1949), 7:861.

74. "Secret" report by U. A. Johnson.

75. Roger Buckley, *Occupation Diplomacy: Britain, the United States and Japan, 1945-1952* (Cambridge, 1982), pp. 123-26.

76. A. G. Donnithorne, *Economic Developments since 1937 in Eastern and Southeastern Asia and Their Effects on the United Kingdom* (London: Royal Institute of International Affairs, 1950), p. 35; memo of conversation between British and American officials, July 8, 1949, PSA, Box 5; Espenshade, "Present Conditions," p. 75.

77. F. R. Hoyer Millar to Sir Roger Makins, Nov. 16, 1949, FO 371, F17668/10345/61G.

78. Memo of conversation by Sir Geoffrey Thompson, Feb. 20, 1950, FO 371, FZ 11345/3.

3. *Great Britain and the*
   Dollar Gap: The Malayan Link

1. Letter from May and Samuel Charles Wright to Truman, Feb. 4, 1949, 841.5151/2-449, Box 5841, RG 59.

2. In 1949, the sterling nations, besides the United Kingdom, were New Zealand, Australia, the Solomon Islands, New Guinea, British Borneo, British Malaya, Burma, Pakistan, India, Ceylon, Iraq, Kuwait, Bahrain, Qatar, Oman, Aden, Cyprus, Gibralter, Iceland, British Somaliland, Uganda, Kenya, Pemba, Seychelles, Mauritius, Zanzibar, Tanganyika, Nyasaland, Rhodesia, Basutoland, Union of South Africa, Swaziland, South-West Africa, Nigeria, Gold Coast, Sierra Leone, Gambia, Bermuda, Bahamas, Barbados, Trinidad, Tobago, British Guiana, Jamaica, and British Honduras.

3. Lord Gladwyn, *The Memoirs of Lord Gladwyn* (New York, 1972), p. 208.

4. Avi Shlaim, "Ernest Bevin," in Shlaim, Peter Jones, and Keith Sainsbury, eds., *British Foreign Secretaries since 1945* (Newton Abbot, 1977), p. 57.

5. Richard N. Gardner, *Sterling-Dollar Diplomacy*, rev. ed. (New York, 1969), p. 168.

6. Quoted in M. W. Kirby, *The Decline of British Economic Power since 1870* (London, 1981), p. 97.

7. Quoted in Gardner, *Sterling-Dollar Diplomacy,* p. 245.

8. David Marquand, "Sir Stafford Cripps: The Dollar Crisis and Devaluation," in Michael Sissons and Philip French, eds., *Age of Austerity* (London, 1963), p. 170; Gardner, *Sterling-Dollar Diplomacy,* pp. 312–24.

9. Thomas Balogh, *The Dollar Crisis: Causes and Cure* (Oxford, 1949), pp. 22–27.

10. "Economic Survey for 1949," Feb. 16, 1949, CAB 129, CP(49)29.

11. Quotation in "Expansion of Exports to North America," Mar. 29, 1949, PREM 8/1185, EPC(49)31, PRO. See also CAB 128, CM 5(49)5, Jan. 20, 1949.

12. U.S. Economic Cooperation Administration, *Country Data Book: United Kingdom, 1950* (Washington, 1950), p. 2; minute by J. P. E. C. Henniker, June 16, 1949, FO 371, UE 3830/150/53G; Julius C. Holmes and Thomas K. Finletter to Lewis Douglas and W. Averell Harriman, June 21, 1949, 841.51/6–2149, Box C-555, RG 59.

13. *NYT,* May 29, 1949.

14. Douglas cables of June 16 and June 22, 1949, in *FRUS* (1949), vol. 4, *Western Europe,* pp. 784–90; *NYT,* July 1, 11, 12, 1949.

15. Bevin to Acheson, June 22, 1949, FO 371, UE 4007/150/53G.

16. "Post-War Policy: American and British Views," July 22, 1949, T 236, 110/196/05, WD(49)17.

17. Snyder to Acheson, July 9 and 10, 1949, *FRUS* (1949), 4:799–802. Text of communiqué in *DSB,* Aug. 8, 1949, p. 197. Canada's importance as a potential dollar supplier to Great Britain should not be overlooked, but note Douglas's statement to Acheson that "Abbott . . . took a position which is almost identical with ours." Douglas to Acheson, July 19, 1949, 841.5151/7–1949, Box C-556, RG 59.

18. Board of Trade brief on the future of multilateral international economic cooperation, Aug. 12, 1949, FO 371, UE 5410/150/53.

19. Cripps's report in 466 H. C. Deb. 5s., col. 2149–55.

20. Board of Trade brief, Aug. 12, 1949: "Cuts in the U.K. Dollar Import Programme for 1949/50," Aug. 17, 1949, T 236, 110/196/05.

21. "Sterling Balances," Nov. 14, 1949, PREM 8/1187, EPC(49)137; Cripps's devaluation announcement, Sept. 18, 1949, FO 371, UE 6044/150/53.

22. "Anglo-Canadian-American Economic Talks: Second Meeting," July 8, 1949, FO 371, UE 4292/150/53G; Douglas to Acheson, July 20, 1949, 841.51/7–2049, Box 5838, RG 59.

23. For descriptions of triangular trade, see Claude A. Buss, "New Relationships: Economics and Diplomacy in Southeast Asia," in Philip W. Thayer, ed., *Southeast Asia in the Coming World* (Baltimore, 1953), p. 85; *FEER,* Sept. 8, Oct. 20, Dec. 22, 1949; U.N., ECAFE, *Economic Survey of Asia and the Far East* (1948), p. 45, 259; European Recovery Program, *Second Report of the Organization for European Economic Cooperation* (Paris, n.d. [February 1950]), p. 16.

24. U.S. Dept. of Commerce, *Foreign Commerce Yearbook, 1949* (Washington, 1951), p. 520; ECA, Special Commission to the United Kingdom, *The Sterling Area: An American Analysis* (London, 1951), p. 79; "Table VIII: Sterling Area Trade with USA and Canada," Aug. 15, 1949, T 236, 110/196/06.

25. Note of Discussion, "The Dollar Situation: Canada's Attitude," Aug. 11, 1949, CAB 129, CP(49)174. Quotation from "Economic War Potential of British and Foreign Territories in South East Asia," Dec. 23, 1948, FO 371, F 1068/1102/61; ECA, *The Sterling Area,* p. 79.

26. "Malaya as Dollar Earner and Raw Material Supplier," Apr. 13, 1949, FO 371, UE 2836/150/53G; memo by A. Creech Jones, June 30, 1948, PREM 8/1406; E. A. Radice,

"The Sterling Area Dollar Problem," Aug. 15, 1949, T 236, 110/196/06, TT(49)1.

27. CO 717/155-156, 187/52275; Mr. Watson to Roderick Barclay, Dec. 23, 1949, FO 371, FZ 1102/22; U.K. Central Office of Information, *An Economic Review of Malaya, 1945-1949* (London, 1950), pp. 22, 30-31; "Analysis of the Situation and Policy in Malaya," unattributed, n.d., PSA, Box 14; *FEER* Feb. 2, 1950; *Draft Development Plan of the Federation of Malaya* (Kuala Lumpur, 1950).

28. *Economic Review of Malaya*, p. 22.

29. Ibid., pp. 30-31; "Analysis of the Situation and Policy in Malaya."

30. *Economic Review of Malaya*, pp. 22, 30-31; "Analysis of the Situation and Policy in Malaya."

31. *Draft Development Plan of the Federation of Malaya*; North Borneo Rubber Commission, Report (Singapore, 1949); Douglas to Acheson, Aug. 10, 1949, *FRUS* (1949), vol. 9, *The Far East: China*, pp. 55-56; speech by Federation High Commissioner H. L. G. Gurley, Nov. 15, 1949, in *FEER*, Feb. 2, 1950.

32. Glenn H. Snyder, *Stockpiling Strategic Materials: Politics and National Defense* (San Francisco, 1966), pp. 11-12.

33. Quotation in minutes of Cabinet meeting, July 25, 1949, CAB 128, CM 48(49)3. See also Cripps to Commonwealth finance ministers, June 27, 1949, FO 371, UE 4161/150/53G.

34. Brief for tripartite talks, "U.S. Stockpiling," Aug. 13, 1949, T 236, 110/196/05.

35. "Under What Conditions May the Rest of the Sterling Area Make a Net Contribution to the United Kingdom?," Aug. 10, 1949, T 236, 110/196/06.

36. "Notes for the Secretary of State on the Rubber Position," June 22, 1949, CO 852, 921/1/47; *The Economist*, No. 12, 1949; *FEER*, Feb. 2, Mar. 23, 1950.

37. Under secretary's meeting, "Implementation of U.S. Rubber Policy," June 1, 1949, PSA, Box 14; U.S. Dept. of Commerce, *Rubber: First Annual Report* (Washington, 1949), pp. 3-4.

38. Minutes of Cabinet meeting, Mar. 28, 1949, CAB 128, CM 23(49)2; memo of conversation between Sir Roger Makins and Lewis Douglas, Aug. 18, 1949, FO 371, UE 5328/150/53; British Rubber Development Board, "Rubber Developments," September 1949, CO 852, 923/1/50.

39. "Under What Conditions?" Aug. 10, 1949; Charles S. Reed to W. Walton Butterworth, July 9, 1948, PSA, Box 14; "Brief for Ministerial Talks in Washington," Aug. 29, 1949, CAB 129, CP(49)185.

40. Statement by Jones from cabinet meeting, Mar. 8, 1948, CAB 128, CM18(49)2. Memo by Colonial Office, "Security Situation in the Federation of Malaya," April 1949, PREM 8/1406.

41. Statement by L. D. Gammans, Sept. 27, 1949, 468 H. C. Deb. 5s., col. 102-3.

42. Reed to Butterworth, July 9, 1948; *Annual Report on the Federation of Malaya, 1949* (London, 1950), p. 205; Douglas to Acheson, July 7, 1949, 841.51/7-749, Box 5838, RG 59.

43. Brief for secretary of state, "Political Situation in South East Asia," Jan. 11, 1949, FO 371, F1545/1016/61.

44. Shinwell to Attlee, Mar. 24, 1949, PREM 8/1406. Monthly report to secretary of state and foreign secretary, August 1949, FO 371, F13028/10134/61G.

45. *Annual Report on the Federation of Malaya, 1949*, intro., p. 123.

46. See Ellen J. Hammer, *The Struggle for Indochina, 1940-1955* (Stanford, 1966), pp. 207-44.

47. Ashley Clarke to Mr. Esler Dening, Jan. 7, 1949, FO 371, F720/1015/86; British embassy in Paris to Foreign Office, Jan. 17, 1949, FO 371, F1540/1015/86.

48. Quotation is in minute by R. C. Blackham, Foreign Office, June 8, 1949, FO 371,

F8210/1015/86. See also Viscount Hood (Paris) to Dening, Feb. 10, 1949, FO 371, F2277/1015/10; brief for Dening by R. H. Scott, "Recognition of Viet Nam," Sept. 3, 1949, FO 371, F13255/1015/86.

49. Minute by Bevin on memo, "United Kingdom Policy in South-East Asia and the Far East," Oct. 22, 1949, FO 371, F15857/1055/61G.

50. Brief for Bevin by Dening, Mar. 23, 1949, FO 371, F4487/1023/61G.

51. Minutes of meeting between Malcolm MacDonald and members of Foreign and Colonial Offices, May 24, 1949, FO 371, F8338/1075/61G.

52. Scott to Frank S. Gibbs (Saigon), Feb. 24, 1949, FO 371, F2347/1015/86; "Economic War Potential of . . . South East Asia," Dec. 23, 1948; MacDonald to Foreign Office, Dec. 19, 1949, FO 371, F19106/1055/86.

53. Minute by John Russell, Foreign Office, on military intelligence report of Feb. 28, Mar. 17, 1949, FO 371, F3423/1015/86.

54. Hayter to Dening, Dec. 23, 1949, FO 371, F19625/1055/86.

55. Minute on telegram from MacDonald, Nov. 16, 1949, FO 371, F16662/1015/86.

56. Morrison to Attlee, June 20, 1949, PREM 8/977.

57. Report on the tripartite economic discussions, Oct. 4, 1949, FO 371, UE 6327/150/53G; report by the Ad Hoc Interdepartmental Committee on U.S. Investment in the Sterling Area, Nov. 23, 1949, FO 371, UEE 43/1.

58. MacDonald to Foreign Office, Sept. 2, 1949, FO 371, F13136/1024/61.

59. "Strategic perimeter" in "Minutes of Meeting of the Secretary and the Consultants on the Far East," Oct. 27, 1949, 890.00/11-1749, Box C-846, RG 59; "without any clear policy" in Dening to Sir Cecil Syers, Mar. 18, 1949, FO 371, F4468/1023/61G; "having burnt their fingers" in H. A. Graves (Washington) to Dening, Apr. 16, 1949, FO 371, F5743/1023/61G.

60. Bevin to Acheson, "South East Asia," Apr. 2, 1949, *FRUS* (1949), vol. 7, *The Far East and Australasia*, pp. 1135–37; Graves to Dening, Apr. 16, 1949.

61. Dening to Sir Ralph Stevenson (Nanking), Apr. 5, 1949, FO 371, F5095/1123/61G.

62. U.N., ECAFE, *Survey of Asia* (1948), p. 45; *NYT*, Sept. 10, 1949.

63. Kok Wah Fong, "Economic Relations between Malaya and the United States of America," M.A. thesis, Stanford Univ., 1953, p. 42.

64. William L. Blue (Kuala Lumpur) to Acheson, Feb. 10, 1949, PSA, Box 14.

65. William R. Langdon (Singapore) to DOS, Jan. 18, 1949, PSA, Box 14.

66. Memo by Willard L. Thorp, "Background and Preparations for U.S.-U.K.-Canadian Discussions regarding the Economic and Financial Crisis of the Sterling Area," Aug. 15, 1949, OES, Box 5; George F. Kennan, *Memoirs: 1925–1950* (Boston, 1967), p. 485.

67. Thorp to Acheson, June 27, 1949, *FRUS* (1949), 4:793–97.

68. Acheson to Douglas, June 30, 1949, *FRUS* (1949), 4:798–99.

69. Webb to Kennan, Aug. 26, 1949, *FRUS* (1949), 4:820–21.

70. *NYT*, Sept. 21, 1949.

71. Langdon to DOS, Jan. 18, 1949.

72. Douglas to Acheson, June 18, 1949, 841.51/6-1849, Box C-555, RG 59.

73. *DSB*, July 4, 1949, p. 862.

74. Memo by Thorp, "Background and Preparations," Aug. 15, 1949.

75. Oliver Franks to Foreign Office, Aug. 12, 1949, FO 371, UE 5131/150/53.

76. Acheson to Douglas, July 6, 1949, 841.5151/7-649, Box C-556, RG 59.

77. Harriman to Acheson, June 25, 1949, *FRUS* (1949), 4:792–93.

78. Acheson to Douglas, June 17, 1949, *FRUS* (1949), 4:796–97.

79. Memo by Thorp, "Background and Preparations, Aug. 15, 1949.

80. Policy Planning Staff, "Position Paper for the Discussions with the British and Canadians on Pound-Dollar Problems," Sept. 3, 1949, *FRUS* (1949), 4:822–30.

81. *NYT,* Sept. 6, 1949.

82. Under secretary's meeting, "Implementation of U.S. Rubber Policy," June 1, 1949; minutes of under secretary's meeting, June 3, 1949, OES, Box 9.

83. "Implications of the Sterling Area Crisis to the U.K. and the U.S.," Aug. 18, 1949, *FRUS* (1949), 4:806–20.

84. Douglas to Acheson, Aug. 15, 1949, Acheson Papers, Memos of Conversation, 1949, Box 64, HSTL.

85. Memo of conversation between Makins and Douglas, Aug. 18, 1949.

86. Draft recommendations of Commonwealth finance ministers, July 18, 1949, FO 371, UE 4667/150/53.

87. Franks to Foreign Office, May 18, 1949, FO 371, UE 3089/150/53.

88. Acheson to Douglas, June 27, 1949.

4. *The United States, Nationalism, and Colonialism in Postwar Southeast Asia*

1. Minutes of meeting of the Cabinet's China and South East Asia Committee, Apr. 29, 1949, SAC(49)3, CAB 134/669; "SEA Fortnightly Summary," Acheson to Bangkok, May 6, 1949, 890.00/5-649, Box C-846, RG 59.

2. *FEER*, Sept. 29, 1949, p. 409; Dept. of Commerce, *Foreign Commerce Yearbook, 1949*, p. 521.

3. *NYT,* Jan. 14, 1949.

4. CIA, "Review of the World Situation," June 15, 1949, NSC Meetings, Truman Papers, PSF, Box 206, HSTL; Hugh Tinker, *The Union of Burma*, 3d. ed., (London, 1961), p. 97; John F. Cady, *The History of Post-War Southeast Asia* (Athens, Ohio, 1974), p. 68.

5. R. L. Clifford, "Burma" papers for use at New Delhi Foreign Service Conference, Feb. 25, 1949, 890.00/2-2549, Box C-845, RG 59.

6. J. Klahr Huddle (Rangoon) to DOS, June 1, 1949, 890.00/6-149, Box C-846, RG 59.

7. Ne Win's call on Acheson, July 25, 1949, Acheson Papers, Memos of Conversation, 1949, Box 64, HSTL.

8. U E Maung's call on Acheson, Aug. 23, 1949, Acheson Papers, Memos of Conversation, 1949, Box 64.

9. Report of Representative Charles B. Deane, member of the Special Subcommittee of the House Committee on Expenditures in the Executive Departments, on trip to the Far East, Oct. 19, 1949, Truman Papers, PSF, Box 177, HSTL.

10. The foregoing draws on the following studies: Tinker, *Union of Burma*; Jan Pluvier, *South-East Asia from Colonialism to Independence* (Kuala Lumpur, 1974), pp. 346–49, 389–94; 396–400; Cady, *History*, pp. 66–68; David Joel Steinberg, ed., *In Search of Southeast Asia* (New York, 1971), pp. 343–47; Russell H. Fifield, *The Diplomacy of Southeast Asia: 1945-1958* (New York, 1958), pp. 167–229; Saul R. Rose, *Britain and South East Asia* (Baltimore, 1962), pp. 109–25.

11. The foregoing is based on Pluvier, *South-East Asia*, pp. 405–8; Cady, *History*, pp. 85–97; Frank C. Darling, *Thailand and the United States* (Washington, 1965), pp. 11–68; Edwin F. Stanton, *Brief Authority: Excursions of a Common Man in an Uncommon World* (New York, 1956), pp. 216–22.

12. Stanton, *Brief Authority*, p. 219.

13. Ibid., pp. 221-22.

14. *NYT,* Jan. 26, 1949.

15. Quotations in Sir G. Thompson to Foreign Office, Apr. 23, 1949, FO 371, F5735/1017/61; and Thompson to Foreign Office, Apr. 27, 1949, FO 371, F6009/1017/61. See also *Annual Report on the Federation of Malaya, 1949* (London, 1950), p. 205; memo of conversation between H. A. Graves and Kenneth P. Landon, Jan. 5, 1949, PSA, Box 18.

16. Darling, *Thailand*, p. 72; Stanton, *Brief Authority*, pp. 224-26.

17. PPS-51, "United States Policy toward Southeast Asia," Mar. 29, 1949, *FRUS* (1949), vol. 7, *The Far East and Australasia*, pp. 1128-33. This paper became the basis for UM D-26, "To Define U.S. Policy toward South East Asia," Apr. 4, 1949, OES, Box 5, and NSC-51, July 1, 1949 (cited in *FRUS* [1949], vol. 7, 1128-29). For an extended analysis of PPS-51, see Michael Schaller, *The American Occupation of Japan: The Origins of the Cold War in Asia* (New York, 1985), pp. 158-63, and Robert M. Blum, *Drawing the Line: The Origin of the American Containment Policy in East Asia* (New York, 1982), pp. 112-24.

18. Memo left by Bevin for Acheson, Apr. 2, 1949, *FRUS* (1949), 7:1135-37.

19. In PSA, Box 5, see Lacy to Reed, May 13, 1949; Reed to Butterworth, May 17, 1949.

20. Stanton to Acheson, June 14, 1949, *FRUS* (1949), 7:50-53.

21. Thorpe, "Quarterly Military Survey," June 1, 1949, PSA, Box 19.

22. Acheson to Bangkok, July 28, 1949, PSA, Box 19.

23. Davies, "Suggested Course of Action in East and South Asia," July 7, 1949, *FRUS* (1949), 7:1148-51.

24. Wilfred Malenbaum to Willard Thorp, May 31, 1949, PSA, Box 18; *DSB,* Aug. 22, 1949, p. 277.

25. Memo from Acheson to Truman, Aug. 18, 1949, *FRUS* (1949), 7:844-45.

26. *FEER,* Sept. 8, 1949, p. 319.

27. Quoted in Darling, *Thailand*, p. 82.

28. In PSA, Box 19, see Stanton to Acheson, Aug. 2, 1949 and Butterworth to Jessup, Aug. 5, 1949; Reed to Jessup, Aug. 22, 1949, PSA, Box 5. Stanton is quoted.

29. Acheson to Bangkok, June 22, 1949, 851G.01/6-2249, Box 6181; memo of conversation including Butterworth and Prince Wiwat, Sept. 22, 1949, 851G.00B/9-2249, Box 6181, RG 59.

30. Bureau of Far Eastern Affairs, "Military Assistance on Reimbursable Basis under MAP," n.d. [autumn 1949], PSA, Box 4.

31. *Foreign Commerce Yearbook, 1949,* p. 128.

32. Quoted in Anthony J. S. Reid, *The Indonesian National Revolution, 1945-1950* (Longman, Australia, 1974), p. 43.

33. Robert J. McMahon, *Colonialism and Cold War: The United States and the Struggle for Indonesian Independence, 1945-49* (Ithaca, 1981), p. 170. My account of U.S. policy toward Indonesia, here and in Chapter 9, relies heavily on McMahon's excellent study. Because of it, I have not thought it necessary to recapitulate in detail the evolution of American policy.

34. Robert J. McMahon, "Anglo-American Diplomacy and the Reoccupation of the Netherlands East Indies," *Diplomatic History,* 2 (1978):14; Russell H. Fifield, *Americans in Southeast Asia: The Roots of Commitment* (New York, 1973) pp. 79-86.

35. Robert Lovett to Charles A. Livengood (consulate general at Batavia), Dec. 20, 1948, *FRUS* (1948), vol. 6, *The Far East and Australasia*, pp. 592-93; Evelyn Colbert, "The Road Not Taken: Decolonization and Independence in Indonesia and Indochina," *Foreign Affairs,* 51 (1973):608-28.

36. In *FRUS* (1949), vol. 7, see Butterworth to Charles E. Bohlen, Jan. 7 (pp. 136-

37); memo of conversation between U.S. and Dutch officials, Jan. 11 (pp. 139–41); Livengood to Acheson, Mar. 25 (pp. 343–46); Acheson to Batavia, June 24 (p. 454). See also *NYT*, Jan. 12, 1949.

37. Quotation in memo of conversation by Acheson, Mar. 31, 1949, *FRUS* (1949), vol. 4, *Western Europe*, pp. 258–61. See also McMahon, *Colonialism and Cold War*, pp. 276–78, 282–95.

38. Colbert, "Road Not Taken," p. 617; McMahon, *Colonialism and Cold War*, p. 314.

39. In *FRUS* (1948), vol. 6, see Lovett to Livengood, May 28 (pp. 191–92); Livengood to secretary of state, June 2 (pp. 207–8).

40. In *FRUS* (1948), vol. 6, see Lovett to Livengood, Sept. 27 (pp. 378–79); Dec. 30 (pp. 613–16). Quotations in first document.

41. Colbert, "Road Not Taken," pp. 617–22; McMahon, *Colonialism and Cold War*, pp. 314–15.

42. Butterworth, Rusk, and Hickerson to Marshall, Feb. 10, 1948, *FRUS* (1948), 6:91–94.

43. George McTurnan Kahin, *Nationalism and Revolution in Indonesia* (Ithaca, 1952), pp. 214–17.

44. Rusk to Jessup, Dec. 23, 1948, *FRUS* (1948), 6:597–600.

45. Memo of conversation between Indian ambassador to the United States, Butterworth, Rusk, and Joseph Satterthwaite, Jan. 3, 1949, *FRUS* (1949), 7:123–25.

46. Acheson to Herman Baruch (The Hague) and Raymond Lisle (Batavia), Jan. 31, 1949, *FRUS* (1949), 7:198.

47. DOS to Tom Connally, Feb. 11, 1949, *FRUS* (1949), 7:223n.

48. Acheson to Baruch, Aug. 23, 1949, *FRUS* (1949), 7:474–78.

49. Quoted in Ellen J. Hammer, *The Struggle for Indochina, 1940–1955* (Stanford, 1966), p. 173.

50. *Pentagon Papers*, vol. 1, pt. C, p. 3.

51. *The Economist*, Nov. 12, 1949, p. 1073; *Foreign Commerce Yearbook, 1949*, pp. 68–69; *FEER*, Feb. 16, 1950, p. 228; Hammer, *Struggle for Indochina*, p. 13; Robert Shaplen, *The Lost Revolution: The U.S. in Vietnam, 1946–1966*, rev. ed. (New York, 1966), p. 80. Shaplen is quoted.

52. *NYT*, Mar. 12, 1950.

53. Jean Lartéguy, *The Centurions*, trans. Xan Fielding (New York, 1961), p. 26.

54. Hammer, *Struggle for Indochina*, pp. 168–69, 183.

55. Ibid., pp. 298–99.

56. *Le Monde*, Apr. 6, 1949; Truman, *Memoirs*, vol. 2, *Years of Trial and Hope* (Garden City, 1956), p. 256. See also Chapter 8, below.

57. Quoted in Hammer, *Struggle for Indochina*, p. 216.

58. Jefferson Caffery to Marshall, Jan. 16, 1948, 851G.00/1-1648, Box 80, RG 59.

59. Joseph Buttinger, *Vietnam: A Dragon Embattled*, vol. 2, (New York, 1967), p. 726.

60. Consulate general at Saigon (George M. Abbott) to Acheson, Mar. 18, 1949, 851.01/3-1849, Box 6181, RG 59.

61. D. C. Hopson to Foreign Office, June 14, 1949, FO 371, F9639/1015/86.

62. Lucien Bodard, *The Quicksand War: Prelude to Vietnam*, trans. Patrick O'Brian (Boston, 1967), p. 169.

63. *NYT*, Jan. 3, 1949; CIA, "Review of the World Situation," May 17, 1949, NSC Meetings, Truman Papers, PSF, Box 206.

64. M. A. Colebrook, Saigon consulate, "Labor Report, July 1949, South Vietnam–Indochina," Aug. 22, 1949, 851G.504/8-2249, Box 6184, RG 59.

65. Caffery to Acheson, Jan. 10, 1949, 851G.00/1-1049, Box 80, RG 59.

66. Memo of conversation between Daridan, Butterworth, and Reed, Apr. 13, 1949, *FRUS* (1949), 7:19–20.

67. Edward R. Drachman, *United States Policy toward Vietnam, 1940–1945* (Rutherford, N.J., 1970), p. 51.

68. Walter LaFeber, "Roosevelt, Churchill, and Indochina: 1942–45," *American Historical Review*, 80 (1975):1293.

69. The scholarship on FDR's policy toward Indochina is excellent. With Drachman and LaFeber, see Gary R. Hess, "Franklin Roosevelt and Indochina," *Journal of American History*, 59 (1972):353–68; Christopher Thorne, "Indochina and Anglo-American Relations, 1942–1945," *Pacific Historical Review*, 45 (1976):73–96; George C. Herring, "The Truman Administration and the Restoration of French Sovereignty in Indochina," *Diplomatic History*, 1 (1977):97–117.

70. See statement of John Carter Vincent, *DSB*, Oct. 21, 1945, pp. 644–46.

71. Reed to DOS, Aug. 6, 1946, 851G.50/8–646, Box 6184, RG 59.

72. Edward H. Foley, Jr., to Marshall, Oct. 21, 1948, 851G.114NARCOTICS/10–2148, Box 6182, RG 59; Colebrook to Acheson, Apr. 14, 1949, 851G.114NARCOTICS/4–1449, Box 6182, RG 59.

73. Caffery to Acheson, Jan. 14, 1949, 851G.00/1–1449, Box 80, RG 59.

74. Reed to Butterworth, Feb. 23, 1949, PSA, Box 5.

75. William Gibson (Hanoi) to Acheson, June 30, 1949, 851G.01/6–3049, Box 6181, RG 59.

76. Bodard, *Quicksand War*, p. 234.

77. Memo of conversation between A. G. Trevor Wilson, British consul at Hanoi, and Arthur Ringwalt, U.S. embassy, London, Oct. 20, 1949, 851G.00/10–2049, Box 80, RG 59.

78. Memo of conversation between Stanton and Count J. de la Grandville, counselor of the French embassy in Bangkok, Nov. 25, 1949, 851G.01/11–2549, Box 6182, RG 59.

79. Acheson to Caffery, Feb. 25, 1949, *FRUS* (1949), 7:8–9.

80. Caffery to Acheson, Mar. 16, 1949, *FRUS* (1949) 7:12–14.

81. PPS-51, pp. 1128–33.

82. UM D-26, "To Define U.S. Policy toward South East Asia," Apr. 4, 1949, OES, Box 5. See also Blum, *Drawing the Line*, pp. 112–14.

83. Reed to Butterworth, Apr. 14, 1949, 851G.00/4–1449, Box 80, RG 59.

84. Ogburn, "Requirements for the Security of the Countries of Southeast Asia," Apr. 20, 1949, PSA, Box 4; memo of conversation between H. A. Graves and Reed, Apr. 26, 1949, 851G.01/4–2649, Box 6181, RG 59.

85. "Solution of Indochinese Problem as Proposed by Miss DuBois," attached to covering memo from Reed to Davies, May 9, 1949, PSA, Box 5.

86. Reed to Butterworth, May 16, 1949, PSA, Box 5.

87. Acheson to Abbott, May 2, 1949, *FRUS* (1949), 7:21–22; Acheson to Abbott, May 10, 1949, *FRUS* (1949), 7:23–25; Acheson to Abbott, May 15, 1949, *Pentagon Papers*, 8:194–95. Abbott to Acheson, May 6, 1949, *FRUS* (1949), 7:22–23; Abbott, "Country Paper on Indochina Prepared for the New Delhi Foreign Service Conference," transmitted to Acheson May 6, 1949, *Pentagon Papers*, 8:157.

88. Dean Acheson, *Present at the Creation: My Years in the State Department* (New York, 1969), p. 386.

89. In *FRUS* (1949), vol. 7, see Bruce to secretary of state, May 30 (p. 34); Bruce to secretary of state, June 2 (pp. 36–38); Abbott to secretary of state, June 10 (p. 45).

90. Ibid., "Memorandum by the Department of State to the French Foreign Office," sent to Bruce, June 6 (pp. 38–45). Bruce to secretary of state, June 13 (pp. 45–46); Webb to Bruce, June 16 (pp. 56–57).

91. Ibid., Webb to certain diplomatic and consular offices abroad, June 14 (pp. 53–54). Ibid., Webb to Abbott, June 14 (p. 47); Stanton to secretary of state, June 17 (pp. 58–59). Text of statement of support in *DSB*, July 18, 1949, p. 75.

92. Ogburn to Reed and James L. O'Sullivan, June 28, 1949, PSA, Box 5.

93. Acheson to Abbott, June 29, 1949, *FRUS* (1949), 7:64; Abbott to Acheson, July 5, 1949, *FRUS* (1949) 7:67–68.

94. Reed to Butterworth, July 11, 1949, PSA, Box 5; Gibson to Acheson, July 8, 1949, 851G.01/7–849, Box 6182, RG 59.

95. Bruce to Acheson, July 1, 1949, 851G.01/7–149, Box 6182, RG 59.

96. Butterworth to Rusk, July 22, 1949, PSA, Box 5.

97. Acheson to certain diplomatic and consular offices, July 20, 1949, *FRUS* (1949), 7:1170–71.

98. Text of treaty in *FRUS* (1949), 4:281–85. The North Atlantic Treaty did not immediately create an organization. Instead, it was in early 1949 a statement of trans-Atlantic cooperation designed as a psychological umbrella for Western Europeans fearing Soviet invasion or Communist subversion. See also Timothy Ireland, *Creating the Entangling Alliance: The Origins of the North Atlantic Treaty Organization* (Westport, Conn., 1981); Andrew J. Rotter, "The Origins of the North Atlantic Treaty," *USA Today* (November 1983), pp. 62–64.

99. *Le Monde*, Mar. 26, Apr. 1, 6, and 12, July 24–25, 27, and 28, 1949; Edmond Delage, "Defense de l'Europe de l'Ouest," *Revue de Defense Nationale* (March 1949):316.

100. Final draft of position paper of U.S.–U.K.–Canada Security Conversations, ca. Apr. 1, 1948, *FRUS* (1948), vol. 3, *Western Europe*, p. 75; memo of conversation by the secretary of state, Feb. 14, 1949, *FRUS* (1949), 4:108–110; George W. Perkins to Acheson, Oct. 11, 1949, *FRUS* (1949), vol. 3, *Council of Foreign Ministers: Germany and Austria*, pp. 285–86; Bruce to Acheson, Nov. 21, 1949, *FRUS* (1949), 3:342–43.

101. In *FRUS* (1949), vol. 3, see Acheson to John J. McCloy (high commissioner for Germany), Nov. 21 (pp. 340–42); memo from R. M. Cheseldine (special assistant to the director of the Bureau of German affairs) to Henry Byroade (director of the Bureau of German Affairs), Dec. 14, 1949 (pp. 355–360). See also Truman, *Memoirs*, 2:253; Acheson, *Present at the Creation*, p. 442.

102. *Pentagon Papers*, vol. 1, pt. C, p. 4; Hammer, *Struggle for Indochina*, p. 164; Bernard Fall, ed., *Ho Chi Minh on Revolution* (New York, 1967), p. 442; Archimedes L. A. Patti, *Why Viet Nam? Prelude to America's Albatross* (Berkeley, 1980).

103. Quotation from DOS, *Round Table Discussion on American Policy toward China*, Oct. 7, 1949, p. 226; Acheson to Bruce, "Transcript of Radio Interview with Ho Chi Minh by Harold Isaacs," Apr. 27, 1949, 851G.01/4–2749, Box 6181, RG 59; *New York Herald-Tribune*, Oct. 14, 1949.

104. King C. Chen, *Vietnam and China, 1938–1954* (Princeton, 1969), pp. 195–228.

105. U.S. Congress, Senate Foreign Relations Committee, *Causes, Origins, and Lessons of the Vietnam War: Hearings*, 92d Cong., 2d sess., May 9, 10, 11, 1972, p. 182. A major who served with the OSS in Tonkin likened filing favorable reports on Ho Chi Minh to "dropping stones down a bottomless well."

106. Acheson to Reed, Oct. 9, 1946, *FRUS* (1946), vol. 8, *The Far East*, p. 61.

107. *Pentagon Papers*, vol. 1, pt. C, p. 4.

108. Memo of conversation between H. A. Graves, Butterworth, and others, Mar. 17, 1948, 851G.00/3–1748, Box 80, RG 59.

109. *Pentagon Papers*, vol. 1, pt. A, p. 6.

110. Ibid., vol. 1, pt. B, p. 64.

111. Acheson to consulate at Hanoi, May 20, 1949, *FRUS* (1949), 7:29–30.

112. Charles Yost to Jessup, Aug. 22, 1949, 890.00/11-849, Box C-846, RG 59.

113. Rusk to Acheson, July 16, 1949, 890.00/7-1649, Box C-846, RG 59.

114. "Economic Implementation of U.S. Policy with Respect to South and East Asia," transmitted from R. H. Whitman to Jessup, Aug. 22, 1949, 890.00/8-2249, Box 6923, RG 59.

115. Ogburn to Reed, July 1, 1949, PSA, Box 4.

5. *Shifts in United States Policy toward the Far East and the World, Autumn 1949*

1. *DSB*, Sept. 5, 1949, p. 323-24.

2. Arthur J. Vandenberg, Jr., ed., *The Private Papers of Senator Vandenberg* (Boston, 1952), p. 518.

3. Acheson to Jessup, July 18, 1949, 890.00/7-1849, Box 6923, RG 59.

4. Jessup to Rusk, July 21, 1949, 890.00/7-2149, Box 6923, RG 59; Philip C. Jessup, *The Birth of Nations* (New York, 1974), pp. 26-27; *DSB* Aug. 15, 1949, p. 237.

5. Case to Jessup and Fosdick, Sept. 6, 1949, FW890.00/11-1849, Box C-846, RG 59.

6. Tang Tsou, *America's Failure in China, 1941-1950*, 2 vols. (Chicago, 1963), p. 513.

7. Memo by Jessup, Sept. 30, 1949, 890.00/8-1849, Box 6923, RG 59; DOS, *Round Table Discussion on American Policy toward China*, Oct. 6, 1949, pp. 129-30; memo by Gerald Stryker, Nov. 2, 1949, *FRUS* (1949), vol. 9, *The Far East: China*, pp. 154-60.

8. "Minutes of Meeting of the Secretary and Consultants on the Far East," Oct. 26, 1949, FW 890.00/11-1749, Box C-846, RG 59; Charles W. Yost to Jessup, Aug. 29 (359E), Sept. 1 (359F), 1949, DDRS.

9. Memo by Acheson, "Conversation with the President, Item 1: China and the Far East," Nov. 17, 1949, Acheson Papers, Memos of Conversation, 1949, Box 64, HSTL.

10. Nancy Bernkopf Tucker, "American Policy toward Sino-Japanese Trade in the Postwar Years: Politics and Prosperity," *Diplomatic History*, 8 (1984):183-208.

11. Memo of conversation by Acheson, Oct. 12, 1949, *FRUS* (1949), 9:124-25; memo of conversation by Charlton Ogburn, Jr., Nov. 2, 1949, *FRUS* (1949), 9:160-61; Sir O. Harvey (Paris) to Foreign Office, Nov. 11, 1949, FO 371, F17671/1015/86.

12. Tang Tsou, *America's Failure*, pp. 504-5.

13. See the account by John Leighton Stuart in *Fifty Years in China* (New York, 1954), pp. 239-40.

14. Tang Tsou, *America's Failure*, p. 517; *DSB*, Nov. 28, 1949, p. 799, Jan. 23, 1950, pp. 119-22.

15. Roger Lapham to H. Medill Sarkisan, Jan. 27, 1950, R. Allen Griffin Papers, Hoover Institution on War, Revolution, and Peace, Stanford, Calif., Box 2.

16. Acheson to Stuart, May 15, 1949, *FRUS* (1949), 9:23-24.

17. Memo of conversation by Acheson, Oct. 12, 1949, *FRUS* (1949), 9:124-25.

18. Sir O. Harvey to Foreign Office, Nov. 11, 1949. Acheson also considered supplying arms to anti-Communist guerrillas in China. See "Minutes of Meeting," Oct. 26, 1949.

19. Acheson to the chargé in the Philippines, Oct. 14, 1949, *FRUS* (1949), 9:129-30.

20. Nancy Bernkopf Tucker claims that both Acheson and Ambassador to India Loy Henderson redefined "international obligations" in early 1950 to make them more easily satisfied by the PRC. In my view, she has misread their statements. See Tucker, *Patterns in the Dust: Chinese-American Relations and the Recognition Controversy, 1949-1950* (New York, 1983), p. 192, and my review in *Reviews in American History*, 12 (1984):266-73.

21. "Minutes of Meeting," Oct. 26, 1949.

22. Minutes of Foreign Relations Committee meeting, Jan. 10, 1950, in U.S. Con-

gress, Senate Subcommittee of the Committee on Foreign Relations, *Hearings on the Nomination of Philip C. Jessup to Be United States Representative to the United Nations*, 82d Cong., 1st sess., 1951, p. 792.

23. Quoted in Robert M. Blum, *The United States and Communist China in 1949 and 1950: The Question of Rapprochement and Recognition*, a staff study prepared for the Senate Committee on Foreign Relations (Washington, 1973), p. 4.

24. On the administration's refusal to bolster Taiwan, see Robert M. Blum, *Drawing the Line: The Origin of the American Containment Policy in East Asia* (New York, 1982), pp. 173–77; Tucker, *Patterns In the Dust*, pp. 184–87; William Whitney Stueck, Jr., *The Road to Confrontation: American Policy toward China and Korea, 1947–1950* (Chapel Hill, 1981), pp. 140–42; Warren I. Cohen, "Acheson, His Advisers, and China, 1949–1950" in Dorothy Borg and Waldo Heinrichs, eds., *Uncertain Years: Chinese American Relations, 1947–1950* (New York, 1980), pp. 29–30.

25. Abbott to Acheson, Dec. 29, 1949, 851G.01/12-2949, Box 6182, RG 59; *NYT,* Feb. 2, 1950.

26. Kirk to DOS, Nov. 9, 1949, *FRUS* (1949), vol. 5, *Eastern Europe: The Soviet Union*, p. 673.

27. Memo by George Perkins (assistant secretary of state for European Affairs) to Durward V. Sandifer (deputy assistant secretary of state for U.N. affairs) drafted by Llewellyn E. Thompson (deputy assistant secretary for European affairs), Sept. 23, 1949, *FRUS* (1949), vol. 1, *National Security Affairs: Foreign Economic Policy*, pp. 170–71.

28. Truman, *Memoirs*, vol. 2, *Years of Trial and Hope* (Garden City, 1956), pp. 306–10; Dean Acheson, *Present at the Creation: My Years in the State Department* (New York, 1969), pp. 450–53.

29. "Minutes of the First Meeting of the Policy Planning Staff on the International Control of Atomic Energy," Oct. 12, 1949, *FRUS* (1949), 1:191–92. In *FRUS* (1949), vol. 4, *Western Europe*, see Acheson to Webb, Sept. 26 (pp. 338–39); Acheson to embassy in United Kingdom, Oct. 24 (pp. 344–45).

30. Report of Representative Charles B. Deane, member of the Special Subcommittee of House Committee on Expenditures in the Executive Departments, on trip to the Far East, Oct. 19, 1949, Truman Papers, PSF, Box 177, HSTL.

31. Fosdick to Jessup, Dec. 3, 1949, FW890.00/12-349, Box 6923, RG 59.

32. Rusk to Acheson, July 16, 1949, 890.00/7-1649, Box C-846, RG 59.

33. All quotations from "Minutes of Meeting of the Secretary and the Consultants on the Far East," Oct. 27, 1949, FW890.00/11-1749, Box C-846, RG 59. See also "United States Policy in the Far East," unattributed report, Oct. 18, 1949, 538C, DDRS; Case to Fosdick, Oct. 28, 1949, 474E, DDRS; Jessup to Acheson, "Outline of Far Eastern and Asian Policy for Review with the President," Nov. 14, 1949, *FRUS* (1949), vol. 7, *The Far East and Australasia*, pp. 1209–14.

34. Reed to Butterworth, Apr. 14, 1949, 851.00/4-1449, Box 80, RG 59; "Minutes of Meeting," Oct. 27, 1949.

35. Shohan to Joseph Coppock, May 3, 1949, PSA, Box 5. See also DOS, *Round Table Discussion*, Oct. 7 (pp. 298–99), Oct. 8 (p. 467), 1949.

36. "Minutes of Meeting," Oct. 27, 1949.

37. Case, Fosdick, and Jessup to Acheson, "Tentative Findings on U.S. Policy in the Far East," Sept. 2, 1949, 474B, DDRS.

38. "Minutes of Meeting," Oct. 26, 1949.

39. Abstract of speech by Salant, Dec. 28, 1949 (transmitted Jan. 11, 1950), FO 371, UEE 22/3.

40. Seymour E. Harris, *Foreign Aid and Our Economy,* (Washington, 1950), pp. 39–40.

41. ECA, *Report of the ECA-Commerce Mission to Investigate Possibilities of Increasing Western Europe's Dollar Earnings* (Washington, October 1949), p. 8.

42. Whitney address quoted in *NYT,* May 26, 1949; Steelman address in *DSB,* June 12, 1949, p. 761.

43. Harris, *Foreign Aid,* pp. 7, 11, 72.

44. Charles P. Kindleberger, *The Dollar Shortage* (Boston, 1950), pp. 94, 130–33, 142–43.

45. For an insightful discussion of international Keynesianism during this period, see William S. Borden, *The Pacific Alliance: United States Foreign Economic Policy and Japanese Trade Recovery, 1947–1955* (Madison, Wis., 1984), pp. 9, 19–50. Borden notes the growing influence of Keynesianism on the administration by 1950.

46. Lloyd to Elsey, Dec. 1, 1949, Elsey Papers, Box 61, HSTL.

47. Memo by Lloyd, "Overseas Investment in Point IV," Dec. 3, 1949, Truman Papers, David D. Lloyd Files, Box 20, HSTL.

48. *DSB,* Oct. 10, 1949, p. 550.

49. *DSB,* Sept. 26, 1949, pp. 473–74.

50. Fosdick to Jessup, Oct. 7, 1949, 890.00/11–1849, Box C-846, RG 59; Blum, *Drawing the Line,* pp. 25–30, 125–42.

51. DOS, *Round Table Discussion,* Oct. 6, 1949, pp. 5–6.

52. Case, Fosdick, and Yost to Jessup, Oct. 25, 1949, 890.00/11–1849, Box C-846, RG 59.

53. Case, Fosdick, and Jessup to Acheson, "Tentative Findings," Sept. 2, 1949.

54. "Minutes of Meeting[s]," Oct. 26 and 27, 1949.

55. Yost to Jessup, Case, and Fosdick, Nov. 1, 1949, 538E, DDRS.

56. Fosdick to Jessup, Nov. 4, 1949, 890.00/11–1849, Box C-846, RG 59.

57. Jessup to Butterworth, Nov. 4, 1949, 890.00/11–1849, Box C-846, RG 59.

58. Yost to Fosdick, Jessup, and Case, Nov. 7, 1949, 538G, DDRS.

59. Jessup, *Birth of Nations,* p. 166; Fosdick to Jessup, Nov. 4, 1949.

60. Butterworth to Fosdick, Nov. 17, 1949, PSA, Box 5.

61. Charles Reed to Jessup, Aug. 22, 1949, 851G.00/8–2249, Box 80, RG 59; Case, Fosdick, and Jessup to Acheson, "Tentative Findings," Sept. 2, 1949.

62. Case to Jessup and Fosdick, Sept. 15, 1949, 474C, DDRS; "Minutes of Meeting," Oct. 27, 1949; Case to Fosdick, Oct. 28, 1949.

63. "United States Policy in the Far East," Oct. 18, 1949.

64. Quotations from Fosdick to Jessup, Oct. 7, 1949, 890.00/11–1849, Box C-846, RG 59. See also Fosdick to Jessup, Oct. 25, 1949, 538D, DDRS.

65. Fosdick to Jessup, Dec. 3, 1949 (emphasis in original).

66. Jessup to Acheson, "Outline of Far Eastern and Asian Policy," Nov. 14, 1949; "Minutes of Meeting," Oct. 27, 1949.

67. Davies, "Suggested Course of Action in East and South Asia," July 7, 1949, *FRUS* (1949), vol. 7, *The Far East and Australasia,* pp. 1148–51.

68. Fosdick to Jessup, Nov. 4, 1949; Jessup, *Birth of Nations,* p. 28.

69. Schedule of Ambassador Philip C. Jessup, Jan. 5, 1950, Philip C. Jessup Papers, General Correspondence, 1919–1958, Box 47, Library of Congress.

70. Mark Ethridge to Marshall, Feb. 17, 1947, *FRUS* (1947), vol. 5, *The Near East and Africa,* p. 24; statement by Under Secretary of State for Economic Affairs Will Clayton in Barton J. Bernstein, "Commentary," in Richard S. Kirkendall, ed., *The Truman Period as a Research Field: A Reappraisal, 1972* (Columbia, Mo., 1974), pp. 176–77.

71. *Pentagon Papers,* vol. 1, pt. 4, A-4; *NYT,* Jan. 11, 1949; DOS, *Round Table Discussion,* Oct. 7, 1949, p. 204.

72. Memo of conversation by Butterworth, Sept. 9, 1949, *FRUS* (1949), 7:76–79. The administration was not confident that the French could hold Indochina. See Yost to

Jessup, Case, and Fosdick, Nov. 1, 1949; William Gibson (Hanoi) to Acheson, Nov. 12, 1949, 851G.00/11-1249, Box 80, RG 59; Acheson to embassy in Hanoi, Nov. 12, 1949, 851G.00/11-1249, Box 80, RG 59.

73. CIA, "Review of the World Situation," Oct. 19, 1949, NSC Meetings, Truman Papers, PSF, Box 206, HSTL.

74. Johnson to NSC, June 10, 1949, *Pentagon Papers*, 8:218.

75. PPS-51, "United States Policy toward Southeast Asia," Mar. 29, 1949, *FRUS* (1949), 7:1128-33.

76. For a discussion of the shaping of NSC-48, see Blum, *Drawing the Line*, pp. 165-77, and Michael Schaller, *The American Occupation of Japan: The Origins of the Cold War in Asia* (New York, 1985), pp. 206-7.

77. NSC-48/1, Dec. 23, 1949, *Pentagon Papers*, 8:225-65; NSC-48/2, Dec. 30, 1949, ibid., pp. 265-72. For joint chiefs of staff and Truman quotations see Kenneth W. Condit, *The History of the Joint Chiefs of Staff: The Joint Chiefs of Staff and National Policy*, 4 vols. (Wilmington, 1979), 2:518-19.

78. Acheson, *Present at the Creation*, pp. 457-60, 462.

79. *NYT*, Mar. 2, 1949; "Minutes of Meeting," Oct. 27, 1949; *Pentagon Papers*, 8:257.

80. *NYT*, Jan. 11, 1950; Princeton Seminars (a series of conferences held by Acheson and other members of the Truman administration at Princeton Univ., 1953 and 1954), Feb. 13, 1954, microfilm, Green Library, Stanford Univ.

81. Text of Acheson's National Press Club Speech in *DSB*, Jan. 23, 1950, pp. 111-18.

82. State of the union address, Jan. 4, 1950, *Public Papers of the Presidents of the United States*, Harry S Truman, 1950 (Washington, 1965), p. 5.

83. Charles Wolf, Jr., *Foreign Aid: Theory and Practice in Southern Asia* (Princeton, 1960), p. 44.

84. *DSB*, Jan. 23, 1950, p. 114.

6. The Reconstruction of Japan: The Southeast Asia Connection

1. NSC-41, Feb. 28, 1949, *FRUS* (1949), vol. 9, *The Far East: China*, pp. 826-34. In *FRUS* (1950), vol. 6, *East Asia and the Pacific*, see Johnson to Acheson, Mar. 24 (pp. 625-26); Livingston Merchant to Acheson, Apr. 20 (pp. 628-32); Acheson to Johnson, Apr. 28 (pp. 632-36).

2. Report by Charles H. Boehringer, "Integration of Japan's Economy with Economies of South Asian Countries," n.d. [late January-early February 1950], PSA, Box 2.

3. *NYT*, Jan. 31, 1950; Jerome B. Cohen, *Japan's Postwar Economy* (Bloomington, Ind., 1958), p. 15.

4. Joseph M. Dodge, handwritten notes, n.d., Joseph M. Dodge Papers, Japan, 1950, Box 7, Burton Historical Collection, Detroit Public Library.

5. Boehringer, "Integration of Japan's Economy."

6. Memo from Reid to Tracy Voorhees, Apr. 5, 1950, Dodge Papers, Japan, 1950, Box 1. See also Ada V. Espenshade, "Present Conditions and Future Outlook of Japan's Foreign Trade," *FEER*, Jan. 19, 1950, pp. 68-75; Robert A. Fearey, *The Occupation of Japan: Second Phase, 1948-50* (New York, 1950), p. 137; Joseph M. Dodge, typescript, n.d., Dodge Papers, Japan, 1950, Box 7.

7. Boehringer, "Integration of Japan's Economy."

8. N. Wycoff, "Summary of Selected Countries' Trade with Japan during the Period January through April 1950," Sept. 20, 1950, John D. Sumner Papers, Box 7, HSTL.

9. Stanley Andrews, "Special Report: Coordination of American Economic Aid in

South and Southeast Asia" (draft), Apr. 20, 1950, Stanley Andrews Papers, Box 2, HSTL.

10. Reid to Voorhees, Feb. 27, 1950, Dodge Papers, Japan, 1950, Box 1; Charles J. Shohan to Merchant, Mar. 16, 1950, *FRUS* (1950), 6:58–62; Ogburn to Jessup and Butterworth, Mar. 29, 1950, PSA, Box 5.

11. Memo of conversation by the Advisory Committee on Fiscal and Monetary Problems, Apr. 28, 1950, Dodge Papers, Japan, 1950, Box 5. See also Dodge's handwritten notes (n. 4 above).

12. Doherty to John M. Allison (director of the Office of Northeast Asian Affairs), Mar. 29, 1950, PSA, Box 2.

13. Joyce and Gabriel Kolko, *The Limits of Power: The World and United States Foreign Policy, 1945–1954* (New York, 1972), p. 523; Fearey, *Occupation,* p. 173.

14. Fearey, *Occupation,* pp. 142–43; General Headquarters, Supreme Commander for the Allied Powers, *SCAPINS: Supreme Commander for the Allied Powers' Instructions to the Japanese Government, from 4 September 1945 to 8 March 1952* (Mar. 20, 1952), pp. 491–92, 495–96.

15. *NYT,* Jan. 14, 1949; *SCAPINS,* p. 454; Fearey, *Occupation,* p. 198.

16. *FEER,* Sept. 8, 1949,(p. 308), Dec. 29, 1949 (p. 828); Fearey, *Occupation,* pp. 138–39; N. Wycoff, "Summary of Selected Countries' Trade."

17. Quotation from *NYT,* Mar. 17, 1950. See also *FEER,* Nov. 3, 1949, p. 587; *The Economist,* Dec. 24, 1949, p. 1395; Russell H. Fifield, *The Diplomacy of Southeast Asia: 1945–1958* (New York, 1958), p. 202; *NYT,* Jan. 4, 1950.

18. "Revised Final Draft of the Trade Agreement between the Union of Burma and Occupied Japan," Jan. 20, 1950, PSA, Box 2; "Japanese Trade Agreements," July 19, 1951, R. Allen Griffin Papers, Hoover Institution on War, Revolution, and Peace, Stanford, Calif., Box 10; *The Economist,* Feb. 25, 1950, p. 435; *DSB,* Apr. 3, 1950, p. 525; *FEER,* Mar. 16 (p. 340), May 25 (p. 671), and June 15 (p. 784), 1950.

19. Memo of conversation between Thai Finance Minister Prince Wiwat and officials in the DOS, Sept. 22, 1949, PSA, Box 18.

20. "Analysis of the Situation and Policy in Thailand," unattributed, n.d. [autumn 1949], PSA, Box 19; "Japanese Trade Agreements," July 19, 1951; Boehringer, "Integration of Japan's Economy"; *FEER,* Mar. 9, 1950, p. 318; "State Department Policy Statement on Thailand," Oct. 15, 1950, *FRUS* (1950), 6:1529–39. Japan also signed a trade agreement with the French Union, including Indochina, in May, 1948. See the report by the Foreign Trade and Commerce Division of SCAP, n.d., in Dodge Papers, Japan, 1949, Box 6.

21. Sebald to DOS, Aug. 20, 1949, *FRUS* (1949), vol. 7, *The Far East and Australasia,* pp. 830–40.

22. Butterworth to Acheson, Nov. 30, 1949, *FRUS* (1949), 7:907–8.

23. Jessup to Acheson, Jan. 10, 1950, *FRUS* (1950), 6:1114–15.

24. Memo of conversation by Acheson, Sept. 13, 1949, *FRUS* (1949), 7:858–59.

25. Memo of conversation by Sebald, Sept. 21, 1949, *FRUS* (1949), 7:862–64.

26. Johnson to Acheson and enclosure, Dec. 23, 1949, *FRUS* (1949), 7:922–23. Dean Acheson, *Present at the Creation: My Years in the State Department* (New York, 1969), pp. 558–60.

27. In *FRUS* (1950), vol. 6, see Acheson, memo of conversation with Truman, Feb. 20 (p. 1139); memo of conversation by John Howard (special assistant to the secretary), Apr. 24 (pp. 1175–82). See also Acheson, *Present at the Creation,* pp. 558–60; John Dower, "The Eye of the Beholder," *Bulletin of Concerned Asian Scholars,* 2 (October 1969).

28. Butterworth to Acheson (with attachments), Jan. 18, 1950, *FRUS* (1950), 6:117–29; *DSB,* Apr. 24, 1950, p. 661.

29. Report by Whitman for Jessup, Fosdick, and Case, "Implementation of 'Economic Aspects of U.S. Policy with Respect to South and East Asia,' " Aug. 22, 1949, 890.00/8–2249, Box 6923, RG 59.

30. Shohan to Lacy and Merchant, "Increasing Japanese Trade: Another Way to Skin the Cat," Mar. 9, 1950, PSA, Box 1; Doherty to Allison, Mar. 29, 1950, PSA, Box 2; Shohan to Allison, Apr. 14, 1950, PSA, Box 4.

31. "Possible Methods of Increasing Intra-Regional Trade and Commerce among Countries of South and East Asia," unattributed, n.d. [early April 1950], PSA, Box 3. See also Allison to Butterworth, Mar. 14, 1950, *FRUS* (1950), 6:1223n.2.

32. Doherty to Dodge, June 16, 1950, *FRUS* (1950), 6:1223n.2. Japan's finance minister, Hideo Ikeda, made a similar proposal during a visit to the United States in the spring of 1950. Joseph Dodge regarded it with interest but never energetically promoted it. Dodge to Marquat, May 16, 1950, Dodge Papers, Japan, 1950, Box 3.

33. NSC-61, "A Report to the National Security Council by the Departments of State and Defense on U.S. Economic Aid to Far Eastern Areas," Jan. 27, 1950, NSC Meetings, Truman Papers, PSF, Box 206; Shohan and Lacy to Merchant, Mar. 8, 1950, PSA, Box 1; Reid to Voorhees, Apr. 5, 1950, Dodge Papers, Japan, 1950, Box 1; memo of conversation by the Advisory Committee on Fiscal and Monetary Problems, Apr. 28, 1950. Voorhees's scheme was backed by the findings of a mission to Southeast Asia in early 1950, led by Voorhees's deputy, Robert West, and Agriculture Department official Stanley Andrews. For documentation, see R. W. E. Reid to West and enclosures, Aug. 30, 1949, Dodge Papers, Japan, 1949, Box 3; Voorhees to John P. Loomis, Dec. 22, 1949, and Voorhees to MacArthur, Dec. 31, 1949, "Special Report: Coordination of American Economic Aid in South and Southeast Asia," all in Andrews Papers, Box 2; William S. Borden, *The Pacific Alliance: United States Foreign Economic Policy and Japanese Trade Recovery, 1947–1955* (Madison, Wis., 1984), pp. 126–30; Michael Schaller, *The American Occupation of Japan: The Origins of the Cold War in Asia* (New York, 1985), pp. 223–24.

34. Shohan to Lacy and Merchant, "Increasing Japanese Trade," Mar. 9, 1950.

35. Doherty to Allison, Mar. 29, 1950.

36. "Possible Methods of Increasing Intra-Regional Trade." Shaw to MacArthur, "Commercial Arrangements for Conducting the Foreign Trade of Occupied Japan," Oct. 24, 1949, Dodge Papers, Japan, 1949, Box 4.

37. George H. Owen to Merchant, "DS Views Re Econ. Aspects U.S. Policy toward SEA," Sept. 13, 1949, PSA, Box 5.

38. Acheson to MacArthur, Sept. 9, 1949, *FRUS* (1949), 7:850–52.

39. *New York Herald-Tribune*, Jan. 9, 1950.

40. "Possible Methods of Increasing Intra-Regional Trade."

41. UM D-74, "Development of U.S.–Burma Policy," Dec. 16, 1949, OES, Box 6; *NYT*, Mar. 5, 15, 1950.

42. Case, Fosdick, and Yost to Jessup, Oct. 25, 1949, 890.00/11–1849, Box C-846, RG 59.

43. UM D-74.

44. McGhee to Rusk and Acheson, "U.S. Policy for Burma," Jan. 25, 1950, PSA, Box 7.

45. DOS to embassy in Burma, Feb. 13, 1950, *FRUS* (1950), 6:233.

46. "Needs for United States Economic and Technical Aid in Burma," in Samuel P. Hayes, ed., *The Beginning of American Aid to Southeast Asia: The Griffin Mission of 1950* (Lexington, Mass., 1971), pp. 151–99.

47. Report by Kenneth P. Landon, "Thailand," Nov. 22, 1949, PSA, Box 5; Acheson to Truman, Mar. 9, 1950, *FRUS* (1950), 6:40–43.

48. "Needs for United States Economic and Technical Aid in Thailand," in Hayes, *Beginning of American Aid*, p. 227.

49. Fifield, *Diplomacy,* p. 250.

50. N. Wycoff, "Summary of Selected Countries' Trade."

51. Memo of conversation by Butterworth, Feb. 5, 1950, *FRUS* (1950), 6:1134.

52. Shohan and Lacy to Merchant, Mar. 8, 1950, PSA, Box 1.

53. Acheson, *Present at the Creation,* p. 560; Dodge to MacArthur, May 8, 1950, Dodge Papers, Japan, 1950, Box 3; E. D. Johnson to Dodge, June 7, 1950, Dodge Papers, Japan, 1950, Box 4.

54. Shohan to Lacy and Merchant, "Increasing Japanese Trade," Mar. 9, 1950; Doherty to Allison, Mar. 29, 1950.

55. Shohan and Lacy to Merchant, Mar. 8, 1950; Diehl to Sebald, June 20, 1950, *FRUS* (1950), 6:1223–27; Borden, *Pacific Alliance,* pp. 138–39.

56. Paper by Shohan, "Economic Regionalism in the Far East," Jan. 5, 1950, PSA, Box 5; Reed to Butterworth, Jan. 5, 1950, PSA, Box 4; Shohan to Merchant, Gay, and Lacy, Apr. 26, 1950, PSA, Box 2.

57. Allison to Merchant, Apr. 5, 1950, PSA, Box 3.

58. NSC-61/1, "A Report to the National Security Council by the Executive Secretary on Coordination of U.S. Aid Programs for Far Eastern Areas," May 16, 1950, NSC Meetings, Truman Papers, PSF, Box 206.

59. Report by Sumner, "Coordination of U.S. Assistance in the Far East," Apr. 22, 1950, Sumner Papers, Box 6. See also Michael Schaller, "Securing the Great Crescent: Occupied Japan and the Origins of Containment in Southeast Asia," *Journal of American History,* 69 (1982):409; Schaller, *American Occupation,* pp. 228–29; Borden, *Pacific Alliance,* pp. 130–31.

60. Shohan to Allison, Apr. 14, 1950, PSA, Box 4.

61. "Possible Methods of Increasing Intra-Regional Trade"; Diehl to Sebald, June 20, 1950.

62. Memo of conversation between Jessup and representatives of the British Foreign Office, Mar. 11, 1950, *FRUS* (1950), 6:46–47; Franks to Foreign Office, July 24, 1950, FO 371, FZ 11345/5.

63. British embassy document, "Rice Situation in South East Asia," Mar. 16, 1950, PSA, Box 7. For an earlier clash on the same issue, see Roger Buckley, *Occupation Diplomacy: Britain, the United States, and Japan, 1945–1952* (Cambridge, 1982), pp. 137–39.

64. Memo by W. M. Clyde, Apr. 4, 1950, PSA, Box 2.

65. *The Economist,* June 17, 1950, p. 1316.

7. The Reconstruction of Great Britain: Triangular Trade and the Limits of American Commitment

1. *NYT,* July 15, 1949.

2. Text of communiqué in *DSB,* Aug. 8, 1949, p. 197. Bevin and Cripps quoted in *Business Week,* Oct. 22, 1949, p. 92.

3. *DSB,* Sept. 5, 1949, p. 354; "Tripartite Economic Discussions (Washington), Combined Official Group, Minutes of the First Meeting," Aug. 27, 1949, Council of Foreign Ministers (CFM) Files, Lot M-88, Box 143, RG 59.

4. Interview with Lord Franks, Oral History Interview Collection, HSTL.

5. Hoyer Millar to Roger Makins, Aug. 5, 1949, FO 371, UE 5182/150/53.

6. Summary of secretary's daily meeting, Aug. 8, 15, and 17, 1949, OES, Box 1.

7. Oral History Interview with Lord Franks: Hoyer Millar to Makins, July 2, 1949, FO 371, UE 4272/150/53G; Hoyer Millar to Makins, Aug. 24, 1949, FO 371, UE 5526/150/53G.

8. Memo of conversation with Norris Dodd by John Strachey, July 20, 1949, UE 5327/150/53.

9. Truman's speech in *NYT*, Aug. 30, 1949. Quotation from minute by K. Pridham, Aug. 31, 1949, FO 371, UE 5541/150/53.

10. George F. Kennan, *Memoirs: 1925–1950* (Boston, 1967), p. 487; Policy Planning Staff, "Position Paper for the Discussions with the British and Canadians on Pound-Dollar Problems," Sept. 3, 1949, *FRUS* (1949), vol. 4, *Western Europe*, pp. 822–30.

11. "Draft: Possible Final Comuniqué of U.S.-U.K.-Canadian Financial Talks," Sept. 7, 1949, John W. Snyder Papers, Turkey–United Kingdom (Dollar Crisis), Box 34, HSTL; text of communiqué, Anglo-American-Canadian Financial Talks, *DSB*, Sept. 26, 1949, pp. 473–75.

12. See series of telegrams, Franks to Foreign Office, Sept. 7, 1949 (FO 371, UE 5674/150/53); Sept. 13 (FO 371, UE 5940/150/53); Sept. 18 (FO 371, UE 5898/150/53).

13. Makins to Sir William Strang, Apr. 6, 1949, FO 371, UE 2264/150/53G.

14. "Anglo-Canadian-American Economic Talks: Second Meeting," July 8, 1949, FO 371, UE 4292/150/53G.

15. Quotation in Foreign Office to embassy in Washington, Sept. 16, 1949, FO 371, UE 5898/150/53. See also minutes of cabinet meeting, Aug. 29, 1949, CAB 128, CM53(49)1; statement by Cripps to U.S. and Canadian ministers, Sept. 7, 1949, CAB 129, CP(49)191; Wilson-Smith to Foreign Office, Sept. 13, 1949, FO 371, UE 5953/150/53; memo of conversation between U.S. and U.K. officials, Sept. 20, 1949, 890.00/10-1449, Box C-846, RG 59.

16. *NYT*, Jan. 3, 1950.

17. Text of communiqué, Anglo-American-Canadian Financial Talks, pp. 473–74.

18. *NYT*, Aug. 27, 1949.

19. *NYT*, Aug. 28, 1949; ECA, *Report of ECA-Commerce Mission to Investigate Possibilities of Increasing Western Europe's Dollar Earnings* (Washington, October 1949).

20. Quotation in *NYT*, Oct. 23, 1949. See also "Tripartite Economic Discussions".

21. *NYT*, Nov. 13, 1949; ECA, Special Commission to the United Kingdom, *The Sterling Area: An American Analysis* (London, 1951), p. 101.

22. Memo of conversation between Acheson and Robert Schuman, Sept. 26, 1949, Acheson Papers, Memos of Conversation, 1949, Box 64, HSTL.

23. Memo of conversation between Acheson and Sir Oliver Franks, Oct. 18, 1949, Acheson Papers, Memos of Conversation, 1949, Box 64.

24. Address before the convention of the National Foreign Trade Council, Nov. 2, 1949, *DSB*, Nov. 14, 1949, p. 747. ECA, *Sterling Area*, p. 101.

25. *NYT*, Aug. 30, 1949.

26. The president's economic report to Congress, Jan. 6, 1950, *Public Papers of the President's of the United States*, Harry S Truman, 1950 (Washington, 1965), pp. 29–30.

27. *NYT*, Jan. 3, 1950.

28. Memo from Acheson to Truman and attachment, Feb. 16, 1950, *FRUS* (1950), vol. 1, "National Security Affairs; Foreign Economic Policy," pp. 834–46.

29. Truman to Gray, Apr. 3, 1950, *Public Papers*, Truman, 1950, p. 239. See also William S. Borden, *The Pacific Alliance: United States Foreign Economic Policy and Japanese Trade Recovery, 1947–1955* (Madison, Wis., 1984), pp. 35–43.

30. DOS, *Round Table Discussion on American Policy toward China*, Oct. 6, 1949, pp. 31–32.

31. *NYT*, Nov. 13, 1949.

32. Lloyd to Elsey, Dec. 1, 1949, Elsey Papers, Box 61.

33. Oral history interview with Franks; Acheson notes, "The Uncommitted Peo-

ples," Princeton Seminars (held by Acheson and other members of Truman administration at Princeton Univ., 1953 and 1954), microfilm, Green Library, Stanford Univ.

34. Quotations in *NYT*, Aug. 30, 1949. See also the president's midyear economic report, July 11, 1949, *Public Papers of the Presidents, Harry S Truman, 1949* (Washington, 1964), p. 366.

35. U.K. delegation at Colombo to Foreign Office, Jan. 9, 1950, FO 371, UEE 2/4.

36. Note by Robert Hall, Treasury, "Exports to the United States," Jan. 11, 1950, PREM 8/1185.

37. Minutes of cabinet meeting, Apr. 3, 1950, CAB 128, CM17(50)3.

38. *FEER*, June 1, 1950, p. 705.

39. Comment by Nitze, Oct. 10, 1953, Princeton Seminars. For the effects of devaluation on British economic problems, see also *NYT*, Jan. 4, 1950; *FEER*, Feb. 16, 1950, p. 202; minutes of a meeting of the DOS Rubber Advisory Panel, Mar. 6, 1950, PSA, Box 2; *Business Week*, Apr. 15, 1950, p. 129; *The Economist*, June 24, 1950, p. 1404; Raymond F. Mikesell, *Foreign Exchange in the Postwar World* (New York, 1954), p. 149.

40. *NYT*, July 7, 1949; Douglas to Acheson, July 7, 1949, 841.5151/7–749, Box C-556, RG 59; summary of secretary's daily meeting, July 8, 1949, OES, Box 1; "Malaya: Possible Projects from MAP $75,000,000," unattributed, n.d., PSA, Box 4.

41. Summary of secretary's daily meeting, Sept. 8, 1949, OES, Box 1.

42. "Tripartite Economic Discussions (Washington): Report from the Working Group on Commodities and Stockpiling," Sept. 10, 1949, CFM Files, Lot M-88, Box 143, RG 59.

43. Text of communiqué, Anglo-American-Canadian Financial Talks, p. 474.

44. "Report on the Tripartite Economic Discussions at the Official Level in Washington, from 27th August to 2nd September, 1949," Oct. 4, 1949, FO 371, UE 6327/150/53G.

45. Franks to Foreign Office, Sept. 19, 1949, FO 371, UE 5984/150/53G.

46. Harlan P. Bramble to Henry R. Labouisse, Jr., Nov. 30, 1949, PSA, Box 2; Donald D. Kennedy, "Implementation of Rubber Policy," n.d. [late 1949], PSA, Box 2; Glenn H. Snyder, *Stockpiling Strategic Materials: Politics and National Defense* (San Francisco, 1966), pp. 105–13.

47. Statement by Webb, Sept. 27, 1949, U.S. Congress, House Committee on Foreign Affairs, *International Technical Cooperation Act: Hearings*, 81st Cong., 1st sess., 1950, pp. 38–39; address by Joseph C. Satterthwaite to 330th Field Artillery Association, Oct. 1, 1949, *DSB*, Oct. 10, 1949, p. 556; *NYT*, Jan. 3, 1950.

48. First Kennedy quotation in memo by Donald D. Kennedy, "Proposed Department of Commerce Action with Respect to Synthetic Rubber," Sept. 23, 1949, OES, Box 5. Second Kennedy quotation in Kennedy, "Implementation of Rubber Policy." See also Winthrop G. Brown to Webb, "Implementation of U.S. Rubber Policy," Aug. 4, 1949, PSA, Box 14; summary of secretary's daily meeting, Sept. 13, 1949, OES, Box 1.

49. Kennedy to Robert C. Turner, n.d. [mid-November, 1949], PSA, Box 2; F. G. Jarvis and Lacy to Rusk, May 1, 1950, PSA, Box 4; Armstrong, Bramble, Alexander, and Thorp to Webb and Acheson, Dec. 19. 1949, PSA, Box 4; U.K. record of informal meeting of Continuing Consultative Committee, Nov. 23, 1949, T 236, 110/196/05.

50. Statement by Webb, Sept. 27, 1949, Committee on Foreign Affairs, *Technical Cooperation Act*, p. 38.

51. U.S. Dept. of Commerce, *Rubber: Second Annual Report* (Washington, 1950), pp. 18–19; U.K. record of informal meeting of Continuing Consultative Committee, Jan. 4, 1950, FO 371, UEE 53/2.

52. *NYT*, Mar. 4, 1950.

53. Ibid., April 13, June 16, 1950; Kok Wah Fong, "Economic Relations between

Malaya and the United States of America," M.A. thesis, Stanford Univ., 1953, p. 48; *The Economist*, May 6, 1950, pp. 1013–17.

54. *WSJ*, Dec. 16, 1949.

55. U.S. Dept. of the Interior, Bureau of Mines, *Minerals Yearbook: 1950* (Washington, 1953), p. 1221.

56. Ibid., p. 1217; International Tin Study Group, *Tin and the Tin Study Group, 1948–52,* (The Hague, 1953), p. 4, and *Tin, 1950–1951: A Review of the World Tin Industry* (The Hague, 1952), p. 56; Fong, "Economic Relations," pp. 93, 99–100; U.K. record of informal meeting of Continuing Consultative Committee, Nov. 30, 1949, T 236, OF 110/196/08.

57. William Fox, *Tin: The Working of a Commodity Agreement* (London, 1974), pp. 210–11; memo, "Proposed Position for the United States Delegation at the Fifth Meeting of the International Tin Study Group," Feb. 15, 1950, PSA, Box 3; *The Economist*, Apr. 1, 1950, p. 734.

58. Minutes of meeting including Brown, Labouisse, Bramble, and others, Nov. 3, 1949, PSA, Box 3.

59. Labouisse to Webb, Nov. 15, 1949, 841.5151/11-1549, Box C-556, RG 59; Jarvis and Shohan to Reed, Dec. 14, 1949, PSA, Box 3.

60. ECA, *Sterling Area*, p. 77.

61. *NYT*, Apr. 5 and 13, June 16, 1950; Fong, "Economic Relations," p. 48.

62. U.S. Congress, House Committee on Armed Services, *President's Recommendations Concerning Synthetic Rubber: Hearings before a Special Subcommittee,* 81st Cong., 2d sess., Feb. 23, 1950, pp. 5431–52, 5463–72. Firestone quotation, p. 5495.

63. Ibid., Feb. 20, 1950, p. 5358.

64. Princeton Seminars, Oct. 10, 1953.

65. Jarvis and Lacy to Rusk, May 1, 1950.

66. House Committee on Armed Services, *President's Recommendations,* Mar. 14, 1950, pp. 5557–64.

67. Great Britain, Colonial Office, *Annual Report on North Borneo* (London, 1949), p. 6; *NYT*, Sept. 14, 1949, Apr. 12, May 15, 1950; *The Economist*, Nov. 12, 1949, p. 1045, and May 13, 1950, p. 1083.

68. Statement by Elliot, June 30, 1950, U.S. Congress, House Committee on Armed Services, *Stockpiling of Strategic and Critical Materials: Hearings before a Special Subcommittee,* 81st Cong., 2d sess., 1950, p. 7664.

69. *Annual Report on the Federation of Malaya, 1950* (London, 1951), p. 73.

70. Statement by Elliot, June 30, 1950, Committee on Armed Services, *Stockpiling,* p. 7664; memo of conversation including Shohan, Jarvis, and Thai Ambassador Kridakon, July 5, 1950, PSA, Box 2.

71. *WSJ*, Feb. 20, 1950; *Annual Report on the Federation of Malaya, 1950,* p. 74; *The Economist*, Apr. 8, 1950, p. 792; "United States Tin Stockpile Negotiations," joint note by the secretary of state for the colonies and the minister of supply, Jan. 9, 1950, FO 371, UES 1541/8; United Kingdom delegation at Colombo to Foreign Office, Jan. 10, 1950, FO 371, UEE 2/5; Foreign Office to embassy in Washington, Jan. 19, 1950, FO 371, UES 1541/5; Hoyer Millar to Foreign Office, Feb. 8, 1950, FO 371, UES 1541/15; Hoyer Millar to Foreign Office, Feb. 13, 1950; FO 371, UES 1541/17.

72. Princeton Seminars, Oct. 10, 1953. See also memo by Shohan, "Trade Policy and Its Implementation," Aug. 23, 1949, PSA, Box 4; *NYT*, Sept. 7, 1949.

73. J. W. F. Rowe, *Primary Commodities in International Trade* (Cambridge, 1965), p. 156; Fong, "Economic Relations," p. 103; Fox, *Tin,* pp. 216–18; John J. Schanz, Jr., "The United States and a Post War Tin Control Agreement," Ph.D. diss., Pennsylvania

State Univ., 1954, pp. 193–96; *The Economist*, July 30, 1949, pp. 254–56, Dec. 3, 1949, p. 1260, May 6, 1950, p. 1026; International Tin Study Group, *Tin and the Tin Study Group, 1948–52* (The Hague, 1953), pp. 14–15.

74. Quotation from statement by Sir G. Clauson, Foreign Office, Feb. 24, 1950, FO 371, UES 1541/21. See also Colonial Office, weekly report on Malaya Feb. 10–16, 1950, FO 371, FZ 1015/9.

75. "Sterling Assets of Overseas Countries" (table), Nov. 14, 1949, PREM 8/1187.

76. *NYT*, Dec. 28, 1949, Apr. 25, 1950.

77. Memo by Treasury, "Sterling Balances of the Sterling Area," Aug. 24, 1949, CAB 129, CP(49)179; Webb to Kennan, Aug. 26, 1949, *FRUS* (1949) 4:820–21.

78. Text of communiqué, Anglo-American-Canadian Financial Talks, pp. 474–75; Labouisse to Webb, Nov. 15, 1949.

79. Memo of conversation by Acheson, Jan. 6, 1950, Acheson Papers, Memos of Conversation, 1950, Box 65.

80. Memo of conversation by Acheson, Jan. 24, 1950, Acheson Papers, Memos of Conversation, 1950, Box 65.

81. Paper prepared by British embassy, "Sterling Balances and South East Asia," Apr. 17, 1950, *FRUS* (1950), vol. 3, *Western Europe*, pp. 1632–39. See also Franks to Foreign Office, Apr. 13, 1950, FO 371, FZ 1112/10.

82. Memo of conversation by Acheson, May 5, 1950, *FRUS* (1950), 3:1639–41.

83. Memo by the chancellor of the exchequer, "The Sterling Balances," May 23, 1950, PREM 8/1187, EPC(50)58.

84. Malaya Monthly Political Intelligence Reports, February–April 1950, FO 371, FZ 10116/3–6; 473 H.C. Deb. 5s., Apr. 6, 1950, col. 1368–76.

85. *NYT*, Apr. 13 and 16, 1950. (Quotation from latter.)

86. MacDonald to Foreign Office, Mar. 23, 1949, FO 371, F 4545/1073/61G. See also William Langdon to DOS, "Meeting of the British Defence Coordination Committee, Far East," May 6, 1949, PSA, Box 14.

87. MacDonald to Foreign Office, Nov. 6, 1949, FO 371, F 16662/1015/86; memo by Bevin, Nov. 26, 1949, CAB 129, CP(49)244; MacDonald to Foreign Office, "Summary of Impressions and Suggestions" following a trip to Indochina, Nov. 28, 1949, FO 371, F 17833/1026/86; MacDonald to Foreign Office, Dec. 19, 1949, FO 371, F 19106/1055/86.

88. Quotation in Bruce to Acheson, Nov. 23, 1949, 851G.01/11-2349, Box 6182, RG 59. See also George M. Abbott to Acheson, Nov. 18, 1949, 851G.00/11-1849, Box 80, RG 59; excerpt from telegram from Malcolm MacDonald, ca. Dec. 6, 1949, PSA, Box 5.

89. Julius Holmes to Acheson, Dec. 5, 1949, 851G.01/12-549, Box 6182, RG 59.

90. Record of meeting at the DOS, Sept. 13, 1949, RO 371, F 14115/1025/86G.

91. R. H. Scott to Attlee, Dec. 29, 1949, FO 371, FF 1051/4.

92. Memo of conversation with Bevin by Dening, Dec. 29, 1949, FO 371, F 19627/1055/86.

93. Paper by British embassy, "French Indo-China," Jan. 6, 1950, PSA, Box 7.

94. Statement by Bevin at Colombo conference, Jan. 12, 1950, FO 371, FF 1051/22. Arthur R. Ringwalt (U.S. embassy, London), to R. H. Scott, Jan. 21, 1950, FO 371, FF 1016/31.

95. Memo of conversation between Bevin and French ambassador, Feb. 8, 1950, FO 371, FF 1051/47; Gibbs (Saigon) to Foreign Office, Mar. 6, 1950, FO 371, FF 1195/1.

96. Quotations from Ministry of Defence to GHQ, Far East Land Forces, June 28, 1950, FO 371, FF 1194/24. See also MacDonald to Dening, Feb. 7, 1950, FO 371, FF 1103/1; "Supply of Arms for French Indo China," July 7, 1950, FO 371, FF 1194/24G.

97. Roderick Barclay, *Ernest Bevin and the Foreign Office, 1932–1969* (London, 1975), p. 69.

98. Percy Spender, *Exercises in Diplomacy* (New York, 1969), p. 194; memo of conversation between Roger Makins, Sir Percivale Liesching, and Percy Spender, Jan. 9, 1950, FO 371, FZ 1102/4.

99. Quotations from Spender, *Exercises*, pp. 196, 200, 216, 251, and draft paper by Spender, "Economic Policy in South-East Asia," Jan. 10, 1950, FO 371, FZ 1102/4. See also Guy Wint, *Southeast Asia and Its Future* (London, 1951), pp. 30–31.

100. Quotation from Spender, *Exercises*, p. 218. See also extract of 8th meeting of Commonwealth conference at Colombo, Jan. 12, 1950, FO 371, FZ 1102/15.

101. Spender, *Exercises*, p. 195.

102. Memo of conversation by Acheson, Jan. 6, 1950, Acheson Papers, Memos of Conversation, 1950, Box 65.

103. Lord Strang, *Home and Abroad* (London, 1956), p. 240.

104. Commonwealth Relations Office (Symon) to high commissioner in Australia (Garnett), Apr. 4, 1950, FO 371, FZ 1102/55. Sir Leslie Rowan to E. A. Hitchman, Apr. 21, 1950, FO 371, FZ 1102/89.

105. Memo of conversation between Bevin and MacDonald, Apr. 27, 1950, FO 371, FZ 1102/92.

106. Gay to Merchant, June 21, 1950, PSA, Box 1.

107. Address by George McGhee to Annual Press Institute, Jan. 19, 1950, *DSB*, Jan. 30, 1950, p. 170. McGhee's speech was much appreciated by the British embassy. See Hoyer Millar to Foreign Office, Jan. 30, 1950, FO 371, FZ 10345/2.

108. Minute by R. H. Scott for Strang, Mar. 10, 1950, FO 371, FZ 1022/15.

109. Memo of conversation between Plimsoll and Edmund H. Kellogg, Mar. 29, 1950, PSA, Box 2.

110. In *FRUS* (1950), vol. 6, *East Asia and the Pacific,* see Pete Jarman to Acheson, Mar. 13 (pp. 53–54), Webb to embassy in Australia, Mar. 18 (p. 63), Acheson to embassy in Australia, Apr. 19 (pp. 81–82).

111. Memo of conversation by Butterworth, Sept. 9, 1949, *FRUS* (1949), vol. 7, *The Far East and Australasia,* pp. 76–79.

8. The Reconstruction of Western Europe and the Beginning of United States Aid to Southeast Asia

1. Merchant to Butterworth, Mar. 7, 1950, *FRUS* (1950), vol. 6, *East Asia and the Pacific,* pp. 750–51.

2. Memo by James L. O'Sullivan, "Preliminary Talks as to Indochina," Sept. 28, 1949, *FRUS* (1949), vol. 7, *The Far East and Australasia,* pp. 83–89; Bruce to Acheson, Sept. 23, 1949, 851G.01/9–2349, Box 6182, RG 59.

3. Kenneth P. Landon to Merchant, Oct. 11, 1949, PSA, Box 4, memo by O'Sullivan, Sept. 28, 1949, PSA, Box 4.

4. In *FRUS* (1949), vol. 7, see memo by O'Sullivan, Sept. 28 (p. 85); Butterworth to Acheson, Oct. 20 (pp. 92–94); Acheson to Arthur S. Abbott, Oct. 21 (p. 94).

5. Memo by O'Sullivan, Sept. 28, 1949.

6. Acheson to Abbott, June 29, 1949, *FRUS* (1949), 7:64; "Minutes of Meeting of the Secretary and the Consultants on the Far East," Oct. 26, 1949, FW 890.00/11–1749, Box C–846, RG 59.

7. Quotation from Acheson to Bruce, Dec. 1, 1949, *FRUS* (1949), 7:101–2. Memo of conversation by Charles S. Reed, Nov. 28, 1949, 851G.01/11–2849, Box 6182, RG 59.

8. Memo of conversation by Butterworth, Sept. 9, 1949, *FRUS* (1949), 7:76–79.

9. J. L. O'Sullivan, "French Indochina," Nov. 25, 1949, PSA, Box 5.

10. William M. Gibson to DOS, Nov. 19, 1949, 851G.00/11-1949, Box 80, RG 59; Dallas M. Coors to DOS, Dec. 7, 1949, 851G.00/12-749, Box 80, RG 59.

11. Summary record of meeting of U.S. ambassadors at Paris, Oct. 22, 1949, *FRUS* (1949), vol. 4, *Western Europe,* pp. 494-96.

12. Bruce to Acheson, Dec. 11, 1949, *FRUS* (1949), 7:105-10.

13. Franks to Foreign Office, Dec. 17, 1949, FO 371, F 18982/10345/61.

14. Butterworth to Rusk, Jan. 5, 1950, *FRUS* (1950), 6:690-91.

15. Acheson to embassy in the Philippines, Jan. 7, 1950, *FRUS* (1950), 6:691-92.

16. In *FRUS* (1950), vol. 6, see Butterworth to Abbott Jan. 20 (pp. 698-700); memo by Edmund A. Gullion, Jan. 26 (pp. 700-702).

17. In *FRUS* (1950), vol. 6, see Abbott to Acheson, Jan. 29, and editor's footnote (p. 702); Acheson to embassy in the United Kingdom, Jan. 30 (pp. 703-4); memo from Acheson to Truman, Feb. 2 (pp. 716-17); memo of conversation by Acheson, Feb. 3 (p. 719).

18. Bruce to Acheson, Feb. 6, 1950, *FRUS* (1950), 6:721-22.

19. Arthur Ringwalt to R. H. Scott, Jan. 21, 1950, FO 371, FF 1016/31.

20. Dening to Sir Geoffrey Thompson (Bangkok), Jan. 26, 1950, FO 371, FZ 1022/3.

21. Ringwalt to Scott, Jan. 31, 1950, FO 371, FF 1051/31.

22. Kinna to embassy in Paris, Feb. 1, 1950, FO 371, FF 1051/33.

23. Bruce to Acheson, Dec. 22, 1949, *FRUS* (1949), 7:112-13.

24. "Roof off everything" in Princeton Seminars (held by Acheson and other members of Truman administration at Princeton Univ., 1953 and 1954), Oct. 10, 1953, microfilm, Green Library, Stanford Univ. See also Dean Acheson, *Present at the Creation: My Years in the State Department* (New York, 1969), pp. 469-70.

25. Edwin Stanton to Acheson, Aug. 31, 1949, 851G.01/8-3149, Box 6182, RG 59.

26. King C. Chen, *Vietnam and China: 1938-1954* (Princeton, 1969), pp. 229-32; Yano Tōru, "Who Set the Stage for the Cold War in Southeast Asia?" in Yōnosuke Nagai and Akira Iriye, eds., *The Origins of the Cold War in Asia* (New York, 1977), pp. 330-31, 335.

27. *NYT,* Feb. 1, 1950.

28. Charles Yost to George W. Perkins, Jan. 31, 1950, *FRUS* (1950), 6:710-11.

29. *NYT,* Feb. 2, 4, 1950.

30. Lacy to Merchant, Feb. 14, 1950, PSA, Box 7; Merchant to Lacy, Mar. 10, 1950, PSA, Box 8.

31. Stanton to Acheson, Mar. 1, 1950, *FRUS* (1950), 6:747-48; Lacy to Merchant, Mar. 10, 1950, PSA, Box 8.

32. Lacy to Merchant, Feb. 14, 1950.

33. All but the last quotation in memo of conversation by Acheson, Feb. 16, 1950, *FRUS* (1950), 6:730-33; last quotation in memo of conversation by Merchant, Feb. 16, 1950, *FRUS* (1950), 6:733.

34. Quotations in draft telegram by Lacy and Elim O'Shaughnessy, Mar. 7, 1950, ibid.; and Merchant to Lacy, Mar. 10, 1950. See also Butterworth to Merchant, Feb. 17, 1950, *FRUS* (1950), 6:738-39; Charles J. Shohan to Merchant, Mar. 16, 1950, ibid., p. 59; Charlton Ogburn to Butterworth, Mar. 21, 1950, ibid., pp. 766-67; memo of conversation between U.S. and French officials, Mar. 16, 1950, PSA, Box 8. The difference between Lacy's strong advocacy of an evolutionary statement on Feb. 14 and the "milk and water" draft of the telegram of Mar. 7 was O'Shaughnessy's participation in the latter.

35. Stanton to Acheson, Feb. 17, 1950, *FRUS* (1950), 6:738-39.

36. Jessup to Butterworth, Mar. 20, 1950, PSA, Box 8. See also memo by William Gibson, Mar. 20, 1950, ibid.

37. Butterworth to Jessup, Mar. 21, 1950, PSA, Box 8.

38. In *FRUS* (1950), vol. 6, see Acheson to Bruce, Mar. 29 (pp. 768–71); Gullion to DOS, Apr. 4 (p. 771n.); Bruce to DOS, Apr. 7 (p. 771n.); Gullion to DOS, Apr. 8 (pp. 773–76). In late March, under attack by Joseph McCarthy, Butterworth was relieved of his job at Far East and made a special adviser on Japan. In early May he was appointed ambassador to Sweden. Dean Rusk took over at Far East.

39. Speech to the American Legion, Aug. 29, 1949, *NYT*, Aug. 30, 1949. See also state of the union address, Jan. 4, 1950, *Public Papers of the Presidents of the United States, Harry S Truman, 1950* (Washington, 1965), p. 5; annual budget message, Jan. 9, 1950, ibid., p. 59.

40. European Recovery Program, *Second Report of the Organization for European Economic Cooperation* (Paris, n.d. [February 1950]), pp. 23, 208.

41. Bonesteel to John Ohly, Mar. 29, 1950, *FRUS* (1950), vol. 3, *Western Europe*, pp. 36–40.

42. Salant to Willard Thorp, Mar. 20, Apr. 27, 1950, Salant Papers, Box 2, HSTL.

43. Statement by Acheson, Mar. 30, 1950, U.S. Congress, Senate Committee on Foreign Relations, *An Act for International Development: Hearings*, 81st Cong., 2d sess., p. 5.

44. James Webb to embassy in the Netherlands, Sept. 29, 1949, *FRUS* (1949), 7:500; *NYT*, Aug. 25, 1949.

45. George McTurnan Kahin, *Nationalism and Revolution in Indonesia* (Ithaca, 1952), p. 442.

46. Robert J. McMahon, *Colonialism and Cold War: The United States and the Struggle for Indonesian Independence, 1945–49* (Ithaca, 1981), pp. 302–3.

47. Chapin to Acheson, Nov. 1, 1949, *FRUS* (1949), 7:558–59.

48. In *FRUS* (1949), vol. 7, see Chapin to Acheson, Nov. 2 (pp. 562–63); Chapin to Acheson, Dec. 22 (p. 584); Acheson to consulate general at Batavia, Dec. 27 (p. 587); *NYT*, Dec. 25, 1949.

49. Memo from Acheson to Truman, Jan. 9, 1950, *FRUS* (1950), 6:954–66.

50. Jessup to Rusk, Feb. 3, 1950, *FRUS* (1950), 6:978n.; Acheson to embassy in Indonesia, Feb. 7, 1950, *FRUS* (1950), 6:978.

51. Letter from Herbert E. Gaston to R. Djuanda, Feb. 10, 1950, Sumner Papers, Box 6, HSTL.

52. Samuel P. Hayes, ed., *The Beginning of American Aid to Southeast Asia: The Griffin Mission of 1950* (Lexington, Mass., 1971), pp. 281, 294–95.

53. Report of Rep. Charles B. Deane, member of the Special Subcommittee of House Committee on Expenditures in the Executive Departments, on trip to the Far East, Oct. 19, 1949, Truman Papers, PSF, Box 177.

54. F. G. Jarvis to Shohan and O'Sullivan, Feb. 2, 1950, PSA, Box 2. When an American entrepreneur named Matthew Fox persuaded the Indonesians to give him virtual control over the islands' foreign trade for ten years—Fox exchanged a $100,000 loan for 51 percent of the voting stock in a monopoly trading corporation—the State Department threatened to prosecute. The department argued Fox's arrangement restricted access to the Indonesian market. See A. Merle Cochran to Acheson, Jan. 19, 1950, *FRUS* (1950), 6:967–69; Acheson to Cochran, Feb. 10, 1950, ibid., p. 979; Roger C. Dixon to Winthrop G. Brown, Mar. 9, 1949, 851G.602/2–949, Box 6184, RG 59.

55. Cochran to Webb, May 18, 1950, *FRUS* (1950), 6:1023–25.

56. Abbott to DOS, Dec. 17, 1949, 851G.5045/12–1749, Box 6184, RG 59.

57. Chen, *Vietnam and China*, pp. 235–36; *NYT,* Mar. 1, 1950; Merchant to Butterworth, Mar. 7, 1950, *FRUS* (1950), 6:750–51; Lacy to Rusk, Mar. 30, 1950, PSA, Box 7.

58. *NYT,* Apr. 2, 1950.

59. *FEER,* Apr. 27, 1950, p. 540; *NYT,* Jan. 12, Mar. 1, Apr. 23, 24, 1950.

60. *Pentagon Papers*, vol. 1, sec. 2, pt. A, pp. 17–18.

61. Bruce to Acheson, Jan. 31, 1950, *FRUS* (1950), 6:704–5.

62. *NYT,* Feb. 15, 1950.

63. Country report by the Bureau of Far Eastern Affairs for the director of the Mutual Defense Assistance Program (James Bruce), n.d. [Feb. 16, 1950], *FRUS* (1950), 6:735–38.

64. Griffin to Acheson, May 4, 1950, *FRUS* (1950) 6:794–98. See also *Pentagon Papers*, Gravel ed., 4 vols. (Boston, 1971), 1:76: "A Communist take-over in France was a real possibility."

65. U.S. delegation at Tripartite Foreign Ministers Conference (London) to Webb, May 9, 13, 1950, *FRUS* (1950), 3:1021, 1056.

66. See, for example, Acheson to Bruce, Oct. 19, 1949, *FRUS* (1949), 4:469–72.

67. Memo of conversation by Acheson, Feb. 14, 1949, *FRUS* (1949), 4:469–72.

68. Stephen E. Ambrose, *Rise to Globalism: American Foreign Policy, 1938–1976*, rev. ed. (New York, 1976), p. 181.

69. Harry S Truman, *Memoirs*, vol. 2, *Years of Trial and Hope* (Garden City, 1956), p. 253.

70. John Foster Dulles, *War or Peace?* (New York, 1950), p. 157.

71. Truman to Acheson, Jan. 31, 1950, *FRUS* (1950), vol. 1, *National Security Affairs; Foreign Economic Policy*, pp. 141–42.

72. See, for example, Ambrose, *Rise to Globalism*, pp. 188–91; Walter LaFeber, *America, Russia and the Cold War: 1945–1971*, 2d ed. (New York, 1971), pp. 90–91; Acheson, *Present at the Creation*, pp. 486–97; Paul Y. Hammond, "NSC-68: Prologue to Rearmament," in Warner R. Schilling, Paul Y. Hammond, and Glenn H. Snyder, *Strategy, Politics, and Defense Budgets* (New York, 1962), pp. 267–378; John Lewis Gaddis, *Strategies of Containment: A Critical Appraisal of Postwar American National Security Policy* (New York, 1982), pp. 89–126.

73. NSC-68 is reprinted in *FRUS* (1950), 1:234–92.

74. Acheson, *Present at the Creation*, p. 489.

75. See Acheson to Bruce, Apr. 21, 1950, *FRUS* (1950), 3:59.

76. *Le Monde*, Apr. 6, 1949.

77. Dulles to the under secretary of state, Apr. 21, 1950, *FRUS* (1950), 3:60.

78. Bruce to Acheson, Apr. 22, 1950, *FRUS* (1950), 3:61–62.

79. *L'Année Politique, 1950* (Paris, 1950), p. 112.

80. William Hayter (Paris) to Dening, Dec. 23, 1949, FO 371, F19625/1015/86.

81. Sir Alvary Gascoigne to Foreign Office, May 1, 1950, FO 371, FF 1194/19.

82. U.S. delegation at Tripartite Preparatory Meetings to Acheson, Apr. 25, 1950, *FRUS* (1950), 3:860–63.

83. Minutes of cabinet meeting, May 8, 1950, CAB 128, CM29(50)3.

84. *NYT,* Jan. 28, 1950; record of interdepartmental meeting on the Far East at DOS, May 11, 1950, *FRUS* (1950), 6:87–92.

85. Memo of conversation at Quai d'Orsay, Mar. 13, 1950, *FRUS* (1950), 6:754–57.

86. U.S. delegation at Tripartite Preparatory Meetings to Acheson, Apr. 29, 1950, *FRUS* (1950), 3:896–98.

87. Memo of conversation by Acheson, Mar. 7, 1950, Acheson Papers, Memos of Conversation, 1950, Box 65, HSTL.

88. Statement by Bohlen to Voorhees group, Apr. 3, 1950, *FRUS* (1950), 3:1369–72. See also Voorhees to Acheson, Apr. 10, 1950, *FRUS* (1950), 3:43–45.

89. U.S. delegation at Tripartite Preparatory Meetings to Acheson, Apr. 29, 1950.

90. Memo by O'Sullivan, "Preliminary Talks as to Indochina," Sept. 28, 1949, *FRUS* (1949), 7:83–89.

91. Edwin M. Wright to Butterworth, Sept. 21, 1949, PSA, Box 6.

92. Franks to Foreign Office, Dec. 17, 1949, Fo 371, F 18982/10345/61. See also memo of conversation by Acheson, Dec. 24, 1949, Acheson Papers, Memos of Conversation, 1949, Box 64.

93. Butterworth to Rusk, Jan. 5, 1950, *FRUS* (1950), 6:690.

94. Memo of conversation by Jessup, Jan. 9, 1950, *FRUS* (1950), 6:1109–14; Jessup to Acheson, Jan. 10, 1950, ibid., pp. 1114–16.

95. Gascoigne to Foreign Office, Jan. 17, 1950, FO 371, FZ 1022/1.

96. Memo by Jessup, Jan. 14, 1950, *FRUS* (1950), vol. 7, *Korea*, pp. 1–7.

97. Memo of conversation by Jessup, Jan. 16, 1950, *FRUS* (1950), 6:280–283.

98. In 539D, DDRS, see Jessup, "Memorandum of Conversation with High Commissioner Pignon and Associates," Saigon, Jan. 25, 1950 ("our problems" quotation); Jessup, "Second interview with High Commissioner Pignon," Jan. 26, 1950 ("we've had it" quotation); and Jessup, "Notes on Visit to Saigon and Hanoi, Indochina, Jan. 24–28, 1950." Quotation "convinced of the urgency" in Frank S. Gibbs to Foreign Office, Feb. 3, 1950, FO 371, FF 1016/57.

99. "American flags" quotation in Jessup, "Notes on Visit to Saigon and Hanoi, Indochina—Jan. 24–28, 1950," DDRS, 539D. Other quotations in Jessup to Acheson, Jan. 29, 1950, *FRUS* (1950), 6:702–3. See also Abbott to Acheson, Jan. 31, 1950 (two telegrams), *FRUS* (1950), 6:705–9; Philip C. Jessup, *The Birth of Nations* (New York, 1974), pp. 172–82.

100. Quotation in Jessup, *Birth of Nations*, pp. 184, 186. See also memo by Gibson, Mar. 14, 1950, *FRUS* (1950), 6:759–61; *NYT*, Mar. 12, 1950.

101. Memo of conversation by Jessup, Feb. 6, 1950, *FRUS* (1950), 6:11–18; *NYT*, Feb. 7, 1950.

102. MacDonald to Foreign Office, Feb. 18, 1950, FO 371, FZ 1022/12; Jessup, *Birth of Nations*, p. 186.

103. Memo of conversation by Jessup, Feb. 8, 1950, *FRUS* (1950), 6:229–32.

104. *NYT*, Feb. 13, 15, 16, 1950; Jessup, *Birth of Nations*, p. 189 ("strategic importance" quotation); Acheson, "Daily Digest," Apr. 4, 1950, excerpted in Princeton Seminars; USIS publication, Feb. 16, 1950, Myron M. Cowen Papers, Box 2, HSTL; five telegrams from Stanton to Acheson, Feb. 17, 18, 27, 1950, *FRUS* (1950), 6:18–20, 27–30. Jessup's closing remarks quoted in Stanton's Feb. 27 telegram.

105. Bruce to Acheson (two telegrams), Feb. 22, 1950, *FRUS* (1950), 6:739–43; Jessup, *Birth of Nations*, pp. 183–84. Jessup cites the French official (Parodi) but not Schuman in his memoirs.

106. Jessup, *Birth of Nations*, pp. 186–87.

107. Ibid., p. 185.

108. Conversation at Quai d'Orsay, Mar. 13, 1950, and memo by Gibson, Mar. 14, 1950, *FRUS* (1950), 6:754–57, 759–61; Sir O. Harvey to Foreign Office, Mar. 14, 1950, FO 371, FF 1016/88.

109. Memo of conversation by Ogburn, Mar. 23, 1950, *FRUS* (1950), 6:68–76.

110. *NYT*, Mar. 30, 1950.

111. Joint chiefs of staff to Louis Johnson, Jan. 20, 1950, *FRUS* (1950), 6:5–8.

112. Acheson to Abbott, Jan. 27, 1950, *FRUS* (1950), 6:3–4; Butterworth to Acheson, Jan. 16, 1950, PSA, Box 4; Robert E. Hoey, "Indochina: Notes for Secretary's Press Conference," Jan. 24, 1950, PSA, Box 2; Hayes, *Beginning of American Aid*, p. 11.

113. Griffin to Hayes, May 19, 1968, R. Allen Griffin Papers, Box 1, Hoover Institu-

tion of War, Revolution, and Peace, Stanford, Calif.; Hayes, *Beginning of American Aid*, p. 11. Truman bridled at giving Republicans positions of responsibility and resisted Griffin's appointment for nearly three weeks.

114. Memo of conversation by Acheson, Feb. 20, 1950, *FRUS* (1950), 6:25n.; Truman to Griffin, Feb. 28, 1950, Truman Papers, Official File 2639, HSTL.

115. *DSB*, March 13, 1950, p. 411.

116. Memo of conversation by Acheson, Feb. 20, 1950; Acheson to Southeast Asian embassies, Feb. 24, 1950, *FRUS* (1950), 6:24–25; Webb to Griffin, Mar. 1, 1950, *Pentagon Papers*, 8:286–87.

117. Webb to Griffin, Mar. 1, 1950; Merrill C. Gay, "The Proposed Griffin Mission to Southeast Asia," Feb. 7, 1950, Griffin Papers, Box 10.

118. Hayes, *Beginning of American Aid*, pp. 12, 19, 21–22.

119. Interview with author, Feb. 1, 1977.

120. Hayes, *Beginning of American Aid*, p. 12.

121. *NYT*, Mar. 9, 10, 1950.

122. Griffin to DOS, Mar. 9, 1950, PSA, Box 7.

123. Griffin and Gullion to Acheson, Mar. 13, 1950, *Pentagon Papers*, 8:289–91. Acheson to Griffin and others, Mar. 10, 1950, ibid.

124. Report no. 1 of the Griffin mission appears in various forms in Hayes, *Beginning of American Aid*, pp. 61–109; *FRUS* (1950), 6:762–63 (conclusions only); *Pentagon Papers*, 8:292–300; Griffin Papers, unfiled.

125. First two quotations from Gullion to Hoey, Mar. 18, 1950, PSA, Box 7. Merchant to Captain H. E. Orem, Feb. 21, 1950, PSA, Box 7; Gullion to Acheson, Mar. 19, 1950, *FRUS* (1950), 6:765–66; *NYT*, Mar. 17, 20, 21, 24 and Apr. 8, 1950. ("Shoved around" quotation in *NYT*, Mar. 21.)

126. Griffin quotations from interview with author; MacDonald quoted in Griffin to Acheson, Mar. 21, 1950, *FRUS*, 6:64–65; all other quotations in "Needs for United States Economic and Technical Aid in the Colony of Singapore and the Federation of Malaya," in Hayes, *Beginning of American Aid*, pp. 127–49.

127. "Not . . . as bad" quotation in record of an interdepartmental meeting on the Far East, May 11, 1950, *FRUS* (1950), 6:87–92; "might well prove" quotation in "Needs for United States Economic and Technical Aid in Burma," in Hayes, *Beginning of American Aid*, pp. 151–99; "turned the corner" quotation in Hla Maung, "Beginning of American Aid to Burma," ibid., pp. 201–22.

128. Quotations in "Needs for United States Economic and Technical Aid in Thailand," in Hayes, *Beginning of American Aid*, pp. 223–67. See also Griffin and Stanton to Acheson, Apr. 12, 1950, *FRUS* (1950), 6:79–81; and record of interdepartmental meeting, May 11, 1950.

129. "Law and order" quotation in record of interdepartmental meeting, May 11, 1950; other quotations in "Needs for United States Economic and Technical Aid in Indonesia," in Hayes, *Beginning of American Aid*, pp. 269–326. See also Griffin to Acheson, Apr. 22, 1950, *FRUS* (1950), 6:1011–16.

130. For NSC-64, see *FRUS* (1950), 6:744–47, 786–87.

131. Address by Acheson in *DSB*, Mar. 27, 1950, pp. 467–72.

132. *NYT*, Mar. 16, 1950.

133. Franks to Foreign Office, Mar. 21, 1950, FO 371, FZ 10345/6.

134. Hayes, *Beginning of American Aid*, pp. 6–8; Wright to Butterworth, Sept. 21, 1949, PSA, Box 6; memo of conversation with Truman by Acheson, Oct. 13, 1949, Acheson Papers, Memos of Conversation, 1949, Box 64; Butterworth to Rusk and Acheson, Oct. 24, 1949, PSA, Box 4; outline of U.S. Far Eastern policy prepared by

Ogburn, Mar. 20, 1950, PSA, Box 5. In *FRUS* (1950), vol. 6, see Merchant to Butterworth, Mar. 22 (pp. 750–51); Butterworth to Lacy, Mar. 22 (p. 768).

135. General J. H. Burns to Frederick Nolting, Apr. 7, 1950, PSA, Box 7; material for secretary's press conference, Apr. 12, 1950, PSA, Box 2. In *FRUS* (1950), vol. 6, see Acheson to Truman, Apr. 17 (pp. 785–86); Bruce to Acheson, Apr. 29 (p. 790n.); Gullion to Acheson, Apr. 30 (p. 790); Truman to Acheson, May 1 (p. 791).

136. Legislation in DOS, *American Foreign Policy, 1950–1955: Basic Documents* (Washington, 1957), p. 3048. See also Richard Bissell to Robert Blum, May 5, 1950, *FRUS* (1950), 6:801–2; Robert M. Blum, *Drawing the Line: The Origin of the American Containment Policy in East Asia* (New York, 1982), pp. 200–202; Charles Wolf, Jr., *Foreign Aid: Theory and Practice in Southern Asia* (Princeton, 1960), pp. 44–45; William Adams Brown, Jr. and Redvers Opie, *American Foreign Assistance* (Washington, 1953), pp. 406–8, 412–14; statement by Truman, June 5, 1950, *DSB*, June 26, 1950, p. 1042; ECA, Div. of Statistics and Reports, Far East Program Div., *The Role of ECA in Southeast Asia* (Washington, January 1951), p. 2.

137. In *FRUS* (1950), vol. 3, see Acheson to Webb, May 9 (pp. 691–92); Acheson to Webb, May 10 (pp. 694–95); Dulles to Acheson, May 10 (695–96). See also Acheson, *Present at the Creation*, pp. 498–501; Truman's statement on coal-steel community, *DSB*, May 29, 1950, p. 828.

138. Quotations in Acheson to Webb, May 8, 1950, *FRUS*(1950), 3:1007–12. See also Gaddis Smith, *Dean Acheson* (Totowa, N.J., 1972), p. 314.

139. Bruce to Acheson, May 16, 1950, *FRUS* (1950), 6:815–16.

140. Statement by Webb, May 11, 1950, *DSB*, May 22, 1950, p. 791; Webb to legation at Saigon, May 15, 1950, *FRUS* (1950), 6:93–94; U.S. note of May 24, *DSB*, June 12, 1950, p. 977; Hayes, *Beginning of American Aid*, pp. 43–44; Wolf, *Foreign Aid*, p. 81.

141. Merchant to Reed and others, Sept. 29, 1949, PSA, Box 5; Bureau of Far Eastern Affairs, "Military Assistance on Reimbursable Basis under MAP: Vietnam," and ibid., "Thailand," n.d., PSA, Box 4.

142. Butterworth to Rusk and Acheson, Oct. 24, 1949, PSA, Box 4.

143. Memo by joint chiefs of staff, Jan. 20, 1950, sent by Johnson to Acheson on Feb. 1, *FRUS* (1950), 6:5–8.

144. "Report on Indochina," unattributed, Feb. 20, 1950, 540A, DDRS; Lacy to John V. Bell, Apr. 5, 1950, PSA, Box 8. In *FRUS* (1950), vol. 6, see Abbott to Acheson, Jan. 31 (pp. 707–9); "Problem Paper Prepared by Working Group in State Department," Feb. 1 (pp. 711–15); Bruce to Acheson, Feb. 22 (pp. 739–42); Acheson to Truman and annexes A and B, Mar. 9 (pp. 40–44); Truman to Acheson, May 1 (p. 791); Webb to Stanton, May 23 (pp. 96–98); Acheson to Truman, July 10 (pp. 115–17); Acheson to embassy in India, Aug. 3 (pp. 415–16).

145. "Report on Conversations with French and Vietnam Officials during Visit to Saigon," by commander, Seventh Fleet (R. S. Berkey), Apr. 5, 1950, PSA, Box 8.

146. Quotation in Acheson to embassy in United Kingdom, May 3, 1950, *FRUS* (1950), 6:792. See also Lacy to Bell, Apr. 5, 1950; Robert Allen to Samuel Parelman, May 22, 1950, PSA, Box 8.

147. Report on Indochina by Hoey, Apr. 5, 1950, PSA, Box 8.

148. Acheson to Bruce, Mar. 4, 1950, *FRUS* (1950), 6:748–49 ("publicized recipient" quotation); Bell to Nolting, Mar. 30, 1950, PSA, Box 8; Lacy to Bell, Apr. 5, 1950 ("could obviously not" and "political and military" quotations); Allen to Parelman, May 22, 1950; COMMATS, Andrews Air Force Base, to COMGENAMC, Wright-Patterson Air Force Base, June 6, 1950, PSA, Box 8; Lucien Bodard, *The Quicksand War: Prelude to Vietnam*, trans. Patrick O'Brian (Boston, 1967), p. 20 (final quotation).

149. In PSA, Box 8, see Jessup to Merchant, June 2, 1950; Lacy to Merchant, June 7, 1950; Lacy to Rusk, June 28, 1950.

150. Truman's special message to Congress on military aid, June 1, 1950, *Public Papers*, Truman, 1950, p. 448.

151. In *FRUS* (1950), vol. 6, see Rusk to Burns, Mar. 7 (p. 752); Johnson to Acheson, Apr. 14 (pp. 780–85); Webb to Johnson, May 16 (pp. 816–17). See also Omar N. Bradley (chairman, joint chiefs of staff) to Johnson, May 2, 1950 (two memos), *Pentagon Papers*, 8:315–19.

152. Quotation from "Minutes of the First Meeting of the Southeast Asia Aid Policy Committee," July 13, 1950, *FRUS* (1950), 6: 117–19. *Pentagon Papers*, vol. 8, sec. 4, pt. 2, pp. 2, 11.

153. Blum, *Drawing the Line*, p. 203.

154. *Pentagon Papers*, vol. 8, sec. 4, pt. A, pp. 2, 11; Lyman Lemnitzer to James Bruce, Apr. 19, 1950, *FRUS* (1950), 6:787–89; John Ohly to Lemnitzer and Edward T. Dickinson, June 1, 1950, ibid., pp. 98–100; Gullion to Acheson, June 10, 1950, 543G, DDRS.

155. Carlos P. Romulo to Acheson, Mar. 2, 1950, Acheson Papers, Memos of Conversation, 1950, Box 65.

156. Memo of conversation by Acheson, Mar. 10, 1950, *FRUS* (1950), 6:752–53.

157. *Pentagon Papers*, vol. 1, sec. 4, pt. A, p. 11. Emphasis in original.

9. *The Korean Intervention and After*

1. Minutes of meeting at Blair House by Jessup, June 25, 1950, *FRUS* (1950), vol. 7, *Korea*, p. 158.

2. Dodge to Marquat, June 29, 1950, Joseph M. Dodge Papers, Japan, 1950, Box 3, Burton Historical Collection, Detroit Public Library.

3. For the argument that U.S. intervention in Korea was a logical extension of the containment policy in the Far East, see William Whitney Stueck, Jr., *The Road to Confrontation: American Policy toward China and Korea, 1947–1950* (Chapel Hill, N.C., 1981), pp. 146–52.

4. Kano to Dodge, Apr. 7, 1950, Dodge Papers, Japan, 1950, Box 5.

5. In Dodge Papers, Japan, 1950, see "Monthly Economic Report, Japan, July 1950," July 15, 1950, Box 5; press statement by Dodge, Oct. 7, 1950, Box 1; R. W. Hale, "Foreign Trade Policy," Nov. 27, 1950, Box 7. See also Yamamoto Mitsuru, "The Cold War and U.S.-Japan Economic Cooperation," in Yōnosuke Nagai and Akira Iriye, eds., *The Origins of the Cold War in Asia* (New York, 1977), pp. 112–13; Charles A. Willoughby, *MacArthur, 1941–1951* (New York, 1954), p. 348; William Adams Brown, Jr., and Redvers Opie, *American Foreign Assistance* (Washington, 1953), pp. 368–69; William S. Borden, *The Pacific Alliance: United States Foreign Economic Policy and Japanese Trade Recovery, 1947–1955* (Madison, Wis., 1984), pp. 144–47.

6. Quotation from Kano to Dodge, Sept. 7, 1950, Dodge Papers, Japan, 1950, Box 6. Richard Bissell to Ralph W. E. Reid, May 18, 1951, Dodge Papers, Japan, 1950, Box 1; Brown and Opie, *American Foreign Assistance*, p. 369.

7. Letter of transmittal by P. S. Lokanathan, ECAFE, *Economic Survey of Asia and the Far East, 1950*, pp. xv–xvi.

8. Donald MacDougall, *The World Dollar Problem* (London, 1957), p. 289; Frederick T. Koyle, "Export-Import Problems in Southeast Asia," in Philip W. Thayer, ed., *Southeast Asia in the Coming World* (Baltimore, 1953), pp. 115, 118–19.

9. Quotation in memo of conversation by Armstrong, Jan. 5, 1951, PSA, Box 2. See also Acheson to certain diplomatic and consular offices, Aug. 21, 1950, in *FRUS* (1950), vol. 6, *East Asia and the Pacific*, pp. 133–34; Charles J. Shohan to W. C. Armstrong, Aug. 14, 1950, PSA, Box 4; Armstrong to John E. O'Gara, Dec. 6, 1950, PSA, Box 4; memo of conversation by George J. Alexander, Dec. 11, 1950, *FRUS* (1950), 6:174–76.

10. U.S. Congress, Senate Committee on Interior and Insular Affairs, *Stockpile and Accessibility of Strategic and Critical Materials to the United States in Time of War: Hearings before Special Subcommittee on Minerals, Materials, and Fuels Economics*, 83d Cong., 1st sess., Feb. 24, 1954, pt. 7, p. 88; C. W. Nichols, "Proposed United States Position in United Nations Conference on Tin," Sept. 26, 1950, PSA, Box 3; "Agreed Minute" of discussions between U.S. and U.K. officials on tin policy, July 25–Aug. 4, 1950, ibid.; Frederic Benham, *The National Income of Malaya, 1947–49* (Singapore, 1951), p. 198.

11. Quotations from memo of conversation between British officials and members of the Melby-Erskine mission, Singapore, Aug. 8, 1950, FO 371, FZ 1198/8. Acheson to legation at Saigon, July 5, 1950, *FRUS* (1950), 6:114–15.

12. Excerpts from Gray's Report on Foreign Economic Policies" in *DSB*, Nov. 27, 1950, pp. 847–49.

13. Harlan Cleveland to Dean Rusk, Aug. 21, 1950, PSA, Box 1.

14. Percy Spender, *Exercises in Diplomacy* (New York, 1969), p. 272; Lewis Douglas to Acheson, Nov. 14, 1950, and Acheson to Douglas, Nov. 22, 1950, *FRUS* (1950), 6:159–61; Frederic Benham, *The Colombo Plan and Other Essays* (London, 1956), p. 2.

15. Borden, *Pacific Alliance*, pp. 204–10; Lord Ismay, *NATO: The First Five Years* (Utrecht, 1955), p. 40; Harry Bayard Price, *The Marshall Plan and Its Meaning* (Ithaca, 1955), pp. 156–57.

16. Shohan to Rusk, May 10, 1951, PSA, Box 14; Harry B. Price to Henry Bardach, July 9, 1951, PSA, Box 14.

17. F. S. Gibbs to Foreign Office, July 10, 1950, FO 371, FF 10381/2.

18. Lacy to Rusk, June 30, 1950, *FRUS* (1950), 6:106. See also minutes of the first meeting of the Southeast Asia Aid Committee, July 13, ibid., pp. 117–19.

19. Walter S. Salant to David Bell and David Lloyd, Aug. 31, 1950, Walter S. Salant Papers, Box 2, HSTL.

20. Editorial note, *FRUS* (1950), vol. 1, "National Security Affairs; Foreign Economic Policy," p. 864; Samuel T. Parelman to John Emmerson, Nov. 30, 1950, PSA, Box 1.

21. Memo by David Lloyd, Nov. 27, 1950, George M. Elsey Papers, Subject File, Box 61, HSTL.

22. W. W. Blancké to Acheson, Aug. 31, 1950, 546H, DDRS.

23. In *FRUS* (1950), vol. 6, see Acheson to Truman, July 10 (pp. 835–36), and editorial note (p. 893).

24. Quotation in R. E. Hoey to Rusk, Nov. 13, 1950, PSA, Box 8. See also *Pentagon Papers*, vol. 8, sec. 4, pt. A, pp. 11, 15; cover letter with report of Melby-Erskine mission, Aug. 6, 1950, *FRUS* (1950), 6:840–44.

25. Lacy to Merchant, July 19, 1950, PSA, Box 8; *Pentagon Papers*, 8:341–42.

26. In DDRS, see Blancké to Acheson, Aug. 31, 1950, 546H; David Bruce to Acheson, Aug. 12, 1950, 545E; memo of conversation by James Bonbright, July 29, 1950, 545B ("during the first days of August" quotation). See also acting British consul general (Shanghai) to Foreign Office, July 20, 1950, FO 371, FF 1092/1 ("on July 29" quotation); Lacy to Rusk, Aug. 22, 1950, PSA, Box 9; Clubb to Rusk and Merchant, Sept. 27, 1950, PSA, Box 5. On Sept. 11, Rusk wrote Acheson that the Far Eastern Bureau anticipated a Communist offensive in Indochina in late September or early October. The bureau acknowledged the "possibility" that the Chinese would direct the offen-

sive, but thought it more likely that the Viet Minh alone would attack. See Rusk to Acheson, Sept. 11, 1950, *FRUS* (1950), 6:878–80.

27. Bernard Fall, *Street without Joy* (Harrisburg, Pa., 1964), pp. 32–33.

28. Gibbs to Foreign Office, Dec. 6, 1950, FO 371, FF 10381/3; United States minutes, Truman-Attlee conversations, Dec. 4, 1950, *FRUS* (1950), vol. 3, *Western Europe,* pp. 1706–19.

29. Quotation from Timothy P. Ireland, *Creating the Entangling Alliance: The Origins of the North Atlantic Treaty Organization* (Westport, Conn., 1981), p. 179. See also Richard Barnet and Marcus Raskin, *After Twenty Years: The Decline of NATO and the Search for a New Policy in Europe* (New York, 1965), p. 21; minutes of a private conference of French, British, and U.S. foreign ministers, Sept. 14, 1950, *FRUS* (1950), 3:293–301; Acheson to Robert Schuman, Jan. 27, 1951, *DSB,* Feb. 19, 1951; Acheson speech, July 24, 1951, *DSB,* Aug. 6, 1951, p. 205; Truman's 4th report on Mutual Defense Assistance Program, Feb. 12, 1952, *DSB,* Feb. 25, 1952, p. 316.

30. Charles M. Spofford to Acheson, July 28, 1950, *FRUS* (1950), 3:148–50; notes on conversation between Truman and Vincent Auriol, Mar. 29, 1951, PSA, Box 7.

31. Lacy to Merchant, July 19, 1950, PSA, Box 8.

32. Gibbs to R. H. Scott, Mar. 24, 1950, FO 371, FF 1103/3.

33. Robert Shaplen, *The Lost Revolution: The U.S. in Vietnam, 1946–1966,* rev. ed. (New York, 1966), pp. 86–91 (de Lattre quotation and "high contracting parties"); Lucien Bodard, *The Quicksand War: Prelude to Vietnam,* trans. Patrick O'Brian (Boston, 1967), pp. 223–25; R. E. M. Irving, *The First Indochina War* (London, 1975), pp. 101–2; Heath to Acheson, Sept. 1, 1950, 547A, DDRS ("holding out" quotation); Heath to Acheson, June 30, 1951, *FRUS* (1951), vol. 6, *Asia and the Pacific,* pp. 439–41; "Economic Aid Program: Reference Notes," Sept. 1951, R. Allen Griffin Papers, Box 10, Hoover Institution on War, Revolution, and Peace, Stanford, Calif.

34. Lacy to Rusk, Aug. 21, 1950, PSA, Box 7; memo of conversation between Shohan and Griffin, Oct. 17, 1950, PSA, Box 7; K. T. Young to General Malony, Oct. 13, 1950, *Pentagon Papers,* 8:370.

35. Memo of conversation by Charlton Ogburn, Apr. 17, 1950, PSA, Box 9.

36. H. A. Osborn to Hoey, Oct. 16, 1950, PSA, Box 7.

37. Memo of conversation by Ogburn, Jan. 19, 1951, PSA, Box 6.

38. Ogburn to Rusk, Jan. 15, 1951, PSA, Box 6.

39. Borden, *Pacific Alliance,* pp. 159–65; John W. Dower, *Empire and Aftermath: Yoshida Shigeru and the Japanese Experience, 1878–1954* (Cambridge, Mass., 1979), pp. 369–427; Michael Schaller, *The American Occupation of Japan: The Origins of the Cold War in Asia* (New York, 1985), pp. 293–95; handwritten notes, n.d., Dodge Papers, Japan, 1950, Box 7.

40. Borden, *Pacific Alliance,* pp. 179, 189, 218, 228.

41. Stephen E. Ambrose, *Rise to Globalism: American Foreign Policy, 1938–1976,* rev. ed. (New York, 1976), pp. 206, 226; F. S. Northedge, *Descent from Power: British Foreign Policy, 1945–1973* (London, 1974), p. 201.

42. In *FRUS* (1952–1954), vol. 13, *Indochina,* see U.S. minute of tripartite foreign ministers meeting with France and U.K., Paris, May 28, 1952, pp.157–66; Dulles to DOS, Oct. 17, 1953, pp. 830–32; Dulles to DOS, Dec. 17, 1954, pp. 2385–87. See also George C. Herring, *America's Longest War: The United States and Vietnam, 1950–1975* (New York, 1979), pp. 26–28.

43. Anthony Eden, *Full Circle* (Boston, 1960), p. 97.

44. Memo of conversation by DOS Counselor Douglas MacArthur II, Apr. 11, 1954, *FRUS* (1952–1954), 13:1307–9; George C. Herring and Richard H. Immerman, "Eisen-

hower, Dulles, and Dienbienphu: 'The Day We Didn't Go to War' Revisited," *Journal of American History,* 71:343–63.

45. Memo of conference at White House, May 5, 1954, *FRUS* (1952–1954), 13:1466–70.

46. Eden, *Full Circle,* pp. 86–119; Dulles to DOS, Apr. 13, 1954, *FRUS* (1952–1954), 13:1319–20; memo of conversation by Merchant, Apr. 24, 1954, ibid., pp. 1386–91; memo of conversation by Dulles, Apr. 25, 1954, *FRUS* (1952–1954), vol. 16, *The Geneva Conference,* pp. 553–57; Dulles to DOS, Apr. 27, 1954, ibid., pp. 576–77. The British were not, as Dulles charged, "uninterested" in Indochina. At a dinner party on Apr. 26, Churchill was apparently philosophical when he said, "I have known many reverses myself. I have not given in. I have suffered Singapore, Hong-Kong, Tobruk; the French will have Dien Bien Phu." Great Britain regained all three places, of course— two of them as colonies. Churchill quoted in Herring and Immerman, "Eisenhower, Dulles, and Dienbienphu," p. 360. See also Dulles to embassy in Australia, Apr. 1, 1954, *FRUS* (1952–1954), 13:1204–5.

47. J. M. Gullick, *Malaysia: Economic Expansion and National Unity* (Boulder, Colo. 1981), pp. 85–102, 213–16, 260; Roy F. Harrod, *The British Economy* (New York, 1963), pp. 147–48; U.N. Statistical Office, *Yearbook of International Trade, 1956,* pp 596, 608.

48. Phillipe Devillers and Jean Lacouture, *End of a War: Indochina, 1954,* trans. Alexander Lieven and Adam Roberts (New York, 1969), p. 331.

49. NIE-35/2, "Probable Developments in Indochina through Mid-1953," Aug. 29, 1952, *FRUS* (1952–1954), 13:243–49.

50. Bernard Fall, *The Two Vietnams: A Political and Military Analysis* (New York, 1963), p. 318; Walter LaFeber, *America, Russia and the Cold War,: 1945–1971,* 2d ed. (New York, 1972), pp. 102–4, 126–27, 169–71 ("agonizing reappraisal," p. 169); Dwight D. Eisenhower, *Mandate for Change, 1953–1956* (Garden City, 1963), pp. 397–409; Eden, *Full Circle,* ch. 5–7.

51. Fall, *Two Vietnams,* pp. 318–22.

52. LaFeber, *America, Russia and the Cold War,* pp. 166–67.

53. Memo of conversation by Edward Page, Jr., June 7, 1954, *FRUS* (1952–1954), 16:1059–60.

54. *The Pentagon Papers,* NYT ed. (New York, 1971), pp. 53–66.

55. Herring, *America's Longest War,* p. 56.

56. Graham Greene, *The Quiet American* (New York, 1956), p. 13.

57. Record of conversation between Jessup and representatives of the British Foreign Office, Mar. 11, 1950, *FRUS* (1950), 6:46–51.

58. Princeton Seminars (held by Acheson and other members of Truman administration at Princeton Univ., 1953 and 1954), May 15, 1954, microfilm, Green Library, Stanford Univ.

Bibliography

ARCHIVES

Harry S Truman Library, Independence, Missouri

Papers
    Dean Acheson
    Stanley Andrews
    Myron M. Cowen
    George M. Elsey
    Walter S. Salant
    John D. Sumner
    Harry S Truman
        David D. Lloyd Files
        Charles S. Murphy Files
        Post-presidential Files
        President's Secretary's Files
        White House Central Files
    James G. Webb

Oral History Interview Collection
    Robert W. Barnett
    Winthrop G. Brown
    John M. Cabot
    Lord Franks
    Raymond W. Miller
    Walter S. Salant

National Archives, Washington, D.C.

    All the following are in Record Group 59.
    State Department Decimal Files

Lot Files, Records of the Philippines and Southeast Asia Division
Lot Files, Office of the Executive Secretariat
Lot Files, Council of Foreign Ministers

Library of Congress, Washington, D.C.

Philip C. Jessup Papers

Burton Historical Collection, Detroit Public Library

Joseph M. Dodge Papers

Green Library, Stanford University

The Princeton Seminars. These seminars were a series of conferences held by Dean Acheson and other high-ranking members of the Truman administration at Princeton University during 1953 and 1954. Transcripts of these meetings are available on microfilm.

Hoover Institution on War, Revolution and Peace, Stanford, California

R. Allen Griffin Papers
Roger Lapham Papers

Public Record Office, Kew, England

Cabinet minutes and conclusions (CAB 128)
Cabinet papers or memoranda (CAB 129)
Foreign Office records (FO 371)
Papers of the Prime Minister's Private Office (PREM 8)
Treasury records (T 188, T 236, T 238)
Colonial Office records (CO 717, CO 852)
Records of the Board of Trade (BT 11)

GOVERNMENT DOCUMENTS

All are published by Government Printing Office unless otherwise noted.

United States

President
Public Papers of the Presidents of the United States. Harry S Truman, 1949, 1950; Dwight D. Eisenhower, 1954.

Congress, Senate
Committee on Foreign Relations. *An Act for International Development: Hearings,* 81st Cong., 2d sess., 1950.
_____. *A Decade of American Foreign Policy: Basic Documents, 1941–1949,* 1950.

Bibliography

Committee on Armed Services and Committee on Foreign Relations. *Military Situation in the Far East,* 82d Cong., 1st sess., 1951.

Subcommittee of the Committee on Foreign Relations. *Hearings on the Nomination of Philip C. Jessup to Be United States Representative to the United Nations,* 82d Cong., 1st sess., 1951.

Committee on Interior and Insular Affairs. *Stockpile and Accessibility of Strategic and Critical Materials to the United States in Time of War: Hearings before Special Subcommittee on Minerals, Materials, and Fuels Economics,* 83d Cong., 1st sess., 1953–1954.

Committee on Foreign Relations. *The United States and Vietnam: 1944–1947.* Staff study based on the *Pentagon Papers,* 92d Cong., 2d sess., 1972.

———. *Causes, Origins and Lessons of the Vietnam War: Hearings,* 92d Cong., 2d sess., 1972.

———. *The United States and Communist China in 1949 and 1950: The Question of Rapprochement and Recognition,* by Robert M. Blum. Staff study, 1973.

Congress, House

Committee on Foreign Affairs. *Point Four: Background and Program,* July 1949.

Special Subcommittee of Committee on Expenditures in the Executive Departments. *Report of Representative Charles B. Deane on a Trip to the Far East,* Oct. 19, 1949.

Committee on Foreign Affairs. *International Technical Cooperation Act: Hearings,* 81st Cong., 1st sess., 1950.

Committee on Armed Services. *President's Recommendations Concerning Synthetic Rubber: Hearings before a Special Subcommittee of the Committee on Armed Services,* 81st Cong., 2d sess., 1950.

———. *Stockpiling of Strategic and Critical Materials: Hearings before a Special Subcommittee of the Committee on Armed Services,* 81st Cong., 2d sess., 1950.

Committee on Foreign Affairs. *Report of the Special Study Mission to Pakistan, Thailand and Indochina.* 83d Cong., 1st sess., 1953.

Committee on Armed Services. *United States–Vietnam Relations, 1945–1967: A Study Prepared by the Department of Defense.* 12 vols., 1971 (*Pentagon Papers*). Also editions by Senator Mike Gravel, 4 vols. (Boston: Beacon Press, 1971), and *New York Times* (New York: Bantam, 1971).

Department of State

American Foreign Policy 1950–1955: Basic Documents, 1957.

The China White Paper, August 1949. Reissued with a new introduction by Lyman P. Van Slyke. 2 vols. Stanford: Stanford Univ. Press, 1967.

Department of State Bulletin, 1948–1954.

Foreign Relations of the United States, 1945–1954.

Round Table Discussion on American Policy toward China. Oct. 6, 7, and 8, 1949.

Department of Commerce

Foreign Commerce Yearbook, 1947–1951.

Rubber: Annual Report, 1949, 1950.

Department of the Interior

Bureau of Mines. *Minerals Yearbook: 1950.*

Economic Cooperation Administration

Report of the ECA-Commerce Mission to Investigate Possibilities of Increasing Western Europe's Dollar Earnings, October 1949.

Division of Statistics and Reports, Far East Program Division. *The Role of ECA in Southeast Asia,* January 1951.

Special Commission to the United Kingdom. *The Sterling Area: An American Analysis,* London, 1951.

Country Data Book: United Kingdom, 1950.

European Recovery Program
Second Report of the Organization for European Economic Cooperation (OEEC). Paris: Imprimerie Administrative Centrale, n.d. [February 1950].

General Headquarters, Supreme Commander for the Allied Powers
SCAPINS: Supreme Commander for the Allied Powers' Instructions to the Japanese Government, From 4 September, 1945 to 8 March, 1952, Mar. 20, 1952.

Great Britain and Colonies

All are published by His Majesty's Stationery Office, unless otherwise noted.

Central Office of Information, *An Economic Review of Malaya, 1945–1949* (1950).

Colonial Office, Brunei. *Annual Report on Brunei,* 1949, 1950.

_____. *Annual Report on North Borneo,* 1949, 1950.

Commonwealth Consultative Committee on South and South-East Asia. *The Colombo Plan for Cooperative Economic Development in South and South-East Asia,* 1950.

Parliament. *Parliamentary Debates* (Commons), 5th ser., vol. 468, Sept. 27–Oct. 28, 1949.

Secretary of State for the Colonies. *Report: British Dependencies in the Far East, 1945–1949,* 1949.

Malaya (Federation). *Annual Report on the Federation at Malaya, 1949, 1950.* London: His Majesty's Stationery Office, 1950, 1951.

Malaya (Federation). *Draft Development Plan for the Federation of Malaya.* Kuala Lumpur: Government Printing Office, 1950.

North Borneo Rubber Commission. *Report.* Singapore: Government Printers, 1949.

Japan

Bureau of Statistics, Office of the Prime Minister. *Japan Statistical Yearbook.* Tokyo 1960.

United Nations

Economic Commission for Asia and Far East. *Economic Survey of Asia and the Far East,* 1948–1950.

Statistical Office. *Yearbook of International Trade,* 1952–1960.

BOOKS

Acheson, Dean. *Present at the Creation: My Years in the State Department.* New York: W. W. Norton, 1969.

Ambrose, Stephen E. *Rise to Globalism: American Foreign Policy, 1938–1976.* Rev. ed., New York: Penguin, 1976.

Bachrack, Stanley. *The Committee of One Million: The "China Lobby" and U.S. Policy, 1953–1971.* New York: Columbia Univ. Press, 1971.

Baerwald, Hans H. *The Purge of Japanese Leaders under the Occupation.* Berkeley: Univ. of California Press, 1959.

Bibliography

Ball, W. MacMahon. *Japan: Enemy or Ally?* New York: John Day, 1949.

Balogh, Thomas. *The Dollar Crisis: Causes and Cure.* Oxford: Oxford Univ. Press, 1949.

Barclay, Roderick. *Ernest Bevin and the Foreign Office, 1932–1969.* London: Butler & Tanner, 1975.

Barnet, Richard, and Raskin, Marcus. *After Twenty Years: The Decline of NATO and the Search for a New Policy in Europe.* New York: Random House, 1965.

Bauer, P. T. *Report on a Visit to the Rubber Growing Smallholdings of Malaya, July–September 1946.* London: His Majesty's Stationery Office, 1948.

Benham, Frederic. *The National Income of Malaya, 1947–49.* Singapore: Government Printing Office, 1951.

———. *The Colombo Plan and Other Essays.* London: Royal Institute of International Affairs, 1956.

Bland, D. E. and Watkins, K. W. *Can Britain Survive?* London: Joseph, 1971.

Block, Fred L. *The Origins of International Economic Disorder.* Berkeley: Univ. of California Press, 1977.

Blum, Robert M. *Drawing the Line: The Origin of the American Containment Policy in East Asia.* New York: W. W. Norton, 1982.

Bodard, Lucien. *The Quicksand War: Prelude to Vietnam.* Translated and with an introduction by Patrick O'Brian. Boston: Little, Brown, 1967.

Borden, William S. *The Pacific Alliance: United States Foreign Economic Policy and Japanese Trade Recovery, 1947–1955.* Madison: Univ. of Wisconsin Press, 1984.

Borg, Dorothy, and Heinrichs, Waldo, eds. *Uncertain Years: Chinese-American Relations, 1947–1950.* New York: Columbia Univ. Press, 1980.

Brown, William Adams, Jr. *The United States and the Restoration of World Trade.* Washington: Brookings, 1950.

Brown, William Adams, Jr., and Opie, Redvers. *American Foreign Assistance.* Washington: Brookings, 1953.

Buckley, Roger. *Occupation Diplomacy: Britain, the United States and Japan, 1945–1952.* Cambridge: Cambridge Univ. Press, 1982.

Buttinger, Joseph. *Vietnam: A Dragon Embattled.* 2 vols. New York: Praeger, 1967.

———. *Vietnam: The Unforgettable Tragedy.* New York: Horizon, 1977.

Cady, John F. *The History of Post-War Southeast Asia.* Athens: Ohio Univ. Press, 1974.

Chassin, Lionel Max. *The Communist Conquest of China.* Cambridge, Mass.: Harvard Univ. Press, 1965.

Chen, King C. *Vietnam and China, 1938–1954.* Princeton: Princeton Univ. Press, 1969.

Chesneaux, Jean. *The Vietnamese Nation.* Sydney: Current Books, 1966.

Cleveland, Harlan. *The Obligations of Power.* New York: Harper & Row, 1966.

Cohen, Jerome B. *Japan's Postwar Economy.* Bloomington: Indiana Univ. Press, 1958.

Cohen, Warren. *Dean Rusk.* Totowa, N.J.: Cooper Square, 1980.

Colbert, Evelyn. *Southeast Asia in International Politics, 1941–1956.* Ithaca: Cornell Univ. Press, 1977.

Condit, Kenneth W. *The History of the Joint Chiefs of Staff: The Joint Chiefs of Staff and National Policy.* 4 vols. Wilmington: Michael Glazier, 1979.

Connell-Smith, Gordon. *The Inter-American System.* London: Oxford Univ. Press, 1966.

———. *The United States and Latin America.* London: Heineman, 1974.

Cooke, Colin, *The Life of Richard Stafford Cripps.* London: Hodder & Stoughton, 1957.

Darling, Frank D. *Thailand and the United States.* Washington: Public Affairs Institute Press, 1965.

Davies, John Paton, Jr. *Dragon by the Tail: American, British, Japanese and Russian Encounters with China and One Another.* New York W. W. Norton, 1972.

Devillers, Philippe, and Lacouture, Jean. *End of a War: Indochina, 1954*. Translated by Alexander Lieven and Adam Roberts. New York: Praeger, 1969.

Dietrich, Ethel B. *Far Eastern Trade of the United States*. New York: Institute of Pacific Relations, 1940.

Donnithorne , Audrey Gladys. *Economic Developments since 1937 in Eastern and Southeastern Asia and Their Effects on the United Kingdom*. London: Royal Institute of International Affairs, 1950.

Dower, John W. *Empire and Aftermath: Yoshida Shigeru and the Japanese Experience, 1878–1954*. Cambridge, Mass.: Harvard Univ. Press, 1979.

Drachman, Edward R. *United States Policy toward Vietnam, 1940–1945*. Rutherford, N.J.: Fairleigh Dickinson Univ. Press, 1970.

Dulles, John Foster. *War or Peace?* New York: Macmillan, 1950.

Eckes, Alfred E., Jr. *A Search for Solvency: Bretton Woods and the International Monetary System, 1941–1971*. Austin: Univ. of Texas Press, 1975.

Eden, Anthony. *Full Circle*. Boston: Houghton-Mifflin, 1960.

Eisenhower, Dwight D. *Mandate for Change, 1953–1956*. Garden City: Doubleday, 1963.

Emerson, Rupert. *Africa and United States Policy*. Englewood Cliffs, N.J.: Prentice-Hall, 1967.

Fall, Bernard. *The Two Vietnams: A Political And Military Analysis*. New York: Praeger, 1963.

_____. *Street without Joy*. Harrisburg, Pa.: Stackpole, 1964.

_____. ed. *Ho Chi Minh on Revolution*. New York: Praeger, 1967.

Fearey, Robert A. *The Occupation of Japan: Second Phase, 1948–50*. New York: Macmillan, 1950.

Ferrell, Robert H., ed. *Off the Record: The Private Papers of Harry S Truman*. New York: Harper & Row, 1980.

Fifield, Russell H. *The Diplomacy of Southeast Asia: 1945–1958*. New York: Harper & Row, 1958.

_____. *Americans in Southeast Asia: The Roots of Commitment*. New York: Thomas Crowell, 1973.

Fox, William. *Tin: The Working of a Commodity Agreement*. London: Mining Journal Books, 1974.

Frankel, Joseph. *British Foreign Policy 1945–1973*. London: Oxford Univ. Press, 1975.

Friedman, Edward, and Selden, Mark, eds. *America's Asia: Dissenting Essays on Asian-American Relations*. New York: Pantheon, 1969.

Gaddis, John Lewis. *Strategies of Containment: A Critical Appraisal of Postwar American National Security Policy*. New York: Oxford Univ. Press, 1982.

Gardner, Richard N. *Sterling-Dollar Diplomacy*. Rev. ed. New York: Oxford Univ. Press, 1969.

Gelb, Leslie H., and Betts, Richard K. *The Irony of Vietnam: The System Worked*. Washington: Brookings, 1979.

Gladwyn, Hubert Miles Gladwyn Jebb, Baron. *The Memoirs of Lord Gladwyn*. New York: Weybright & Talley, 1972.

Goodman, Grant K., comp. *The American Occupation of Japan: A Retrospective View*. Lawrence: Univ. of Kansas Press, 1968.

Gullick, J. M. *Malaya*. New York: Praeger, 1963.

_____. *Malaysia: Economic Expansion and National Unity*. Boulder: Westview Press, 1981.

Hadley, Eleanor M. *Antitrust in Japan*. Princeton: Princeton Univ. Press, 1970.

Hammer, Ellen J. *The Struggle for Indochina 1940–1955*. Stanford: Stanford Univ. Press, 1966.

Harris, Seymour E. *Foreign Aid and Our Economy.* Washington: Public Affairs Institute Press, 1950.

Harrod, Roy F. *The Life of John Maynard Keynes.* New York: Harcourt, Brace, 1951.

_____. *The British Economy.* New York: McGraw-Hill, 1963.

Havighurst, Arthur F. *Britain in Transition: The Twentieth Century.* 3d ed. Chicago: Univ. of Chicago Press, 1979.

Hawes, Grace M. *The Marshall Plan for China: Economic Cooperation Administration, 1948–1949.* Cambridge, Mass.: Schenkman, 1977.

Hayes, Samuel P., ed. *The Beginning of American Aid to Southeast Asia: The Griffin Mission of 1950.* Lexington, Mass.: Heath, 1971.

Heller, Francis H., ed. *The Truman White House: The Administration of the Presidency, 1945–1953.* Lawrence: Regents Press of Kansas, 1980.

Herring, George C. *America's Longest War: The United States and Vietnam, 1950–1975.* New York: Wiley, 1979.

Ho Chi Minh. *On Revolution.* Edited and with an introduction by Bernard Fall. New York: Praeger, 1967.

International Tin Study Group. *Review of the World Tin Position, 1947–1948.* The Hague, 1948.

_____. *Tin, 1950–1951: A Review of the World Tin Industry.* The Hague, 1952.

_____. *Tin and the Tin Study Group, 1948–1952.* The Hague, 1953.

Ireland, Timothy P. *Creating the Entangling Alliance: The Origins of the North Atlantic Treaty Organization.* Westport, Conn.: Greenwood Press, 1981.

Iriye, Akira. *The Cold War in Asia: A Historical Introduction.* Englewood Cliffs, N.J.: Prentice-Hall, 1974.

Irving, R. E. M. *The First Indochina War.* London: Croon Helm, 1975.

Ismay, Hastings Lionel Ismay, Baron. *NATO: The First Five Years.* Utrecht: Bosch, 1955.

Jessup, Philip C. *The Birth of Nations.* New York: Columbia Univ. Press, 1974.

Kahin, George McTurnan. *Nationalism and Revolution in Indonesia.* Ithaca: Cornell Univ. Press, 1952.

Kahin, George McTurnan, and Lewis, John W. *The United States in Vietnam.* Rev. ed. New York: Dial Press, 1969.

Kahn, E. J., Jr. *The China Hands.* New York: Random House, 1972.

Kaplan, Lawrence S., and Clawson, Robert W., eds. *NATO after Thirty Years.* Wilmington: Scholarly Resources, 1981.

Kawai, Kazuo. *Japan's American Interlude.* Chicago: Univ. of Chicago Press, 1960.

Kennan, George F. *Memoirs: 1925–1950.* Boston: Little, Brown, 1967.

Kindleberger, Charles P. *The Dollar Shortage.* Boston: MIT Press, 1950.

Kirby, M. W. *The Decline of British Economic Power since 1870.* London: George Allen & Unwin, 1981.

Kirkendall, Richard S., ed. *The Truman Period as a Research Field: A Reappraisal, 1972.* Columbia: Univ. of Missouri Press, 1974.

Koen, Ross. *The China Lobby in American Politics.* New York: Macmillan, 1960.

Kolko, Gabriel. *The Politics of War: The World and United States Foreign Policy, 1943–1945.* New York: Random House, 1968.

_____. *The Roots of American Foreign Policy.* Boston: Beacon, 1969.

Kolko, Joyce and Gabriel. *The Limits of Power: The World and United States Foreign Policy, 1945–1954.* New York: Harper & Row, 1972.

Krasner, Stephen D. *Defending the National Interest: Raw Materials Investments and U.S. Foreign Policy.* Princeton: Princeton Univ. Press, 1978.

LaFeber, Walter. *America, Russia and the Cold War: 1945–1971.* 2d ed. New York: Wiley, 1972.

Lartéguy, Jean. *The Centurions.* Translated by Xan Fielding. New York: E. P. Dutton, 1961.

Lekachman, Robert. *The Age of Keynes.* New York: Random House, 1966.

Levin, N. Gordon. *Woodrow Wilson and World Politics.* New York: Oxford Univ. Press, 1968.

Lief, Alfred. *The Firestone Story.* New York: McGraw-Hill, 1951.

_____. *Harvey Firestone: Free Man of Enterprise.* New York: McGraw-Hill, 1951.

Livingston, Jon; Moore, Joe; and Oldfather, Felicia, eds. *The Japan Reader, vol. 2, Postwar Japan: 1945 to the Present.* New York: Pantheon, 1973.

MacDougall, Donald. *The World Dollar Problem.* London: Macmillan, 1957.

McGeehan, Robert. *The German Rearmament Question.* Urbana: Univ. of Illinois Press, 1971.

McLellan, David. *Dean Acheson: The State Department Years.* New York: Dodd, Mead, 1976.

McMahon, Robert J. *Colonialism and Cold War: The United States and the Struggle for Indonesian Independence, 1945–49.* Ithaca: Cornell Univ. Press, 1981.

Mallalieu, William C. *British Reconstruction and American Policy, 1945–1955.* New York: Scarecrow Press, 1956.

Marshall's Mission to China, December 1945–January 1947. Introduction by Lyman P. Van Slyke. 2 vols. Arlington, Va.: University Publications of America, 1976.

May, Ernest R. *The Truman Administration and China, 1945–1950.* Philadelphia: Lippincott, 1975.

Mecham, J. Lloyd. *A Survey of United States–Latin American Relations.* Boston: Houghton Mifflin, 1965.

Melby, John F. *The Mandate of Heaven: Record of a Civil War, China, 1945–1949.* Toronto: Univ. of Toronto Press, 1967.

Mikesell, Raymond F. *United States Economic Policy and International Relations.* New York: McGraw-Hill, 1952.

_____. *Foreign Exchange in the Postwar World.* New York: Twentieth Century Fund, 1954.

Nagai, Yōnosuke, and Iriye, Akira, eds. *The Origins of the Cold War in Asia.* New York: Columbia Univ. Press, 1977.

Northedge, F. S. *Descent from Power: British Foreign Policy, 1945–1973.* London: George Allen & Unwin, 1974.

Packenham, Robert A. *Liberal America and the Third World: Political Development Ideas in Foreign Aid and Social Science.* Princeton: Princeton Univ. Press, 1973.

Palmier, Leslie H. *Indonesia and the Dutch.* London: Oxford Univ. Press, 1962.

Patti, Archimedes L. A. *Why Viet Nam? Prelude to America's Albatross.* Berkeley: Univ. of California Press, 1980.

Phillips, Cabell. *The Truman Presidency.* New York: Macmillan, 1966.

Pluvier, Jan. *South-East Asia from Colonialism to Independence.* Kuala Lumpur: Oxford Univ. Press, 1974.

Price, Harry Bayard. *The Marshall Plan and Its Meaning.* Ithaca: Cornell Univ. Press, 1955.

Pye, Lucian W. *Guerrilla Communism in Malaya.* Princeton: Princeton Univ. Press, 1956.

Reid, Anthony J. S. *The Indonesian National Revolution, 1945–1950.* Longman, Australia: Hawthorn, 1974.

Rose, Saul R. *Britain and South-East Asia.* Baltimore: Johns Hopkins Univ. Press, 1962.

Rowe, J. W. F. *Primary Commodities in International Trade.* Cambridge: Cambridge Univ. Press, 1965.

Sawyer, Charles. *Concerns of a Conservative Democrat.* Carbondale: Southern Illinois

Univ. Press, 1968.

Schaller, Michael. *The U.S. Crusade in China, 1938–1945*. New York: Columbia Univ. Press, 1979.

———. *The American Occupation of Japan: The Origins of the Cold War in Asia*. New York: Oxford Univ. Press, 1985.

Schilling, Warner R.; Hammond Paul Y.; and Snyder, Glenn H. *Strategy, Politics and Defense Budgets*. New York: Columbia Univ. Press, 1962.

Sebald, William J. *With MacArthur in Japan: A Personal History of the Occupation*. New York: W. W. Norton, 1965.

Shaplen, Robert. *The Lost Revolution: The U.S. in Vietnam, 1946–1966*. Rev. ed., New York: Harper & Row, 1966.

Shlaim, Avi; Jones, Peter; and Sainsbury, Keith, eds. *British Foreign Secretaries since 1945*. Newton Abbott, England: David & Charles, 1977.

Sissons, Michael, and French, Philip, eds. *Age of Austerity*. London: Hodder & Stoughton, 1963.

Smith, Gaddis. *Dean Acheson*. Totowa, N.J.: Cooper Square, 1972.

Snyder, Glenn H. *Stockpiling Strategic Materials: Politics and National Defense*. San Francisco: Chandler, 1966.

Spender, Percy. *Exercises in Diplomacy*. New York: New York Univ. Press, 1969.

Stanton, Edwin F. *Brief Authority: Excursions of a Common Man in an Uncommon World*. New York: Harper & Row, 1956.

Steinberg, David Joel, ed. *In Search of Southeast Asia*. New York: Praeger, 1971.

Strang, William Strang, Baron. *Home and Abroad*. London: André Deutsch, 1956.

Stuart, John Leighton. *Fifty Years in China*. New York: Random House, 1954.

Stueck, William Whitney, Jr. *The Road to Confrontation: American Policy toward China and Korea, 1947–1950*. Chapel Hill: Univ. of North Carolina Press, 1981.

Sullivan, Mariana P. *France's Vietnam Policy*. Westport: Greenwood Press, 1978.

Tang Tsou. *America's Failure in China, 1941–1950*. 2 vols. Chicago: Univ. of Chicago Press, 1963.

Thayer, Philip W., ed. *Southeast Asia in the Coming World*. Baltimore: Johns Hopkins Univ. Press, 1953.

Thorp, Willard R. *Trade, Aid, or What?* Baltimore: Johns Hopkins Univ. Press, 1954.

Tinker, Hugh. *The Union of Burma*. 3d ed. London: Oxford Univ. Press, 1961.

Topping, Seymour. *Journey between Two Chinas*. New York: Harper & Row, 1972.

Truman, Harry S. *Memoirs*, vol. 2, *Years of Trial and Hope*. Garden City: Doubleday, 1956.

Tucker, Nancy Bernkopf. *Patterns in the Dust: Chinese-American Relations and the Recognition Controversy, 1949–1950*. New York: Columbia Univ. Press, 1983.

Vandenberg, Arthur J., Jr., ed. *The Private Papers of Senator Vandenberg*. Boston: Houghton Mifflin, 1952.

Vinacke, Harold M. *The United States and the Far East, 1945–1951*. Stanford: Stanford University Press, 1952.

———. *The History of the Far East in Modern Times*. 6th ed. New York: Appleton-Century-Crofts, 1959.

Westerfield, H. Bradford. *The Instruments of America's Foreign Policy*. New York: Thomas Crowell, 1963.

Wildes, Harry Emerson. *Typhoon in Tokyo: The Occupation and Its Aftermath*. New York: Macmillan, 1954.

Williams, William Appleman. *The Tragedy of American Diplomacy*. 2d rev. ed. New York: Dell, 1972.

Willoughby, Charles A. *MacArthur, 1941–1951*. New York: McGraw-Hill, 1954.

Wint, Guy. *Southeast Asia and Its Future*. London: Batchworth, 1951.

_____. *The British in Asia*. Rev. ed. London: Faber & Faber, 1954.

Wolf, Charles, Jr. *Foreign Aid: Theory and Practice in Southern Asia*. Princeton: Princeton Univ. Press, 1960.

Woodhouse, C. M. *British Foreign Policy since the Second World War*. London: Hutchinson, 1961.

Yeager, Leland B. *International Monetary Relations: Theory, History and Policy*. 2d ed. New York: Harper & Row, 1966.

Yergin, Daniel. *Shattered Peace: The Origins of the Cold War and the National Security State*. Boston: Houghton Mifflin, 1978.

Yoshida Shigeru. *The Yoshida Memoirs*. Cambridge, Mass.: Riverside, 1962.

ARTICLES

Colbert, Evelyn. "The Road Not Taken: Decolonization and Independence in Indonesia and Indochina." *Foreign Affairs*, 51 (April 1973):608–28.

Delage, Edmond. "Defense de l'Europe de l'Ouest," *Revue de Defense Nationale*, March 1949, pp. 312–29.

Dower, John. "The Eye of the Beholder." *Bulletin of Concerned Asian Scholars*, October 1969.

Gelb, Leslie H. "On Schlesinger and Ellsberg: A Reply." *New York Review of Books*, Oct. 21, 1971, pp. 31–34.

_____. "The Essential Domino: American Politics and Vietnam." *Foreign Affairs*, 50 (1972):459–75.

George, Alexander L. "The 'Operational Code': A Neglected Approach to the Study of Political Decisionmaking." *International Studies Quarterly*, 12 (1969):190–222.

Herring, George C. "The Truman Administration and the Restoration of French Sovereignty in Indochina." *Diplomatic History*, 1 (1977):97–117.

Herring, George C., and Immerman, Richard H. "Eisenhower, Dulles, and Dienbienphu: 'The Day We Didn't Go to War' Revisited." *Journal of American History*, 71 (1984):343–63.

Hess, Gary R. "Franklin Roosevelt and Indochina." *Journal of American History*, 59 (1972):353–68.

_____. "The First American Commitment in Indochina: The Acceptance of the 'Bao Dai Solution,' 1950." *Diplomatic History*, 2 (1978), 331–50.

Ireland, Timothy. "Year of Departure: 1950." *Fletcher Forum*, May 1978, pp. 114–38.

Kahin, George McTurnan. "The Pentagon Papers: A Critical Evaluation." *American Political Science Review*, 69 (1975):675–84.

LaFeber, Walter. "Roosevelt, Churchill, and Indochina: 1942–45." *American Historical Review*, 80 (1975):1277–95.

Leffler, Melvyn P. "The American Conception of National Security and the Beginnings of the Cold War, 1945–48." *American Historical Review*, 89 (1984): 346–81.

Levine, Steven I. "A New Look at American Mediation in the Chinese Civil War: The Marshall Mission and Manchuria." *Diplomatic History*, 3 (1979):349–75.

McLean, David. "American Nationalism, the China Myth, and the Truman Doctrine: The Question of Accommodation with Peking, 1949–50." *Diplomatic History*, 10 (1986):25–42.

McMahon, Robert J. "Anglo-American Diplomacy and the Reoccupation of the Netherlands East Indies." *Diplomatic History,* 2 (1978):1–23.
Melby, John F. "Vietnam: 1950." *Diplomatic History,* 6 (1982):97–109.
Ninkovich, Frank. "Ideology, the Open Door, and Foreign Policy." *Diplomatic History,* 6 (1982):185–208.
Paterson, Thomas G. "Foreign Aid under Wraps: The Point Four Program." *Wisconsin Magazine of History,* 56 (1972–73):119–26.
Rabe, Stephen G. "The Elusive Conference: United States Economic Relations with Latin America, 1945–1952." *Diplomatic History,* 2 (1978):279–94.
Schaller, Michael. "Securing the Great Crescent: Occupied Japan and the Origins of Containment in Southeast Asia." *Journal of American History,* 69 (1982):392–414.
Schlesinger, Arthur M., Jr. "Eyeless in Indochina." *New York Review of Books,* Oct. 21, 1971, pp. 23–32.
Siracusa, Joseph M. "The United States, Viet-Nam and the Cold War: A Reappraisal." *Journal of Southeast Asian Studies,* 5 (1974):82–101.
Smith, Gaddis. "How the American War Began." *New Republic,* Feb. 10, 1973, pp. 29–31.
Thorne, Christopher. "Indochina and Anglo-American Relations, 1942–1945." *Pacific Historical Review,* 45 (1976):73–96.
Tucker, Nancy Bernkopf. "American Policy toward Sino-Japanese Trade in the Postwar Years: Politics and Prosperity." *Diplomatic History,* 8 (1984):183–208.
Warner, Geoffrey. "The United States and Vietnam 1945–65, Part I: 1945–1954." *International Affairs,* 48 (1972):379–94.
Westerfield, H. Bradford. "What Use Are Three Versions of the Pentagon Papers?" *American Political Science Review,* 69 (1975):685–96.
Yasuhara, Yoko. "Japan, Communist China, and Export Controls in Asia, 1948–1952." *Diplomatic History,* 10 (1986):75–89.

UNPUBLISHED WORKS

Fong, Kok Wah. "Economic Relations between Malaya and the United States of America." M.A. thesis, Stanford Univ., 1953.
Immerman, Richard H. "Perceptions of U.S. Interest in Indochina." Draft chapter, in author's possession.
Schanz, John J., Jr. "The United States and a Post War Tin Control Agreement." Ph.D. dissertation, Pennsylvania State Univ., 1954.
Tai-Hsun Tsuan. "An Explanation of the Change in United States Policy toward China in 1950." Ph.D. dissertation, Univ. of Pennsylvania, 1970.

Index

Library of Congress Cataloging-in-Publication Data

Rotter, Andrew Jon.
    The path to Vietnam.

    Bibliography: p.
    Includes index.
    1. Asia, Southeastern—Foreign relations—United States. 2. United
States—Foreign relations—Asia, Southeastern. 3. Asia, Southeastern—
Foreign economic relations—United States. 4. United States—Foreign
economic relations—Asia, Southeastern. 5. United States—Foreign
relations—1945–   . 6. United States—Foreign economic relations.
I. Title.
DS525.9.U6R67   1987   327.73059   87-47603
ISBN 0-8014-1958-1 (alk. paper)